T0114800

Praise for

In the Ruins of Empire

"Ronald Spector is an excellent writer. . . . With *In the Ruins of Empire*, an unruly, hopelessly complicated Asia comes alive. Spector etches memorable portraits not only of the major characters but of several of the minor ones as well [in] many poignant and gripping vignettes. . . . We all know the cliché about how 'history repeats itself,' but successful historians show us how. . . . Spector's book is not only about the past and present. He also enables us to imagine the future."

—*The New York Times Book Review*

"A useful look at the shaping of the modern world." —*Kirkus Reviews*

"*In the Ruins of Empire* describes the political twists and historical tangles that produced years of postwar bloodshed. It is a complicated story, and historian Ronald H. Spector does a good job identifying major players and events." —*Pittsburgh Post-Gazette*

"A groundbreaking study of post-1945 occupations across Asia. It is a resounding lesson for our time about the failure of postwar operations in countries we were little prepared to reconstruct. Ronald Spector's book is a cautionary tale that should be read by anyone interested in how we need to think about future involvements in distant lands we enter at our peril."

—Robert Dallek, author of *Nixon and Kissinger*

"A vivid account." —*Foreign Affairs*

ALSO BY RONALD H. SPECTOR

AT WAR AT SEA: SAILORS AND
NAVAL COMBAT IN THE TWENTIETH CENTURY

THE OXFORD COMPANION TO
AMERICAN MILITARY HISTORY (co-editor)

AFTER TET: THE BLOODIEST YEAR IN VIETNAM

EAGLE AGAINST THE SUN:
THE AMERICAN WAR WITH JAPAN

IN THE RUINS OF EMPIRE

RANDOM HOUSE TRADE PAPERBACKS | NEW YORK

IN THE RUINS OF EMPIRE

THE JAPANESE SURRENDER AND THE BATTLE FOR POSTWAR ASIA

RONALD H. SPECTOR

2008 Random House Trade Paperback Edition

Published in the United States by
Random House Trade Paperbacks,
an imprint of The Random House Publishing Group,
a division of Random House, Inc., New York.

RANDOM HOUSE TRADE PAPERBACKS and colophon
are trademarks of Random House, Inc.

Originally published in hardcover in the United States
by Random House, an imprint of The Random House
Publishing Group, a division of Random House,
Inc., in 2007.

Grateful acknowledgment is made to the following for
permission to reprint previously published material:

University of California Press: Excerpts from *Why Viet Nam?: Prelude to America's Albatross* by Archimedes L. A. Patti, copyright © 1980 by Archimedes L. A. Patti. Reprinted by permission of University of California Press.

George Wickes: Excerpts from two memoirs by George Wickes entitled "Saigon 1945" and "Hanoi 1946." Reprinted by permission of the author.

LIBRARY OF CONGRESS
CATALOGING-IN-PUBLICATION DATA

Spector, Ronald H.
In the ruins of empire : the Japanese surrender and the
battle for postwar Asia/Ronald H. Spector.
p. cm.
Includes bibliographical references and index.
ISBN 978-0-8129-6732-6
1. East Asia—History—1945- 2. Southeast Asia—
History—1945- I. Title.
DS518.1.S64 2007
950.4'24—dc22 2006051048

www.atrandom.com

Title-page photograph courtesy of the Signal Corps

Book design by Barbara M. Bachman

147468846

In memory of my mother, Ethel Spector Davis

CONTENTS

INTRODUCTION

Americans are accustomed to thinking of World War II as having ended on August 14, 1945, when Japan surrendered unconditionally. The finality of this action seemed to be appropriately symbolized in the solemn ceremony aboard the USS *Missouri* on September 2 in which Japan's representatives signed the instrument of surrender under the watchful eyes of General MacArthur and in the shadow of the *Missouri*'s sixteen-inch guns.

That was the end of the war so far as most Americans were concerned. Yet on the mainland of Asia, in the vast arc of countries and territories stretching from Manchuria to Burma, peace was at best a brief interlude. In some parts of Asia, such as Java and southern Indochina, peace lasted less than two months. In China, a fragile and incomplete peace lasted less than a year. In northern Indochina, peace lasted about fifteen months, and in Korea, about three years. Indeed, 1945–46 in Asia may have appeared to many not as a time when war ended, but as a time when the various protagonists switched sides.

Why did peace in Asia prove so elusive? What were the elements that contributed to the long postwar years of grim struggle during which many suffered far more than they had during World War II itself? This book attempts to address these questions through an examination of events in five countries that previously formed a part of the Japanese Empire. With one exception, they were places in which things went disastrously wrong and gave birth to long-term problems that sometimes outlived the Cold War. This is largely a story about military occupations and their consequences. After the American experience in Iraq it is unnecessary to explain that military occupations that follow on the complete disruption of a country's old order are often ill-conceived, confused, messy affairs that can result in unforeseen consequences for both the occupied and the occupiers. At the conclusion of the war against Japan, the victorious Allies—Britain, China, the United States, and the USSR—all sent troops to occupy or reclaim vast areas of mainland Asia that had formed part of Japan's empire.

The British and Americans saw their most important task as disarming the Japanese military forces in China, Korea, and Southeast Asia and sending them back to Japan. Another pressing concern was to liberate thousands of Allied prisoners of war and civilian internees who had been starved, beaten, and otherwise ill treated by the Japanese in prison camps throughout Asia. The greatest threat to these policies was anticipated to be the Japanese. Most of their well-armed forces on the mainland of Asia had never suffered any direct military setbacks and could not be counted on to behave as a defeated enemy. In addition, die-hard Pan-Asianists and former members of the secret police and intelligence organizations might stay on to help stir up trouble among the local populations.

The Chinese and Soviets also saw the occupations as an opportunity to assert what they believed to be their historic rights and interests in East Asia. For the Americans and the British, it was simply a matter of reestablishing stability and order through the implementation of policies recently agreed upon by the Allies. Few anticipated that the Japanese forces themselves might be utilized to help in the restoration of order through those policies, or that local people would seriously oppose them.

All of the soldiers who brought their various versions of liberation to the countries of Greater East Asia were members of famous military units, veterans of the most difficult campaigns of World War II. They were unprepared for their new role as occupiers and had at best an imperfect knowledge of the places they were going. They wanted most to go home. Their governments were often little better prepared, and these soldiers would soon become acquainted with the consequences of ignorance, inattention, and indecisiveness in London, Moscow, and Washington. Their theaters of operation were the countries of Japan's former empire of Greater East Asia, built on the wreckage of the European colonial empires they had defeated and occupied in 1942.

The British, French, and Dutch colonial empires that had been displaced by the Japanese with unexpected ease and dispatch had themselves been relatively recent creations, despite their pretensions to age and permanence. So were the Japanese colonies in Korea and Manchuria. The final French conquests in Indochina had ended only in the 1880s. The Dutch had added sizable portions of the Indonesian archipelago, including Kalimantan, Bali, and Sumatra, to the Netherlands Indies only in the mid- to late nineteenth century and were still battling stubborn resistance forces in Aceh into the early twentieth century. In Korea, many were still alive in 1945 who could remember Korea as an independent state. "The world was fluid and about to be remade," recalled an American journalist. "An empire had vanished. A half dozen victors raced for the spoils."[1] More than a half dozen; for old class antagonisms, regional rivalries, ethnic and religious conflicts were still alive. They had survived both European colonialism and the Japanese imperial project, although sometimes in new or altered form. The war and the Japanese conquest transformed political and personal alignments, ideologies, and institutions in the nations that became part of Greater East Asia, but the basis of postwar suspicions, and ambitions, remained.

THE
JAPANESE EMPIRE
IN AUGUST 1945
SOVIET UNION
MONGOLIA
MANCHUKUO
(MANCHURIA)
Mukden
Vladivostok
Peiping
Sea of
Japan
KOREA
Keijo (Seoul)
Yellow River
Yellow
Sea
JAPAN
Tokyo
CHINA
Nanking
Hankow
Shanghai
Chungking
Yangtze River
East
China
Sea
OKINAWA
Kunming
BURMA
FORMOSA
Hanoi
Hong Kong
PACIFIC
OCEAN
THAILAND
Bangkok
FRENCH
INDOCHINA
Saigon
South China Sea
Manila
PHILIPPINES
N. BORNEO
(Br.)
MALAYA
(Br.)
SARAWAK
(Br.)
Singapore
SUMATRA
BORNEO
CELEBES
Palembang
NETHERLANDS INDIES
NEW
(Neth.)
GUINEA
(Br.)
Batavia
Java Sea
JAVA
PAPUA
(Aus.)
TIMOR
(Port.)
Arafura Sea
INDIAN
OCEAN
AUSTRALIA

CHINA AND MANCHURIA
SOVIET UNION
MONGOLIA
AFGHANISTAN
SINKIANG
INNER MONGOLIA
HEILUNGKIANG
Harbin
Changchun
KIRIN
Mukden
LIAONING
Sea of Japan
JAPAN
KOREA
(Japan)
Peiping
Tienjin
HOPEH
NINGSIA
SHANXI
SHANTUNG
Tsingtao
CH'ING-HAI
KANSU
Xian
SHENSI
HONAN
KIANGSU
Yellow Sea
TIBET
BHUTAN
Nanking
ANHWEI
Shanghai
Ch'eng-tu
HUPEH
Wuhan
SZECHUAN
Chungking
CHEKIANG
Ch'ang-sha
KIANGSI
INDIA
Kuei-yang
HUNAN
Foochow
PACIFIC OCEAN
KUEI-CHOU
FUKIEN
Kunming
FORMOSA
(Japan)
YUNNAN
KWANGSI
Kuang-chou
KWANGTUNG
BURMA
South China Sea
INDOCHINA
INDIAN OCEAN
THAILAND
HAINAN

Allied Intelligence Estimate of
PRISONER OF WAR CAMPS
in China and Korea, 1945
SIBERIA
MONGOLIA
MANCHUKUO
Hoten
Mukden
Peiping
Sea of
Japan
KOREA
Chefoo
Keijo (Seoul)
Weihsien
Yellow River
Tsingtao
JAPAN
Yellow
Sea
CHINA
Yangtze River
Shanghai
East
China
Sea
FORMOSA
Hong Kong
PACIFIC
OCEAN
South
China
Sea
PHILIPPINES

VIETNAM
CHINA
Red River
Mekong River
BURMA
TONKIN
(North Vietnam)
Lang Son
Hanoi
Phu Yen
Haiphong
RED RIVER
DELTA
Gulf
of
Tonkin
Mekong River
LAOS
Mekong River
ANNAM
(Central Vietnam)
Hue
Danang
THAILAND
CENTRAL
HIGHLANDS
CAMBODIA
Ban Me Thuot
Mekong River
Dalat
COCHINCHINA
(South Vietnam)
Tay Ninh
Saigon
CAPE ST. JACQUES
Gulf
of
Thailand
MEKONG RIVER
DELTA
South
China Sea

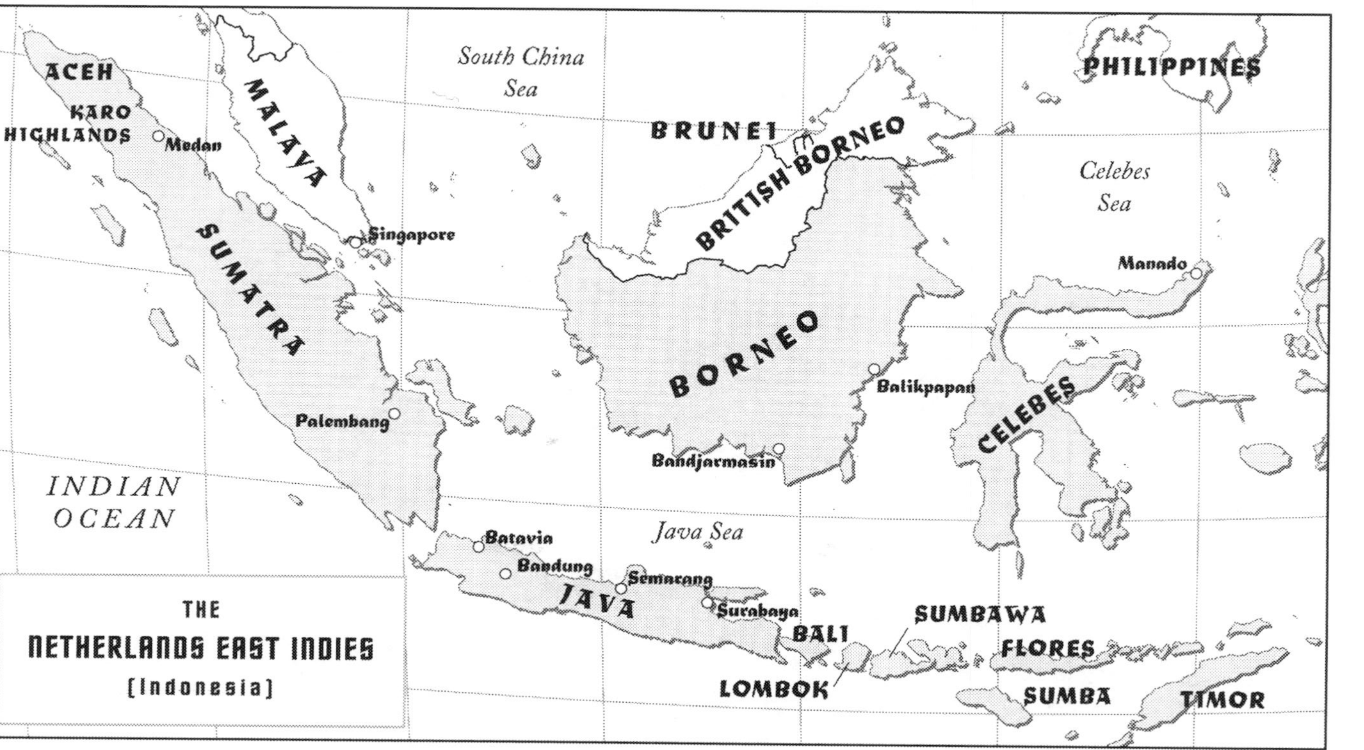

ACEH
KARO
HIGHLANDS
Medan
MALAYA
SUMATRA
Singapore
Palembang
South China
Sea
INDIAN
OCEAN
BRUNEI
BRITISH BORNEO
BORNEO
Balikpapan
Bandjarmasin
PHILIPPINES
Celebes
Sea
Manado
CELEBES
Java Sea
Batavia
Bandung
Semarang
JAVA
Surabaya
BALI
LOMBOK
SUMBAWA
FLORES
SUMBA
TIMOR
THE
NETHERLANDS EAST INDIES
(Indonesia)

IN THE RUINS OF EMPIRE

CHAPTER ONE

"SHOOT THE WORKS!"

NO ONE EXPECTED THE WAR TO END WHEN IT DID. EVEN AFTER the two atomic bombs and the entry of the Soviet Union into the war on August 9, the Japanese, though doomed, were expected to fight on for some considerable time. Suddenly, on August 10, the Domei News Agency broadcast a statement by the Japanese Foreign Ministry that Japan was ready to accept the surrender terms presented by the Allies in the so-called Potsdam Declaration on July 26, "provided that the said declaration does not comprise any demand which prejudices the prerogatives of His Majesty as a Sovereign Ruler." The announcement surprised even top officials in Washington. "When the Japanese surrendered it caught the whole goddamn administrative machinery with their pants down," recalled a colonel in the Army high command.[1] At the time the official notification was received via neutral embassies, Secretary of War Henry Stimson was about to leave on vacation, and the army and navy were opening another round in their continuing squabble about command arrangements for the impending invasion of Japan.[2]

One of those slated for that invasion, Marine sergeant David F. Earle, a veteran of the campaigns on Guam and Okinawa, listened with his tentmates to the radio. "Our station," he told his parents, "which secures at 2200, was back on the air with Japan's unconfirmed peace offer. It seemed almost too good to be true, beyond all realization. . . . Men shook hands, embraced and beer was drug out. Each time the commentor announced the same commentary, even though the men had heard the same thing over and over there was complete silence, as if we weren't able to hear it often enough. This morning the announcement was confirmed and now it's either accepted or not. To those who don't want to accept the terms because of the Emperor—I haven't got words in my vocabulary to fit my contempt and scorn for their attitude. I know damn well that twenty-eight months out here would change their minds but fast. Anyway, we in my tent have already accepted the surrender and if the country hasn't we've decided to sue for a separate peace."[3]

Many in Washington shared Sergeant Earle's sentiments. In July, Stimson and Undersecretary of State Joseph C. Grew, former ambassador to Japan, had urged President Truman to include an explicit promise in the Potsdam Declaration that it might be possible for Japan to retain "a constitutional Monarchy under the present dynasty" following its surrender.[4] There was strong opposition to such a guarantee, however, from many of the president's advisers, including Secretary of State James F. Byrnes, who believed that it would compromise the longstanding Allied agreement on "unconditional surrender" by the Axis powers. "Too much like appeasement," former secretary of state Cordell Hull observed. Other Americans saw no reason to retain the outmoded reactionary institutions that had encouraged Japanese militarism and aggression.[5] The emperor had been portrayed in the American media as a symbol of Japanese fanaticism, a partner of Hitler and Mussolini. A Gallup poll published in *The Washington Post* at the end of June had revealed that 33 percent of Americans wanted the emperor executed, 17 percent favored a trial, 20 percent were for imprisonment or exile, and only 7 percent favored his retention, even as a figurehead.[6]

Truman was well aware of these sentiments when he hastily convened a meeting at the White House to discuss the Japanese surrender offer. Present at the meeting were Byrnes, Stimson, the president's military aides, Navy Secretary James V. Forrestal, John Snyder, a Missouri friend of Truman's who was serving as head of the Office of War Mobilization, and the president's military adviser and chairman of the Joint Chiefs of Staff, Admiral William D. Leahy. Stimson urged acceptance of the Japanese stipulation, pointing out that the emperor was "the only source of authority in Japan." He argued that "something like this use of the Emperor must be made in order to save us from a score of bloody Iwo Jimas and Okinawas all over China and the New Netherlands [Indonesia]."[7] Leahy and Snyder agreed. Byrnes, however, warned that public opinion and the Allied powers might not understand or accept such a concession. Abandonment of unconditional surrender could lead to "the crucifixion of the President" at the hands of public opinion. Truman informed the meeting that since news of the Japanese proposal, the White House had received 170 telegrams, all but seventeen of which had urged the harshest surrender terms.[8] On the other hand, millions more Americans like Sergeant Earle might be equally infuriated if Truman and his advisers allowed this opportunity for peace to slip away.

At that point Forrestal suggested a compromise: The United States should send a reply that reaffirmed the Potsdam demands while neither rejecting the Japanese offer nor discouraging hope that the emperor could remain. Byrnes, aided by his special assistant, Benjamin Cohen, was given primary responsibility for drafting a reply, though Forrestal, Leahy, Stimson, and Truman himself all lent a hand, as did Undersecretary Grew. Grew had not been at the White House meeting, but he was the government's highest-ranking expert on Japan and had always stressed the crucial role of the emperor in any surrender scheme. Now "Grew, mastering his personal pride, opened the door between his office and Byrnes' and said, 'Mr. Secretary, if you are working on the Japanese note I believe I and some others could be helpful.'" Byrnes agreed.[9]

Unlike most products of a committee, Byrnes's reply was a masterpiece. Addressing the key Japanese reservation on the emperor, the note was intentionally ambiguous, asserting, "From the moment of surrender, the authority of the emperor and the Japanese government to rule the state shall be subject to the authority of the Supreme Commander of the Allied powers, who will take such steps as he deems proper to effectuate the surrender terms." But the note also promised, "The ultimate form of government of Japan shall, in accordance with the Potsdam Declaration, be established in accordance with the freely expressed will of the Japanese people." At a meeting of the full Cabinet, Truman approved the note.[10] The British and the other Allies quickly agreed, and, after only momentary hesitation, so did the Soviets.

A more significant Allied disagreement, although it appeared small at the time, briefly arose over the question of the surrender ceremony. The draft of the note submitted to the Allies had provided for the emperor to sign the surrender documents personally. Grew had unsuccessfully argued against this provision, but when the British raised doubts about its advisability, Byrnes dropped it. The Chinese government, which had been especially enthusiastic about this symbolic humbling of Japan, was not informed of the "slight change" until after the revised note had actually been dispatched to Japan.[11] Stalin made no formal objection, but he later cautioned Ambassador Averell Harriman that the American plan to stage the surrender ceremony in Tokyo Bay entailed "considerable risks." The Japanese, Stalin observed, "were treacherous people." He was sure "there were some crazy cutthroats left" and advised the Americans to take several hostages to "guard against incidents."[12]

In Tokyo, the receipt of the Byrnes note touched off a crisis within the highest circles of the government. Japanese Army leaders argued that the demands of the note were intolerable and that Japan must fight on, while most of the civilian ministers urged acceptance of the Allied terms.[13] With the government deadlocked and American B-29s raining leaflets on Japanese cities containing copies of the Japanese note of August 10 with Byrnes's reply, the emperor met with the Cabinet and other senior military and political advisers to announce that it was his wish that Japan "accept the Allied reply as it stands."[14]

IN THE LATE AFTERNOON of August 14, an RCA messenger carrying a telegram to the Swiss legation in Washington was stopped by police for making an illegal U-turn on Connecticut Avenue. After ten minutes he was allowed to proceed. The messenger was carrying Tokyo's acceptance of the surrender terms. At 7:00 P.M. Truman announced to the reporters who jammed the president's office that he had received from the Japanese government "a full acceptance of the Potsdam Declaration which specifies the unconditional surrender of Japan."[15]

Even before President Truman's announcement of Japan's final surrender, the thoughts of many Americans had turned to the twenty-two thousand Americans and the hundred and ten thousand other Allied prisoners of war in Japanese hands. It was unclear how many were still alive. Many were known to be suffering severely from disease, malnutrition, and exposure even where they were not being subjected to torture, brutality, and other forms of abuse by the Japanese.[16] The story of the appalling Bataan Death March, in which six hundred Americans and five to ten thousand Filipinos who had surrendered in the Philippines perished in a brutal sixty-five-mile forced-march evacuation to their prison camps, became widely known in the United States by early 1944.[17] Americans believed, with good reason, that with their impending defeat the Japanese might decide to massacre all the surviving prisoners, many of whom had by this time been moved to northern China, Manchuria, and Japan. U.S. intelligence estimated that there were about nine thousand Allied prisoners in China and Manchuria, with another fifty-five hundred in Indochina and one thousand in Korea.[18]

In April the War Department had ordered Lieutenant General Albert C. Wedemeyer, the top American commander in China, to be prepared to locate, assist, and repatriate Allied POWs in China and Manchuria as quickly as possible. This had been a comparatively simple task in the European Theater, where almost all Axis territory had already fallen and Allied forces reached most camps within a few days. Conditions were far different in General Wedemeyer's China Theater, an enormous expanse of territory that included China, Manchuria, Korea, and at least half of Indochina. Much of this area was still in the hands of the Japanese, who as recently as the previous fall had conducted a series of devastating offensives into central China that brought thousands more square miles under their control.

Within the Japanese-held areas were large and small pockets of land controlled or influenced by the Chinese Communist forces of Mao Tse-tung (Mao Zedong), who conducted guerrilla warfare, propaganda, and subversion against the Japanese. Nominally allied to Chiang Kai-shek (Jiang Jieshi), the American-backed leader of "Free China," the Communists remained in fact his bitter rivals in an ongoing struggle for control of China that had been only temporarily interrupted by the Japanese. Finally, there were the Soviets, who had entered the war against Japan on August 9. Led by experienced commanders who had helped destroy the German Wehrmacht a few months before, the Soviet armies swept aside the ill-prepared Japanese in Manchuria and advanced rapidly toward the main cities and rail lines.

American planners estimated that it might take a month or more for relief forces traveling overland to reach some of the largest prison camps, which were located hundreds of miles from the nearest American bases in China. Such a delay was completely unacceptable, however. The United States, Wedemeyer's staff reminded him, "has consistently maintained that China Theater is their [special] responsibility and we have in many cases pointed this out in no uncertain terms to the other Allied nations. . . . A failure to discharge the humanitarian aspects of this responsibility can never be condoned."[19]

In Europe, the British and Americans had employed special teams immediately after the surrender to locate POW camps, contact the internees, report on conditions, and provide emergency support. That concept appeared to be the solution to the problem of POW relief in Asia as well. Yet in Asia such teams would have to travel immense distances into relatively unknown territory and confront armies whose attitudes and intentions were likely to be problematic at best. Only one American organization in East Asia was both prepared and equipped to carry out such missions: the Office of Strategic Services.

Like many other activities in the China Theater, intelligence operations there had been characterized by contention, confused organization, and byzantine personal and political rivalries. By 1945 no fewer than fourteen different agencies were contributing intelligence information to theater headquarters.[20] Until a few months before the surrender, the Office of Strategic Services, widely referred to as "OSS," had scarcely existed as a major contender in the bureaucratic Olympics incessantly played out in China's wartime capital, Chungking (Chongqing). The brainchild of Colonel William J. Donovan, a Wall Street lawyer, Republican political operator, and hero of World War I, OSS was conceived as a single agency that would coordinate the collection and analysis of foreign intelligence and conduct special operations such as commando raids and disinformation campaigns and work with partisan and guerrilla groups behind enemy lines.[21] Older organizations like the Office of Naval Intelligence, the FBI, and the Army's Military Intelligence Service viewed Donovan's organization of former college professors, gangsters, corporate lawyers, and European émigrés with suspicion. The two Pacific commanders, General Douglas MacArthur and Admiral Chester Nimitz, barred Donovan's organization from their theaters. Yet OSS proved its value in the North African campaign, and in November 1942 Donovan received a broad charter from the Joint Chiefs of Staff to act as their agent for espionage, sabotage, and psychological and guerrilla warfare.

In China also, OSS got off to a rocky start. (Its first head of intelligence reportedly went around Chungking passing out business cards with "American Intelligence Office" printed under his name.)[22] In the summer of 1944, when Patrick J. Hurley, a prominent Republican and former secretary of war, arrived as the new U.S. ambassador at Chungking, Donovan's prospects improved. Hurley and Donovan had served together in the Hoover administration. Wedemeyer, who assumed command of the China Theater that October, was an outstanding staff officer and planner who valued centralization and orderly organization. He readily accepted Donovan's arguments on the value of a single U.S. intelligence agency under the direct control of the theater commander. With Hurley and Wedemeyer's support, OSS grew from a small organization with a strength of about one hundred in October 1944 to about nineteen hundred in July 1945. More important, at the time of the Japanese surrender, OSS had been about to undertake a series of secret operations to penetrate what its leaders referred to as "Japan's inner zone." From its advance base at Xian in Shanxi Province of west-central China, OSS was completing preparations to send teams to operate in the furthest parts of Japanese-occupied China as well as to Manchuria and Korea. It already had small groups of agents operating in Shantung (Shandong), Shanxi, Hebei, and Peiping (Beijing).[23]

On August 14 the head of Strategic Services in the China Theater proposed to General Wedemeyer's chief of staff that OSS contact teams be parachuted in to distant points believed to have prisoner-of-war camps, such as Peiping and Weihsien (Weifang) in northern China, Mukden (Shenyang) in Manchuria, Hanoi in northern Vietnam, and Vientiane in Laos.[24] OSS commanders in Xian and Kunming were already making preparations for such missions. The Air Ground Aid Service of the U.S. Army Air Forces, China Theater, was the organization primarily responsible for aiding American prisoners, evaders, and escapees behind enemy lines. But the Air Ground Aid Service had no parachute-qualified personnel and lacked OSS firsthand experience in the northern areas.

Wedemeyer quickly agreed to the proposal and directed his commanders to give highest priority to the task of landing teams at camps throughout the theater. Their targets would be Peiping, Weihsien, and Shanghai in China, Mukden and Harbin in Manchuria, Vientiane in Laos, and Hainan Island in the Gulf of Tonkin. The mission of the teams was to render immediate aid and medical assistance to the prisoners of war and other interned personnel, to prepare accurate lists of those being held, to coordinate the distribution of supplies to be dropped in, and to furnish information to theater headquarters about the extent, location, size, and conditions of each camp. The teams also had intelligence missions assigned to them and were expected to report on political and military conditions in their areas; however, they were prohibited from discussing surrender terms or arrangements with the Japanese.[25] OSS was to have exclusive responsibility for camps north of the Yellow River and would operate with the Air Ground Aid Service in other areas.

Shortly after dawn on August 15, Teletype machines in Xian and Kunming began to clatter out a short message from Chungking: "Commanding General, China Theater, directs provisions of directive, re contact with POW camps be implemented. Shoot the works! Implement to fullest! Good Luck!"[26] Four missions were considered most critical: Team Cardinal to camps around Mukden in Manchuria; Team Duck to POW camps near the city of Weihsien on the Shantung Peninsula; Team Magpie to camps near the former imperial capital of Peiping; and Team Eagle to Keijo (Seoul) in Korea. All of these places were deep in Japanese territory, garrisoned by thousands of Japanese soldiers, many of whom had never been defeated in battle.

Early on the sixteenth of August a B-24 bomber left Xian carrying the Cardinal team: Major James T. Hennessy, the team leader; Major Robert F. Lamar, the medical officer; Tec4 Edward A. Starz, the radio operator; Corporal Fomio Kido, a Japanese American interpreter; Corporal Harold B. Leith, a Russian and Chinese linguist; and Chong Shih-wu, a Chinese Army officer and interpreter. Cardinal's destination was Hoten, near Mukden, almost nine hundred miles from Xian. They were followed on the seventeenth by Duck and Magpie and on the eighteenth by Eagle.

The Hoten camp was rumored to house a large number of American prisoners including Lieutenant General Jonathan Wainwright, the last American commander in the Philippines, who had surrendered

Corregidor to the Japanese in 1942. There were also high-ranking British and Dutch officers captured during the Japanese conquest of Southeast Asia. In the Hoten area were at least thirty thousand men of the Japanese Kwantung Army. The Russians were still some hundred miles away but were coming fast. It is a mark of the supreme confidence and determination, and perhaps the supreme cluelessness, of Americans in that summer of '45 that no one hesitated to launch a team of six men armed with pistols, only one of whom spoke Japanese, into the midst of a Japanese Army still at war and in the path of an advancing Soviet juggernaut.

Major Hennessy's men landed safely less than two miles from Hoten and successfully retrieved all seventeen of their cargo parachutes bearing emergency medicine and other supplies. "Because of the overcast, we couldn't see the plane," recalled Pfc. Robert Brown, an American airman held at Hoten. "We heard it, though, and it wasn't Japanese. Four engines are four engines and American engines are American engines. Off in the distance we saw about twelve parachutes. . . . Oh boy, the rumors began flying. In prison camp you live on rumors. They started on Bataan and never ended."[27]

The Japanese at Hoten were sullen and abusive. Lamar, Starz, and Chong were taken into custody near their airdrop site and ordered to strip. Lamar was "stood up against a wall where several Japs made feints at him with their bayonets." The rest of the team was blindfolded and ordered into a truck, where one Japanese soldier continued to pummel Hennessy in the shoulder with his closed fist.[28] A short time later, however, the Japanese at Hoten received confirmation of the surrender, and their behavior abruptly changed.

Now smiling and courteous, the Japanese military police allowed the team to visit the prison, but the camp commander refused to furnish any information to Hennessy or to allow him to talk with the prisoners. After an afternoon of futile argument, the camp commander agreed to send a message to Kwantung Army headquarters relaying Hennessy's demand that custody of the prisoners and command of the camp be turned over to the Americans. Accompanied by a squad of military police, the team then were driven to Mukden, where they were quartered in the Yamato Hotel for the night.[29]

Returning to the camp next morning, Hennessy found that the

Japanese camp commander's "attitude had changed entirely and he gave us all the information we desired."[30] There were reported to be 1,673 prisoners at Hoten, of whom about 1,300 were Americans, 240 British, and the remainder from various other Allied countries. There were also 45 civilian internees, mostly Belgians.[31] A small number of very high-ranking Allied prisoners, including General Wainwright and the former governor of the Straits Settlements, Sir Shenton Thomas, were being held at a satellite camp at Xian, 160 miles northwest of Mukden.[32]

The Cardinal team toured the camp and met with Major General George M. Parker, the senior American officer. Starz set up his radio gear in the prison compound and Lamar made a quick evaluation of the patients in the prison hospital. Hennessy found "the majority of the prisoners were underweight and undernourished . . . all 'beds' (consisting of mats on the wooden floors of the cubicles) were full of fleas. The windows had been blacked out until we arrived when the paper was removed to allow light and air to circulate." The prisoners nevertheless declared "this was the best camp they had been in." Hennessy reported that he "ate a meal with the prisoners which they thought was wonderful food but which almost nauseated me. It consisted of dry corn bread, watery stew and rice. Previous to this they had been served one bun a day with three meals consisting mostly of watery soup and polished rice."[33] General Parker, the former commander of II Corps on Bataan, called a meeting of all senior officers at which Hennessy confirmed to the jubilant prisoners that the war was over and they would soon be going home. Major Lamar and Corporal Leith departed the following morning for Xian, to contact Wainwright, and Starz, who had been having difficulty with his relatively low-powered radio, finally made contact with Xian, on the morning of August 18 with a breakdown of prisoners and a list of requested supplies.

On August 20 a B-24 landed at Mukden airfield bringing supplies and three more men for the Cardinal team: Major Robert B. Helm, a communications specialist, and two medics, Pharmacist's Mate 2nd Class Ray Sutton and Master Sergeant Philip J. Malmstedt. The day also witnessed the arrival of the Russians. Soviet fighters swept over the area as an advance party of about a hundred paratroopers landed from C-47s that afternoon and seized control of the airfield. The Japanese promptly surrendered to the Soviets.[34] At Hoten the Russians "ordered the Japanese to bring in all their arms and ammunition," recalled Robert Brown. "Then they told the American officers they were going to shoot the guards. Of course General Parker talked them out of it."[35]

As additional units of the Soviet Sixth Guards Tank Army under Lieutenant General Toomanyan arrived, the Russians promptly commandeered all available vehicles, leaving Major Hennessy stranded at the Yamato Hotel. The Russians invited the Americans to join them in an impromptu victory party at the hotel that evening, and the following morning the Soviet commander issued the Cardinal team passes enabling them to move freely about the Mukden area but refused them the use of any vehicles. Fortunately, Major Lamar had now returned from his trip to Xian in possession of a Japanese car he had been furnished along the way, and the Cardinal team drove back to Hoten. On arrival, Hennessy found that the Russians had disarmed and imprisoned the Japanese and left the Americans in charge of the camp. Taking possession of three of the camp vehicles, the team began to prepare the most critically ill prisoners for evacuation.

Hennessy's main concern was now the VIP prisoners still at Xian, particularly General Wainwright, because he and Lieutenant General A. E. Percival, the former British commander at Singapore, were scheduled to be present with General MacArthur at the official surrender ceremony in September. Lamar and Corporal Leith had located the prisoners at Xian on the nineteenth. They included, in addition to Wainwright and Percival, Major General E. P. King; Major General G. E. Moore; two additional British generals; three Dutch generals including Lieutenant General H. ten Poorten, the former commander in chief in the Netherlands Indies; former governor-general Tsarda Van Starkenborg; two former British colonial governors including Sir Shenton Thomas; and other high-ranking officials. The OSS men found Wainwright frail and worn but alert and eager for news. Major Lamar attempted to contact Hennessy by radio but was unsuccessful. Lamar decided that attempting to move the prisoners to Mukden would be too risky. The Soviets were closing in on Xian, and the attitude of the rapidly disintegrating Japanese Army and nearby Communist Chinese units was uncertain.

Leaving Leith, a Russian linguist, at Xian to interpret for the prisoners, Lamar left for Mukden to organize a safer evacuation. His return trip proved his caution to have been amply justified. Starting for Mukden by rail, Lamar found his train halted at the Russian lines. Securing a car, Lamar and his Japanese interpreter were repeatedly stopped at Japanese and Communist Chinese roadblocks and occasionally fired at as they passed between the lines.[36]

It took two days following Lamar's return to Mukden to persuade the Soviets to provide a special train to bring the prisoners from Xian to Mukden.[37] The train carrying Lamar with a detachment of Russian guards arrived to find that the prisoners had left with a convoy of Russian trucks only hours before. Wainwright and his fellow prisoners endured a nightmarish three-day trip to Hoten by road and rail that made Lamar's earlier travels seem easy. Finally, at midnight on the twenty-sixth, a tired but exultant Corporal Leith walked into Hennessy's hotel room to announce that the prisoners had finally arrived at Mukden.

The following morning Wainwright posed for pictures at the airport and dispatched a personal message of thanks to Donovan before boarding a plane that would carry him to Xian on the first leg of his journey to the surrender ceremony in Tokyo Bay. For hundreds of other newly liberated Allied prisoners, however, there were no special planes or quick evacuations. "Our POWs are keyed up and becoming extremely hard to handle," reported Major Helm. "They have been jumping the fence, although guarded by their own men and wandering aimlessly about the city. . . . After three and a half years in one spot they want to walk and look."[38] Brigadier General William E. Brougher, a survivor of Bataan, recorded in his diary that men returned from town with "truck loads of beer . . . much celebrating."[39] That the former POWs were finding more than beer in Mukden was reflected in Major Hennessy's message to Xian urgently requesting "venereal prophylactic kits for 1500 men for 21 days."[40]

At the end of August, a much larger POW processing team relieved Cardinal of much of their POW work, but team members continued to collect intelligence under the increasingly suspicious eyes of the Russians. Except for a few urgent cases who were evacuated by air, most of the fourteen hundred prisoners at Hoten were moved by rail during early September to the port of Dairen (Dalian), from where the U.S. Navy hospital ship *Saint Olaf* and three destroyers carried them to Okinawa. By that time, the Hoten prison camp had received a new prisoner population of five thousand Japanese who had fallen into Soviet hands.[41]

ONE DAY AFTER CARDINAL had landed in Manchuria, B-24s brought other OSS teams to north China. The Magpie team, commanded by Major Ray Nichols, was assigned to liberate the prisoners and internees at Fengtai Prison near the center of Beijing, then called Peiping. Fengtai was believed to hold more than three hundred captives, including the survivors of General James H. Doolittle's famous raid on Tokyo in April 1942. Three of these aviators who had fallen into Japanese hands had been executed and a fourth deliberately starved to death, but four others had survived and were at Fengtai, as was Commander Scott W. Cunningham, who had commanded the stubborn defense of Wake Island by the Marines in December 1941. Both Wake Island and the Doolittle Raid held enormous symbolic and emotional importance for Americans in 1945, and both had been commemorated in popular movies.

Nichols's team made an "excellent landing" near Fengtai in the late afternoon of August 17. The Americans were quickly surrounded by Japanese troops but were spared the roughing up Hennessy's men had received. The Peiping area commander, Lieutenant General Takahashi, argued that because the war was "not officially over" he needed permission from his superiors to allow the team to visit the prisoners, but he did agree that Nichols could give the captives cigarettes, food, and medical supplies. He also agreed to allow the team to send radio messages in clear, and he housed them at a first-class hotel in downtown Peiping.[42] The following day, Nichols reported that Commander Cunningham and about a dozen other American POWs had been located and would be transported to hotels in Peiping the next morning. Three hundred seventeen Allied internees in Peiping were also released. The four Doolittle flyers, who had been held in especially harsh conditions, were released on the evening of the twentieth and taken to the Grand Hôtel des Wagons-Lits. Army Air Forces bombardier Jacob DeShazer ate a hearty dinner, then instinctively hid some extra cans of C rations in his clothes.[43]

News of the location of the former Doolittle raiders was flashed to

General Wedemeyer and on to Washington. On August 23, the three flyers who were fit to travel flew to Chungking, where they received a heroes' welcome. By that time Major Nichols's concerns had shifted from the Japanese to safeguarding his internees against warring factions of Chinese. The Japanese surrender had been a signal for Chinese Communist troops to move to seize control of the north before Chiang's troops could arrive in strength. Both sides bid for the support of the so-called puppet troops, Chinese military forces that had fought under the control of the Japanese-sponsored puppet government of Wang Ching-wei (Wang Jingwei). On the twenty-third, Nichols advised a quick evacuation of all remaining Allied internees "in view of the military situation" and rumors that Chinese Communist troops were infiltrating the city.[44] The Japanese, he reported one week later, were confused about "who in this area is to be the real representative of the Chinese government. . . . I would also like to know who is to be real Chinese commander. Many claim to be."[45] Nichols's charges were in no real danger, and the Communists failed to seize Peiping, but the question of who held real authority in China was one that was about to be decided in a protracted and sanguinary fashion over the next four years.

The Shantung Peninsula, where Team Duck landed early on August 17, was another area in which the struggle for control of China was well under way. The team, commanded by Major Stanley A. Staiger, landed near a POW camp about two miles from Weihsien, a town not far from Tsingtao, where a former Presbyterian mission enclosed by a barbed wire fence held about fifteen hundred mostly civilian internees. In contrast to Hoten and Fengtai, the Japanese at the Weihsien camp, though "sullen," readily turned over the camp to the team. A "surging mass of prisoners" surrounded Major Staiger's men, "wringing their hands, embracing them, pounding their shoulders, kissing them."[46] The camp commander was described by Staiger as "stupid and scared stiff," and all real liaison work for the team was handled by Mr. Koga, the Japanese vice-consul at Tsingtao (Qingdao), who spoke excellent English but appeared "tricky" and "very anti-foreign."[47]

Staiger's men found about two hundred Americans in the camp along with British, Canadians, Belgians, Cubans, Dutch, Filipinos, and nine other nationalities ranging in age from ninety years to five days. Families of four, sometimes including young children, occupied a single room. A council of nine men administered camp affairs, and the prisoners had an efficient hospital with medicines procured through the Red Cross and the Swiss and Swedish consulates. Morale in the camp was described as good. Internees were able to go to church and hold dances. Only about two dozen prisoners were sick enough to require hospitalization, but all suffered from shortages of food. Staiger requested that all aircraft bringing supplies "buzz the camp on arrival," since "the sight of an American plane does wonders for them."[48]

As at Fengtai, rival Chinese forces appeared more of an immediate danger than did the Japanese. Colonel Jimbo Noruhiko, commander of the Japanese Army forces in the area, warned the Americans that the rapidly advancing forces of the Chinese Communist Eighth Route Army might soon be in a position to interdict most of the roads on the Shantung Peninsula. Staiger reported that the camp itself was in no immediate danger: "Chinese forces are guarding the area outside of the camp, Japanese forces were guarding the surrounding wall and internees are guarding the interior of the camp."[49] Away from the immediate area, however, the situation became more problematic because of the presence of bands of "dejected and nervous Japanese soldiers" and the reported appearance of units of the Eighth Route Army only five to seven miles away.[50] By August 29, however, the Duck team was reporting that the Communist forces appeared to be withdrawing into Hopeh (Hebei) Province. The following day, processing of prisoners and internees for evacuation through Tsingtao began.[51]

Like its successor, the Central Intelligence Agency, in which some of its people later served, OSS was a secret organization that seemed irresistibly drawn to publicity. The POW relief teams were considered a highly confidential project. Many team members had the secondary mission of intelligence reporting on political conditions, personalities, and alignments in their area. Yet the missions to Manchuria and northern China seemed too successful and dramatic to keep under cover. Observing the arrival of General Wainwright and other high-ranking Allied leaders at Xian, fresh from rescue by Cardinal, one OSS officer exulted, "It was a completely OSS show. . . . All of these people were pathetic in their gratitude for the things we were able to do for them. . . . No matter what honors or entertainment is provided for them from now until they reach home, they will all remember Xian and the OSS officers there as the highlight. . . ."[52] The commander of the Xian base, Major Gustave Krause, assured Colonel Richard P. Heppner, the chief of OSS China, that he would "see that OSS gets all credit possible. . . . Have full photo coverage of entire Wainwright trip. . . . All pictures have OSS personnel in them."[53]

The status of these pictures and accompanying sound recordings soon proved "tricky" since they had been "made in violation of regulations" during the "secret" missions.[54] Nothing daunted, Donovan proposed releasing them to the news media.[55] The task of publicizing OSS achievements proved complicated, however. Heppner discover to his distress that the Luce publications ran the story of Wainwright's rescue "without any reference to the leading role of OSS." He proposed that Washington leak the correct story to some rival publication.[56] Similarly, an Office of War Information news story on the liberation of Weihsien internment camp by Staiger's Team Duck failed to mention OSS by name.[57]

These frustrations in ensuring proper publicity for OSS soon paled beside the much larger problem of unwelcome publicity concerning OSS's operations in Korea. Lieutenant Colonel Willis H. Bird, the deputy director of OSS, was assigned the difficult task of leading POW operations in Korea. Bird's Team Eagle, composed of twenty-two men, was too large to be accommodated aboard a B-24, but a C-47 crew had volunteered to fly the mission even though the plane could carry only enough fuel for a one-way trip and would have to land in Korea in order to refuel.

Bird's team departed for Keijo, the capital of Korea, in the early hours of August 16, 1945, accompanied by Office of War Information reporter Henry R. Lieberman. There were believed to be as many as seven POW camps in Korea, and Keijo appeared to Bird to be the logical starting point for obtaining information on the location and status of these facilities.[58] About halfway to Keijo the plane picked up news broadcasts reporting that Japanese planes were still attacking American ships, and that fighting was continuing elsewhere. That was enough for Bird, who ordered a return to Xian.

After closely monitoring broadcasts for the next two days, Bird decided that the mission could proceed. He again departed Xian with his team and OWI reporter Henry Lieberman on the morning of the eighteenth.[59] No American had been to Korea since 1941. The Japanese Army there was still unblooded by the war. As their plane approached Keijo field, the team "could see factory smokestacks and buildings unmolested by the bombs that had devastated industrial facilities in Japan. . . . There about 50 planes, including about 20 Zeros, parked on the field with flight patrols taking off and landing regularly."[60]

The Japanese allowed Eagle's C-47 to land at an airfield outside Keijo, where they were met by a large delegation headed by a lieutenant general. Once they discovered that Bird had no authority to negotiate surrender terms, the Japanese became stubborn and uncooperative. The Americans were treated courteously but kept under guard at the airfield. The general flatly refused to furnish any information about Allied POWs except to assert that they were safe and being properly treated. As for Bird's men, they were to leave at once. The general insisted that although he was aware of the cease-fire, he had no authority from Tokyo to negotiate with Bird. When the American suggested that the team might be interned so that they could carry out their relief activities, the Japanese general refused, observing that it "was not safe" for them to remain. "One glance around the airfield" appeared to correspondent Lieberman to be "enough to support the general's contention. . . . On the field platoons and companies marched back and forth with Japanese sergeants barking their orders. . . . Japanese enlisted men in and about the hangars stared at the Americans with immobile expressions. In front of one barracks a white-shirted officer was practicing executioner sweeps with his long samurai sword."[61]

Bird then pointed out that if the Americans were to depart they would need gasoline for their C-47. Because the type of gasoline needed would have to be obtained from another field, Bird and his men were detained for the night at the airfield. The Japanese colonel left in charge of the Americans, whom Lieberman remembered as Shibuda, turned out to be an excellent host. After a dinner in which exceedingly polite enlisted men waited on the Americans with numerous bottles of sake and Kirin beer, one of the Japanese officers, a graduate of the military academy, called on the Americans to sing "the American air force song." Bird's men responded with a rousing rendition of "Wild Blue Yonder" with the Japanese beating time on the tables. A loud chorus of the Japanese air force song followed this.

Despite the conviviality of the dinner, Bird found the Japanese still unyielding the following morning. As the C-47 was being fueled, the Japanese brought up two tanks as well as mortars and deployed them around the plane. A frustrated Bird departed Keijo on the late afternoon of August 19.[62]

Almost immediately Bird received new orders from OSS to return with his team to Korea even if they had to be interned. By this point Bird, having seen the attitude of the Japanese at Keijo and the guns pointed at his team, had become convinced that an attempt to return to Korea would mean almost certain annihilation for his men, and he flew to Chungking to discuss the situation directly with General Wedemeyer. On August 22, Bird met with Wedemeyer, but while the China Theater was still weighing the future of the Eagle operation, a news story by Lieberman appeared in the media. Listening to the radio the following morning, Wedemeyer was flabbergasted to hear "about the Japs entertaining our people with beer and sake and each nationality singing their own national songs."[63] Wedemeyer, who felt uneasy having American troops associated even with the French and British, was infuriated at this evidence of apparent fraternization with the Japanese. "Colonel Byrd [*sic*] was rather stupid," Wedemeyer later recalled. "He was a temporary officer who wanted to solve problems his own way."[64]

Donovan instructed Heppner to "make sure [disciplinary] action [was] taken" against Bird.[65] While OSS and Wedemeyer's staff pondered ways to deal with the public relations catastrophe, further missions to Korea were shelved. An entire American corps was scheduled to land in that country in a few weeks in any case. OSS director Heppner hastily appointed a new public relations officer and instructed OSS personnel not to discuss their activities with the media.

By late September almost all former captives of the Japanese liberated by OSS had begun their journey home. Despite the debacle of the Eagle mission, the OSS teams on the whole had achieved remarkable success. A small number of determined young Americans, launched into the vastness of Asia, had performed notable feats of courage and improvisation that would be long remembered by those whose lives had been saved or imprisonments ended by the appearance of a lone B-24 bomber and a handful of parachutes. Yet the OSS missions in the north of China were tiny, fleeting episodes in comparison with the enormous drama that was about to unfold in East and Southeast Asia.

The Japanese had "lost"; the British, Chinese, French, Dutch, and Americans had "won." Yet there were still four million Japanese, many of them armed, on the mainland of Asia, and the Europeans remained shut out of most of their former colonies for the time being. All along the vast arc of countries stretching from Manchuria to Burma that constituted the ruins of the Japanese Empire, new ideas and ambitions were stirring, while old feuds were renewed with greater vigor. "I view Asia as an enormous pot, seething and boiling," wrote General Wedemeyer on the day after Japan's surrender. In this great drama now commencing, the Americans were not simply bit players. They were more like wealthy producers or prominent drama critics, often influential but with little control over how the play was performed or the actors behaved.

CHAPTER TWO

"An Enormous Pot, Seething and Boiling"

At noon Tokyo time on August 15, 1945, a brief radio address by the emperor announced the end of the war to millions of astounded Japanese in the Home Islands and all across Japan's still-vast empire, from the rolling plains of Manchuria to the jungles of Southeast Asia. Hours before, die-hard officers had persuaded or tricked leaders of the army's Imperial Guards Division into seizing the palace and destroying the discs of the emperor's prepared broadcast. But the hotheads never found the discs, cleverly concealed in the blacked-out palace, and the coup fizzled.

The emperor's broadcast did not use the words "defeat" or "surrender," observing only that despite the best efforts of all his soldiers and subjects, "the situation has developed not necessarily to Japan's advantage, while the general trends of the world have all turned against her interest." Japan would accept the Allied demands and the Japanese must "pave the way for a grand peace for all the generations to come by enduring the unendurable and suffering the insufferable."

To Japanese abroad, as to those at home, the sudden end of the war came as a severe shock. In the Southern Army, which was responsible for the defense of Southeast Asia, officers had heard reports of peace negotiations on foreign radio broadcasts, but all queries to Tokyo had been met with instructions to continue fighting to the end. As late as August 12, two days after the Japanese government had informed the Allies of its readiness to surrender subject to the retention of the emperor, Imperial General Headquarters had advised Southern Army commanders that "to continue the war with one mind is the only strategy for us and each soldier should follow this spirit."[1] As the emperor prepared his surrender broadcast, the commander of the China Expeditionary Army, General Okamura Yasuji, telegraphed to the chief of the Army General Staff, "The humiliating peace terms which have been reported by foreign broadcasts are tantamount to liquidating the Japanese empire which is now shining in all its glory and no subject of the empire can on any account submit to them."[2]

In the end, the generals and Japanese everywhere had to confront the fact of defeat. On the fifteenth of August, naval headquarters advised commanders in Southeast Asia that there was "nothing else to do but to adhere to the imperial order" and warned them to "take special care to see that all personnel act accordingly." The following morning the chief of the Army General Staff told the principal army commanders "a cease-fire order was about to be issued by the emperor."[3] General Itagaki Seishiro, the Japanese military commander in Singapore, reportedly refused to surrender until ordered to do so by his superior, Field Marshal Count Terauchi, "for the honor of his country."[4] Members of the imperial family were dispatched to China, Manchuria, and Southeast Asia to convey the emperor's desire for an orderly surrender and to emphasize that "to follow his wishes was the greatest act of allegiance to him."[5]

Among ordinary Japanese, reactions varied. At Hangchow (Hangzhou) the OSS reported that when the emperor's message was broadcast, Japanese soldiers "went down on their knees and wept bitterly." As in Japan, some Japanese abroad chose the path of suicide. A total of nine majors, seven captains, thirty-one other junior officers, eighty-eight noncommissioned officers, and twenty-six privates in Hangchow committed suicide during the month following the surrender.[6] Arthur Thompson, a Eurasian living in Singapore, recalled that a group of Japanese officers gathered at a large house on Bukit Timah Road. "They put a bomb under the house. They ate and they drank and drank and got drunk making a hell of a noise singing and shouting. And at a certain time the time bomb was set. The time bomb blasted right through the house, blew the roof off and they all died."[7]

Other Japanese felt angry and betrayed. "The imperial edict . . . has been brought about because the emperor sold his country to retain his throne," wrote one young officer.[8] On the other hand, General Imamura Hitoshi felt "officially great disappointment that even after digging an underground fortress our efforts were in vain. However my personal reaction was one of great relief. I could send 70,000 of our men back to their homeland alive."[9]

Some Japanese chose to regard the surrender as a temporary setback. "The Japanese people have no way to relieve the shame of the war except by rising again," wrote a Japanese officer in Korea. "I deeply believe the gods will help us. 1948 will probably be the year."[10] Foreign Minister Shigemitsu Mamoru observed that though China was among the victorious powers, she "is well aware that her future will not be easy and she will ultimately come to realize the necessity of a coalition with Japan." He added, "We still cherish the desire to see Korea revert to the empire."[11] OSS Counter-Intelligence reported rumors of the existence of a secret "Young Officers Alliance" composed of fanatical junior officers and other "rightist elements." The organization was reportedly financed by selling old army equipment, metals, and jewelry and was planning an armed uprising for 1948.[12] A high-ranking Chinese officer told his American adviser of rumors that "Jap aviators had gotten in touch with Chinese Air Force officers and advanced many reasons why China should cooperate with Japs in the future and not with Americans."[13]

In general, Japanese officers and men obeyed Tokyo's instructions to maintain discipline. In a few instances, however, Japanese troops took out their frustration and anger on the local population. At a village near Kuantan in Malaya, Japanese soldiers broke into several Chinese houses and "killed some Chinese in their beds . . . a small child was seized by a Japanese soldier who cut off his head and drank his blood."[14]

Most of the people of Greater East Asia learned of the war's end in less violent ways. Chin Sin Chong learned of the surrender from a leaflet dropped by a B-29 during an air raid on Singapore.[15] In Malaya and Singapore, many heard the news even before the emperor's broadcast through clandestine radios or through rumors. "Often we heard rumors," recalled Tan Ben Chang. "Sometimes they were believed, sometimes not. But when the news of the surrender came, I think most of us thought it was true. Because I don't think people would pass that sort of rumor."[16] Others heard later from newspapers or even public announcements.

In China an American general, hearing news of the atomic bombs and Japan's surrender offer, decided to stage an early victory parade for the benefit of the news cameras. In this way pictures of the "victory" in China might arrive in the United States in time for the actual celebration of VJ Day. Enlisting the support of his counterparts among the Nationalist forces stationed nearby, the general assembled several hundred Chinese and American troops for a parade through the town of Liuchow [Liuzhou], in south-central China, which was still in ruins from the effects of the devastating Japanese offensive of the previous summer. "Just before the parade I found that nobody had thought of telling the Liuchow public what was in store for them or why," recalled Graham Peck, an officer with the Office of War Information and a Chinese linguist.

> So I walked ahead to see the response in a little square where the country people sold food. . . . A few minutes after I reached the square . . . the khaki column of elite troops with their new American equipment could be seen approaching behind large Kuomintang [Guomindang] and American flags. The people in the market stared dumbfounded, then began to murmur among themselves:
>
> "Who are they?"
>
> "What do you suppose they want in Liuchow?"
>
> "Do you think they have come to take anything away from us?"
>
> "No, look at their fine clothes. Everything here is too poor for them."
>
> The parade began to pass through the square and soon delivered up an American general smiling in his jeep.
>
> "Peculiar, isn't it," the ragged man beside me said to his neighbor on the other side. "What do you make of it?"
>
> The other man gave him an utterly inscrutable look. "I think they have caught some bandits and are going to take them out and shoot them," he said.[17]

Many people learned of the surrender only weeks later. Ng Seng Yong, a pawnbroker and rice importer in a rural Malay village, learned of the surrender only on September 2, when he heard a broadcast of the surrender ceremony in Tokyo Bay over a radio hidden in his neighbor's attic.[18]

THE WAR HAD BEEN WON in the Pacific. In Asia, Japan's army was largely intact. It had large numbers of troops in northern and western China and, until August 9, Manchuria and Korea as well. Japanese armies had been badly mauled in Burma, but all of Indochina, Malaya, and the Netherlands Indies were still under Japanese control. At the moment of surrender there were approximately six and a half million Japanese soldiers and civilians—about one in every twenty Japanese—in the western Pacific and on the mainland of Asia. They included about 1,200,000 in Manchuria, 750,000 in Korea, 1,500,000 in China proper, and at least 700,000 in various parts of Southeast Asia.[19]

Allied policy was that all these Japanese were to be returned to Japan.[20] In principle, Allied forces would occupy the whole of Japan's former empire, where they would receive formal surrenders from various commands and disarm and repatriate the Japanese. The basic surrender document, General Order No. 1, hastily drafted in the State Department and the Pentagon during the night of August 10, provided that Japanese forces in China, Taiwan, and northern Indochina, but not Manchuria, were to surrender to Chiang Kai-shek. All Japanese forces in Manchuria and in Korea north of the 38th parallel were to surrender to the commander in chief of Soviet forces in the Far East. Japanese forces in Southeast Asia and the southwest Pacific were instructed to surrender to the Supreme Allied Commander, Admiral Lord Louis Mountbatten, and those in other parts of the Pacific to Admiral Chester Nimitz, commander in chief of the U.S. Pacific Fleet. The Japanese government and all forces in the Home Islands were to surrender to General Douglas MacArthur, designated the Supreme Allied Commander in Japan. Japanese forces in Korea south of the 38th parallel and in the Philippines would also surrender to MacArthur.

President Truman approved the order on August 14 and it was dispatched to Japan for the emperor to issue to his troops. At the suggestion of Assistant Secretary of War John J. McCloy, a provision had been added instructing the Japanese that the Allied commanders listed in the order were "the only representatives empowered to accept the surrender and all surrenders of Japanese forces shall be made only to them or their designated representatives."[21]

Yet it would be some time before the forces of the victorious powers could arrive in all the various quarters of former Greater East Asia. In a few places, that interval was relatively short; in many others it was a matter of some weeks or more. The timing of these Allied appearances proved to be of critical importance.

The Soviets were the first to arrive. They had entered the war on August 9, when more than a million and a half Soviet troops, accompanied by 3,700 tanks and 1,900 self-propelled guns, swept into Manchuria from the north, east, and west. Their approach obscured by heavy rainstorms, the Soviets achieved complete surprise. Across supposedly impassable deserts, mountains, and swamp land eleven Soviet armies thrust into the heart of the country, relentlessly crushing or outflanking the unprepared and outgunned soldiers of the Japanese Kwantung Army. Japanese soldiers discovered that their guns were often powerless to stop Soviet T-34 tanks. "Our artillery laid fire on the tanks in the rear," recalled a Japanese officer, while suicide assault teams attacked from the roadside. "However, even though the tanks were hit, since the projectiles were not armor-piercing, the actual damage was almost nil. . . . The enemy calmly repaired his tanks on a spot exposed to us. His behavior was arrogant and insolent in the face of our impotence."[22]

By the time of the emperor's surrender broadcast, the Soviets had advanced hundreds of miles into Manchuria, captured the key cities of Mutanchiang (Mudanjiang) and Wangching (Wangjing) and completely encircled the hapless Kwantung Army. The Soviets claimed to have killed about 84,000 Japanese soldiers, including Manchurian and Chinese puppet troops, and captured almost 600,000. Soviet losses were about 12,000.[23]

The Kwantung Army reacted slowly to Tokyo's surrender announcement. On August 16, Imperial General Headquarters instructed Kwantung Army commanders to contact local Russian commanders to negotiate surrender arrangements. Communications were poor, and the Soviets refused to allow the Japanese free movement between units. As a result, some fighting continued into August 20. Russian advances did not completely end until the last days of August, by which time the Soviets had occupied the city of Kalgan, the main railway junction of the northeast, and Red Army columns were moving into the Chinese provinces of Hopeh (Hebei) and Jehol (Rehe). Roughly one and a half million Japanese in Manchuria, Korea, and northern China became prisoners of the Soviets. Many spent years in Soviet prison camps, and at least three hundred thousand are still unaccounted for. For many other Japanese as well, the war in Manchuria was far from over.

For forty years Manchuria had been the focus of Japanese dreams and ambitions for industrial development, economic independence, social engineering, and Pan-Asian betterment under Japanese leadership.[24] Between 1931 and 1941, Japan had expended the equivalent of six billion dollars on factories, hydroelectric plants, railways, mines, shipyards, and other industrial development projects in Manchuria.[25] Japanese corporations controlled most of the country's mining, fishing, manufacturing, and communications.[26] The majority of the 1,200,000 Japanese in Manchuria were soldiers of the Kwantung Army, but there were also large numbers of civilians engaged in business, manufacturing, and banking. Several thousand were employees of the South Manchuria Railroad and more than three thousand were advisers to, or employees of, the puppet Manchukuo (Manzhouguo) government.[27]

Only about 2 percent of the Japanese in Manchuria were engaged in agriculture, but those 2 percent were included in an elaborate scheme of social planning. They were part of a project for the large-scale colonization of the area by land-poor farmers from Japan, "soldiers of the hoe" resettled on agricultural lands in Manchuria. About half of the settlements were located along the Soviet-Manchurian frontier. Many were established for younger colonists who had come to Manchuria through service in the Patriotic Youth Brigade, an organization that recruited young men aged fourteen to twenty-one for three years of paramilitary and agricultural training. With their young brides, also brought from Japan, they were considered the ideal means of spreading the Japanese spirit abroad and relieving rural poverty at home as well as "serving as a reserve for Imperial Army operations" in the event of war with Russia.[28]

Once placed in their new homes, the settlers found themselves the owners of prime agricultural land far in excess of anything they might have dreamed of at home. The Manchukuo government secured a considerable portion of the land from its former Chinese owners through "price manipulation, coerced sales and forced evictions." Now possessed of more land than they could farm with only their families, the Japanese colonists proceeded to hire large numbers of Chinese and Korean laborers or even to lease back some of the recently appropriated land to its former owners.[29] Not surprisingly, relations between the settlers and older Chinese and Korean residents were at best uneasy, sometimes hostile. The colonists were allowed to carry firearms and to take action against Chinese or Koreans who appeared menacing. Fukushima Yoshi, the young wife of a prosperous store owner in northeast Manchuria, was cautioned by her husband to treat the Manchurians kindly, "but in your heart you cannot completely trust them. . . . They're likely to have vengeful feelings toward Japan. Even the kids who worked for us would sometimes blurt out to me that Japan was bad for taking their land." Yoshi's family had a large German shepherd trained "to bite only Manchurians. They'd dress someone up in Manchu clothes and they trained the dog to attack when he came into a room, taking a big bite out of his calf."[30]

As the possibility of Soviet attack loomed ever larger, the settlements were progressively denuded of their able-bodied manpower. Reservists and young men from the Youth Brigade were called up in 1944. In a final "bottom-scraping" (*nekosoki*) mobilization in July and August 1945, most of the settlements lost their few remaining men.[31] "The draft in Manchuria was crazy," recalled one writer. "Even the elderly and sick were included and they did not receive uniforms or conventional arms. Instead they were ordered to bring with them any arms at home including swords, spears and hunting guns. . . . The undrafted people up to age forty-five were forced to train to conduct suicide attacks and serve as part of a bucket brigade in case of fire and to use wooden spears. . . ."[32] Meanwhile, the Kwantung Army completed plans to fall back to defensive positions in the south and east, abandoning most of the agricultural settlements to the Soviets.

Settlers near the Soviet border learned of the Russian attack only when they were suddenly ordered to evacuate or by accident through encountering other settlers fleeing south. The residents of Fukushima Yoshi's settlement "had no idea which way to escape. Everyone just wanted to go whatever way the Soviets weren't said to be coming. . . .

From that first night you were totally on your own. If you ran into someone familiar you greeted them and maybe walked together but soon enough you were separated. I had no idea where we were. Perhaps the railroad tracks would take us to Mukden. I found them and walked along them. Those who collapsed just died by the roadbed. But it wasn't long before you couldn't walk the rails any more. The Soviets started using them. . . . We had to move into the mountains. They were a wilderness, sometimes even a primeval forest, and there were dead bodies all over the trails. . . . If the Manchus found you, you'd be stripped of all you had. But the Soviets were the most frightening. They killed Japanese just for the sake of killing. I saw many who'd been bayoneted. Heaps and heaps of bodies."[33]

Ono Eiko, a fourth-grader living in a settlement a few miles from the Soviet border, fled south with her father, grandfather, mother, and two younger sisters after the Japanese Army and police had commandeered all the available horses for their own flight. After walking all night toward the nearest railroad station, they were strafed by Soviet aircraft. Arriving at the railroad station, they learned the trains had stopped running and decided to take the rugged route through the mountains to avoid Soviet troops. While on the mountain trail, the settler groups were strafed several more times and attacked by armed bands of Chinese. Food ran out and the settlers subsisted on grass and roots. Only fifteen of Eiko's party of more than a hundred settlers survived to return to Japan.[34] In all, it is estimated that at least eleven thousand settlers lost their lives as a result of Russian attacks, local assaults by Chinese and Koreans, and on the trek south. More than four thousand of these deaths were suicides.[35] Ironically, 73 percent of the male settlers called up for military service survived the Soviet invasion, but only 27 percent of those remaining in the settlements were as fortunate.[36]

Young children and infants were the most likely to die on the long flight to the south. A baby's crying could endanger an entire group by betraying their location to the Russians or to Chinese brigands.[37] Fatigue and malnutrition frequently made it impossible for mothers to nurse. "The babies were the most pitiful," recalled one former refugee. "Because of the hunger they no longer had the power to cry, and when closely examined they were cold with their shrunken bony fingers in their mouths."[38] Many of the hapless refugees felt obliged to leave their youngest children with friendly Chinese families as the only way to ensure that they would survive the wreckage of Manchukuo.

Most of those who completed the nightmare journey to the south found only further hardship in the crowded cities of Manchuria and northern China. A Japanese consular official reported, "Some refugees have walked over a thousand miles to get to the refugee camps. Many are emaciated; some literally naked. There are few adult males in the camps. Many of the sick have committed suicide along the way so as not to be a burden to their relatives. Some of the women have agreed to have sex in order to obtain a ride on a train."[39] The new arrivals were covered "with lice which caused typhus. They smelled so bad that one could not go near them," recalled one journalist. "They had no shoes of course and the soles of their feet were black with mud, sweat and grease."[40] By the end of August the Japanese ambassador in Manchuria estimated that there were about half a million refugees from both city and countryside in Mukden. "They have been robbed of all but what they could bring with them. They are housed without food; sometimes not being able to eat for days at a time."[41]

The Japanese neighborhood associations in Mukden and other large cities pooled their resources to set up self-help organizations in the camps, which attempted to provide food, medical care, and burial services, kept records, and ran rudimentary hospitals and even a credit union.[42] But with the old Manchukuo currency rapidly becoming worthless and the Soviet occupation forces flooding the market with military scrip of dubious value, most Japanese were hard hit by inflation even when they escaped shakedowns by the Russians.

Disease ravaged the camps during the winter and spring of 1945–46. In one refugee camp near Harbin all 1,020 people contracted typhus. One makeshift graveyard on the grounds of an old school was at one point adding a hundred graves a day.[43] In all, about 15 percent of the Japanese in the Harbin area died between August 1945 and March 1946.[44]

Though the Japanese suffered most, all those who had the misfortune to be living in Manchuria that fateful August were to undergo a difficult ordeal. In Mukden the Chinese, Manchurians, and Koreans greeted the arrival of Russian troops with enthusiasm. Attacks on and looting of Japanese-owned shops and businesses soon began, unhindered by Soviet troops. Japanese houses and buildings were sometimes burned to the ground. In the city of Jinzhou, south of Mukden, "Japanese houses were looted and my mother noticed that one of her poor neighbors suddenly had a lot of valuable things for sale. Schoolchildren revenged themselves on their Japanese teachers and beat them up ferociously. Some Japanese women left their babies on the doorsteps of local families in the hope that they would be saved."[45]

Chinese mobs, often armed with rifles left behind by the fleeing Japanese, roamed the city beating, robbing, and raping. Many Japanese resisted as best they could and, according to an American observer of the OSS Cardinal Team, "casualties ran into the hundreds on both sides."[46] In Mukden, Corporal Hal Leith came upon "a mob of Chinese trying to kill a Japanese child—maybe twelve years old. . . . I bawled out the Chinese mob (called them turtle eggs and said that they were acting as bad as the Japanese!). Some of the Chinese took my side and some commented on my good Chinese accent. . . . I turned the boy over to the hospital authorities. . . . I was really mad—went back to the RR station and waded into the Chinese mob and took their clubs away from them and broke them against the curbing. . . . How I got away with it I will never know. . . . The people in the mob again all commented on my being an American and on my good Chinese accent."[47] After three days, the Soviets stepped in to demand that all weapons be surrendered within the next seventy-two hours. The penalty for noncompliance was death.

The Soviets quickly rounded up all the Japanese police officials, prosecutors, judges, bank presidents, and company heads. In all, about nineteen hundred civilian officials were detained, facing an uncertain fate.[48] Former Chinese and Manchurian functionaries of the Manchukuo government "besieged the Soviet occupation authorities with gifts, begging to be granted an audience. The Soviets accepted the gifts but granted no audience."[49]

Soviet soldiers swiftly took up where the local residents had left off, cheerfully robbing both Chinese and Japanese houses. In the opinion of the OSS team, "The Russians excelled the Chinese in large scale housebreaking, looting and, in numerous cases, rape."[50] The Japanese consulate reported that women were raped at bus stops, in railroad stations, and simply by Russians passing on the roads. Rumors held that local authorities had been instructed "to offer up a certain number of women each night" to the Soviets."[51] Women cut their hair and put ink and bandages on their face to make themselves as unattractive as possible.[52] To the Soviets, recently arrived from a country that had long lacked consumer goods of all kinds, Manchuria appeared far more opulent than Russia. They set out immediately to right this imbalance. Russian soldiers "burst into private homes and ransacked the house, removing everything of value except the furniture. Then a military truck would come and haul away the furniture."[53] Soviet officers seldom attempted to restrain their men from looting and indeed often joined in.[54]

"All they do is loot and kill," declared Hal Leith, "and they don't stick to looting from the Japanese. Some soldiers wear as many as ten watches. . . . I have met some very nice Soviet military in Mukden but they are about 1 in 10."[55] A Soviet general excused the rapacious behavior of his troops to an American by explaining that they were "shock troops" formed from those who had had their families butchered by the Germans and were most eager for revenge. After the German surrender they were dispatched to the Far East. " 'Not being normal in their minds,' they were bent on looting, killing and rape."[56]

The Japanese vice-consul in Port Arthur (Lunchun) reported that Chinese citizens had stolen arms from the naval base in order to arm themselves as a militia to stop Russian looting.[57] Even the Chinese Communists protested to the Soviets that Red Army troops "were engaging in activities inconsistent with the practices of a proletarian army, in particular raping women and depriving peasants of their livelihood." The secretary of the Party's Northeast Committee, Hu Fujia (Hu Fuchia), urged the Red Army commanders to issue orders promising strict punishment for violations of discipline. Hu believed it would require a massive propaganda campaign to win back the goodwill of the Chinese toward the Soviets.[58]

Surprisingly, the Japanese discovered some Soviet soldiers "to be simple and friendly as individuals. They loved children and were constantly asking women with children in their arms if they could hold their babies, even while on duty." Young mothers with children were reportedly safe from rape.[59] Another peculiarity was the Soviet partiality to the performing arts. The Soviet deputy commanding general was reported to be a lover of the theater, and actors, dancers, singers, and musicians were accorded many special privileges. The performing arts troupe, which had been organized to entertain the Kwantung Army, quickly reconstituted itself as the "peace art association" under the leadership of a former official of the Manchuria Film Association. Performers were housed in a former luxury hotel and were guarded day and night by armed sentries. Their food and clothing were far better than those of other surviving Japanese and elicited more than a little envy and animosity from their fellow countrymen.[60]

While most of its residents struggled to find enough food for survival and Soviet soldiers prowled the streets in search of overlooked items to loot, Mukden enjoyed a vibrant cultural life. There were four legitimate theaters and several cinemas. All revenue from the theaters was allocated for the arts. The deputy commanding general provided coal for heating. An art institute was in operation with separate departments of drama, dance, vocal music, and instrumental music. "All Soviet troops at the theaters were gentlemen. They took off their hats and treated the theaters as sacred places."

The individual Red Army soldier's adventures in larceny paled into insignificance beside the systematic deindustrialization of Manchuria by the Soviet authorities. Working around the clock, the Soviets dismantled entire factories and power plants and sent them north to Siberia on endless trains of flatcars. *New York Times* correspondent Hallett Abend reported that even the giant locomotive and railway-car building plants at Dairen "were transported bodily north of the Amur River."[61] The Soviets concentrated on power-generating equipment, electric motors, laboratories, and hospitals as well as the latest machine tools.[62] About $3 million in gold bullion disappeared from Mukden banks. "It is probably safe to assume," wrote Major Lamar of the Cardinal mission, "that the Soviets are intent on taking control of all factories and sending their equipment to Russia before their withdrawal from the country."[63]

Over the next few weeks the Soviets almost met Major Lamar's predictions. Of 972 factories in Mukden, only twenty had sufficient machinery to continue functioning six months later. Waterworks and sewage plants were inoperable for lack of power, and mines needed to supply coal for the coming winter were unable to continue production for lack of machinery.[64] "They had taken everything that could be taken," recalled Robert Seck, a U.S. Marine flight mechanic who flew into the city just after the Soviets departed. "The only thing they left was a memorial to themselves with a tank on top in the center of town."[65] American experts estimated the direct damage done to the economy of China by the Soviet removals to be around $850 million.[66] The Russians also used their occupation currency to buy up most of the important property in Manchuria. Arriving in Mukden in March 1946, Hallett Abend found that several modern office buildings, two paper mills, an aircraft plant, the largest hotel, and, of course, the four theaters, were all Russian-owned.[67] "The damage which Manchurian industry has sustained since V-J Day," concluded the economics experts, "has set back China's industrial progress for a generation."[68]

As the Soviet advance continued into Jehol and Hopeh, the Russians repeated their performances farther north. The city of Pingchuan in Jehol Province had been expecting the arrival of Chiang's troops and were surprised to find their town occupied instead by the Red Army. Former members of the puppet army and police were rounded up and imprisoned without adequate food while the Russians ransacked every house and carried away all the livestock. Local residents reported that Soviet soldiers "forcibly took people's wristwatches. If they refused to give them up, they were sentenced to be shot. . . . The Russian Army forced the farmers to find women for them. When some failed to produce the women, the Russians, unable to satisfy their desires, shot two laborers and one farmer."[69]

The devastating Soviet sojourn in northern China was only one of the unintended consequences of the U.S. and British invitation to the Russians to enter the war against Japan. When Churchill, Roosevelt, and Stalin had met at Yalta in February 1945, Soviet help to subdue Japan still appeared very important. The Japanese were on their last legs in the Pacific with American forces preparing to land on Okinawa, but Tokyo still had large armies on the continent who might have to be engaged at some point to prevent their participation in the battle for the Japanese Home Islands.

Stalin's price was the restoration of all the special privileges that Czarist Russia had held in Manchuria before she had been deprived of them "by the treacherous attack of Japan in 1904." This included control of Dairen and Port Arthur and joint operation of the Manchurian railroads. The Soviets would recognize China's "full sovereignty" in Manchuria, but China would have to accept the continued existence of the Soviet-sponsored regime in Outer Mongolia, the Mongolian People's Republic. This agreement on the Far East was reached without any consultation with the Chinese government.

Roosevelt promised to obtain Chiang Kai-shek's consent to the agreement, and the Soviets promised to sign a "treaty of friendship and alliance" with China. Such a treaty would explicitly recognize Chiang's Kuomintang regime as the only legitimate government of China and, in effect, abandon the Chinese Communists. Negotiations over the treaty in Moscow dragged on from June through August. The Soviets were alternately contemptuous and wheedling, the Chinese worried but unflappable. Finally on August 10 Stalin warned Chiang's representatives that they had better sign the treaty quickly because the Chinese Communist armies were moving into Manchuria in the wake of the Soviet invasion.[70] On August 14, the day of Japan's final surrender announcement, the Chinese and Soviet foreign ministers signed the treaty. The price to Chiang was high: everything agreed at Yalta and then some; but the Chinese Communists had been isolated, and the world's two strongest powers were now formally tied to Chungking.

Although he had his treaty, as well as General Order No. 1 directing the Japanese generals to obey only him, Chiang was not well positioned to push his advantage. During the spring and summer of 1945, the Japanese had conducted a far-reaching series of offensives called Ichigo that left Chiang in control of even less territory than after the Japanese victories of 1937–38. His remaining power lay mainly in the southwest corner of a disunited China. As diplomat John Paton Davies, a veteran of many years in East Asia, recalled, "Chiang's regime and the Communists were the principal elements," but there were also "a number of residual warlords, semiautonomous provincial factions and generals, and, in occupied China and Manchuria, puppet governments set up by the Japanese. Political brokers, agents, and provocateurs moved among these varied elements making deals, buying and selling expedient allegiances and betrayal."[71] Altogether, at the time of the Japanese surrender there were five functioning governments in China: Chiang's, the Communists, and three Japanese-created puppet regimes. Each of the five had its own currency, legal system, and taxes, in addition to its own army. The puppet regimes in Manchukuo, Peiping, and Nanking (Nanjing) had a total of about one and a half million men in their armies. Mao Tse-tung's army was reported to number about nine hundred thousand with a two-million-man militia.[72] Communist forces surrounded the major cities of Peiping, Hankow (Hankou), Tsingtao, Shanghai, and Nanking, as the OSS POW teams had quickly discovered, and the Communists controlled hundreds of miles of rail line.

In the reoccupation of China, Chiang was, as one American officer put it, "starting from the flat of his back."[73] The Generalissimo's armies were more than a thousand miles from the great cities in the north and east. His forces were very large on paper, with a total of four million men, but General Wedemeyer estimated that only about twenty divisions had been properly trained and equipped, nineteen others were partly equipped and trained, and the rest "scarcely worth a damn by the standards of modern warfare."[74] After eight years of war, Chiang's Nationalist government was weary, ill organized, and corrupt, at once ineffective and oppressive. "If peace comes suddenly, it is reasonable to expect widespread confusion and disorder," declared General Wedemeyer at the beginning of August. "The Chinese have no plans for rehabilitation, prevention of epidemics, restoration of utilities, establishment of a balanced economy and redisposition of millions of refugees."[75]

Chiang himself had been hailed in the American media as a brave and dedicated national hero. Yet to many who knew him, he was not a figure to inspire confidence. "I had the feeling he was not a modern man," recalled one of his close advisers. "[He] had the traditional Confucian mentality that relies first on men and personal relationships rather than institutions."[76] A Kuomintang minister observed that Chiang "always selected his commanders less because of their ability than because of their personal loyalty. So long as a man was faithful to him he wouldn't mind a little corruption."[77] Proud and rigid, with supreme confidence in his own ability, Chiang "thought he could never be wrong. . . . When anybody reported any facts which did not tally with his own observations, he never thought they could be true. If any mistakes were committed, he deemed that these mistakes had happened because of the failings of his subordinates."[78]

Wedemeyer, whose main mission had been organizing, training, and equipping Chiang's troops for an offensive intended to progressively win back east China from the Japanese, now found himself with a new task as the end of the war approached. Washington instructed him that after a Japanese capitulation he was to continue military aid to Chiang and assist his forces in reoccupying all the former Japanese-held areas of China as well as Taiwan. American naval and Marine forces would take control of key ports on the China coast to facilitate the disarming of the Japanese and the arrival of Chiang's Nationalist troops. Wedemeyer was to do all this while at the same time ensuring that U.S. forces did not become involved in "fratricidal war."[79]

In the north, Mao Tse-tung did not even know of the Sino-Soviet treaty, but he wasted no time. Even before General Order No. 1 had been issued, General Chu Teh (Zhu De), commander of the Communist forces in the north, had announced that "any anti-Japanese armed forces can take the surrender of the Japanese." In notes to the Allied embassies in Chungking, the Communists claimed that it was they who had done all the fighting in the war against Japan. Their radio broadcasts declared that "the Fascist chieftain," Chiang Kai-shek, "cannot represent the Chinese people and Chinese troops which really oppose the Japanese."[80] Troops of Mao's Eighth Route Army moved forward to disarm the Japanese and north to meet the victorious Russians. Communist forces also occupied, or threatened to occupy, some of the large cities and seized even more of the railroads.

Chiang ordered the Communists to stand fast and await his orders. He reminded the Japanese to surrender only to him. The Communists ignored these instructions and were soon fighting those Japanese who refused to yield to them while confiscating the weapons and equipment of those who did. Some of the latter were soon recruited into the Eighth Route Army. Alarmed at these developments, Wedemeyer urged Washington to give China first priority in allocation of U.S. occupation forces. After describing the advances of Communist troops, he also raised the possibility that some of the Japanese troops might continue to fight. In any case, former enemy forces and civilians would have to be concentrated in the major port areas for shipment back to Japan. Wedemeyer wanted seven American divisions sent to China and requested, as "an absolute minimum," that two American divisions be sent to Taku (Dagu), a port near Peiping, one to Shanghai, and elements of a fourth to Canton.[81] Marshall promptly advised Wedemeyer that "your proposal that we give China first priority over Japan and Korea will not be acceptable" and that the most he could expect would be two U.S. divisions, whose arrival would be dependent on the availability of shipping.[82]

By the time Wedemeyer read this reply, his headquarters was receiving reports of "armed clashes between Central Government and Communist Forces in several areas." One and a half million Communists were reportedly "deployed for the occupation of Shanghai-Nanking-Hangchow area, the bulk interposed between Japs and Central Government."[83] In view of these developments, Wedemeyer believed it was urgent to lift Chiang's armies by sea and air to eastern and northern China as soon as possible. Admiral Nimitz reported that an amphibious task force would be available to transport two Marine divisions to China, but only after all available assault shipping had been used to lift MacArthur's forces to Japan and Korea.[84] All this would take time. In the interim, Chiang and his American allies would have to depend to a great extent on their erstwhile enemies, the Japanese and the "puppets," to hold back the Red tide.

Most of the Japanese generals in China viewed the Communists with distaste and the Nationalists with disdain. They felt no sense of having been defeated by Chiang or by the Communist guerrillas. An American general concluded that "the Japanese officers that he met [to arrange details of the surrender] are representative of a Japanese Army that has not been defeated. Every mannerism indicates that they were obediently attending to a conference, and formally surrendering but that's all."[85] For weeks in Shanghai and Peiping, Japanese troops with polished bayonets continued to patrol the streets and Japanese officers still drove about in their staff cars.[86] As late as September 4, an OSS officer reported from Shanghai that "to date the Japs have not in any way relinquished control of the city."[87]

On August 23, General Ho Ying-chin (He Yingqin), commander of the Nationalist armies, ordered the Japanese generals in northern and eastern China to hold and defend all areas they occupied against the Communists pending the arrival of Chiang's forces. Despite their contempt for China's military, the Japanese generals were more than willing to comply in return for implicit understandings that the Japanese in China and their property would be well taken care of.

For many months before the Japanese surrender, rumors had been flying concerning secret understandings between Chiang, the puppet regimes, and the Japanese to form a common front against the Communists. "In China," observed one Chinese journalist, "no matter what happens there is always the same set of career bureaucrats."[88] With the Allied victory, high officials who had collaborated with the Japanese now proclaimed themselves advance agents charged to "maintain order" by the Nationalist government. In Hopeh Province, the former Japanese-controlled puppet army now became the Kuomintang's "Hopeh Advance Army," commanded by a former collaborationist official.[89] Japanese messages decrypted by American intelligence revealed that the Nanking puppet government and a Nationalist government representative, Ku Chu-tung, "had been in contact for over a year." Ku and General Ho Ying-chin had reportedly "secretly proposed to the puppet government a joint defense against the Communists." In Peiping, "the local puppet government, with full knowledge (indeed under the direction) of Chungking, is taking steps to cooperate with the Japanese to keep the Chinese [Communists] from gaining control of the area."[90] In Shanghai, the mayor, Chou Fo-hai, a former high-ranking minister in the collaborationist Wang Ching-wei regime, had run the city for the Japanese. He now announced that he had been instructed by Chiang to maintain public order—of course, in cooperation with the Japanese.[91]

The tacit Japanese realignment with Chiang was made easier by the fact that several of Chiang's top generals had attended military schools in Japan during the 1920s and early 1930s and retained a deep respect for their erstwhile mentors. When Major General Imai Takeo, Okamura's deputy chief of staff, arrived at Chekiang to arrange the formal surrender of Japanese forces, he found that three officers of the Chinese delegation were his former pupils at the Japanese military academy. According to Imai, the head of the Chinese delegation had provided a round table for the surrender conference to imply that the Japanese were to be treated as equals. The Americans, however, had insisted on two long tables facing each other. The American representative at the surrender ceremony was also concerned that the Chinese seemed inclined to allow the Japanese officers to retain their personal swords as they were "family heirlooms." He reminded the Chinese of the "Potsdam declaration that the Jap military caste must be destroyed."[92] The

Chinese officers reportedly were "annoyed at the American lack of understanding of politeness between fellow Orientals. After the conference was over they talked with the Japanese delegates about Japan with great pleasure."[93]

General Okamura himself, despite having carried out one of the largest gas attacks of the war against Chinese troops and having directed a brutal pacification campaign in northern China that caused the deaths of hundreds of thousands of civilians,[94] was cordially received by Chiang's generals. One of General Ho Ying-chin's aides recalled that when Ho arrived in Nanking for the formal surrender ceremony, "he immediately visited General Okamura, who had taught him at the military academy in Tokyo, and, addressing him as 'sensei' [teacher], apologized profusely for having to subject him to the indignity of surrendering."[95] Ho's senior interpreter, Major Wang Yao-wu, was so distressed by Ho's conduct that he confided to an American adviser his fear that "his countrymen had forgotten about the rape of Nanking."[96] The Nationalist general Yen His-shan (Yan Xishan), warlord of Shanxi Province, had been a classmate of Okamura's at the military academy and remarked to one of Okamura's staff officers that he did not believe that Japan had really been defeated in Asia.[97]

Thanks largely to the Japanese and the puppet regimes, the Communists were kept out of the largest cities in north China and forcefully expelled from many smaller ones. The Japanese patrolled the rail lines, protected key installations, and used bayonets to suppress a Communist-organized strike in Shanghai.[98] "There is nothing in Nanking that indicates its liberation," wrote a Chinese journalist at the end of August. "Okamura is still enthroned in the Foreign Ministry building. Japanese gendarmes still occupy the former premises of the Judicial Yuan. Japanese sentries are posted everywhere."[99] Communist newspapers reported more than a hundred armed clashes with Japanese or puppet troops between late August and the end of September.[100] In the area of Kaifeng, the OSS reported that about 130 troops of the Japanese Twelfth Army had been killed in fighting with the Communists between the Japanese surrender and late November 1945. Though the Japanese fought well, "they have nothing but contempt for Chinese inefficiency and their only desire is to return home."[101]

For many, that return was still far off. An American naval officer reported, following a meeting with Chiang, that "the Generalissimo does not desire to disarm and repatriate additional Japanese troops from North China at this time as he is fearful that if sufficient Chinese national troops are not available to prevent it, the Chinese Communists will move into areas evacuated by the Japanese."[102] As late as December 1946, an American diplomat estimated there were still at least eighty thousand Japanese troops operating under Nationalist command in China.[103]

In addition to the Japanese, Mao Tse-tung faced another problem in the north: the Russians. News of the Soviet treaty with Chiang flabbergasted many in Yenan (Yan'an). Despite differences in doctrine, the Chinese Communists had always aligned themselves ideologically and politically with the Soviet Union. The Chinese Communist Party was part of the Communist International. As recently as April, Mao had called the Soviet Union "the best friend of the Chinese People."[104] Officially the Party accepted the treaty as "beneficial to China and the world," but, as one Party cadre added after repeating the official line in a lecture, "We do not understand actual Russian policy."[105] An American newsman who managed to reach Manchuria in early October was "impressed by the fact that the Communists were puzzled and disappointed by Soviet policy."[106] Privately some Party leaders speculated that Stalin had been frightened by the U.S. atomic bombs and was eager to avoid anything that could lead to a clash with the Americans.[107]

On August 14, as the Japanese surrender was announced, Chiang, bolstered by assurances of continued American military and political support and his treaty with the Russians, invited Mao Tse-tung to Chungking for talks. Both Chiang and Mao were aware that the people of China, exhausted by eight years of war, were strongly opposed to the prospect of further military strife, but Mao was less than thrilled by the invitation. Given Chiang's ideas of diplomacy and the past history between the two men, it was possible that Mao might not leave Chungking alive. But U.S. ambassador Patrick J. Hurley arrived at Yenan in his plane to personally escort Mao to Chungking, thus guaranteeing his safety. More importantly, Stalin made it clear to Mao that he must talk to Chiang. In a secret message from Moscow, Stalin warned that a civil war would destroy the Chinese nation. This was followed several hours later by an even stronger message: If Mao refused to negotiate, "his stand would be repudiated in China and abroad."[108] On August 28, Mao flew with Hurley to Chungking.

It was Mao's first airplane ride, but it was not Hurley's first visit to Yenan. Appointed President Roosevelt's special representative to China in August 1944, and ambassador a few months later, Hurley was a prominent Republican politician, National Guard general, and former secretary of war from Oklahoma. On his first visit to Yenan, Hurley, resplendent in major general's uniform with full medals, had greeted Mao Tse-tung and other Communist leaders with a loud Choctaw war whoop as he disembarked from his plane. Hurley had important supporters in Washington, but to many of those who came in contact with him in China, his behavior seemed something beyond eccentric. "Hurley was crazy," concluded John F. Melby, a State Department political officer in Chungking. "I think he was beginning to get a little senile. . . . He wasn't ambassador for very long [but] he sure raised a lot of hell while he was there."[109]

Even the circumspect General Wedemeyer confided to Marshall that Hurley was "at times too garrulous for he talks continually and he is not always discreet as to what he says and to whom he relates information. . . . Between you and me I think he is failing in health and it affects his perspective at times in his relations with others."[110] Hot-tempered and suspicious, Hurley was constantly at odds with many of the embassy's China experts, whom he considered wrong-headed and probably disloyal. "Many of the American correspondents [in China] were communistically inclined," he told Navy Secretary James Forrestal, "as well as many of the people of the State Department . . . who felt no obligation for the United States except to draw their pay."[111]

For almost a year Hurley had been working to bring about a settlement between the Nationalists and Communists that would end the strife between them and unite China under Chiang's leadership. But while Hurley was devoted to achieving a peaceful end to internal struggle in China, he was equally devoted to Chiang, who he believed should never be pressured or coerced into accepting any arrangements Chiang deemed unacceptable. Not surprisingly, Hurley was making little progress with this approach when the war suddenly ended. Now he saw a new opportunity to achieve a settlement. On a visit to Moscow in

April, Hurley had been assured by Stalin that the Soviets deplored the possibility of civil war in China and would recognize the Nationalists as the legitimate government of China. With such support guaranteed by the Sino-Soviet Treaty, Hurley reasoned, the Communists would have nowhere to go.

Mao arrived in Chungking wearing a topee and appearing calm and confident, giving little indication of his contempt and loathing for the Nationalists. While Chou En-lai (Zhou Enlai), the Communist permanent liaison officer in Chungking, nervously checked Mao's quarters for bombs and sniffed his food for poison, Mao went calmly about his talks, attended a Chinese opera performance, and exchanged toasts with Chiang—the last occasion on which the two would ever see each other face to face.[112]

While Hurley was anxiously following the negotiations, a new problem arose. On August 25, an American OSS officer, Captain John Birch, was murdered by Communist soldiers near Suchow (Suzhou). Birch had been on his way to the Shantung Peninsula to survey the area's former Japanese airfields for possible use in POW operations and to establish radio communications for OSS in the region.[113] In the town of Hwang Ko (Hankuo), Birch's small detachment was stopped by Communist soldiers, who demanded that the OSS party surrender its arms. Birch, who spoke fluent Chinese, refused, and demanded to speak to the officer in charge. An angry altercation followed. Birch and his deputy, Lieutenant Tung Chin-seng, a Nationalist officer, were shot by the Communists and their bodies dumped in a pit. Birch's body was later mutilated by the Communists, probably in an effort to make identification impossible. Lieutenant Tung survived, however, and, helped by local people, made his way to a nearby Nationalist unit.[114]

The news of Birch's death sent shock waves through American headquarters in Chungking. General Chu Teh explained to an infuriated Wedemeyer that he had alerted the Communist New Fourth Army command to Birch's expected arrival at the town of Ninchuan (Nanchang), but Birch showed up at Hwang-ko station, 250 miles north of Ninchuan, in an area still under the control of Chinese puppet troops. Communist forces in the area were part of the Eighth Route Army and had not been informed of Birch's arrival.[115] A more likely explanation for the Eighth Route Army's behavior is that the American was scheduled to meet with General Hu Peng-chu, the commander of the former puppet Sixth Army. The Communists were at the time in the midst of delicate maneuvers to subvert the Sixth Army headquarters and bring the former puppet troops over to the Eighth Route Army.[116]

Wedemeyer confronted Mao and Chou En-lai directly at Hurley's quarters in Chungking five days after Birch's murder. The two professed to have no knowledge of the incident. Wedemeyer told the Communist leaders that "I am going to use whatever force is necessary to protect American lives." He warned that there would be grave consequence if the American public were to learn of Birch's death at the hands of the Communists. Mao replied in a conciliatory tone, reminding the Americans that the Communists had helped to rescue downed flyers and had welcomed an American observer group to Yenan. He suggested that the shooting may have been by "local guerillas who were fighting the Japanese and during the fighting some misunderstanding may have happened."[117] Angry as he was, Wedemeyer was not inclined to force a showdown with Mao over the incident, especially since he privately believed that Birch "actually provoked the unfortunate altercation with the Chinese Communists which resulted in his death."[118] Years later some hard-line anticommunists in the United States would come to regard Birch as the first casualty of the Cold War, and the extremist right-wing John Birch Society was named in his honor.

At Chungking, Mao recognized that he was temporarily in a tight position. He had little doubt about the long-term outcome of a contest with the Nationalists. His movement was dynamic, growing, and highly motivated, with good leaders and a proven strategy, while Chiang's was increasingly isolated, corrupt, reactionary, and incompetent. Yet for the moment, with the Americans backing Chiang and Russian attitudes uncertain, he was prepared to make concessions. The Communists dropped their earlier demand to share power with Chiang in a coalition government and agreed to give up a few of their base areas in some provinces. The Nationalists recognized the Communists as a legal and equal political party and promised democratization of their government and a political consultative assembly to draft a new constitution.

Hurley urged the two sides to agree on basic principles and leave the details for later. That is what they did—then promptly began fighting about the details. The Communists refused to place their armed forces under Nationalist command or to disband them, and they were of course unwilling to surrender control of their remaining base areas, the foundation of their regional power, to the Chungking government's control. On October 10, Mao departed Chungking, leaving Chou En-lai to continue the talks. Hurley had already departed for Washington a few weeks before, hopeful that his efforts had at last been successful.

"Chiang has lost his soul," Mao declared on his return from Chungking. "He is merely a corpse and no one believes him anymore."[119] Yet while Mao felt confident in his ability to read Chiang, understanding Stalin's intentions was a different matter. The first contacts between the Soviets and the Eighth Route Army were not auspicious. Chinese Communist units that encountered the Red Army early in the campaign in Manchuria found themselves unable to establish real contact because they could not speak Russian and the Red Army had no Chinese interpreters until early September, when a few Soviet consular officials arrived.[120] Wang Zi-feng, a young Communist cadre, attended a dinner party for the Soviets in October. There was only one interpreter present, a nineteen-year-old Russian nurse. The Chinese soldiers were "amazed at the Soviets' capacity to drink. They finished off bowl after bowl." During the party Wang "could see the differences" between the two nations' soldiers. The Soviets quickly lost their inhibitions and began singing and dancing, while the Chinese remained "wary of openly expressing emotions."[121]

Soviet generals were unimpressed by the appearance of the poorly equipped Chinese Communist troops, who often lacked even uniforms, and sometimes referred to them as "irregulars."[122] For their part, the Chinese Communists sometimes found it politically and psychologically disastrous to be associated with the rapacious Soviet troops who had alienated broad segments of the local people.[123]

Adding to their anger and concern about the Soviet pillage and abuse of the population, Chinese Communist leaders soon discovered that the Red Army could be less than cooperative in helping the Party's armed forces to establish themselves in Manchuria. Although ordinary Red Army officers and soldiers, graduates of Soviet ideological indoctrination, were inclined to be friendly to their brother proletarians of the Eighth Route Army, the higher Soviet command knew that

Moscow had its own interests in Manchuria and was unwilling to endanger its very good deal with Chiang. In some towns and regions, the Red Army welcomed Chinese Communist cadres and turned over captured Japanese arms and equipment to them. In Jehol, local residents reported that the Soviets kept the best arms for themselves, turned over the next best to the Communists, and destroyed the rest.[124] Nevertheless, officially and sometimes in practice, the Soviet generals supported Chungking.

In early September, Moscow directed Marshal Vasilevskii to send a delegate to Yenan to try to set the ground rules for Chinese Communist–Soviet military relations in Manchuria. Vasilevskii's representative told Yenan leaders that the Soviets were obliged to observe the terms of the Sino-Soviet Treaty and hold the large cities of Mukden, Changchun, and Harbin plus the railroads for the Nationalists. Elsewhere the Communists were free to move and receive Soviet help if they agreed to avoid the large cities, not to openly carry on their activities in Soviet-occupied areas, and not to allow their forces to operate under the name of the Eighth Route Army.[125]

It was not a great bargain, but it was enough. On the first night after their meeting with the Soviet representative, the Party Politburo agreed to gamble on an all-out effort to gain control of Manchuria. From Shantung, from the Yangtze and central China, thousands of soldiers and party cadres converged on the northeast. "So long as we place the Northeast and Jehol and Chahar [Changsha] provinces under our control," wrote Liu Shao-chi (Liu Shaoqi), who had chaired the Politburo meeting, "we will ensure the victory of the Chinese people." By December there were four hundred thousand soldiers and cadres in Manchuria ready to try.

CHAPTER THREE

"GRAFT AND CORRUPTION PREVAIL"

WHILE MAO'S FORCES WERE CONVERGING ON MANCHURIA, OTHER forces were also preparing to move north. On Guam and Okinawa, U.S. Marines of the III Amphibious Corps were packing their gear and receiving a new round of inoculations. The III Amphibious Corps was all that Wedemeyer had received in response to his request for seven American divisions in China. To be sure, this was no small force. It consisted of two Marine divisions, veterans of Iwo Jima and Okinawa, with their air wing and various logistical and support units. But it was far less than seven divisions, and the Marines were not expected to reach north China until the end of September.

Once ashore, one division of Marines would secure the important commercial hub of Tientsin (Tianjing) and its ocean port of Tangku (Tanggu) along with the Tientsin–Peiping rail line and the key deep-water harbor of Chinwangtao (Qinhuangdao), the port for much of northern China's coal supplies. A second Marine division would land at Tsingtao on the Shantung Peninsula, which had the best port north of Shanghai. Meanwhile, Chiang's forces would be airlifted into the cities of Nanking and Shanghai in central China. Finally, the ships that had brought the Marines would transport Nationalist troops to the north, where they would arrive sometime in October or November.

The Marines' mission was to assist the Nationalists in reoccupying key areas in the north and to supervise the disarmament and evacuation of the Japanese Army and civilians. While the presence of the Marines would have the practical effect of denying the cities and railroads in the north to the Communists, Wedemeyer's instructions from Washington insisted that American forces avoid involvement in China's civil war.

On Guam and Okinawa, men of the 1st Marine Division, many of them survivors of grim battles on Peleliu and Okinawa, greeted V-J Day quietly. "These combat-tested men were perfectly content to let the rear-echelon troops do the celebrating," wrote one Marine. "As I recall most . . . spent the day writing letters and visiting the 1st Marine Division cemetery where [our] company had served as the honor guard."[1] "Most of us felt it was too solemn an occasion to celebrate," recalled Pfc. Eugene Sledge; "the memory of so many dead friends was still fresh in our minds."[2]

Speculation and rumors flew thick and fast. "The most oft-repeated rumor . . . was that the entire First Marine Division was to be flown in a huge fleet of B-29s back to the States, each man issued dress blues, and then we would have a victory parade down Fifth Avenue in New York City. The more we talked the more logical it seemed to us in our mental state of wishful thinking."[3] Whether or not they believed that there would be a victory parade in New York, all Marines were aware that under the newly instituted "point system," based on time overseas, a large number of them would have first priority in returning home. "Many of us had over the 85 points needed to get sent stateside," recalled Sergeant David Earle. "We counted our points over and over again to assure ourselves of the correct count. Finally we would be going home!!"[4] On Guam, however, General Keller E. Rockey's III Marine Amphibious Corps headquarters was monitoring the message traffic between Wedemeyer, Nimitz, and the Joint Chiefs of Staff. It was soon apparent that China and not the United States was the likely destination for most of Rockey's Marines.[5]

Like most big secrets in the Corps, this one was almost immediately known to thousands of Marines by the time III Amphibious Corps received its warning order from Pacific headquarters on August 22. "What a bummer!" recorded Sergeant Earle. "Some of the men were really bummed about the prospect of not going home and started to report to sick-bay with 'battle fatigue.' We did have a couple of men who I thought needed to be transferred out, but there really was nothing seriously wrong with most of them." Earle's company commander called his sergeants together. "The first thing he did was . . . to give the order that he would court-martial any man reporting to sick bay with combat fatigue. We passed the word and there were no more combat fatigues."

"We were not happy," recalled Corporal Calvin Decker, "but Marines are trained to take their duty as it comes."[6]

Along with disappointment there was more than a little enthusiasm. China was an exotic land that few ordinary Americans could ever hope to visit. The very word "China" was almost a synonym in American slang for distance and remoteness. Pfc. Joe Shipman, a radio operator in the 1st Marine Division, felt "awe" at the prospect of going to China.[7] The Marines had a long association with China stretching back to the first years of the century. "China duty" with the legation guard in Peiping and Tientsin or the 4th Marines in Shanghai was the most glamorous, most desirable, and most prestigious assignment in the "old Corps." Platoon Sergeant George H. Haertlein remembered "feeling great" about going. "When I enlisted in June 1941 I hoped that some day I would go to China."[8] Of the eight generals assigned to III Amphibious Corps and its subordinate units, seven had served prewar tours in China.[9] In both Marine divisions, officers and enlisted men who had spent time in China before the war had passed on their colorful tales of life in the Orient to the younger Marines. "China duty became the constant topic of conversation," recalled Eugene Sledge.[10] First Sergeant John T. Demoss of the 6th Marine Division, assigned to secure Tsingtao, was "overjoyed" at the opportunity to be a China Marine.[11] "I decided I was going to enjoy the trip to China," recalled Sergeant Earle. "I asked myself, when would I ever get to see China again? I think, after the fact, that all of the men were glad to have had the opportunity."[12]

In mid-September, ships of Vice Admiral Daniel E. Barbey's Seventh Amphibious Force returned from carrying American occupation forces to Korea and began loading the 1st Marine Division on Okinawa and Guam. Brigadier General William A. Worton, the III Amphibious Corps chief of staff, was already in Tientsin with an advance party to reconnoiter and select buildings and barracks for the Marines. Several dozen former Japanese barracks, schools, hospitals, hotels, and cinemas were taken over by the Americans, and the entire Japanese garrison at Taku was withdrawn.[13] As part of his building requisitions for III Corps, Worton, a veteran of twelve years' service in China and the only member of the Tientsin Race Club not in a Japanese internment camp, voted unanimous approval of his own action in taking over the club's building and racetrack.[14]

It was quickly apparent to Worton that the single primitive airfield at Tientsin would not be adequate to support the large number of fighters and transport aircraft that the Marines would bring to China.[15] Peiping, with its two large military air bases, would also have to be occupied. Wedemeyer's headquarters promptly authorized General Rockey to "occupy such intermediate and adjacent areas as he deems necessary."[16] Much of the countryside surrounding Tientsin and Peiping was held by the Communists, who were unhappy to see the Marines and aware that they would probably be followed by Nationalist troops. During his visit, Worton held a heated meeting with Communist representatives, who warned of trouble if the Marines tried to occupy Peiping. Worton responded that III Corps "was combat experienced and ready and would have overwhelming aerial support, and that it was quite capable of driving straight on through any force that the Communists mustered in its path."[17]

On September 26, landing craft carrying the first battalions of the 1st Marine Division crossed the shallow Taku bar at the mouth of the Hai River headed for the town of Tangku, where the Marines boarded trains for Tientsin. Disembarking from their trains, they were greeted by cheering crowds waving small American flags. "It seemed that each one of Tientsin's two million people turned out for the parade," wrote an American correspondent. "Bottles of Vodka, Chinese lanterns, flags and stray pieces of women's clothing were handed up to men on the tanks."[18] On their way to their billets in the old British barracks of Tientsin, the 1st Marines encountered "huge masses of people lining the streets rows and rows deep. Cheering, crying, mothers and fathers thrusting their babies into our arms. . . . The number of Chinese people was so great they managed to infiltrate our ranks in the parade and some of the Marine units towards the end of the parade got lost," recalled Pfc. Leo Bouchard, "and once we arrived at the old British Barracks [my section] was sent out to retrace the parade route and find the lost units."[19] Watching the tumultuous welcome as American landing craft sailed up the Hai River, Sergeant Earle wondered whether the Chinese "had done the same thing with all their many conquerors."[20]

A few days after the Tangku landings, a battalion of the 7th Marines came ashore at Chinwangtao, and on the eleventh of October the 6th Marine Division began unloading from transports in the harbor of

Tsingtao. In the city, buildings lining the main street were covered with posters reading "Welcome the U.S. Navy," "The cooperation of the United States and China is ernest [*sic*]," and "The Allies are the angeles [*sic*] of peace,"[21] and after a few days, "Chinese restaurants which once served shark's fin or eight precious grains were now offering steak with or without eggs."[22]

Tsingtao was packed with thousands of refugees from the fighting in the countryside as well as renegade puppet soldiers, some still in uniform. Rioting and looting had broken out in the Japanese and German sections of the city. Within a few days of their arrival, heavily armed squads of Marines were patrolling the streets of Tsingtao, bringing an abrupt end to the widespread unrest in the city.[23] While the Marines were suppressing rioting, the city's mayor was concerned with more pressing problems, namely "cabarets, dancing girls and prostitutes for the American forces." Cabarets were available, but there were no dancing girls in the city. The mayor tactfully suggested to his American liaison officer that the Americans "import a boatload from Shanghai." Meanwhile, to meet the emergency, he had ordered "an inventory of White Russian girls" in Tsingtao.[24]

In moving into their occupation areas, the Marines encountered opposition only on the road from Tientsin to Peiping. While attempting to remove a series of roadblocks on a narrow space of the road, a party of engineers was fired on by forty or fifty Chinese Communists. The engineers withdrew and returned the following day with a platoon of tanks and an entire company of Marines. As Navy fighters circled overhead, the Marines dismantled the roadblocks and proceeded to Peiping without incident.[25]

At Peiping the Marines "headed straight for the very old but still elegant Marine Barracks. . . . The Japanese had several battalions in formation. The Japanese officer in charge had planned a ceremony to hand over the keys to our general and then vacate the barracks. . . . Our Marine General [Keller E.] Rockey . . . looked the Japanese general right in the eye and said to him, 'Give the g—dam keys to my sergeant.' He then did an about face and walked away."[26]

Despite the incident on the Tientsin–Peiping road, the Communists initially had no real plans to try to oppose the Marines by force, although they believed that the American presence in north China could only hurt their struggle for control of the region. The American landings had come as a surprise to Mao. He knew the Americans were withdrawing army and air force units from China and did not believe the United States would risk a rupture with the Soviets by sending troops to the doorstep of Manchuria.[27]

Mao's confusion was understandable. The United States was demobilizing its forces worldwide at a pace that Undersecretary of State Dean Acheson said "amounted almost to disintegration." In China, the Pentagon was rapidly disbanding Wedemeyer's Chinese Combat Command, the primary organization for providing American military advice and training to Chiang's officers.[28] Yet the United States was far from disengagement in China. General suspicion and fear of the Soviets had been growing in Washington during the spring and summer of 1945, primarily in reaction to Russian actions in Eastern Europe. This had spilled over into misgivings by some about Russian actions in China and Manchuria as well. In the final stages of the negotiations for the Sino-Soviet Treaty in Moscow, Truman and Secretary of State Byrnes had become convinced that the Russians were attempting to squeeze additional concessions out of Chiang beyond anything contemplated in the original agreement at Yalta. In a meeting on the day the Soviets entered the war, U.S. ambassador to the USSR Averell Harriman told Stalin that the United States supported the Chinese position and would insist on the observance of the Open Door policy in Manchuria. Following the conclusion of the treaty, Harriman warned that the United States must take steps to prevent Soviet dominance of northeast Asia.

In Washington, Assistant Secretary of War John J. McCloy and Navy Secretary James V. Forrestal shared Harriman's concerns. Truman and his advisers had already decided to have U.S. troops occupy the southern half of Korea in order to prevent Soviet dominance of the peninsula. Byrnes and McCloy had also planned to have American troops land at the key port of Dairen on the Liaotung (Liaodong) Peninsula of Manchuria, but it soon became clear that the Soviets would get there first.[29] Concern about Soviet expansion in East Asia thus made it easy for some in Washington to see the Marines' presence in northern China not simply as a necessary measure for handling the Japanese surrender but as a positive move to shore up Chiang and counter the Soviet presence in Manchuria.[30]

Whatever Washington's motives, the Chinese Communist leaders knew that their forces were in no way up to a military confrontation with the Americans. The Central Committee instructed Party leaders in Shantung, Tientsin, and Peiping to "try to be on good terms with, and not appear hostile to U.S. intelligence and military personnel. . . . If the Americans open fire on us, commit illegal acts or assist the Kuomintang in suppressing the people, make reports so that we may alert international public opinion." Party loyalists were assured that while Hurley and Wedemeyer were "very reactionary . . . U.S. political circles and public opinion sympathize with us to a high degree."[31]

The single exception to the Communist policy of temporary passivity came at the port of Yantai, then called Chefoo, on the north coast of Shantung, across the Gulf of Chili from Dairen. At Chefoo, unlike other cities in northern China, the Japanese garrison did not continue to hold the town, but withdrew one week after the surrender, leaving Chefoo in the hands of the puppet troops, who quickly capitulated to the Communists. From Chefoo, the Communists could ferry troops across the gulf into Manchuria. The local Communist commander was instructed to resist an American landing at all costs. "Only when not able to hinder or beat back their advance should you retreat."[32] When the American convoy carrying the 29th Marines and escorted by cruisers and destroyers appeared on October 4, however, the local Party leaders opted to negotiate and invited the senior American to come ashore for talks.

The American commanders, Admiral Barbey and General Rockey, were also in a tight spot despite the menacing guns of their warships and the presence of a heavily armed regiment that had fought at Okinawa. They had no authorization to force a landing and were under instructions not to become involved in a Chinese civil war. The Communist "mayor" of Chefoo told Barbey that the Communists held Americans in high esteem and desired to cooperate with the United States, but that he could see no reason for American forces to land there since there were no Japanese forces in the city and Chefoo was in the hands of "Chinese troops supported by the people of the province who have fought the enemy many years with many sacrifices." Kuomintang troops would be resisted to the last man. He expressed the hope that the

United States would not mar its long friendship with China by interfering in Chinese internal affairs.[33]

Two days of negotiations convinced Admiral Barbey that "any landing of the Marines with or without Chinese Nationalist troops, would be opposed."[34] Barbey was ready to land but believed that "this explosive situation should be appreciated in all aspects by higher commanders." The admiral also expressed concern about the fate of Allied prisoners and internees still in Communist-held areas.[35] General Rockey recommended to Wedemeyer's headquarters that the landing at Chefoo be canceled and the 29th Marines be landed with the rest of the 6th Marine Division at Tsingtao. General George C. Stratemeyer, Wedemeyer's deputy and acting theater commander, took the recommendation to Chiang for his opinion. Chiang, who perfectly understood the strategic importance of Chefoo, was privately furious, but nevertheless quickly agreed.[36]

Later Party histories referred to this episode as "the Victory of Yantai," and in important ways it was. But Barbey and Rockey may have avoided worse. As Rockey observed, while the Communist opposition "would not have been very serious," there would have been "serious repercussions."[37] The United States would have been involved in combat against the Communists at the very time it was cheering on the peace talks between Chiang and Mao in Chungking. The Central Committee had in fact hoped that heroic fighting at Chefoo would cause "international public opinion to become greatly disturbed." The Chefoo incident was an early illustration of the mutually contradictory aspects of American policy in China: to help Chiang while remaining neutral in the civil war, to thwart the Communists but not to fight them, to confront the Soviets militarily in northern China while carrying out worldwide demobilization.

Happily unaware of the larger implications of their mission, the Marines settled in for what they believed would be a fairly short period of occupation duty in northern China. Although they had heard many stories, most Marines were totally unprepared for the new world they would encounter in China. "A mysterious country full of people and strange smells," recalled Corporal Jack McManus, "especially for a young Marine who grew up in a village of 95 people."[38] Corporal Edmund J. Bardy, a machine gunner in the 5th Marines, succinctly expressed the principal reactions of most Marines: "filthy, poverty stricken, unhealthy sanitary conditions, backward, plenty of history."[39] Many found the smells and crowded conditions in the cities disconcerting, but what impressed the Americans most was the desperate poverty. "We would have young children trying to sneak into our barracks to raid the garbage cans so they could get something to eat," recalled Sergeant Warren Beaster. "Also, the mothers with young girls came up to our guard stations to offer these little girls of theirs and trade them for candy bars and cigarettes."[40] "The vast majority of Chinese were poor beyond [our] comprehension," wrote Corporal Harold Henneman. "Being poor in the U.S. is no comparison. You could purchase almost anything for 5 to 10 cents. A young woman could be purchased for $20.00 including ownership papers."[41] Even when they failed to purchase anything, the Marines could be of economic value to the Chinese, as Sergeant Earle discovered when he moved into former Japanese barracks in Peiping. "It was very disconcerting to be using the head and to look down between the slit in the floor boards and see a Chinese man standing there with a shovel in his hand waiting for you to do your do," observed Earle. "They would fill up their 'honey wagons,' usually drawn by mules, and off they would go to their farms . . . human manure was the richest in those qualities needed to produce fine fruits and vegetables."[42]

While they found these practices appalling, or simply incomprehensible, most Marines recognized that the Chinese were engaged in "a struggle for survival."[43] Corporal Louis R. Weibl observed that Tsingtao had "very proficient thieves," but that was "due to their circumstances and need to survive."[44] The Marines' attitude toward Chinese civilians—though not always Chinese soldiers—was generally positive.[45] Recalling their experiences decades later, the Americans used words such as "friendly," "hard-working," "cooperative," "polite," and "efficient"[46] in describing their encounters with the Chinese. "Very cooperative and pleasant," "I never met an unfriendly person in my tour in China," "They were delightful people even with all their hardships" were representative comments. Paul Nolan of the 1st Marines "found most of the people quite warm and friendly. The soldiers were also pleasant . . . that is until we met them again in Korea."[47] Many Marines expressed admiration for Chinese ingenuity and industry. Master Sergeant William Hill was impressed by how a Chinese man "could perform any task with his hands that the average American would require power tools and numerous special [equipment] to even begin."[48]

There are, of course, good reasons not to take these statements at face value. Most, although by no means all, of the Chinese civilians with whom the Marines had any extended contact were servants, girlfriends, shopkeepers, or prostitutes, for whom friendliness toward Americans was an essential survival trait. In addition, the Marines, like most of their contemporaries, tended to view China and the Chinese in ways that reflected common American racial stereotypes and categories. Donald C. Behrens of the 11th Marines recalled that Marines regularly used racial epithets in referring to the Chinese.[49]

A widespread view was that Chinese society was "backward," "centuries behind ours," and had "always been that way." In case the Marines had any doubts about the general hopelessness of Chinese society, they were quickly reassured by the White Russians and members of the other various derelict foreign communities in Tsingtao and Peiping for whom the universal inferiority and dishonesty of the Chinese was an article of faith.[50] Nevertheless the generally positive feelings of the Marines toward China and the Chinese, which persisted even among Marines who later faced the Chinese armies in Korea, provide a significant contrast to the rancor, animosity, and contempt that GIs manifested toward Koreans and Vietnamese in later wars. This positive view helped to keep morale high all through the Marines' difficult four-year stay in northern China.

Evidence is lacking about whether ordinary Chinese reciprocated the relatively friendly feelings of the Marines, but there is reason for doubt. Constant squabbles between Marines and rickshaw pullers over fares created an atmosphere of mutual annoyance and distrust between American servicemen and the Chinese workingmen with whom they were most often in contact. Chinese students and intellectuals in Peiping resented the stationing of foreign troops in China's traditional center of culture and learning. All Chinese complained of numerous deaths and injuries resulting from traffic accidents involving American military vehicles. (In China the traditional practice gave the right of way to slower-moving vehicles like rickshaws and carts, but the Americans seemed to remain ignorant of this custom.) Accident victims often received compensation from the Americans, but both sides expressed anger and impatience at what they saw as the gross carelessness of the other. "In reality our life is treated as having less value than grass," complained one citizen of Tsingtao. "The tragedies resulting from traffic accidents cannot be explained away as accidental; if so why is there no end of them?"[51] Chinese intellectuals and members of the upper classes believed that Americans conducted themselves like barbarians because of the generally lower standards of civilization in the United States.[52]

On October 6, General Rockey, representing Chiang Kai-shek and the Allied powers, received the swords of Lieutenant General Uchida Ginnosuke and his staff in a formal ceremony marking the surrender of all Japanese troops in the Tientsin area. The surrender touched off a series of riots aimed at the former Japanese concession in the city. Bands of Chinese roamed the Japanese quarter attacking Japanese nationals on sight. The worst incidents occurred on the thirteenth of October, when Chinese thugs set up roadblocks, claiming to be acting for the Americans, and relieved Japanese and other citizens of their valuables. The Marines responded with motorized patrols and ordered Chinese police to protect the Japanese residents. The Japanese consul reported that two to three thousand people suffered losses of property in the riots, and forty or fifty were seriously injured.[53] The Marines now held Tsingtao as well as Peiping, Tientsin, and Chinwangtao, with their large Japanese garrisons and their connecting railroads. Vast areas of the surrounding countryside belonged to the Communists, who continued to feed troops into Manchuria by land and by ship from Chefoo.

As the leathernecks settled into their ambiguous mission, Chiang's troops, many airlifted in by American transport planes, began to return to the cities of central China and the north. With them came officials of the Chungking government eager to reassert control over areas long held by the Japanese. *Chieh-shou* (*jieshu*), the process whereby the Kuomintang carried out the takeover of government in the former Japanese-occupied regions as well as the property and other assets of the Japanese and their collaborators, was, in principle, to be managed by a collection of ad hoc agencies governed by elaborate and complex decrees issued by Chungking.[54] In practice, "it was turned into a racket with official position treated as an opportunity rather than a responsibility."[55] Those appointed to supervise *chieh-shou* were favorites, relatives, or close political allies of the Generalissimo. If they possessed any managerial or political abilities, that was pure coincidence.

The grander bureaucrats came by air, on American transport planes, accompanied by "families, servants, hangers-on and fantastic quantities of luggage including hams from Kunming and nets full of oranges from Chungking."[56] These fortunate officials descended on the relatively wealthy cities of the north and east like rapacious hawks. They brought with them large amounts of Nationalist paper money, now the only legal tender in the formerly occupied territories. They were vested with authority to judge the wartime conduct and loyalty of the millions of Chinese who had lived under Japanese occupation for more than eight years. They were charged with the disposition of millions of dollars in Japanese-owned factories, houses, businesses, and other property as well as those of Chinese collaborators. The possibilities of the situation were endless.

"To describe the liberation of Shanghai," wrote one American correspondent, "is to strain the English language. . . . For weeks the money-changers flew a circle of roundtrips exchanging bales of American dollars, each one worth 1,500 Chinese dollars in Chungking but only $700 in Shanghai. . . . The prosperous Japanese community in Shanghai was systematically stripped. American Lend-Lease trucks rumbled through the streets carrying loot from one place to another."[57] Any building or property that had been occupied by the Japanese or by a "collaborator" was fair game for the acquisitive managers of *chieh-shou.* "It was common for individuals to take advantage of their official position first to occupy a building and then to manipulate things in such a way as to have the building sold to them," recalled one of Chiang's advisers.[58] Even the Americans and British had to take action to prevent their consulates from being requisitioned as former enemy property.

What became of seized enemy property is illustrated by the case of 3,500 former Japanese vehicles taken over by the War Transportation Board in the south-central province of Hunan. One thousand of these seized vehicles were supposed to be turned over to the Hunan Highway Department. The first 50 trucks turned over were found to have about 20 percent of their parts missing; 250 others were missing half of their parts, and the remaining 700 had been so thoroughly stripped that they "no longer looked like vehicles." In a relatively short time the missing parts began to turn up for sale in auto and hardware stores.[59]

Throughout the newly "liberated" parts of China the story was much the same. "When the people in the recovered areas . . . saw the flag of the motherland they were frantically overjoyed," observed a Chinese newspaper editorial. "But after several nights of sleep they discovered that most of them had lost their home and property. . . . Wealth which had taken generations to accumulate was transferred in a twinkling to those who held gold dollars and Nationalist dollars in their hands."[60] In Hankow, captured Japanese property including sizable stocks of cigarettes and cloth were "auctioned off in such large quantities that the only people who have capital to bid are those in official positions who can use civil and military funds long enough to purchase and dispose of the goods and have military vehicles at their disposal."[61] From Kaifeng in north-central China, an OSS officer reported that "every building of any size that is repaired by the local businessmen is taken over by Nationalist troops; thus killing any desire upon the part of business people to repair property destroyed in the war."[62] An investigating committee headed by Shao Tsung-en, leader of a small independent party, concluded, "Officials down to the soldiers are using the resources of the country as their personal property."[63]

Chiang's officials believed that "as public functionaries they had suffered so much hardship and privation in the interior during the seven years of war that they had a right to indulge themselves . . . but actually they behaved like conquerors to their own people."[64] Kuomintang officials often came from parts of China distant from those they now governed and spoke different dialects. They treated the locals with disdain and suspicion, frequently reminding them that it was they who had saved them from the Japanese. Nationalist officials in Jinzhou referred to the Chinese of Manchuria as *wang-guo-nu* (slaves without a country of their own).[65] The locals returned these feelings, referring to the Kuomintang officials as "Chungking Man," a biting reference to "Peking Man," the famous archaeological find of a primitive ape-like creature near Peiping.[66]

The matter of collaboration also lent itself to easy exploitation by the enterprising bureaucrats of the Chiang regime. In principle, the

Kuomintang regarded all those who had lived under the Japanese as lacking the patriotism and dedication of those who were lucky enough to have lived in unoccupied areas or had opted to follow Chiang on the long retreat into southwest China. Their wartime conduct required careful scrutiny. Active collaborators were to be identified and punished. In practice, the concept of collaboration was subject to limitless modification depending on the needs of the regime and the ability of those under scrutiny to pay. "Every Chinese who remained in Hankow or any occupied area during the Japanese Occupation and who has sufficient resources to make his arrest worthwhile is a potential collaborator in the eyes of the arresting agencies," wrote an OSS observer. During one week, sixty-five arrests were carried out in the city, ranging from an ordinary merchant who had carried out small sales to the Japanese to a magistrate who had headed a campaign for contributions to buy airplanes for the Japanese Army. Twenty of those arrested were quickly released after paying fines ranging from one to five million Chinese dollars. The air-minded magistrate was released after paying three million but was later rearrested. Chinese military authorities preferred to try to keep the names of those arrested and released from the newspapers so that they could be rearrested later for the same offense.[67]

Chinese too poor to be of interest to Chiang's bureaucrats still had to cope with the arrival of Chiang's armies from the south. "About the end of October the Nationalists began to appear in Tientsin in force," recalled Sergeant Earle. "There was no compassion with these troops at all. . . . In one case I witnessed an old Chinese lady wanting to get from one side of the street to the other close to where the Nationalists were setting up their machine guns. These army men began beating her to the ground. It was awful. All of us wanted to go over and knock their blocks off but we were under strict orders to turn the other way."[68] "The population of Tientsin and vicinity are utterly disgusted with the Central Government's officials and troops," declared an OSS officer. "Graft and corruption prevail and the only winners are the Communists."[69]

As Chiang's officials settled in to make their fortunes in the cities of the east and north, American ships took aboard the first of the Chinese armies bound for Manchuria. In mid-October, transports of Admiral Barbey's Seventh Amphibious Force began loading troops of the Thirteenth and Fifty-second Chinese Armies at Kowloon and at Haiphong in former French Indochina. When U.S. Navy representatives met with Chinese officers earlier in the month to plan the movement, it appeared likely that there would be problems. Each ship would require American liaison officers who spoke Chinese. Yet the China Theater's "Chinese Combat Command," Wedemeyer's training and military advisory organization, was being rapidly disbanded, creating an acute shortage of qualified interpreters.[70]

The lack of communication may have accounted for some of the unwelcome surprises that occurred as the loading began. The Chinese soldiers had brought with them large quantities of fresh meat and vegetables, but American doctors refused to allow these provisions to be stored in the ships' refrigerated spaces because the animal products were suspected of carrying parasites and the vegetables had been grown using night soil fertilizers. In addition to their edible animals, each Chinese division expected to bring with them approximately twenty-five hundred horses, which the American ships, mostly assault transports, could not accommodate. After hurried negotiations it was agreed that the Chinese soldiers would be given American canned meat and vegetables to supplement their rice ration in place of the fresh produce, and that each division would receive three dozen U.S. Army trucks along with American drivers to substitute for their horses.[71]

As the Chinese, many of whom had never seen a ship before, began to come aboard, medical officers gave them only a cursory inspection "designed to spot the very obvious unfit. . . . A more rigid screening would have reduced the troops carried to a very small number." Navy doctors believed "the fact has to be accepted that Chinese troops are rife with disease and body parasites." Consequently, they would have to exercise "extreme vigilance to prevent common and inherent Chinese diseases from spreading to the ship's personnel."[72] To achieve this, the Chinese soldiers were literally walled off in segregated spaces aboard ship. The Chinese soldiers had their own mess, heads, and sick bay, and any type of fraternization with American sailors was strictly prohibited. Because most Chinese were totally unfamiliar with Western-style toilets and "sea sickness was prevalent," the smells emanating from the Chinese berthing spaces were especially pungent. By the end of October all of Barbey's ships, crammed with Chinese troops earmarked for

Manchuria, were at sea bound for the port of Dairen at the tip of the Liaotung Peninsula in southern Manchuria.

While Chiang's armies sailed north to Manchuria, the Communists walked. The orders from the Central Committee to move to the northeast came as a surprise to many Communist units in central and northern China. With the news of Japan's surrender, Communist guerrilla soldiers, like most of the war's other combatants, desired most of all to go home.[73] This desire was perhaps even stronger among Chinese soldiers who had a special attachment to their region and their families' ancestral land. As for Manchuria, most Chinese from south of the Great Wall regarded that remote northeastern region in much the same way as American GIs from New York regarded the rural South. Communist officers and cadres found it expedient not to mention Manchuria, but to tell the troops that they were moving to a nearby province or city to receive new modern weapons captured from the Japanese or that they were going to a place where they would enjoy better food for their rations.[74]

Despite such blandishments, officers soon found that soldiers were deserting in large numbers. In one case, the sight of a large banner reading "Welcome to the 77th Regiment on its march to the Northeast" revealed to the surprised troops their true destination and set off a wave of desertions from that unit.[75] "Most of those who ran away did so after camp was pitched," wrote one cadre. "So as well as normal sentries we placed secret sentries. . . . Some of us were so desperate we adopted the Japanese method used with their day laborers and collected the men's trousers and stowed them in the company HQ at night."[76]

One Communist division departed Jiangsu on its trip to the northeast with 32,500 troops but arrived with only 28,000. The remainder were reported by the division commander as "either escaped or dead."[77] Many deserters, however, soon returned to their units, prompted by second thoughts about taking their chances in an unfamiliar region where they were liable to be killed or captured by bandits or troops of the Nationalist Army.[78]

Arriving in Manchuria, some Communist soldiers were unhappy to find that the local people, whom they had come to liberate, in fact lived far better than they did. Industrial workers, for example, appeared to enjoy limitless access to cigarettes. Troops of the former puppet army newly recruited to the Communist cause—often with encouragement from the Soviets—had uniforms and weapons far superior to their own. Political officers reported complaints that "these former collaborators are better off than we who have been fighting for eight years."[79] Nor were the promised Japanese weapons always available. Soviet helpfulness in gaining access to weapons and equipment varied from place to place and according to the twists and turns of Moscow's approach to China. On the whole, however, the Communists did benefit from the acquisition of Japanese arms, which even included heavy artillery and aircraft.[80]

As the first Communist formations reluctantly settled into their new missions in Manchuria, Admiral Barbey's ships arrived off the Liaotung Peninsula. The port city of Dairen, the intended landing point, was still in the hands of the Red Army, and the Soviets informed the Chinese government that they would not allow Chiang's troops to land there. They argued that Dairen was a commercial port and the landing of troops there constituted a violation of the Sino-Soviet Treaty. Chungking vigorously disputed this preposterous reading of the treaty but the Soviets still refused. Desperate to get his forces into Manchuria quickly Chiang accepted a Soviet suggestion that the Nationalist troops land at the smaller port of Hulutao. General Stratemeyer (Wedemeyer's acting deputy) agreed and Barbey arrived off Hulutao in his flagship *Catoctin* on October 27.

As the *Catoctin*'s barge, flying the American flag, approached the pier, shots rang out and men could be seen firing from behind barricades on the pier. The barge withdrew, the *Catoctin* went to general quarters, and the destroyer *L. C. Taylor* trained her guns on the shore, where armed men in trenches could be seen. Then a lone man appeared on a promontory near the ship, alternately waving a Chinese and a white flag. Barbey's barge, this time with two Chinese language officers aboard, picked up the soldier and proceeded to the pier. A few hours later, the Communist New Fourth Army general Lau Shek-hai came aboard the *Catoctin* to apologize for the incident, which he termed "a big mistake." He claimed that he had not been notified of the Americans' arrival and had orders to hold the port and prevent "puppet troops" from entering.[81]

The admiral sternly reminded Lau that only the Soviets had been authorized by the Allies to occupy Manchuria in advance of the Nationalists, but Barbey recognized that he was confronted with the same choices as at Chefoo. He opted to avoid actions that might involve American forces in Chinese internal war. At the even smaller port of Yingkou, the American task force again found Chinese Communist forces in control, contrary to assurances from the Soviets. Admiral Barbey believed that his task force could land the Nationalists with only slight resistance but saw that such an action "would cause intense resentment in all Communist areas and definitely identify us as active military participants in the trouble now brewing."[82] China Theater headquarters, anxious to free up the Seventh Fleet's shipping, had earlier suggested that Nationalist forces land at Chinwangtao, already held by the Marines. Chiang reluctantly agreed, and the Thirteenth and Thirty-second Chinese Armies arrived there at the end of October. The Chinese Nationalist forces would now be obliged to fight their way overland into Manchuria through mountain passes and by way of the long and insecure rail lines between Tientsin and Mukden.

Soviet actions at the Manchurian ports were a result of a shift in Stalin's China policy, a policy that changed almost monthly. By the beginning of October, Stalin was frustrated by British and American opposition to his demands in Europe and the exclusion of the Russians from the occupation of Japan. He was also worried by the presence of sizable American forces in northern China. So in October he allowed the Chinese Communists to set up regimes in some Manchurian towns and cities and continued to exclude the Nationalists from Soviet-held areas of Manchuria. At the same time, Red Army generals withheld any cooperation with an advance Nationalist delegation in Changchun that was charged with preparations for the return of Manchuria to Chinese control and administration.

To focus attention on Soviet obstructionism in the northeast, Chiang angrily withdrew his delegation from Changchun in early November, but by then Stalin had flip-flopped once again and now opened secret talks with Chiang to set the withdrawal of Soviet troops and discuss future economic cooperation between China and the Soviets. Chiang wanted the Russians out of Manchuria, but not so quickly as to allow the Chinese Communists to take over before the arrival of his own troops. The Soviets agreed to delay their departure from Manchuria and to facilitate the takeover of the area by the Nationalists.

Stalin, happy to have an excuse to keep his own troops in place while the Americans remained in northern China, now implemented his pledges with a speed and thoroughness that stunned the Chinese Communists. Communist administrations in the towns and cities were unceremoniously evicted from their buildings and offices. P'eng Chen (Peng Zhen), the head of the Party's Northeast Bureau, was informed by the Soviets that the Communists had one week to leave Mukden and its nearby airfields. When he attempted to argue, the Russian commander declared, "If you do not leave, we will use tanks to drive you out." P'eng Chen exploded, "The Army of one Communist Party using tanks to drive out the Army of another Communist Party! Something like this has never happened before. Can this kind of action be acceptable?"[83]

Chiang now turned his attention to wresting Manchuria from the Chinese Communists. He opened an offensive at the strategic pass of Shanhaikuan (Shanhaiguan), where the Great Wall met the sea at the gates of Manchuria. By November 20, both the pass and the town of Shanhaikuan were in the hands of the Nationalists. Two days later, Chiang's armies entered Hulutao, from which they had been barred by sea a month before.[84]

Farther south, the repercussions of the battles for Manchuria threatened to engulf the Marines and the Eighth Route Army forces still carrying on an uneasy coexistence in the Peiping-Tientsin-Chinwangtao triangle. The Marines were charged with keeping rail communications open, ensuring the vital flow of coal into Peiping and Tientsin as well as Shanghai and other cities farther south. But the same rail lines that carried the coal also carried troops and supplies for Chiang into Manchuria.

Nationalist troops were arriving by sea and air in northern China, yet Chiang showed no inclination to use them to relieve the Marines or the Japanese troops who were still patrolling parts of the railways. "The Generalissimo is determined to retain in their present areas the Marines in North China," reported Wedemeyer. "He visualizes using the Marines as a base of maneuver. The Gimo would like to concentrate [on] plans based on conducting a campaign against the Chinese Communists instead of repatriating the Japanese. Such a campaign may require months or years."[85]

The Chinese Communists also saw the Marines as an important ally of the Nationalists. During October and November, Communist saboteurs and raiding parties did their best to destroy track and rolling stock on the Peiping–Mukden rail line. Marine detachments ranging in size from two dozen to a hundred men guarded railroad bridges and stretches of track. Mortars and machine guns defended important crossings. Marine detachments guarding trains were frequently the target of random fire from concealed positions, and Marine aircraft on patrol over Communist-held territory often received ground fire from rifles and machine guns.[86] Incidents were frequent, but most were very brief and involved no casualties. A more serious problem was the weather. The cold northern China winter had begun, and many Marines still had only the lightweight uniforms they had worn in the Pacific campaigns. "As time passed it kept getting colder," recalled Joseph Shipman. "We still had no issue of [winter] clothing so it became common practice for us to take our Marine Corps blanket to a Chinese tailor and have him make a uniform for us. . . . This at least was warmer and the tailoring was reasonable, but the material could not forget that it was just a blanket and trying to keep one's uniform neat and pressed was impossible."[87]

Though it was hard, cold, monotonous work, guarding the trains was a relatively uneventful mission until the end of 1945. The single exception occurred on November 14. On that day, Communist troops concealed in a village near the rail line opened fire on a train guarded by Marines. Major General Dewitt Peck, the 1st Marine Division commander, was aboard the train and immediately called in reinforcements and a simulated air strike against the village. The Communist attack ended as soon as the Marines opened fire with a mortar, but the track bed had been effectively mined and it was more than two days before Chinese workers, under fire from Communist snipers, could repair the damage.[88] Coming on the same day as the opening of the Nationalist attack on Shanhaikuan, the engagement with the Marines, which took place only a few miles away, seemed to the Communists further evidence that the Marines were taking sides in the developing struggle for Manchuria.[89]

Despite the mutual frustration and suspicion, both the Americans and the Chinese Communists made extraordinary efforts to avoid open hostilities. The Communists continued to assist and return American flyers forced down by accidents in their territory. The Central Committee directed that "when we cannot dissuade U.S. military personnel from assisting the GMD [Nationalists] in entering the liberated areas our troops shall act only in self-defense, take up defensive positions and under no circumstances fire first."[90]

The Marines also received very restrictive orders. General Wedemeyer instructed General Rockey that if Marines received fire from a village and American lives were endangered, the Marine commander on the scene was to "inform the military leader or responsible authority in that village in writing that fire from that particular village is endangering American lives and that such firing must be stopped. After insuring that your warning to said military leader or responsible authority has been received and understood, should activity that jeopardizes American lives continue, you are authorized to take appropriate action. . . . Your warning and action should include necessary measures to insure protection of innocent persons."[91] Marine aviators were at first not issued live ammunition for patrols. Later they were permitted to shoot back if fired upon and the source was unmistakable, the target was in the open, "the fire was in some volume," and "innocent people would not be endangered."[92]

On the same day that the Marines were working to reopen the Peiping–Mukden rail line and Chiang's armies were fighting at Shanhaikuan, General Stratemeyer was reporting to Washington that now that Chiang's troops had reached northern China, it might be time to begin planning for the withdrawal of the Marines. Wedemeyer had already argued in messages to the Pentagon that if Washington really wished him to avoid becoming involved in "fraternal strife" in China, the United States must cease acting as the Generalissimo's transportation corps and supply depot. Washington must also withdraw American forces before they found themselves in combat with the Chinese Communists. If, on the other hand, the United States really wished to continue actively supporting Chiang, he would require a new directive.

Wedemeyer wanted Washington to make up its mind. His other concern was Chiang. The American general believed that the Generalissimo ought to concentrate his efforts on reforming his corrupt and ineffective government and bureaucracy, consolidating his control in the south, and gaining control of the north. Control of Manchuria appeared some years off and should not, Wedemeyer believed, be attempted immediately. Even control of northern China could not be achieved for months "or perhaps even years unless a satisfactory settlement with the Chinese Communists is achieved." Yet Wedemeyer considered the chances of a satisfactory settlement "remote."[93]

In Washington, among the handful of men who were privy to the secret cables from China, there was a lack of consensus concerning the purpose of the Marines and their relation to larger policy issues—about which there was also disagreement. There were those who accepted the public explanation, that the Marines were there primarily to manage the surrender and repatriation of the Japanese, of whom there were a large number in northern China, many fully armed. There were those who, like Wedemeyer, saw American forces as indispensable in shoring up the Generalissimo against the Reds and preserving order in China, and there were others, including McCloy and Forrestal, who saw the Marines as a way to keep the Russians in Manchuria from becoming too ambitious. In the State Department, the assistant secretary of state for East Asia, John Carter Vincent, saw the employment of the Marines as a likely path leading the United States deep into the tar pit of China's internal wars. Vincent was a professional diplomat who had spent most of his career in China. He had watched Chiang in action—or inaction—for many years. As early as 1942 he had concluded that the Kuomintang had become "a sterile bureaucracy depending on the monied interests and the military for its support."[94]

The receipt of China Theater's messages touched off a flurry of meetings and memos in Washington. At a meeting of the secretaries of State, War, and Navy on November 6, John J. McCloy called the group's attention to Wedemeyer's recommendations that the United States cease transporting more Nationalist troops to the north and make plans to withdraw the Marines. The United States now faced a "basic decision about how far to back Chiang," McCloy declared. If the Marines were withdrawn, "Chiang's prestige would suffer." The Generalissimo might then have trouble disarming and repatriating the Japanese Army, "still a very cocky and undefeated army."[95] The debate continued over the next three weeks.[96] The service secretaries and the Joint Chiefs of Staff wished to continue supporting Chiang against the Communists by moving additional Chinese troops to the north and keeping the

Marines in place. Vincent argued for withdrawing the Marines as soon as the Japanese had been sent home and pressuring Chiang to negotiate an agreement to end the war. Secretary of State Byrnes characteristically proposed to split the difference: The Marines would stay, but no additional troops would be moved to the north.

Meanwhile, public uneasiness over the presence of the Marines in China was increasing. Congressman Mike Mansfield of Montana returned from a visit to China and delivered a speech on the House floor in which he warned of the United States being inextricably drawn into China's internal affairs. Privately, Mansfield warned the State Department that the Russians might use the Marines as an excuse to stall in evacuating Manchuria.[97] He reminded Truman that if the United States became entangled in the civil war, "it would violate our fundamental policy of noninterference in the internal affairs of other nations and react against us around the world. It would cause trouble among American troops who are already discontented. . . ."[98]

Truman was of course well aware of widespread unhappiness among American troops overseas with what they saw as the slow pace of postwar demobilization. There had been mass protests and demonstrations in Hawaii and the Philippines. The Marines were, however, not so much discontented with being in China, an old and accustomed job, as unhappy with the exceptionally ambiguous and restrictive aspects of their mission. The administration's public explanation of the Marine deployment in China remained that they were to assist in the disarmament and repatriation of the Japanese and that "our armed forces are not in China for assisting any Chinese faction or group."[99] Such announcements were usually coupled with greatly exaggerated estimates of the number of armed Japanese still in China.

On the morning of November 27, the three secretaries met to once again discuss the China issue without reaching agreement. Navy Secretary Forrestal insisted that it would be ill advised to "yank the Marines out of North China now." Byrnes wanted to pressure the Nationalists and the Communists "to get together on a compromise basis."[100] Following their meeting, the three men walked to the White House for a Cabinet meeting. As the Cabinet members were taking their seats, President Truman burst into the room waving a yellow sheet of news copy from the White House pressroom and declared, "See what a son-of-a-bitch did to me." Patrick J. Hurley had made his final erratic contribution to America's China policy. He was frustrated and worn out by his efforts in China and angered by what he saw as the maneuvers of the career men in the State Department to undermine him. In Washington for consultations, Hurley had suddenly announced his resignation at a news conference only a few hours after an amicable conversation with the president. In his resignation letter and statement to the press, Hurley warned that certain professional diplomats in the State Department "continued to side with the Communist armed party and at times with the imperialist bloc against American policy."[101]

Truman was stunned. The event would probably make the front pages and focus attention on the administration's murky China policy. Hurley had many friends, especially among Republicans on the Hill. In the Cabinet discussion, Secretary of Agriculture Clinton Anderson suggested that the president immediately announce the appointment of General George C. Marshall as the new ambassador to China. Marshall had just retired as chief of staff of the army. With Admiral Ernest King, he was regarded as the architect of the Allied victory, and he was the most respected American soldier-statesman. News of his appointment alone would be enough to deflect attention from Hurley's dramatics.

Truman phoned Marshall at his home in Leesburg, Virginia, to which he had retired only six days before. "General, I want you to go to China for me," Truman said. "Yes, Mr. President," Marshall replied, then hung up. A short time later, Mrs. Marshall came downstairs from a nap to hear the radio announce that the president had appointed General Marshall to the post of special ambassador to China and that "he will leave immediately."[102]

"This assignment to China was a bitter blow," Katherine Marshall wrote to a friend. "I give a sickly smile when people say how the country loves and admires my husband. That last week testifying from nine to five every day with the luncheon hours spent with the President and Secretary Byrnes trying to get some idea of what might be done on this mission. Then dumped into his lap to write the whole policy after he got home at night."[103]

Mrs. Marshall's belief that the general had been writing "the whole policy after he got home at night" was an understandable exaggeration. Marshall was getting plenty of help from the Pentagon and the State

Department, though they had still not resolved their differences. Nor were the news media reluctant to provide advice on China. In a single week in November, thirteen newspapers called for the withdrawal of all U.S. troops from China. Eight called for continued support of Chiang Kai-shek, and three warned against intervening in a Chinese civil war.[104]

The eventual decision on China, a result of lengthy discussions that involved the president himself, was a compromise. The United States would continue to transport Chiang's troops to the north and, when necessary, to Manchuria. The Marines would remain for the present. At the same time, Marshall was to use his influence and that of the United States to bring about a cease-fire in the civil war and the peaceful unification of China.

Soon after Marshall left Washington on the first stage of his long trip to China, Truman released a statement on United States China policy. Peace in China, the president declared, was essential to the peace of the world. Consequently, it was "in the most vital interest of the United States and all the United Nations that the people of China overlook no opportunity to adjust their internal differences promptly by means of peaceful negotiations." He called for a national conference of the major political elements to bring about the unification of China. If China showed progress toward peace and unity, the United States was ready to provide economic assistance and other aid. The United States continued to recognize and cooperate with the Nationalist government and to aid it in repatriating the Japanese. "This is the purpose of the maintenance, for the time being, of United States military and naval forces in China."[105]

On December 20, 1945, more than four months after the formal Japanese surrender, Marshall arrived in a China still at war. It was a country partially occupied by troops of the victors and in which significant elements of the Japanese had not so much surrendered as switched sides. The evening of his arrival in Shanghai, Marshall met with Wedemeyer and with Walter Robertson, chargé of the U.S. embassy in China. Years later, Robertson recalled for Marshall's biographer his reaction to Washington's new China policy: "I had the very distinct impression that he had been given a directive . . . which at least the policy makers in Washington thought was possible of achievement. Neither Wedemeyer nor I thought it was possible of achievement."[106]

CHAPTER FOUR

"FREEDOM IS ON THE OFFENSIVE"

"TODAY FREEDOM IS ON THE OFFENSIVE, DEMOCRACY IS ON THE march," General Douglas MacArthur proclaimed in a radio address to the United States shortly after he had presided over the formal surrender of Japan aboard the USS *Missouri* in Tokyo Bay on September 8, 1945. "Today in Asia as well as in Europe unshackled people are tasting the full sweetness of liberty."[1] MacArthur was doubtless referring to the end of Japanese rule, but there were many in the countries of now defunct Greater East Asia who intended to remain unshackled by their former colonial rulers as well.

The majority of the peoples and nations so inclined fell outside MacArthur's sphere and were the responsibility of Admiral Lord Louis Mountbatten, Supreme Allied Commander, Southeast Asia. A tall, handsome naval officer related to the British royal family, with an ego to match MacArthur's, Mountbatten, according to his biographer, "for pleasure rarely took up any book unless it were one of genealogy, most especially relating to his own forebears."[2] Where MacArthur was dignified and aloof, Mountbatten had enormous personal charm to which few, regardless of class, profession, or nationality, proved wholly immune. Where MacArthur was theatrical, Mountbatten was in fact a subject of theater, his adventures in the navy having furnished the story and characters for a successful movie, *In Which We Serve,* starring his friend Noël Coward.

Beneath Mountbatten's charm and flamboyance was an unsentimental realism. The supreme commander saw more clearly than most of the British ruling class, more clearly than most of his own subordinates, that the world before Pearl Harbor and the fall of Singapore was gone forever. His Southeast Asia Command (SEAC) could not restore the old colonial empires, even if it had the forces to try. Mountbatten believed in the vitality and endurance of the new forces of ethnic and national consciousness sweeping Asia even when he did not completely understand them.

At the Potsdam Conference the Allies had agreed that Mountbatten's Southeast Asia Command, which had been mainly concerned with conducting the war in Burma and preparing to attack Malaya, would be enlarged so that it now included not only those countries but virtually all of Southeast Asia except for northern Vietnam and a small portion of the eastern Netherlands Indies. This area comprised over one and a half million square miles of territory and more than 128,000,000 people, at least 120,000 of whom were being held as prisoners or internees by the Japanese under harsh conditions, suffering from near starvation in camps rife with disease.[3] All of it, except for Burma, had been under Japanese occupation for about three and a half years and included almost all of the former Asian colonies of the French, Dutch, and Portuguese.

With the news of the Japanese surrender, SEAC suddenly found itself responsible for an area on the verge of chaos and disintegration. "Appeals from our French and Dutch Allies, cries for help, demands for troops, threats of continued Japanese resistance, apprehensions of wholesale massacre, forebodings of economic collapse, warnings of the starvation of the whole population poured into our headquarters from every quarter," recalled the SEAC ground forces commander, General William Slim.[4]

At the time of the Japanese capitulation, SEAC was in the midst of mounting a large amphibious operation, Operation Zipper, to retake Malaya from the Japanese. Many of the ships in the invasion fleet were already loading or at sea when the war unexpectedly ended. Mountbatten's staff decided to go forward with the Zipper landings as scheduled, since redistributing and reloading the troops would cause delay and confusion. In addition, forces were to be moved by air into Thailand and then into Saigon, in French Indochina, where Field Marshal Count Terauchi's Southern Area Army, responsible for Southeast Asia, had its headquarters.[5]

These plans and preparations were frustrated by an order from General MacArthur that other commands take no action to accept Japanese surrenders or reoccupy Japanese-held territory until after the formal surrender ceremony had taken place in Tokyo Bay at the end of August. MacArthur wanted to make sure that all the far-flung Japanese commands understood unequivocally that Japan had surrendered before any Allied commanders took actions that might complicate the situation. Mountbatten was furious. The occupation forces for Malaya were already at sea. "If any considerable delay is imposed on me, Admiral Power expects 30 to 40 per cent casualties in these small ships and craft due to the Monsoon weather and mechanical breakdown. Delay will add to the suffering of prisoners of war. . . . Moreover I can see no reason why the signature in Tokyo should make my task easier."[6] Nevertheless the Combined Chiefs of Staff backed MacArthur, and the result was a delay of almost two weeks in Operation Zipper. Other parts of Southeast Asia saw no SEAC troops until a month or more after Truman's announcement of Japan's surrender.

This delay proved decisive in determining the shape of events in Southeast Asia over the succeeding months. On the one hand, it provided priceless time for the forces of independence and national self-assertion to establish themselves in preparation for the coming struggle with the returning colonial powers; on the other, it unleashed forces of revenge, racism, political paranoia, greed, and religious fanaticism that would help extend the suffering and violence of the war well into the postwar period. In some portions of Southeast Asia largely bypassed by the military campaigns, the level of death and destruction after the surrender would soon exceed that of the war years.

Not only were SEAC's occupation forces going to be late in arriving, but there were too few of them to assume quickly the entire mission of locating and assisting Allied prisoners, disarming and repatriating the Japanese, and providing military security and civil government functions for the vast areas of Indonesia and mainland Southeast Asia that were now its sphere of responsibility. While American policies in China were influenced by postwar demobilization of the armed forces, demobilization in SEAC had begun even before the fighting ended. With the end of the war in Europe in May, the British government immediately began to return soldiers to civilian life. First to be released would be men with more than three years' service. The ongoing war with

Japan notwithstanding, the program was also to apply to men in SEAC. But this program was still too slow to satisfy a war-weary British public, and on June 8 the government, facing a closely contested general election, announced that for soldiers in Southeast Asia, the term of service required for discharge would be cut from three years and eight months to three years and four months. "This news was a bombshell that shattered all the plans we had been making," wrote General Slim. "The number of men affected was a large one; one third of the officers and men in SEAC and those the most experienced with a high proportion of NCOs would have to be returned to the United Kingdom before 1st October."[7]

A large proportion of Mountbatten's non-British forces were divisions of the Indian Army. The Indian soldiers wanted to go home as much as their British counterparts. However, a good number of the Indians were career soldiers, and many of the rest were in no hurry to be discharged into a civilian economy noted for chronic unemployment.[8] Yet if the Indian soldier was ready, with varying degrees of enthusiasm, to participate in the postwar occupations, his government was much less happy at the prospect. The British still nominally ruled India with a British general, Sir Archibald Wavell, as governor-general, but the new Labour government of Prime Minister Clement Attlee, which came to power in July, soon made clear that it had no wish to hold on to the large and troubled subcontinent. Jawaharlal Nehru and other leaders of the dominant Indian National Congress Party sympathized politically and ideologically with other independence movements in Asia. They saw no reason for Indian soldiers, whose country was on the verge of freedom, to be used to suppress the freedom struggles of others. British authorities in India wanted their troops back as early as possible to deal with growing political and communal unrest on the subcontinent.

On September 4, Royal Marines went ashore at Penang Island off the northwest coast of Malaya. Five days later, the long-planned Zipper landings took place, with troops landing on the southwest coast near Port Dickinson and thirty miles away at Morib near Port Swettenham. At Morib, the British discovered that the apparently firm sand beaches actually concealed layers of soft mud that swallowed many of their tanks and heavy landing vehicles. Many speculated that had the landings not been unopposed, the operation might have been a costly one.[9]

If there was one place where the local people were genuinely happy to see the SEAC troops, it was Malaya. "Enthusiastic and cheering crowds massed along the streets and at the pier to welcome the returning British troops," reported an American OSS officer. "The sincerity of the welcome and joy at the end of Japanese rule appeared to be universal. Stories of terrorism and tortures were heard on every hand."[10] Arthur Thompson, a Eurasian interned at a camp near Changi, first learned of the British landing when he "saw lorry loads of food brought into the camp. . . . The cooks that cooked at the Raffles Hotel, Adelphi Hotel, they brought them into camp." One of the liberated internees, the general manager of Cold Storage, a large Singapore department store for imported foods, went to the warehouse where the butter had been stored. "It wasn't touched for three and a half years and it was good as new. He gave instructions for all the butter to be brought into the camp for the internees. We had so much butter that some used it as hair cream."[11]

During the occupation, the large Chinese population of the Malay states and Singapore was at first singled out for especially harsh treatment by the Japanese. Several thousand were shot or drowned in mass executions in 1942. Others were arrested and tortured. The Chinese community of Singapore was forced to make a large "voluntary" financial contribution to the Japanese war effort. After 1943, the Japanese moderated their practices to some extent, but Chinese suspicion toward the Japanese remained little changed. "Generally speaking, all in all, and for the whole time and for all of Singapore we were living in fear," recalled Lee Tian Soo. "Because [in] our life there is no certainty. Every day when we get up we face our life. . . . Leaving the house to go to work, there is no certainty that we'll come back. Can happen to anybody, something happen."[12]

The Malay population was treated less harshly. The Japanese retained many Malay civil servants in their jobs, appointed some to higher positions, and recruited others as police, informers, or municipal workers. Yet no one was free from the attentions of the Japanese Kempeitai (the secret police) or from arbitrary confiscations, demands for labor, and the casual brutality of Japanese soldiers and officials. When passing a Japanese checkpoint, everyone "had to bow to the sentries. The bow must be executed properly. If the guards were not satisfied they would punish the people by having them stand in the hot sun or slapping them."[13] When asked to describe their memories of the war more than forty years later, Malaysians who responded almost universally used the words "cruel" and "brutal" when referring to the Japanese.[14] "I had a very soft feeling for the Japanese before the war. I considered them very good people, fine and gentlemanly," recalled Ahmed Khan, a Singapore Indian, "but these pro-Japanese feelings disappeared in the very first week of the occupation. There was wholesale cruelty, blind cruelty . . . so all my sympathies for the Japanese, whatever they were before the war, disappeared in a flash."[15]

IT WAS A CHANGED population that welcomed the British back to Malaya in 1945. Watching the British and Indian soldiers come ashore at Singapore, Lee Kip Lin was irritated to "see the arrogant faces of some of the British officers. It's the same old arrogance that you saw before the war. And you felt very annoyed because these swine who were beaten by the Japs and were coming back here without having to fire a shot were still wearing that same kind of arrogant face."[16] "We felt that the British were not supermen as we used to think," observed Gay Wan Guay. "And we remembered seeing them on the long marches to Changi Jail. It was a pitiful sight! . . . Even the older people . . . realized that the white supremacy was a myth; that the Japanese had come and shown that Asians could overthrow the white authority."[17]

Another source of newfound confidence among many Chinese in Malaya, and a source of concern to many other Malayans in 1945, were the activities of the Malayan People's Anti-Japanese Army. The MPAJA was the military wing of the Malayan People's Anti-Japanese Union (AJUF). Both were Communist-led underground organizations formed in 1942 to carry out resistance to the Japanese. The membership of the MPAJA was drawn almost entirely from the Chinese community. Most recruits were former laborers, and about two-thirds had been born in Malaya while the rest were more recent immigrants from China. They were "mostly young Chinese lacking both education and respect for the former leaders of the Chinese community,"[18] according to a British report. The movement suffered an almost fatal setback in its first months when many of its leaders were betrayed to the Japanese by the head of the organization, Lai Tek, a secret informant for the Kempeitai. That the resistance continued to survive and grow was probably due to its decentralized nature. Guerrilla fighting units were organized into provincial groups or regiments and into "troops" of about one hundred armed men and two hundred auxiliaries. These units had little contact with one another and operated almost independently.[19]

A brief look at the activities of the MPAJA 7th Regiment, which operated in the provinces of Kuantan, Kemaman, and Trengganu on the east coast of Malaya, gives some idea of the methods and experiences of the guerrillas. The regiment originated as a small group of Chinese who went into the jungle in 1942 with two rifles. They were able to steal or buy more firearms from rural police stations, and their strength soon grew to one hundred men. By the fall of 1942 they had managed to carry out simultaneous attacks on five police stations and capture additional weapons. The regiment fed itself by maintaining several large vegetable gardens deep in the jungle. Chinese villagers with grievances against the Japanese often moved with their families to the jungle and worked the vegetable gardens. By the end of the year, the guerrillas had become enough of a nuisance for the Japanese to mount a major operation against them supported by mortars and armored personnel carriers. According to the guerrillas' own account, they were encircled for almost two months in their jungle base, but skillful use of terrain and land mines allowed them to survive and inflict heavy casualties on the Japanese.[20]

Whatever the truth of these claims, the 7th Regiment was still active and the following summer staged an ambush in which the governor of Pahang, the Japanese district officer, and a Japanese colonel were killed. During late 1943 and 1944 the Japanese launched an all-out campaign to eliminate the guerrillas, even employing air attacks. Many of the local population fled into the jungle, where they often joined the guerrillas. Most of the vegetable gardens were destroyed and the regiment probably sustained heavy losses, but they remained active into 1945 and at the close of the war had a strength estimated at more than five hundred men.[21]

The total strength of the MPAJA in the eight provinces where it operated was estimated at about ten thousand at the time of the Japanese surrender.[22] There were other resistance forces opposing the Japanese in

Malaya. Small bands of Chinese guerrillas professing loyalty to the Kuomintang operated in northern Malaya near the Thai border, while in parts of the states of Perak, Kedah, and Pahang there were small Malay resistance groups organized by Force 136, the British Special Operations Executive's clandestine operatives in Southeast Asia. The MPAJA, however, was by far the most widespread, numerous, and effective organization.

British officers of Force 136 had been in sporadic contact with the MPAJA since 1943. Mountbatten, planning for the invasion of Malaya, was eager to have the MPAJA in a position to launch diversionary attacks on the Japanese at the time of the landings. If Force 136 liaison teams could arm, train, and lead the guerrillas, they might be even more effective. The SEAC commander was aware of the Communist nature of the MPAJA and the fact that its overwhelmingly Chinese membership could easily antagonize the Malays, but he decided to go ahead with plans for Force 136 to arm the guerrillas. "It is for consideration therefore whether the military advantages to be gained by enlisting the AJUF . . . outweigh the political objections," Mountbatten told the British Chiefs of Staff. I confidently believe that coordinated action by the AJUF . . . accompanied by British liaison officers . . . will be the instrument of saving the lives of many of our own men and hastening the eviction of the Japanese."[23]

In February 1945, Force 136 established direct contact with the MPAJA, and in March 1945 the British agreed to establish liaison teams with each guerrilla group and each patrol. The British also supplied arms to the guerrillas by air from their bases in Ceylon and the Cocos Islands. The MPAJA agreed that "no political questions would be discussed." Two hundred and forty Special Operations Executive (SOE) operatives had been landed in Malaya by airdrops or submarine by the time the war ended.[24] But that was too few to establish liaison teams with all guerrilla units.[25] "The number of liaison officer teams was never enough to escape the innuendo that they were little more than peddlers of arms and welcome sources of money," wrote one SOE officer.[26] Force 136's limited influence with the MPAJA was to prove important in the first days after the Japanese surrender.

On receiving news of the surrender, the Japanese in Malaya withdrew their forces from many locations and regrouped them into a small number of areas to prepare for internment. Those who remained made little effort to maintain law and order. "I think the whole place went totally out of control," recalled Singapore resident Lee Kip Lin. "There were murders everywhere and I knew some of the people who had been collaborators had been murdered. . . . And a lot of personal vendettas went on. You done me harm. I don't like you. Now is the chance. They take a knife and go for you. . . . The police ran off because if there was any revenge the police was a certain victim."[27]

Isolated groups of Japanese soon found themselves confronting MPAJA units that had recently benefited from the delivery of British arms. From the time of the surrender until the end of August, a period of about two weeks, the guerrillas killed about five hundred Japanese and local police, close to the total number they had killed during the entire war.

In many different regions of Malaya the MPAJA emerged from the jungle to take control of local government. By some estimates about 70 percent of the towns and villages were taken over by the guerrillas.[28] The MPAJA's control was particularly strong in the Malay states of Selangor, Negri Sembilan, Perak, Pahang, and Johore. As the Japanese abandoned towns and villages in these areas, the guerrillas quickly moved in. In Kuantan, Force 136 reported that "the general population was absolutely under the thumb of the [MPAJA 7th] regiment."[29] "They fixed prices of commodities and rid those places [they occupied] of anything that bore a trace of Japanese influence. They barricaded the main roads and stopped inter-district road traffic. They took over lorries and vehicles."[30] In Singapore the guerrillas boldly took the former Japanese Club as their headquarters.[31] In Pahang they "took over every department of Civil Administration and occupied most of the large buildings in the town from the Chinese Chamber of Commerce to the police station. They were in complete and absolute control" for almost three weeks, until the first British troops arrived.[32]

Usually the first targets of the MPAJA were police stations and posts. During the war the police forces, composed mainly of Malays and Sikhs, had been used by the Japanese as an antiguerrilla force against the Chinese insurgents. Local police and other suspected collaborators were taken into custody and police stations were frequently burned to the ground. Police and former police who were unable to hide out or flee were dragged through the streets along with other "traitors and running dogs"—suspected informers, black marketeers, mistresses of Japanese soldiers and residents—and given a summary trial. "When the verdict was 'guilty of Death' [*sic*], the convicted were cold-bloodedly executed in public. In certain places in Selangor and Perak they were put into pig's cages, carried round the town, and then butchered before the crowds," wrote one contemporary observer. "What is significant is that the crowds condoned the vengeance of the 'Communists.' Even the slaughter of mistresses of the Japanese, especially MPs' [Kempeitai] paramours, received public approval. Such was public hatred against 'the oppressors of the people.' "[33] Special targets were those associated with the hated secret police. When Allied investigators arrived in Malaya with a list of suspected Kempeitai war criminals, they found that nearly all had disappeared into the hands of the MPAJA and were rumored to be dead.[34]

Although most people approved of the summary justice meted out to the Japanese and to known collaborators, the conduct of the MPAJA soon served to exacerbate tensions between the Malay and Chinese communities in many parts of Malaya. During the war, the Chinese guerrillas' suspicion and contempt for Malays and Indians for working for and cooperating with the Japanese were matched by Malayan fear and resentment of the MPAJA. Malayan leaders complained that the guerrillas, in addition to demanding taxes and "contributions," sometimes used mosques as meeting places and hideouts and that they conscripted Malay women to work for them in the jungle.[35]

The fact that most of the targets of MPAJA punishments and reprisals were Malays helped to fuel this resentment. So did Chinese guerrilla behavior after news of the surrender reached Malaya. "The impression everybody had at that time," recalled Ahmed Khan, "was that the Communists had played a major role in the battle in Malaya and therefore they were going to occupy it and not the British. There were rumors spread by the Communists that China was going to rule over Singapore and Malaya."[36] The seemingly inexplicable delay in the arrival of British troops, long after news had been received that Allied forces had landed in Japan, helped to fuel this speculation.[37] "We Malays thought the Chinese would land on the island [of Singapore] first," recalled one resident. "Some of my Chinese friends expected this to happen. Many Chinese suddenly became quite chauvinistic and arrogant. We were quite worried."[38]

Though some Malay leaders complained of "anarchy" and a "reign of terror" during the brief period of guerrilla rule, regular units of the MPAJA were considered by officers in Force 136 to have been fairly well disciplined and orderly. "The administration, considering the entire lack of experience of the AJA, was fairly satisfactory," wrote Major J. L. Chapman. "Most enemy property stores had been sealed and were under guard. A Special Police Force had been recruited."[39] Yet these officers also admitted that the MPAJA's "methods did not tend to restore confidence to the Malays." One Malay district officer declared to the British that eight days of rule by the MPAJA "was worse than three and a half years under the Japs."[40]

In many areas the MPAJA's actions encouraged communal fears and jealousies, mob violence, and acts of revenge and retaliation. Malays listened to frightening stories of how on a Friday, when Muslim men had gathered at a mosque for prayer, Chinese guerrillas surrounded the building and set it on fire. Then they raped the women of the village. In another version of the story, the Muslim population of a village were rounded up by the guerrillas and brought to the mosque, where they were forced to eat the meat of pigs that the Chinese had slaughtered inside the mosque.[41]

In Singapore, Chinese heard rumors that "an army of Malays from Johore was marching down to kill every Chinese in Singapore." One of Lee Kip Lin's neighbors "appointed himself to be a leader in the neighborhood, as it were, and said, 'Every Chinese in Singapore have to be on the alert. . . . If you hear a gong being sounded . . . we expect every male member of every household to come out and defend the area with anything you like, sticks, knives. Anything you got, you come out.' So of course when you put it that way, what choice have you got except to say, 'Okay.' "[42] Communal antagonism was also encouraged by well-known collaborators, both Chinese and Malay, who had profited during the occupation and hoped to avoid reprisal or punishment by hiding behind the cause of racial solidarity as well as by Malay bureaucrats and politicians who feared that the MPAJA's close cooperation with the British might be rewarded by giving the Chinese greater privileges in postwar Malaya. On August 21, Malays clashed with Chinese guerrillas in various parts of Johore. Houses were burned and some villages completely destroyed. More than four hundred people were killed, and thousands more fled from their homes.[43] Only a week after the Japanese surrender, new fighting had begun in Malaya, which, in some parts of the country, would bring as much death and destruction as the war.

ON SEPTEMBER 12, Admiral Mountbatten, accompanied by his American deputy, General Raymond A. Wheeler, who still wore his World War I–style campaign hat, rode through Singapore in an open car driven by a recently released prisoner of war along streets lined with Royal Marines and sailors in dress uniform.[44] On the steps of the Municipal Building, four Japanese generals and two admirals surrendered their swords to the supreme Allied commander. "I have never seen six more villainous, depraved or brutal faces in my life," the SEAC commander wrote in his diary. "I shudder to think what it would have been like to be in their power. When they got off their chairs and shambled out they looked like a bunch of gorillas with great baggy breeches and knuckles almost trailing the ground."[45] The same Union Jack that had flown over the city at the time of the British surrender was raised again over the ceremony.[46] Japanese prisoners had cleared the large square, or *padang,* fronting the government buildings, which the occupation authorities had used for growing tapioca, and restored some of its former grandeur. "That was a wonderful sight," recalled Arthur Thompson, who watched the surrender ceremony from the upper windows of the supreme court building. "It was wonderful to see the different soldiers outside. . . . There were British soldiers, there were Gurkhas, there were Indians, there were Chinese, there were Dutch, there were Australians and New Zealanders."[47]

Mountbatten had already established a British Military Administration for Malaya under the day-to-day direction of Major General H. R. Hone as chief civil affairs officer. The BMA was responsible for postwar reconstruction and rehabilitation, reestablishing key elements of the civil administration, the police, and the educational system, dealing with economic, financial, and public health issues, supervising the detention and repatriation of the Japanese, and apprehending and trying war criminals. To accomplish these tasks the BMA had a staff of about a thousand military and civilian administrators. Of these, only 244 had previous experience in Malaya—or anywhere else in the British colonial empire.[48] The top people in the BMA were able and experienced, but not a few of their subordinates were incompetents, shysters, and opportunists. One experienced colonial civil servant contrasted "the local populace's joyful welcome" to the returning British forces with their subsequent "disgust at the corruption and looting propensities of the British Military Administration, only a handful of whom knew the country and understood its peoples and had any feeling for them."[49]

SEAC's occupation force, tough British, Indian, and Gurkha soldiers who had just emerged from months of hard jungle fighting, were unprepared temperamentally or by training to become part of a great social and economic reconstruction project. Two Malayan academics who experienced the military government concluded that the British and Commonwealth troops "were hopelessly ill-prepared to resist the temptations of the situation. . . . Their corruption, illegal commandeering of property, gun-play against unarmed civilians and the sale of arms to gangsters, undermined in six months a tradition that had taken a century to build. Guilty individuals were few, the temptations were great. . . . The Army of 1945 was a victim of circumstances no less than the Army of 1942. . . . But those who understand the roots of British prestige in Malaya appreciate that it was 1945 at least as much as 1942 that undermined the confidence of the public."[50]

AFTER THE SURRENDER CEREMONY, Lieutenant General Itagaki Seishiro, commander of the Seventh Area Army, went to Tokyo to stand trial as a war criminal. He was found guilty and eventually executed. Japanese civilians went to Jurong on the southwest outskirts of Singapore to await repatriation to Japan. Japanese soldiers were concentrated at Jurong and Changi Prison, where they traded places with their former Allied captives.

Mountbatten designated all Japanese military forces in his theater as "surrendered Japanese personnel" and put them to work repairing some of the wartime damage and wear in Singapore. As Japanese soldiers filled in holes and bomb craters around the city, crowds sometimes gathered to jeer. "The public . . . some of them . . . just give them a kick . . . showing [their] anger [toward] the Japanese."[51] A Japanese infantryman stationed in northern Malaya recalled that as his unit marched south to be interned, they became the target of stones thrown by the local people and several men received head wounds. Yet acts of violence and revenge against the Japanese by Singapore citizens were relatively few and short-lived. Many Japanese civilians at Jurong recalled that former Chinese employees or friends actually visited the internment camp with food and necessities for their Japanese associates.[52]

The treatment of Japanese soldiers by the British military was far less indulgent. Japanese soldiers were initially concentrated at Jurong and Changi, where they served as working parties. Some working parties were double-timed from Changi to Singapore each morning. There they worked all day cleaning toilets, cutting grass, and carrying cargo from the harbor to warehouses, then were marched back to Changi each night. Other working parties worked at Tengah airfield near Bukit Timah Road, which the Japanese soon renamed Jigoku Tengah (Tengah Hell).

By October all Japanese military personnel in Malaya and Singapore had been transferred to the island of Rempang in the Riau Archipelago. Rempang was completely uninhabited, and the Japanese were forced to clear the trees and undergrowth on the island, build shelters, and attempt to grow vegetables and other crops in Rempang's rather unpromising soil. For the first two months on the island, the Japanese food supply allowed each soldier only about eleven hundred calories a day. Clothing was also in short supply, and most Japanese were soon reduced to what one Japanese officer euphemistically described as "the extremist–simple clothing mode of living."[53] One thing Rempang did possess in abundance was tropical disease. By 1946 it was estimated that about 20 percent of the fifty-nine thousand Japanese on Rempang and Galang were suffering from malaria, dysentery, or beriberi.[54] It was more than a year before the last Japanese left Rempang, many with the feeling that they had been deliberately marooned and starved by the British. There was some truth in these charges, but they would likely have caused small concern to SEAC officers who had recent memories of the thousands of Chinese massacred by the Japanese in Singapore, as well as the tens of thousands of deaths of Allied prisoners and internees in Japanese prison camps and in the construction of the infamous Burma–Siam Railroad.

For Malayans the occupation had been marked by privation, brutality, fear, and uncertainty. With the return of the British, the fear and brutality ended, but the uncertainty and privation continued. Cities and towns were worn and bedraggled after four years of war. Most municipal services had ceased to function. In Kuala Lumpur the public water supply was polluted and pipes were defective, street lighting was out of commission, garbage was not removed, and malarial mosquitoes were breeding in clogged drains and other standing water.[55] In Singapore the harbor was littered with wrecks, most of the warehouses had been destroyed, and none of the harbor cranes was in working order.[56] In all cities, supplies of electricity and fresh water was intermittent and uncertain.

During the war, swarms of people from the countryside had converged on the cities and towns, where rations were reputedly easier to obtain. Hordes of recent migrants occupied tiny, overcrowded apartments or spread their bedding in hallways, under staircases, or in alleys. With the Japanese surrender, large numbers of former POWs, internees, and other displaced persons had taken up temporary residence in Singapore, further contributing to the overcrowding.

Health and sanitary conditions varied from marginal to appalling. The death rate in Singapore for 1945 was more than twice that of 1940. For Indian men in Singapore it was more than seven times as high.[57] Malnutrition was one attribute all the disparate peoples of Malaya had in common. In Kuala Lumpur, Pahang, Kelantan, and Trengganu, 23 percent of schoolchildren were found to be "grossly undersized" for their age, and in Singapore about 40 percent of children were classified as malnourished.[58]

Above all there was the continuing shortage of food supplies. Everywhere in Southeast Asia under Japanese rule there had been a catastrophic drop in rice production. Large-scale requisitioning of rice by the Japanese military in exchange for near-worthless Japanese occupation currency had discouraged rice farmers and encouraged hoarding. At the same time, the breakdown of local and international transport systems during the war had left many farmers with crops that they were unable to get to market. Production plummeted. In 1939 the three principal rice-exporting countries, Thailand, Burma, and Indochina, had sent well over six million tons of rice abroad. For the last six months of 1945, the figure was just 176,000 tons.[59] At the surrender conference in Rangoon on August 27, Terauchi's representatives had "admitted that stocks in the rice-deficient areas were either non-existent or so small they had no idea how they could feed the subject population if the war had continued."[60] Well before the surrender, the British had become aware of the food situation and begun to plan for the emergency, but they overestimated the amount of rice to be found in Malaya and underestimated the size of the population that would have to be fed. In addition, Southeast Asia's needs had to compete with the demands created by food shortages and famine in many other parts of the world.

The British brought in what food they could and introduced a system of free rice distribution and rationing, but this arrangement soon broke down. Prices soared. Those who lived in proximity to Allied occupation troops often benefited from British military rations given, sold, or bartered to them by the troops.[61] The black market flourished. Tan Guan Chuan, a Singapore civil servant, recalled paying the equivalent of six U.S. dollars for a loaf of bread.[62] A common quip was that the British Military Administration's acronym, BMA, actually meant "Black Market Administration."

Further contributing to the economic chaos of the occupation was the British decision to completely demonetize the Japanese occupation currency, which soon became known as "banana money." For many Malayans who held only Japanese currency, this measure meant instant insolvency, while for others who had managed to hold on to some prewar currency or bought it up on speculation it brought equally unexpected riches. As a result of all these developments, the prices paid by a workingman for essential market commodities in 1946 were estimated to have increased more than eight times over what they had been in 1939.[63]

A wave of strikes swept Singapore. Seven thousand dockworkers struck in October in a successful bid for higher wages. That was followed by further strikes by tram workers, hospital employees, firemen, and even bar girls.[64] The strikes culminated in a two-day general strike organized by the Communist-led Singapore General Labour Union, which brought out more than 173,000 workers. Pleased with the success of the general strike, the General Labour Union planned an even larger event for February 15, the anniversary of the British surrender of Singapore to the Japanese. Although Mountbatten regarded strikes about wages and working conditions as "a normal democratic procedure," he recognized that the Communists had more ambitious plans for the labor movement and that they intended to directly challenge the British military government.[65] His subordinates and advisers, far less liberally inclined, had long urged him to arrest the ringleaders of the movement and deport them to China, which was what was done with troublemakers in the good old colonial era. Two days before the planned demonstration, Mountbatten issued a warning calling attention to the fact that while the military administration continued to support the public's right to freedom of expression, it would not allow actions that were deliberately intended to undermine law and order.[66] That night, ten Chinese leaders of the union were arrested, and on the fifteenth, police forcibly dispersed demonstrations called by the strike organizers. However, Mountbatten refused to allow the deportation of the strike leaders to China. If the Communists expected the people to turn out in support of their attempted general strike, they were soon disappointed. Whatever they might think of the British, most urban citizens in Malaya were unready to follow the advocates of class warfare.

Meanwhile, in the countryside, communal violence continued. Anti-Chinese riots were reported in Negri Sembilan, Perak, and Kuala Lumpur. The cause of the riots was described as Malay "discontent with being forced to make contributions to the MPAJA."[67] On the night of November 5, Malays armed with knives attacked the Chinese village of Padang Lobar in Negri Sembilan. Forty women and children were killed. The British deployed troops to protect threatened villages and confined the MPAJA forces to their headquarters area to prevent acts of revenge.[68] During the following month "interracial tensions increased in every state throughout the country."[69] At the end of the month, Chinese on the island of Dindings in the state of Perak attacked two villages, killing seventeen Malays and wounding fourteen. Seven of the dead were children. Twenty Chinese were also killed.[70]

In some states, Malay antagonism toward the Chinese began to take on the form of *sabil Allah*, or holy war. A leading proponent of *sabil Allah* was Kiyai Salleh Bin Abdul Karim of Johore. Religious teaching was Kiyai Salleh's second career, his first, prior to the war, having been as a leader of criminal gangs and inmate of various jails.[71] Since the summer of 1945, Kiyai Salleh had been leading new-style gangs in a holy war against the MPAJA and the Chinese in his district of Batu Pahat and then throughout Johore. His followers were generally believed to have been involved in the massacre at Padang Lobar.

Panglima (Commander in Chief) Salleh, as he was now known, headed a movement of holy warriors known as "the Army of the Red Bands." Kiyai Salleh's message combined highly selective readings of the Koran with Sufi mysticism and traditional Malay beliefs in the supernatural. Kiyai Salleh himself was reported to have impressive supernatural powers. "He cannot be killed by bullets; he can walk dry-shod across rivers; he can burst any bonds that are put on him; his voice can paralyze his assailants."[72] He experienced visions in which a Sufi saint appeared to him, warned him of approaching danger, and advised him on how to overcome his enemies.[73]

A true follower of Kiyai Salleh's teachings could be rendered invulnerable provided he observed certain rituals and was "without pride, did not loot in war, robbed not the dead, and never looked back when fighting."[74] Initiates gathered to recite certain verses of the Koran and were pierced by a golden needle or drank a potion blessed by an imam and were granted invulnerability. Afterward they wore a red band around their arm or as a sash.[75] Kiyai Salleh could also delegate his powers to a few disciples who would then have the ability to confer invulnerability upon new recruits to the movement. Though Kiyai Salleh used the language of religion and magic, British observers believed that there was a strong political component to *sabil Allah*. Kiyai Salleh's three principal lieutenants were all nationalists from the Netherlands Indies and exemplified the violent and xenophobic extremism gaining ascendancy among political activists there. One of them had been implicated in an earlier attack on a Chinese settlement. The British believed that Malay leaders tolerated or even encouraged Kiyai Salleh's activities because they helped to unite Malays in resistance to Chinese political domination.

By early 1946 the "Red Bands" had spread to Malacca, Negri Sembilan, Selangor, Pahang, and Perak.[76] Chinese youths were also reported to be receiving military training from former MPAJA guerrillas.[77]

British intelligence reported "continued racial tensions in most states," especially Kelantan, Perak, and Pahang, where minor incidents were common. In these states, "extreme nervousness is being displayed by the Chinese."[78] On the morning of February 11, another major incident occurred when Malays killed at least twenty Chinese and injured a dozen more in a premeditated attack on the village of Batu Talam.[79] One month later, at Bekor on the lower Perak River, Malays burned down two Chinese houses. In retaliation the Chinese massacred fifty-six Malays. One hundred others were wounded, and the remaining Malay population had to be evacuated to another village. British intelligence reported that only one of the dead had gunshot wounds and the others had been hacked to death by swords and knives.[80] Every incident, indeed every report or rumor of an incident, generated hundreds, sometimes thousands of displaced people who fled their villages or districts after their homes were destroyed or simply out of fear of further attacks.

By this point, others besides the British feared that things were getting out of hand. Leaders of the Malay community began to appeal for tolerance and order and to redirect newly found Malay unity into the political struggle for control of postwar Malaya. The Malay sultans, secretly assured by the British that they would retain many of their prewar prerogatives, began to clamp down on disorders. Wealthy Chinese businessmen, never comfortable with the Communist guerrillas, were also ready for an end to strife. In some districts, Malayan and Chinese leaders organized district boards under a British officer to adjudicate incidents and head off trouble.

The MPAJA had been peacefully demobilized at the beginning of December. Many Communist leaders had argued that conditions were favorable for redirecting their insurgency against the British, but others, principally Lai Tek, argued for a more cautious policy of political organizing, propaganda, and labor agitation. Lai Tek's views prevailed. In a series of formal ceremonies, the MPAJA regiments paraded, medals were distributed, and weapons were turned in (except for the most modern and serviceable, which were buried for future use, many still in the canisters in which they had been airdropped by the British).[81] Former guerrillas received allocations of clothing and money, and the Malayan Communists busied themselves, for the time being, with labor agitation and organizing.

On April 1, 1946, "civil government" was restored to Malaya. The British Military Administration passed into history, unloved and unlamented by those it had governed. A respected historian has observed, "In seven months it destroyed the goodwill which existed at the time of the liberation and brought British prestige in Singapore to a lower point even than in February 1942."[82] A U.S. intelligence summary noted that Mountbatten was reported to be "worried over complaints that conditions in Malaya now are worse than under the Japanese" and had ordered an investigation.[83]

As in China, the Japanese surrender did not mean the end of fighting. "War" between Chinese and Malays simply intensified and continued well into 1946. The incompetents and boodlers in the lower ranks of the BMA were incapable of coping with the monumental problems of food shortages and runaway inflation even when they were not part of the problem. Among the people of Malaya, those who excelled at opportunism, graft, and exploitation thrived in the atmosphere of black marketeering, ethnic tension, and fear as they had during the Japanese occupation. And yet Malaya was among the most successful of postwar British military occupations. In other parts of Southeast Asia there were less welcoming, less forgiving, more impatient peoples awaiting the return of the colonial powers.

CHAPTER FIVE

"LONG LIVE VIETNAM'S INDEPENDENCE"

On September 12, as Mountbatten was receiving the Japanese surrender at the Municipal Building in Singapore, a squadron of Royal Air Force transport planes landed at Tan Son Nhut airport outside Saigon carrying the first of the British occupation forces for Indochina, a battalion of the 20th Indian Division under Major General Douglas Gracey. Crowds of French and Vietnamese cheered the arrival of each plane. Still others lined the road waving Union Jacks as the troops were driven into the city in Japanese trucks.

"The local Indo-Chinese (Annamites for short) and their independence party who were running the local government in the usual feeble WOG fashion thought that we had come to confirm their independence and liberate them from the wicked French," wrote Captain V. M. Sissons. "The local French, all rather futile and vaguely Vichy, who have been terrorized for some months by the Annamites . . . regard us as their liberators."[1]

At Gracey's headquarters, a former girls' school, Gurkhas resplendent in polished white belts and gaiters mounted guard. Local Saigon residents were particularly impressed by the soldiers' kukris, wicked-looking, curved-long-bladed knives, which the Gurkhas wore on their web belts.[2]

While the Gurkhas were being flown into Saigon, another occupation army was moving into Hanoi in northern Indochina. These were Chinese troops from Yunnan under the command of Lieutenant General Lu Han. "All day and all night the troops kept pouring into the city," recalled one Vietnamese observer. "They shocked everyone including the local Chinese community which had organized a formal welcoming ceremony for them. . . . The troops wore shoes of woven straw, cloth, or rubber cut out from tires or even went barefoot. They had tattered uniforms and looked tired and thin. Each unit was accompanied by cooks laden with pots and pans, making a racket."[3] An OSS officer "saw an almost incredible scene of confusion and aimlessly wandering Chinese. Sidewalks, doorways and side streets were cluttered with soldiers and camp followers hovering over bundles of personal belongings, with household furniture and military gear strewn everywhere. Many had staked claims in private gardens and courtyards and settled down to brew tea, do household chores and start the laundry."[4] These contrasting spectacles in northern and southern Vietnam, a country that had not seen a single battle in the war with Japan, were the product of two years of mutual suspicions, geopolitical imaginings, personality clashes, prejudices, and ignorance among the victorious Allies.

In the first months of the Pacific War, the Japanese armies had rolled easily over the British colonies in Malaya, Borneo, and Burma and the Dutch in the East Indies. The Europeans suffered humiliating defeats and many of their former colonial subjects welcomed the Japanese. As for the French colonies in Indochina, these were granted to the Japanese without a fight. Militarily vulnerable and encouraged by the Vichy government to cooperate, the French colonial government in Indochina had made progressively greater concessions to the Japanese, allowing them to station troops in Vietnam and use the ports, airfields, and railroads. By the time of Pearl Harbor, the French had been forced to agree to whatever economic or military demands the Japanese might make in prosecuting their war in Asia.

In return for their acquiescence, the colonial government, headed by Admiral Jean Decoux, was permitted to continue to carry out most of its functions. The French flag still flew over Hanoi, Hue, and Saigon, and French colonials could pursue their usual business, but fifty thousand Japanese troops garrisoned the country, Japanese warplanes flew from the airfields, and the Japanese Navy established a base at Cam Ranh Bay. In the days following Pearl Harbor, Japanese forces had used Indochina as a springboard for attacks against Malaya, the Philippines, and the Netherlands Indies, something the United States would not soon forget. State Department planners observed in 1942 that "the title of France to Indochina was clouded by the failure of the Vichy government to resist Japanese aggression."[5]

Americans saw only one exception to this pattern of collapse and collaboration in Asia. In the Philippines, Japanese troops had been stalled for almost four months by the stubborn defense of Filipino troops fighting alongside the American forces, and even after the latter were forced to surrender, groups of Filipinos continued to wage guerrilla warfare in many parts of the archipelago. To most of those in Washington, the lesson was obvious. The Philippines had been treated well by the United States, had become a self-governing commonwealth in 1935, and had been promised independence in 1945. The result was that Filipinos had rejected Japanese anti-imperialist propaganda, while old-style European imperialism in Southeast Asia had encouraged colonial peoples to side with the Japanese. "Our course in dealing with the Philippines situation . . . offers, I think, a perfect example of how a nation should treat a colony or a dependency," wrote President Franklin Roosevelt in 1942.[6] "Don't think for a minute that Americans would be dying in the Pacific tonight," the president declared to his son, "if it hadn't been for the short-sighted greed of the French and the British and the Dutch."[7]

Roosevelt's determination not to sacrifice American lives and treasure in the war with Japan simply to restore the European colonial empires was shared by many other Americans. *Life* magazine urged the British to "stop fighting for the British Empire and fight for victory."[8] A senior foreign service officer in East Asia warned that European imperialism, based as it was on "subjugation, exploitation, privilege and force," encouraged "a turning by the colonial peoples to any nation or group of nations which can promise them a change, nations to whom the colonial peoples would not turn if it were not for their servitude."[9]

This generalized suspicion of imperialism extended to views of Pacific war strategy. Until 1944, American interest in Asia centered on China, both as a vital symbol that gave the lie to Japan's claim of fighting a war of "Asia for the Asians" and as a future base for aerial bombardment, blockade, and possible invasion of Japan. American military strategists focused their interest on plans and projects to reopen supply routes into China by retaking northern Burma from the Japanese. By contrast, the British sometimes appeared to American leaders to be more interested in efforts to liberate their Asian possessions, especially Singapore. Major General Raymond A. Wheeler, the chief of the American Services of Supply in the China-India Theater, observed, "American interests point north to Japan, British interests south to Singapore."[10] "It is taken for granted on the American side," reported the British ambassador in Washington, "that our dealings in Far Eastern matters [and] our policies are self-seeking and in conflict with the more generous principles of the U.S."[11]

Although the United States agreed, in 1943, to the establishment of a new Allied Southeast Asia Command under Mountbatten to direct operations in Burma, Sumatra, and Malaya, Washington attempted to dissociate itself politically from what some saw as an organization to recapture colonial possessions, and the United States declined to assign diplomatic representatives to Mountbatten's headquarters. Nevertheless, Roosevelt bluntly cautioned London that "the U.S. government would expect to be consulted about any arrangements as to the future of Southeast Asia."[12]

Roosevelt's general animus toward colonialism was most strongly expressed in his attitude toward French Indochina. France's swift collapse before the Nazi onslaught in 1940 convinced the president that France had lost its political genius, social cohesion, and moral fiber. The French willingness to bow to the Japanese without a fight in Indochina seemed only to confirm these conclusions. In Roosevelt's view, the French had done the poorest job of all the colonial powers.[13] The president made no secret of the fact that he believed that at the end of the war, Indochina should be placed under international trusteeship. To foreign ambassadors as well as the British foreign secretary, Roosevelt repeated his belief that "to permit France to return would make bad feeling throughout the Far East; the French had done nothing for the population but had misgoverned and exploited it."[14]

In London, the president's ideas were received with consternation. "I have the impression President Roosevelt is suffering from the same form of megalomania as Wilson and Lloyd George," wrote Sir Victor Cavendish-Bentinck of the Foreign Office. "I trust we will not allow ourselves to quarrel with the French without being on very strong grounds for the benefit of a U.S. President who, in a year's time, may be merely a historical figure."[15] Prime Minister Winston Churchill was skeptical that "international control would work satisfactorily in Indochina" but was unwilling to provoke a quarrel with Roosevelt over the matter and told the Foreign Office that "such questions should be reserved till after the war."[16]

The French were at least equally flabbergasted by the president's remarks. Whatever American views of France, Washington had opted to maintain diplomatic ties with the Vichy government of Marshal Henri Philippe Pétain until 1942. Acting Secretary of State Sumner Welles had also assured the French government in April 1942 that the "United States recognizes the sovereign jurisdiction of the people of France . . . over French possessions overseas." On the eve of the North African landings in November 1942, American diplomats had reiterated these assurances. Roosevelt's blunt pronouncements were in stark contrast to these earlier statements and seemed to signal a sharp change of policy.

Yet in the end the pronouncements remained merely pronouncements. The president never issued clear-cut directives or guidance about what course the United States should follow in regard to Indochina. In Washington, East Asia experts both inside and outside the government tended to share Roosevelt's views, but most of his important and influential advisers and the powerful European bureaus in the State Department did not. Nor did the military. In a conversation at the beginning of 1945, Secretary of War Stimson and the president's confidential adviser Harry Hopkins agreed that the United States should refrain from opposing France's "regrowth."[17] Senior State Department officials were preoccupied with reestablishing a strong France as a counterweight to Soviet expansion into western Europe, or possibly a future resurgent Germany, and with securing French support for the projected postwar United Nations organization.

To confound the confusion, the president refused to discuss the details of his plans for Indochina, simply indicating that it was a matter to be settled at the end of the war.[18] Historians disagree about whether and to what extent Roosevelt may have moderated his stand on a French return to Southeast Asia in the last months before his death in April 1945. But with his passing and the succession of Truman to the presidency, the United States, in effect, abandoned its overt opposition to a French return to Indochina.[19] In May the secretary of state, Edward Stettinius, blandly announced to an astonished French foreign minister that "the record is entirely innocent of any official statement of the U.S. government questioning, even by implication, French sovereignty over Indochina."[20]

Though Roosevelt's approach to colonial questions may have been discarded in Washington after April 1945, it was still very much alive in Chungking, where both Ambassador Hurley and General Wedemeyer continued to view British and French activities in the Far East with deep suspicion. As recently as March 1945, both had visited Washington and conferred with the president only a few weeks before his death. According to Wedemeyer's recollection, the president repeated to them his intention that Indochina be made a trusteeship and warned them to steer clear of any British or French schemes to restore the colonial empires.

The two needed little encouragement. Hurley was a dyed-in-the-wool anti-imperialist, while Wedemeyer had had ample opportunity to hone his anti-British prejudices during three years as a staff officer in Washington and as deputy commander of the Southeast Asia Command. "In General Wedemeyer," wrote a British diplomat, "we have an American who is profoundly distrustful of everything British. And who is convinced that we are a bad number."[21] As for Hurley, he had told the British ambassador in Chungking that in his opinion, U.S.-supplied Lend-Lease equipment "should not be used for the recovery of colonial territory" because this "violated the fundamental principle of self-determination held by the U.S."[22] At Mountbatten's headquarters, one American diplomat characterized relations between the OSS and its British counterpart, the SOE, as "pathologically suspicious."[23] "It becomes increasingly clear," wrote Mountbatten's political adviser, Esler Dening, "that whatever may be the policy in Washington, American anti-imperialists in the armed forces backed by the ubiquitous business man in uniform are determined to do whatever they please in the Far East, both during and after the war."[24]

Indochina provided limitless opportunities for the two Allies to air their mutual suspicions and anxieties. Although it was militarily a backwater in the war, both SEAC and the China Theater were interested in the former French colony. The main Japanese land and air routes for supply and reinforcement of their forces opposing the Southeast Asia Command in Burma and Malaya ran through Indochina. Mountbatten believed that as the battle for those areas proceeded, Indochina "would become of ever-increasing importance to the strategy of SEAC."[25] At the time Mountbatten made this observation, Indochina had also become an important target for air attack by the China Theater's 14th Air Force. American planes operating from south China frequently bombed targets in Vietnam, and by the middle of 1944, B-24 bombers were ranging as far south as Saigon to attack dockyards and rail centers. These air operations required reliable intelligence on weather, air defenses, targets, and Japanese troop movements. Information on troop movements was of special importance because the transfer of Japanese forces in or out of northern Indochina could affect military operations in south China.

There were, therefore, good military reasons for SEAC and the China Theater to conduct clandestine intelligence and guerrilla operations in Indochina, and both had been doing so since 1943. As time passed, however, and the political disputes surrounding the future of colonial Southeast Asia became progressively more bitter and confused, the issue of Mountbatten's operations in Indochina became a subject of heated controversy.

Mountbatten believed that he had secretly received tacit approval for his clandestine missions from both President Roosevelt and Chiang Kai-shek. Wedemeyer, however, claimed to have no knowledge of such understandings, but noted with suspicion that many of SEAC's secret operations appeared to involve the French. Mindful of Roosevelt's charge to "watch carefully to prevent any British and French political activities in Indochina," Wedemeyer feared that secret intelligence missions might be a cover for efforts to help the French influence the political situation in that country.[26]

When the French refused to provide Wedemeyer with the details of their planned operations in Vietnam, the American general closed Kunming airport in southern China to SEAC planes supporting the clandestine operations. This touched off an angry exchange of messages between Kandy (Mountbatten's Ceylon headquarters) and Chungking. Wedemeyer demanded the right to approve all secret operations to be carried out in his theater. Mountbatten agreed to keep Wedemeyer informed but refused to wait for approval in all cases.

Both sides appealed to their respective governments. Wedemeyer argued in a message to army chief of staff General George C. Marshall that the British disregard of his authority as theater commander, their increased activities in Indochina, and the establishment of a French military mission at SEAC headquarters in late 1944 all reflected "a British and French plan to reestablish their pre-war political and economic positions in Southeast Asia."[27] Ambassador Hurley reinforced the general's letter with a warning to President Truman that Mountbatten was attempting to "defeat what we believe to be American policy and reestablish French imperialism."[28]

Washington replied to the China Theater's arguments with a remarkable piece of diplomatic prose. After conveying the president's assurance that "there has been no basic change in the policy" toward Indochina, Undersecretary of State Grew informed Hurley that decisions reached at Yalta and at the San Francisco Conference "would preclude the establishment of a trusteeship in Indo-China except with the consent of the French Government. The latter seems unlikely. Nevertheless it is the President's intention at some appropriate time to ask that the French Government give some positive indication of its intentions in regard to the establishment of civil liberties and increasing measures of self-government in Indo-China. . . . "[29] In a similar message, Marshall advised Wedemeyer, "The State Department's position eliminates the necessity of curtailing Mountbatten's operations in Indo-China." Those operations should be "judged strictly on their military merits and in relation to the stand of the Generalissimo."[30]

What Hurley and Wedemeyer made of these messages is not altogether clear. Hurley ceased sending warnings to Washington, but Wedemeyer recalled that he saw Marshall's message as signaling no fundamental change in policy but as another concession to French pressure. For the future, he still felt himself bound by the instruction about Indochina he had received from President Roosevelt.[31]

Even paranoids have real enemies, and in this case Hurley and Wedemeyer's suspicions were not wholly inappropriate. The British did concur in French intentions to continue their control of Indochina. Like many in Washington, British leaders wished to see a strong postwar France that would have close and cooperative relations with the former wartime Allies. Few in London could take Roosevelt's ideas about international trusteeship and preparation for independence seriously. If they were to be taken seriously, it could easily mean that portions of the British as well as the French Empire might be seen as eligible for trusteeship. "We do not believe there is any satisfactory alternative to France as a stabilizing element," declared the Foreign Office. "Indochina has no geographical or ethnographical unity, no political cohesion aside from that conferred by French rule. It is a mosaic of peoples, tongues and cultures."[32]

Above all there was the belief that Indochina was "not ready" for independence. The Research Branch of the Foreign Office cited a book on Indochina by Virginia Thompson, a well-known American academic expert on Southeast Asia. Thompson was impressed by the "apathy, insensitivity and placidity of the Annamites . . . forced on them by climate and undernourishment. They lack the driving power given by strong desires. Their intelligence is keen but their character weak."[33] Of course, most other regions of Southeast Asia were equally hot and the climate was reported to have the same baleful influence. "One foreign engineer told me that among the natives of all Malaysia, including Siam, there were only half a dozen 'adults,' " wrote bestselling travel writer John Gunther in *Inside Asia.* "Whether this childishness is real or not I don't know. A reason put forward for it is the heat. Often the white man says it is the heat that ruins the natives. It sucks wit and vitality from their blood and gumption from their brains. I have heard Europeans say that true independence is impossible in a tropical country."[34] Walter Foote, longtime American consul general in Batavia and General MacArthur's expert adviser on the Netherlands Indies, also found the Indonesians to be "docile, essentially peaceful, contented and therefore apathetic toward political moves. . . . The natives are definitely not ready for independence. That condition is fifty, perhaps seventy-five, years in the future."[35]

In truth, in the view of the British and the view of most Americans, no one in Asia was "ready" for independence. It was true that the Indians would probably get it soon, but that was only because wartime experience had shown the British that if they failed to deliver independence, the Indians would probably take it for themselves. The Philippines were also to be independent, but still tied to the United States by various obligations and understandings. So the real question appeared to be whether other Asians would be subject to old-style colonialism or some type of new, more enlightened international stewardship that would help prepare them for self-government. Yet the theorizing of Western experts and the prudent calculations of the Foreign Office were about to be overtaken by events, and large numbers of contrary-minded "natives," not noticeably bothered by the heat, were prepared to make the most of them.

On March 9, 1945, the Japanese ambassador to French Indochina, Matsumoto Sunichi, presented Governor-General Decoux with a note. "The possibility of invasion by hostile forces" obliged Tokyo to demand that all French land, sea, and air forces in the colony, as well as the police, be placed under Japanese control. The French were given two hours to comply. Decoux sent a letter suggesting further discussion. By the time it was received, Japanese forces had already moved against French garrisons and forts all over Indochina. Most were quickly disarmed, but in northern Tonkin, where the French commanders had received some warning, there was brief although sometimes fierce resistance, and a sizable number of troops were able to withdraw through the rugged mountain region of western Tonkin into China. Many other less fortunate French soldiers, colonial officials, and functionaries found themselves locked up in their own jails. "Thus the French imperialist wolf was finally devoured by the Japanese fascist hyena," observed Ho Chi Minh in a report to the OSS.[36]

The Japanese takeover, decided on in February, was motivated by fear of an Allied invasion and by increasing evidence that the French colonial government, aware of the course of the war and prompted by the newly established de Gaulle government in Paris, was preparing to switch sides at the opportune moment.[37] With the French disarmed and French leaders behind bars, the Japanese persuaded Bao Dai, the titular emperor of Vietnam, to proclaim his country's "independence." Bao Dai appointed Tran Trong Kim, a well-known author and educator, as prime minister. Kim's Cabinet, consisting mainly of lawyers, physicians, and other well-to-do professionals with no political following, had little real power, but the disappearance of the French security apparatus and the preoccupation of the Japanese with preparing for an Allied invasion encouraged an increase in patriotic and nationalist political activities of all types. The Vanguard Youth, a kind of highly politicized Boy Scout movement for teenagers and young adults, devoted to "national liberation and improving the lives of our countrymen," soon claimed more than a hundred thousand members. Censorship rules were revised, and any political discourse that was not overtly anti-Japanese could be published in the growing number of Vietnamese-language newspapers and journals.[38]

The organization best positioned to capitalize on this situation was the Vietminh, a coalition of nationalist and anti-French groups dominated by the Indochinese Communist Party. Its leader was Ho Chi Minh, a veteran revolutionary who had battled French colonialism for decades. Ho, a founding member of the French Communist Party, had trained in Moscow during the 1920s and guided the establishment of the Indochinese Communist organization in Vietnam in 1930. A patriot and nationalist as well as a revolutionary, Ho combined tenacity of purpose with flexibility in action. A man of great personal charm and magnetism, he left a positive impression with almost everyone he encountered, including those who strongly opposed his politics and purposes. In the final analysis, it was almost certainly due to Ho's extraordinary leadership that the Communists of Vietnam, unlike their counterparts in the rest of Southeast Asia, never strangled on their own dogmatism, brutality, and ineptitude.

In May 1941, near a remote village in northeastern Vietnam, Ho convened the Eighth Plenum of the Communist Party Central Committee. The meeting resulted in a decision to found a new anticolonial nationalist front organization, the Viet Nam Doc Lap Dong Minh, or Vietminh, intended to attract all opponents of the French and Japanese. "The situation was gloomy, the work arduous," recalled Nguyen Khang, a member of the Central Committee. "I was, however, easy in my own mind. World War II had broken out . . . great changes favorable to the revolution would certainly be produced."[39]

Khang's optimism at first seemed unwarranted. Japan swallowed up the rest of Southeast Asia. Warlords arrested Ho Chi Minh while he was trying to organize support in southern China, and the Japanese imposed no obstacles to French colonial measures to suppress the Vietminh "bandits." In September 1943, Chinese warlord General Chang Fa-kwei had Ho released and put him in charge of organizing Vietnamese nationalists in southern China. Across the border in Tonkin, the Vietminh had survived and been able to establish an underground network in remote areas and among intellectuals in the cities.

With the Japanese takeover, the Vietminh saw their opportunity. Vietminh propaganda teams, proclamations, and underground newspapers told the people that the Japanese were now the major enemy and would soon be vanquished like the French. Vietnamese troops of the former French colonial army and militia were encouraged to desert to the Vietminh or sell their arms to them. Government officials, functionaries, educators, and professionals in the north secretly began to align with the Vietminh. Many others joined newly established front groups like the Women's National Salvation League and the Peasants' Salvation Association.

Yet it was neither political organizing nor the Japanese coup that preoccupied most people in northern Vietnam during the spring and summer of 1945, but a devastating famine that would wipe out entire families and depopulate whole villages. Poor rice harvests caused by insects, floods, and bad weather in the spring and fall of 1944 had reduced the stock of rice to the point where it was barely adequate to support the population of Tonkin. However, farmers had been obliged to sell large quantities of that rice at artificially low prices to the French and Japanese authorities, who used it to supply their military forces and as a stockpile against invasion. Speculators and black marketeers bought up a considerable amount of the remainder, causing the price of rice on the Hanoi black market to increase over a thousand percent.[40] The only solution was to ship large quantities of rice from southern Vietnam to the north, as had been done during past food shortages. However, roads and rail lines and coastal shipping had been badly damaged by Allied bombing, and the Japanese had appropriated a large proportion of the available shipping and rail stock to carry military traffic.

By early February 1945, thousands were dying of starvation. Others set off along the roads to other towns and villages in hope of finding food. "They move away in endless file by families," wrote one Frenchman. "The aged, the children, the men, the women, bent under the weight of their misery, shivering all over their denuded skeletons . . . stopping from time to time either to close the eyes of one of theirs that has dropped to get up no more or to strip him of some unnamable rag that occasionally still covers him. . . . To behold these corpses curled up at the roadside having as clothes and shrouds only some stalks of straw one is ashamed of mankind."[41] In the city of Nam Dinh, about ninety miles from Hanoi, oxcarts collected the bodies of the dead for burial in mass graves. "At the height of the famine," recalled Duong Van Mai Elliott, "my mother saw carts piled with dead bodies passing our house every morning. . . . Peasants who could no longer feed their children tried to give them away or just abandoned them in the streets of the city. These emaciated children would rummage through garbage piles for food scraps or they would steal to survive. They would lie in wait and then snatch food packages from people as they left the markets or stores."[42] Even well-to-do middle-class urban residents felt the impact of the famine. Mai Elliott's family subsisted on two meals a day, one of which consisted of thin rice gruel.[43] In all, about one and a half to two million people probably died in the famine, although accurate figures are impossible to come by. Some villages and hamlets lost 30 to 50 percent of their population. In Tay Luong village in Thai Binh Province, more people died as a result of the famine than during the next thirty years of war against the French and Americans.[44]

Vietminh leaders saw the famine as an opportunity to organize the peasants to seize the rice granaries of the colonial regime and to direct popular resentment against the French and Japanese. It was not a tough sell. Everyone knew that the forced requisition of land, compulsory rice sales to the government, and unreasonable taxes had contributed to the dire state of the food supply. The casual cruelty of the Japanese further fueled popular anger. One story told of a woman who had her hand cut off for stealing canned food from the Japanese. Another told of an old woman in Hue who had a job feeding horses for the army. To help her starving family, she had taken some of the rice grain out of the horse feed and replaced it with husks. When her actions were discovered, the Japanese cut open her stomach and stuffed it with husks.[45] Even more than the downfall of the French, more than the impending defeat of the Japanese, it was the famine that enabled the Vietminh to transform their fugitive guerrilla organization into a mass movement. As a respected historian of Vietnam has observed, "The revolution of 1945 matured among the wretched rural population long before the city dwellers perceived it."[46]

Across the border in southern China, the implications of the new situation were only gradually becoming clear to the Allies. The remaining French forces in Indochina frantically radioed for help as they retreated north toward China. Chiang Kai-shek and some of his advisers feared a Japanese move against Kunming. One thing was certain: The customary sources of intelligence about Indochina carefully built on contacts within the French colonial government and the military were now unavailable.

The OSS, following up on Donovan's bureaucratic triumph, which had made it Wedemeyer's premier intelligence agency in China, was at that point completing an elaborate plan for expanding operations into Indochina as well. With the Japanese takeover, Wedemeyer's headquarters became increasingly concerned about the loss of vital intelligence information, just at a time when the Chinese and Americans were preparing an offensive into southeastern China for the coming summer. In addition, there was a continuing need to recover Allied aviators whose planes had been lost over Indochina. Wedemeyer and Hurley were still in Washington, but Wedemeyer's acting chief of staff, Brig. Gen. Melvin E. Gross, was sufficiently concerned about the intelligence blackout to give the OSS a green light to launch operations into Indochina despite the political uncertainties.[47] Initially, the OSS expected to cooperate with French operatives and stay-behind units in Indochina operations. Attempts at cooperation, however, usually led to prolonged bickering with the French over training, command arrangements, supplies, and communications. Those Franco-American operations that were actually carried out generally proved unsuccessful, primarily because the French could never secure the cooperation of the Vietnamese. In July 1945, a Franco-American force attempting to raid the Japanese post at Lang Son was led into a Vietminh ambush by its Vietnamese guides. The Vietminh, reported an American officer, "held the entire area from Langson to the China frontier."[48] Another American officer declared, "I don't think the French will ever do a hell of a lot of good in Indochina because Annamite hatred makes it a more dangerous place for them than for us."[49]

That left the Vietminh. They had already been involved in the rescue and recovery of Allied aviators whose planes had been brought down over Indochina and cooperated with the American Air Ground Aid Service, the organization responsible for the recovery of lost air crews. The OSS chief of intelligence for Indochina, Captain Archimedes L. Patti, had met with Ho Chi Minh near the China border and received assurances that the Vietminh were ready to cooperate with the Americans in fighting the Japanese. In mid-July an OSS team under Major Allison K. Thomas parachuted into Vietminh-held territory near the city of Thai Nguyen, about fifty kilometers from Hanoi. Thomas remained with the Vietminh for more than two months, arming and training select forces for operations against Japanese lines of communication. The war ended before the Vietminh had fought more than a few skirmishes with the Japanese, but their connection with the OSS had bolstered Ho's prestige and helped to identify his movement with the victorious Allies. That connection also infuriated the French and deepened their suspicion of American intentions.

From the Americans at his jungle headquarters, Ho learned on August 12 that the Japanese government had accepted the Potsdam Declaration and that the end of the war was imminent.[50] In two high-level meetings in mid-August, Vietminh leaders accepted Ho's call for a rapid seizure of power in order to confront the Allied occupation forces with a de facto independent government. A National Liberation Committee with Ho as chairman was elected to serve as the core of a provisional government of the new Democratic Republic of Vietnam. A new red national flag with a gold star in the center was adopted and the new national anthem sung for the first time.

Throughout northern Vietnam, months of Vietminh organizing and propaganda and dissatisfaction with the ineffectual Tran Trong Kim government had laid the groundwork for a swift takeover. In Hanoi, where the Vietminh had an estimated hundred thousand sympathizers, a large crowd gathered in front of the municipal theater to hear speakers proclaim that a general insurrection was under way. Large bands of Vietminh supporters took control of government buildings and police posts with little opposition. Within a few days, most of Tonkin in northern Vietnam and a good portion of Annam in the center were in the hands of the Vietminh.[51] The Japanese discreetly remained in the background and, aside from a few minor confrontations, made no move to interfere. Consul General Tsukamoto reported that Japanese officials "were working without stint on measures for protection of the resident Japanese" and were attempting to achieve a compromise with the new government. By the end of August, the Japanese had handed over responsibility for police and for order and control of transportation and public utilities to the Vietminh. They refused, however, to turn over control of the Bank of Indochina.[52] On August 25, Ho Chi Minh arrived in Hanoi from Thai Nguyen and immediately began planning for a mass ceremony to formally declare independence and establish the new government. A few days later, in Hue, Emperor Bao Dai formally abdicated and turned over the imperial seal to representatives of the Vietminh government, indicating that the "mandate of heaven" had now passed from the throne to the nationalists.

On Sunday, September 2, a crowd swollen to three or four hundred thousand by arrivals from the countryside gathered in Ba Dinh Square, near the former governor-general's palace in Hanoi. In the center of the square, organizers had erected a tall platform decked with the new red and gold flags. Vietminh soldiers with drawn pistols encircled the platform and a band in Boy Scout uniforms played military tunes as Vietminh dignitaries mounted the stairs. Vo Nguyen Giap, a former history teacher who now commanded the Vietminh "Liberation Army," introduced Ho to the crowd. As an assistant held a parasol over his head—the traditional symbol of royalty—Ho read the brief declaration announcing Vietnam's independence. At one point in the address he paused and asked his listeners, "Countrymen, can you hear me?" The crowd answered with a roar, "We hear you!" It was a moment that no one present that day ever forgot. That evening an OSS officer who had witnessed the ceremony reported by radio to Kunming, "From what I have seen these people mean business and I am afraid the French will have to deal with them. For that matter we will all have to deal with them."[53]

The Vietminh knew that their new regime was in a race against time. Chinese occupation troops would arrive in a few days. The French were unprepared to relinquish their erstwhile colony. The attitude of the Allies was uncertain. Widespread starvation still remained an immediate threat. Farmers were now eating the seed rice reserved for the next season's planting. In some areas people were eating roots and tree leaves.[54] Rival nationalist groups like the Vietnam Quoc Dan Dang (Vietnamese Nationalist Party), the formerly pro-Japanese Dai Viet, and the pro-Chinese Dong Minh Hoi had been thrown into momentary disarray by the Vietminh's superior boldness and organization but were far from cowed. These groups had a large following, and they retained their own newspapers and radio stations and armed militias.[55]

The Vietminh government did what it could to eliminate its opponents. Hundreds of nationalist supporters were tried as "counterrevolutionaries" or disappeared into the hands of specially formed "honor squads for the elimination of traitors." Prominent members of Bao Dai's government, including the pro-French intellectual Pham Quyen and the Catholic minister Ngo Dinh Khoi, had been executed at the time of the emperor's abdication. Decrees issued on September 5 and 12 outlawed the Quoc Dan Dang and the Dai Viet parties and established military tribunals "to punish counterrevolutionaries." Yet Ho's government dared not go too far in the face of the impending arrival of the occupation forces since many of its rivals, especially the Dong Minh Hoi, had close ties to the Chinese.[56]

In the meantime, there was the worsening famine. Flooding in the Red River Delta in August had left three hundred thousand hectares of land under water, adding to the general distress. To cope with the growing disaster, the new government instituted a series of emergency measures. Agricultural taxes were temporally suspended and rice redistributed from any provinces and districts that had small surpluses. Ho himself announced that he would go without food once every ten days to set an example. People everywhere, even those in cities, were exhorted to grow food on every available piece of land. Crops that matured quickly, such as potatoes, corn, and soybeans, were particularly encouraged. Mai Elliott's brothers in Hanoi had "to go around collecting rice to feed the hungry as part of the 'A Loving Handful of Rice' campaign. The Vietnamese had never seen a mobilization on this scale before. My brothers and their colleagues in the Viet Minh youth association, each carrying a reed basket, would make their rounds knocking on doors and asking for rice donations. Most people cooperated, partly out of sympathy and partly out of fear of antagonizing the Viet Minh."[57]

Another critical issue was education. If the ordinary citizens of Vietnam were going to be persuaded to follow the Vietminh's calls for unity, struggle, and sacrifice over the coming years, the revolution would have to reach them through written media and not simply through slogans, meetings, and speeches. Yet the illiteracy rate among Vietnamese was nearly 90 percent. The Vietminh's goal was to enable all citizens to attain basic literacy within one year. Crash programs were established in hospitals, pagodas, and markets to provide mass literacy training for Vietnamese of all ages. By the fall of 1946, the programs had graduated some two million pupils.[58]

While they waited anxiously for the arrival of the Chinese, the Vietminh attempted to learn what they could about the attitudes of the Americans and the French from the handful of Americans who had arrived in Hanoi on August 22 as part of the OSS–Air Ground Aid Service Mercy Mission operations. The chief of the OSS mission was Captain Archimedes L. Patti, a veteran of service in France and Italy who had run the OSS operations into Indochina in the last months of the war. With Patti's team came five French officers led by the head of French intelligence in Kunming, Major Jean Sainteny. Two days later, eight more men arrived to join Patti's team, followed at the end of the month by a small Civil Affairs/Military Government team under Colonel Stephen Nordlinger.[59]

Who represented whom, and who was in charge of what, was a continuing source of confusion and misunderstanding. Patti reported to the Strategic Services Officer, China Theater, and directly to the OSS Secret Intelligence Branch in Washington. Nordlinger reported to the G-5 (Civil Affairs) division of the China Theater. The Air Ground Aid Service worked for the 14th Air Force. Sainteny claimed to be the official spokesman of the de Gaulle government, but French authorities in SEAC and the China Theater had not confirmed his status.

As he often emphasized during the next few weeks, Patti's mission mainly concerned postwar housekeeping—finding and aiding Allied POWs and internees, searching for war criminals, and arranging the preliminary steps for the surrender of Japanese forces—but he was aware that he was involved in events of great moment and sometimes found it hard to resist becoming involved. Upon his appointment in April 1945, Patti had been instructed to do nothing, which might be construed as helping the French to reestablish their rule in Indochina. Like Wedemeyer, Patti and most of his OSS colleagues were unaware that Washington had, in effect, abandoned Roosevelt's Indochina policy. Patti knew of Acting Secretary Grew's message to Hurley but believed that the operative portion was the statement that there had been "no basic change" and that the United States should take no action to help the French regain their former colony.[60] Throughout his stay in

Hanoi, Patti recalled, "I was conscious of my responsibility to my mission. Wedemeyer, Heppner, and Helliwell [chief of the Special Intelligence Branch, OSS China] were fully cognizant of my orders from Donovan not to assist the French in their designs for reentering Indochina. . . . I felt strongly that if American policy had changed I should have been so advised and recalled."[61]

After landing at Gia Lam airport, Patti and his team were driven by the Japanese through streets festooned with the red and gold flags of the Vietminh. Banners stretched above the streets proclaimed in English, French, and Vietnamese, "Welcome to the Allies," "Long Live Vietnam's Independence," and "Death to the French."

Unhappily observing these scenes was a French team of five members of Sainteny's military mission to Tonkin. Sainteny came from a wealthy banking family with many connections in Vietnam and was married to the daughter of Albert Sarraut, a respected former governor-general of Indochina. Patti and Sainteny had earlier worked together on intelligence and guerrilla warfare projects for Indochina and developed a ripe mutual dislike, which the events of the next two weeks would do nothing to dispel.

French dissatisfaction with the situation in northern Vietnam, however, went well beyond personalities. The French wanted to be treated as one of the victorious Allies in Asia just as they had been in Europe. Never mind that the French colonial regime had collaborated with the Japanese for almost five years; the de Gaulle government insisted that the brief, desperate, and disorganized French response to the Japanese coup of March 1945 constituted "resistance," and France had a right to expect its allies to help her regain what was rightfully hers. If Chinese troops had to take the Japanese surrender in the north, then they should at least be accompanied by the French and colonial troops that had retreated to China in March. The British and Americans should also provide transport to move French troops and equipment to Indochina. The British were sympathetic to these demands, at least in principle, but the Americans, preoccupied with the enormous postsurrender problems in China, Japan, and Korea, not to mention war-devastated Europe, had little time for them. As for the Chinese, they had their own agenda and some old scores to settle.

Patti and Sainteny were taken to the Metropole, a large colonial-style hotel. A crowd of French civilians had gathered at the Metropole to greet the French and American teams, whom they regarded as liberators from both the Japanese and the Vietminh. "There was a frenzy. . . . 'The Americans are here, the Americans are here!' gasped a young boy leaping and jumping at my side, 'and look, they have large revolvers like cowboys.' . . . All who were there whirled about the hallway animated by a boundless excitement. 'He is so big, so blond,' murmured a young girl to her friend as she chewed on her nails. 'Cool! He gave me some chewing gum and some Camels,' cried another, as if the men had parachuted in for the express purpose of supplying the young girls of Hanoi with chewing gum and cigarettes."[62]

Patti's men were billeted at the hotel, but the Japanese insisted that they could not be responsible for the safety of Sainteny's party and suggested that they be moved to the palace of the governor-general. Sainteny readily agreed, believing that the symbolic value of the French once again occupying the palace would prove valuable. Once ensconced in the palace, however, with the grounds patrolled by Japanese sentries, Sainteny and his team found themselves unable to leave or to communicate with the outside world except through Patti and the Americans. They could do little to influence events or to aid their countrymen in Hanoi.

At the time of Patti's arrival there were about twenty-five thousand French in northern Vietnam, the great majority, about twenty-one thousand in Hanoi. About forty-five hundred French prisoners were still confined in the Citadel, an eighteenth-century-style fortress that the Japanese had turned into a prison. Several hundred were housed in the makeshift prison hospital, all suffering from various diseases. About half a dozen were dying every day. One of Patti's men described conditions in the hospital as "incredibly bad."[63] The Air Ground Aid Service, soon joined by a small Civil Affairs team under Colonel Stephen Nordlinger, was able to have about four hundred prisoners under medical treatment transferred to the French hospital in Hanoi and called for medical supplies and food from Kunming. Even so, the situation remained grim. "The American officers are operating with enormous energy and go to a lot of trouble," reported a French military doctor. "But the need for aid is great. From the point of view of sanitation and medical services we have nothing."[64]

Outside the Citadel, most of the French population were still living in their own homes, but they told Americans that they were "terrified of the Annamese," who sometimes stopped Frenchmen on the streets "and under the pretext of searching for arms, they harass and insult the French to the great joy of the onlookers." Many Frenchmen believed "the arrival of the Americans saved their lives for they think the Viet-Minh intended to kill all French."[65] "These Annamites for two thousand years have always been the same, greedy, treacherous and cruel," observed one French resident of Hanoi.[66] Many Frenchmen urgently wished to be evacuated, but General Wedemeyer, undoubtedly preoccupied with the gigantic task of moving thousands of Chinese troops to Manchuria and northern China, responded to French requests for assistance with the reply that "it is the responsibility of the Chinese to provide help for Allied citizens north of the Sixteenth parallel."[67]

While Sainteny remained isolated in the palace, Patti's team, reinforced by eight more men two days later, had become the center of the attention, hopes, and apprehensions of the French, Japanese, and Vietnamese. Although Patti continued to insist that his work concerned mainly prisoners of war, war criminals, and preparations for the surrender, he was seen as the official representative of the victorious Allies.[68] During his first week in Hanoi, Patti was called on by or met with the Japanese commanding general, leaders of the Chinese community, prominent French businessmen, consuls of various European nations, and ministers of the Vietminh government, and dined with Ho Chi Minh.[69] On their first Sunday in Hanoi, Patti and his men were formally welcomed by the Vietminh. "A fifty piece military band had been formed directly across the street facing us. Waving in the breeze were five huge flags representing the Soviet Union, China and the Democratic Republic of Vietnam. To our left was a military unit of about a hundred men standing at 'present arms.' . . . To our right were smaller units of unarmed youths in sparkling white uniforms. . . . Within seconds all flags were dipped except the Stars and Stripes and the band struck up 'The Star Spangled Banner,' and it was the best rendition I had heard in the Far East. On the last note all flags were raised and the procedure repeated in succession for each nation."[70]

On August 25, Patti held a press conference with representatives of Hanoi newspapers and periodicals. Though he repeated his message that "our job is purely a military one and our position is [that] of a neutral nation," he admitted that many of the Vietnamese press representatives believed he "had given them an audience to hear their grievances against the French."[71] The following day, Hanoi papers carried articles repeating alleged assurances by Patti that the French would play no role in the surrender, that the Allies had not agreed to a French military return, and that the Americans recognized Vietnam "as a civilized country."[72] Another headline a few days later announced that "Viet Minh, Fighting with U.S. Troops, Will Soon Be Here to Oust French Oppressors."[73]

Sainteny was angered at the Vietminh's ability to use the Americans for their own propaganda purposes, but he decided to take advantage of Patti's relationship with Ho to try to arrange direct contact between the French mission and the Vietminh. Responding to Sainteny's request for a meeting, Ho agreed to send Giap, his minister of the interior, to the governor-general's palace if Patti was also present. The meeting, held in the ornate salon of the palace, proved inconclusive. Patti reported at the time that "it was apparent from the start that the French had the upper hand and that during the course of the negotiation the Annamites lost considerable ground because of their inferiority complex when confronted with a European."[74] But in his memoirs, written many years later, Patti recalled that Giap had replied to Sainteny's paternal lecture "in perfect French and with absolute self-control" and said "he had not come to be lectured nor to justify the actions of the people of Viet Nam . . . but was prepared to engage in an amicable exchange of views. For the first time in his life Sainteny was meeting face to face a Vietnamese who dared to stand up to a Frenchman."[75]

Whatever the nature of the meeting, Sainteny was becoming increasingly frustrated with his inability to influence the situation and found it easy to blame his problems on Patti and the OSS. On August 28 he warned French headquarters in Calcutta of "a concerted Allied maneuver aimed at eliminating the French from Indochina." The next day he talked of a "total loss of face for France in Indochina."[76] British and French intelligence reports observed, "Having no experience of the Far East, certain Americans have a tendency to show great sympathy to the independence movement and to believe nationalist propaganda," and noted that "the role of mediator in this conflict has been conveniently assumed by the Americans who are especially interested in establishing future commercial relations."[77] Such messages soon drew complaints and protests from the French to Wedemeyer's headquarters about Patti's alleged activities. Colonel William P. Davis, the China Theater deputy director of strategic services, warned his boss, Colonel Richard P. Heppner, "Theater is very much concerned about our activities in Indochina which have no bearing on POWs. . . . Reports coming in that Patti is arranging conferences and mediating between French and Annamites . . . the sort of thing that Theater wants to avoid at all costs since this action puts the U.S. right in the middle."[78] Heppner responded with a blistering message to Patti: "You will not, repeat, not act as mediator or go between or arrange meetings between French, Annamites or Chinese. Confine yourself to POW work and such other special tasks as directed by Chinese Combat Command or this headquarters."[79]

Patti flew to Kunming and Chungking to defend his actions and try to get clarification about current American policy. It seemed to Patti that the fate of the POWs, at least those who were French, was inextricably tied up with the political situation in northern Vietnam. Sainteny and leading French citizens pressed for the immediate release of at least a thousand able-bodied troops from the Citadel so that they could serve as "a protective force" to guard the French community against abuses by the Vietnamese and Japanese. Arms for such a force were reported to have been hidden in various French homes and businesses. Patti strongly opposed any project to arm the French, believing that at best this would lead to incidents between the nationalists and the French and at worst might encourage some Frenchmen to try to reestablish "order" by attempting to seize control of the city. On the other hand, Patti was aware of the need to safeguard the French community from abuses by the Japanese or the Vietnamese. He believed he had to accomplish all that without in any way compromising Donovan's instructions to remain neutral and do nothing that might assist a French reconquest of their colony.[80]

While Patti was en route to China, a full-blown bureaucratic battle broke out among the Americans in Hanoi. Nordlinger and Patti had never gotten on well together, and their relationship was not improved by an earlier incident in which Patti's men, after arranging to rent a house, had returned a few days later to find it occupied by Nordlinger's team. (To the Vietnamese landlord, all Americans looked alike.)[81] Patti considered Nordlinger a capable officer but a hopeless Francophile who "was often used by the French as a front for their political ends,"[82] while Nordlinger considered Patti to be insensitive to the plight of French civilians and overly supportive of the Vietminh. Now Nordlinger attempted a coup claiming that G-5, China Theater, had placed all American military personnel in Hanoi under his direct command and that all would confine themselves to humanitarian and POW activities. Captain Ramon Grelecki, Patti's second in command, coolly replied that Captain Patti's mission might be subject to certain confidential instructions that assigned him tasks beyond the scope of prisoner-of-war work or humanitarian assistance.[83]

At the U.S. embassy in Chungking, Patti, Heppner, and Helliwell met with Second Secretary John Hall Paxton and Brigadier General George Olmstead, representing Wedemeyer. The five men pooled their ignorance and exchanged rumors. Madame Chiang Kai-shek had recently been told by Truman that on his August visit to Washington, General de Gaulle had said that France was taking steps to give Indochina its independence. The OSS liaison officer to Chiang Kai-shek had seen part of a State Department memo in which Truman told Madame Chiang that "no decision" had been reached in regard to Indochina. Olmstead, who headed Wedemeyer's Civil Affairs and Military Government Section, had not even heard of Grew's memo of the previous June.[84] To no one's surprise, the meeting ended inconclusively.

On his return flight to Hanoi a few days later, Patti's plane passed over a long column of troops and vehicles wending its way through the flooded plains of the Red River Delta. "It was a mixture of military vehicles, bicycles, and animal-drawn wagons interspersed with scattered clusters of shuffling nondescript pedestrians. Many bore carrying poles or huge bundles slung over their backs and were leading or prodding livestock."[85] It was the Chinese occupation army. A new layer of complexity, ambition, and greed was about to be superimposed over the suspicions, rivalries, and latent violence that the end of the war had brought to northern Indochina.

CHAPTER SIX

"COCHINCHINA IS BURNING"

TO WEDEMEYER AND CHIANG KAI-SHEK, PREOCCUPIED WITH THE desperate race to reoccupy northern China and Manchuria before the Communists could fill the vacuum created by the Japanese surrender, Indochina appeared a fairly unimportant distraction. Chiang's best troops in southern China were those of General Chang Fa-kwei, who had been Ho's jailer and then patron in 1944. Chang Fa-kwei and his troops in Kwangsi (Guangxi) and Kwangtung (Guangdong) would have seemed the natural choice to undertake operations in Indochina, but his relatively well-trained soldiers with their new American weapons were more urgently needed in the north.

Instead of Chang Fa-kwei, Chiang chose General Lung Yun, commander of the Chinese forces in Yunnan Province on the northern border of Vietnam. Like many warlord generals, Lung had done well from the war. He and his cousin General Lu Han, who commanded the field army, had carried on a profitable contraband trade with the Japanese Army and with the Vichy French in Indochina. Later, after the Americans and Chinese had been able to reopen the Ledo road into southern China, Lung had prospered by hijacking or misappropriating the tons of Lend-Lease arms and equipment that perforce flowed through Yunnan. With the Japanese capitulation, however, the shrewd old warlord allowed greed to get the better of him. Offered command of the Indochina occupation by Chungking, Lung accepted with alacrity and sent his most loyal troops marching off toward Hanoi under the command of Lu Han to reap the profits of postwar peacekeeping.

About one month after the departure of Lu's forces, Lung awoke to find Kunming's military installations surrounded by Chiang's Fifth

Army under one of the Generalissimo's most trusted generals. On walls throughout the city were copies of an order by Chiang Kai-shek removing Lung as governor of Yunnan and "promoting" him to the chairmanship of Chiang's Military Advisory Council in Chungking. After some gestures of resistance, Lung surrendered, and Yunnan came under the direct control of Chiang Kai-shek.

General Lu Han, "the Dragon Cloud," was more of a field soldier and less of a wheeler-dealer than Lung Yun. In 1938, when the Sino-Japanese War was still serious and bloody, he had commanded the Sixtieth Army at the great Chinese victory over the Japanese at Taierzhuang.[1] Under Lu's nominal command in Indochina were three Chinese armies, the Fifty-second, the Sixtieth, and the Ninety-third. Two of these armies were scheduled for early redeployment to Formosa and northern China through the port of Haiphong once they had completed their occupation duties.

To keep an eye on Lu Han and provide him with some local expertise, Chungking had assigned a fourth army to Indochina, the Sixty-second Army, commanded by General Hsiao Wen, who had worked closely with the Vietnamese exiles in southern China and knew Ho Chi Minh well. In addition to commanding the Sixty-second Army, Hsiao was designated Lu's deputy and political adviser. His Sixty-second Army was also scheduled for other duties in the north.

Accompanying Lu Han were American liaison teams of the Chinese Training Combat Command, an American military advisory organization that had been training Chinese units in southern China. All of the teams were under the command of Brig. Gen. Philip E. Gallagher, Lu's adviser. Like Patti, General Gallagher was seen by many French and Vietnamese as some sort of American proconsul with vast powers to resolve all problems. In fact, Wedemeyer's directive to U.S. units with Chinese occupation forces limited their mission to "advising and assisting the Central Government military forces during their movement to their areas of occupation" and "acting in an advisory capacity . . . in the provision of necessary supplies and the administration of civil affairs in the areas occupied by these troops."[2] "The U.S. advisory group . . . had no directive . . . as to who we were to support politically," Gallagher recalled.[3]

On September 14, Gallagher and Lu Han arrived in Hanoi, where

Gallagher was briefed by Patti and Lu assumed direction of the occupation. "He was charged officially with disarming the Japanese," read a French intelligence report on Lu. "Judging by his actions he seemed to have received from his government the mission of helping the Annamites against the French; judging from his behavior, his intention may well have been simply to enhance his personal fortune."[4] Lu Han unceremoniously evicted Sainteny's mission from the governor-general's palace and took up residence there himself. His troops were quartered in public buildings, schools, hospitals, and private homes. "A detachment of about fifty [soldiers] marched into our house," recalled Mai Elliott. "Once again my father put his knowledge of Chinese to good use. He could talk to the commanding officer in writing. The officer was impressed and reined in his soldiers . . . they did not steal any of our belongings as they did throughout Hanoi. But they herded us upstairs and took over the ground floor. The peasant soldiers were not used to urban amenities and at first Giu had to teach them how to turn on the electric lights and ceiling fans. They were so pleased that they would stand by the switches turning them off and on and wondering at the effect."[5]

Ignoring French demands and protests, Lu and Hsiao quickly came to a working agreement with Ho. The Vietminh government was permitted to remain in place. French soldiers stayed locked in the Citadel. Vietminh forces were not disarmed. Ho was pressured but not compelled to include members of Chinese-supported nationalist parties in his government.

The price paid by the Vietminh for this arrangement was high. The entire cost of feeding and maintaining the "Allied" occupation forces in the north was to be born by the Vietnamese, to be compensated later at a "fair" rate of exchange. Despite the famine conditions, OSS reported that the Chinese were actually shipping rice out of the country or selling it on the black market for ten times the Saigon price.[6] According to rumor, Ho Chi Minh also kept the Chinese well supplied with opium and at one point presented Lu Han with a gold opium pipe.

In conversations with General Hsiao Wen and General Lu Han, Ho learned that the Chinese intended to manipulate the local currency to their advantage. The exchange rate between the almost worthless Chinese dollar and the Indochinese piaster was arbitrarily set at 14 to 1, thus making the dollar worth more than three times as much as in southern China. Millions of Chinese dollars soon began to arrive in Indochina. In one instance, $60 million was reported on a single flight from Kunming.[7] "Chinese officers in Viet Nam with business connections at home organized themselves into a closely knit syndicate associated with merchants, bankers and entrepreneurs to buy out at ridiculously little cost, every profitable enterprise they could. . . . Front companies and trusts were quickly formed to acquire outright ownership of or controlling interests in Vietnamese or French-owned plantations, farmland, buildings, mines, and factories, even the small merchant was not spared. . . . If they protested or dared to resist any offer made by the syndicate, the military had ways to persuade."[8] With their bargain shopping and other financial activities, the Chinese, according to one estimate, managed to extract some 400 million piasters from the poorer half of a country whose total gross national product in 1939 had been around 1.1 billion piasters.[9]

In return for these concessions, the Chinese and their American advisers dealt with the Vietminh as the de facto government. "He [Ho] and his provisional government were the only existing semblance of law and order as far as FIC [French Indochina] north of the 16th parallel was concerned," Gallagher recalled, "and the Chinese and I dealt with him accordingly."[10]

Having been briefed by Patti and Nordlinger and received widely divergent views of the Vietminh, Gallagher began a series of informal meetings with Ho. While recognizing that Ho was "an old revolutionist" and "a product of Moscow," Gallagher, like Patti, concluded "the Prime Minister and his party represent the real aspirations of the Vietnamese people for independence. . . . He looks upon the United States as the savior of all small nations and is basing all his actions on the statement in the Atlantic Charter that the independence of the smaller nations would be assured by the major powers. . . . I pointed out frankly that my job was not as a representative of the State Department nor was I interested in the political situation . . . that I was merely working with Lu Han. Confidentially I wish the Vietnamese could be given their independence but of course we have no voice in the matter."[11]

With almost sixty Americans now in Hanoi, considerable progress could be made in evacuating British POWs, in alleviating the conditions at the Citadel, and in improving the newly reopened French military hospital. However, Lu Han and Hsiao Wen both had old grudges against the French and were in no hurry to accommodate them. Both generals were also genuinely concerned about the safety of the large Chinese segment of Hanoi's population should serious fighting break out there.[12] In a meeting with Sainteny on September 21, Lu Han emphasized the fact that the Chinese Army was in charge and would show no partiality to French or Vietnamese.[13]

For the time being an uneasy calm settled over Hanoi, though it seemed to one American observer that "the streets of Hanoi throbbed with tension and agitation. Loudspeakers in many political subheadquarters of the government broadcast the news and commentaries of the government's radio. The streets were heavily placarded, banners proclaimed independence and denounced French imperialism, street meetings took place frequently."[14] Homeowners kept their ground-floor doors and windows tightly shut, French and Vietnamese women seldom appeared in the streets without a male escort, and items of value that might tempt Chinese soldiers to disburse their newly valuable dollars had long since disappeared from the shops.[15]

Contributing to the edginess in the north was the continuing flow of news and rumors about developments south of the 16th parallel. In southern Vietnam as in the north, the Japanese surrender had galvanized nationalists into action. The Communists' position in the south, however, was far shakier than in the north. The Party leadership had been decimated in an unsuccessful uprising in 1940 and the survivors had only begun to regroup following the March 1945 takeover by the Japanese. At the time of the surrender, the Vietminh, under the leadership of Tran Van Giau, had secret cells at several shops and factories in the Saigon area and, more importantly, controlled the Vanguard Youth with its mass membership throughout Cochinchina.[16] Nevertheless, Giau was obliged to compete for leadership of the independence movement with the Trotskyites, who had a solid presence in the south, the pro-Japanese Phuoc Quoc, and two indigenous religious sects, the Cao Dai and the Hoa Hao, which had numerous adherents in and effective control over strategically important parts of the Mekong Delta provinces. Indeed, the main reason that the Communists had been included at all in the nationalist coalition that easily took control of Saigon and most of Cochinchina on August 25 was the widespread belief that the

Allies supported the Vietminh, who, unlike their rivals, had never collaborated or been associated with the Japanese. In the countryside, the sects and the parties competed fiercely, often violently, for control of territory and captured French weapons while maintaining a nervous unity against the return of French imperialism in Saigon.

If southern Vietnam had a government at the time of the arrival of Gracey's troops, it was the thirteen-member Provisional Executive Committee for the South, only four of whose members were from the Vietminh. A delegation from the committee met Gracey's plane at the airport and were completely ignored. Gracey was of course preoccupied with his main mission of controlling and disarming the forty thousand Japanese troops in southern Indochina, who vastly outnumbered his own forces. Gracey's other tasks were to release and repatriate Allied prisoners of war and internees, to maintain law and order, and to "liberate Allied territory in so far as your resources permit."[17]

"Allied territory" in this case meant French territory, for the British government, unlike the Americans and Chinese, had never challenged the right of the French to reassert their rule in Indochina. Indeed, an Anglo-French civil affairs agreement signed at the end of August had specified that among the reasons for stationing Allied troops in Indochina was the restoration of French authority.[18] De Gaulle had appointed General Jacques-Philippe Leclerc, an officer known for his exploits in commanding an armored division in the defeat of Germany, as the commander of French forces in the Far East. He was to retake Indochina by force if necessary. Unfortunately for Leclerc, he had almost no troops with which to do it. The nearest French forces, the 5th Colonial Infantry Regiment on Ceylon, were well trained in jungle warfare, but there were fewer than a thousand of them, with almost no transportation. There were also plans to reconstitute some sort of force from the fifteen hundred to three thousand French soldiers and sailors formerly held by the Japanese, but "these men were tired from long captivity."[19]

So any liberation of "Allied" territory would have to be up to the British. Mountbatten and his staff had some misgivings about where this could lead. "I think we should avoid at all costs the accusation that we are assisting the West to suppress the East," wrote SEAC's political adviser, Sir Esler Dening. "Such accusations will rise very readily to the lips of the Americans and Chinese and are likely to create an unfavorable impression throughout Asia."[20] At the last moment, Gracey's orders were modified to make clear that he was responsible only for controlling key areas in and around Saigon that were directly related to the completion of his mission. But it is doubtful that Gracey received this change before his arrival in Saigon.[21]

Gracey was unimpressed with the nationalist government that claimed to be in charge in Saigon. His chief of staff, after a quick tour of the city, had concluded that the Vietnamese assertion that they controlled civil affairs "was a laugh."[22] Gracey soon decided that the "Annamite government constituted a direct threat to law and order through its police and armed guards."[23] There had been no serious trouble other than during the September 2 Independence Day celebrations when Vietnamese demonstrators, believing they had been fired on by the French, instigated rioting in which several French and Vietnamese were killed and injured. However, there were constant threats to French lives and property, and Vietnamese radio stations and newspapers carried on an incessant campaign of anti-French propaganda.

As Gracey and some of his senior officers saw it, the situation was grave. "It was quite evident," the British general wrote, "that unless the puppet government was evicted and the French government reinstated almost immediately, not only would the puppet government's hold on the country be consolidated . . . but also landing by air and sea of troops and supplies would become daily more hazardous." Gracey's officers believed that "the Vietminh were set to challenge the British for control of Saigon." If the British wavered, they would likely lose all credibility with the Japanese, who were still armed and still outnumbered the Allied forces.[24]

Gracey was not a fool or a grandstander. Nor was he a racist or a reactionary. As a commander of Indian troops, he knew that independence for India, and probably Burma, was near, but Gracey was completely out of his depth. He knew nothing about Indochina, lacked a political officer, and believed French assurances that the nationalists were a minority of troublemakers and former collaborators and that most Vietnamese longed to get back to the old ways. "I am quite sure," wrote Captain Sissons, "that the locals have no real complaint about their treatment by the French; this appears to be the usual European colony with native shopkeepers, native nurses devoted to their white charges and so forth."[25]

Gracey might have learned more about the real situation in Indochina from the OSS. A small OSS detachment with duties similar to Patti's team in the north had been in Indochina since September 1. Besides locating and aiding prisoners of war, particularly Americans, the OSS team, code name Embankment, was to identify and apprehend war criminals and microfilm Japanese documents and code books. Given the absence of any other American presence in Saigon, the team was also to report on political developments and watch for the emergence of any anti-Allied groups or activities by the Japanese to subvert the surrender.[26]

The Embankment team was under the command of Colonel A. Peter Dewey, son of a congressman and a relative of Thomas E. Dewey, the Republican presidential candidate in 1944. Dewey was only twenty-eight years old but had had almost six years of war experience. He had covered the war for the *Chicago Daily News* in 1939–40 and then served with the Polish Ambulance Corps in the Battle of France. After the United States entered the war, Dewey was commissioned a second lieutenant in the army and served on intelligence missions to Acre, Fort Lamy, Khartoum, French Equatorial Africa, and Aden. In 1943 he joined the OSS and was parachuted into occupied France. For his exploits he had received medals from the Polish government and the Croix de Guerre from the French. He spoke almost perfect French and was reported to be "persona grata with De Gaulle."[27]

The advance element of Embankment, a four-man POW evacuation team under First Lieutenant Emile R. Connasse, parachuted into Saigon on September 1. Colonel Dewey followed with the remainder of the team on the fourth and fifth. The small number of American prisoners of war were evacuated by air in the next few days, and Lieutenant Connasse returned to SEAC headquarters. The Americans set up their headquarters at the large Continental Palace Hotel, which soon became a refuge for Frenchmen who sought safety from the threat of Vietnamese violence. "The owner of the hotel, M. Franchini, loved Americans because they were good for business. He sold the hotel to Major Frank White [one of Dewey's officers] for $2, thus placing it under American protection and was then able to demand exorbitant prices of the many terrified French residents who wanted to sleep under the same roof."[28] While maintaining the Continental as a safe haven, and insisting that the Japanese guard it, Dewey soon moved most of his team to a villa on the outskirts of the city that had previously been occupied by a Japanese admiral.

Dewey had no special knowledge of Indochina, and only one member of his team spoke Vietnamese—a few did not even speak French. Having witnessed the disorders of September 2, some members of Connasse's advance team were not overly impressed with the Vietminh's "drugstore revolution." Many of the actions of the provisional government "appeared crazy or inexplicable."[29] Nevertheless, Dewey was determined to carry out the intelligence aspects of his mission and soon established contacts with Vietnamese political leaders. "He sent me several times to meet [with Vietminh leaders]," recalled his crytographer. "The streets were dark. . . . I would go to a house on a quiet street and there meet for perhaps two hours with three or four men who were obviously deeply committed to the liberation of their country. . . . During the war they had listened to the Voice of America broadcasts which spoke of democracy and liberty and they regarded the United States not only as a model but as the champion of self-government that would support their cause."[30] Dewey was particularly impressed with the Dr. Pham Ngoc Thach, the Vietminh founder of the Vanguard Youth, and may have hoped to arrange for Thach to visit the United States incognito.

In retrospect, a meeting of the minds between Gracey and Dewey appears even less likely than a meeting of the minds between de Gaulle and Ho Chi Minh. Gracey could not have been pleased with this brash young American and probably regarded the OSS as a nuisance. They were obviously pursuing activities beyond POW work. Gracey's chief of staff remembered Dewey as "being in a number of places with a number of people which called for an explanation the Control Commission never got."[31] As for Dewey, he was unlikely to find common ground with a general whom one of his officers called "an old-fashioned product of the British Empire."[32]

On September 19, Gracey notified the Vietminh government that he intended to issue a proclamation banning all processions and demonstrations, imposing a nightly curfew, and prohibiting the carrying of arms by any forces not authorized by him. All newspapers were to be closed, and the provisional government was to supply a list of the arms and locations of all Vietnamese police and military units. Beginning on September 21, Gracey's troops began evicting the Vietminh government from public buildings and police stations and disarming Vietminh police and paramilitary forces.

By this time, French officials had convinced Gracey that former French soldiers in the Saigon area who had been imprisoned by the Japanese could be rearmed and easily take control of the city government and services. The Vietnamese would be overawed and offer no resistance. Once it was evident that the French were back in charge, the large number of Vietnamese who desired only a return to normality would lose their fear of the Vietminh and rally to the side of law and order. "There is no doubt that Gracey thought it would be a pushover," his chief of staff recalled. "The information that the British had about the Viet Minh was that they would not resist. The information about the French was that Cédile [de Gaulle's representative in Cochinchina] had tight control over them, that this was not at all a difficult task . . . once done it would provide a substantial useful step forward for the furtherance of the gradual take-over from the British by the French."[33] During the night of September 22–23, the British quietly turned over installations and police posts to the French. The treasury, the main post office, the city hall, and remaining public buildings were taken from the surprised Vietnamese by the French troops with little loss of life but considerable brutality.

On the morning of the twenty-third, residents of the city awoke to find that "Saigon was French again." Cédile had issued detailed instructions to the French community on how they were to conduct themselves after "assuming control." "Arrogant attitudes or triumphalist gestures or speech of a defiant, menacing or provocative nature are absolutely banned. I forbid . . . acts of unjustified brutality, manifestations of resentment or revenge in regard to the Annamites."[34]

Cheerfully ignoring Cédile's rhetoric, the French of Saigon celebrated their victory by going on a rampage in which they expressed all their pent-up feelings of fear, anger, and resentment at the Vietnamese and humiliation at their incarceration by the Japanese. As one of Mountbatten's staff officers reported, "There were wild shootings and Annamites were openly dragged through the streets to be locked up in prisons. Generally speaking there was complete chaos."[35] Soldiers and armed civilians fired into empty buildings. Gangs of French soldiers and civilians roamed the city assaulting Vietnamese, including women and children, at random. Any Vietnamese found on the streets was in danger of being kicked, beaten, and hauled off to a police station.

Gracey was privately furious with the French. He called Cédile in for a tongue-lashing and ordered French "soldiers" partially disarmed and returned to their barracks. To an American officer, Cédile confided that he would have "liked to ship every colonial back to France."[36] Yet the damage was done. British and foreign press representatives reported fully on the antics of the French "assumption of control." At a press conference shortly after the French takeover, Gracey was "given hell" by American and Australian reporters. "Gracey grew angry and said that the reporters 'did not understand the East.' An American replied, 'The East is as inscrutable today as it was yesterday and following this press conference is even more inscrutable.' That really set Gracey off. And about that time the Viet Minh attacked the power station and the lights went off."[37]

Mountbatten, to whom unfavorable press reports were especially unwelcome, suspected that "the stronger we are [in Indochina] the more the French will feel they can take provocative action against the Annamites."[38] He already had misgivings about Gracey's proclamation but backed him as "the man on the spot." Mountbatten now wished the British chiefs of staff to redefine Gracey's mission as narrowly as possible and leave the reconquest of Indochina to the French.

This was far more than a public relations disaster, however. "The Annamites are now thoroughly disillusioned with the British," reported the OSS.[39] The clumsy French coup had led to the very situation Gracey had intended to prevent. Vietnamese of all political persuasions united in a general rising directed at the British and French. The food markets were burned out and there was a sharp increase in kidnappings, murder, and arson. "Life in Saigon was brought to a standstill. Shops and cafes were closed. Many parts of the city were without water."[40]

The bloodiest incident occurred on September 24, when members of the Binh Xuyen, a large Vietnamese criminal syndicate, raided the Cité Herault, a residential suburb populated by well-to-do French and Eurasians, and massacred more than 150 people, mostly women and children. One eyewitness recalled, "The Annamites entered all the houses on Mazet Street. [I] heard screams for an hour after that." The houses were looted and the inhabitants were taken away. "The prisoners were then taken to a village on the banks of the river where the men were tortured in front of their wives and children." Police reported finding the bodies of two women with "eyes put out, teeth pulled out, breasts chopped off, bamboo stakes in their genitalia." A woman who was seven or eight months pregnant "was disemboweled. Her live child was tossed around like a ball and finally run through with a spike." Vietnamese women who were known to be married to Frenchmen were disfigured by daggers.[41]

From that point, civil war was general in the Saigon area. By September 26, the OSS was reporting that many parts of the city were without food or electricity.[42] "Sniping is a nerve-wracking affair in the lightless city," wrote an American reporter. "Shots may be fired from any building or doorway. Half-naked Annamites may suddenly whip out knife or gun from a loin-cloth."[43] "For a time Saigon was a city under siege," recalled George Wickes, communications man for the small OSS detachment in Saigon. "Mostly we heard rather than saw the action. Things were generally calm during the day, but after nightfall we began to hear the sound of gunfire, beginning with the occasional stray shot by a jittery French soldier. . . . Every night we could hear Vietnamese drums signaling across the river and almost on the stroke of 12, there would be an outburst of gunfire and new fires breaking out among the stocks of tea, rubber and tobacco in the dockyards."

With limited numbers of British troops, and French forces few and unreliable, Gracey called on the Japanese to assist in patrolling the city and clearing Vietnamese roadblocks. Rather than being concentrated and disarmed, the Japanese were now informed that they would be responsible for certain areas and for the security of any Europeans needing their aid. One Indian officer recalled that the "Japanese were chiefly used for protecting food convoys which they did with efficiency."[44] How large a role the Japanese played in repelling the Vietnamese attacks on Saigon and breaking the blockade of the city has always been obscure. The British and French had no interest in highlighting their role. However, it is known that by the end of October the Japanese had lost forty-four men, including seven officers, with seventy-nine wounded and fifty missing.[45] By the beginning of December, the Japanese reported a total of 406 casualties in fighting the Vietnamese, including 126 killed.[46]

While the British and French were turning to the Japanese, so were the Vietminh. Somewhere between one thousand and three thousand Japanese soldiers deserted their units and joined the nationalists during August and September 1945.[47] A few joined out of conviction, men who wished to continue the fight for Greater East Asia or who simply could not accept the idea of Japan's defeat. Captain Kanetoshi Toshihide found defeat "unthinkable." He could not bear the thought of returning to Japan when most of his comrades had died for the empire.[48] Many Japanese intelligence officers spoke good Vietnamese and had extensive contacts with Vietnamese organizations, especially the Cao Dai and Hoa Hao. These men, some of whom were graduates of the supersecret Nakano School for espionage and political warfare, were strongly imbued with a Pan-Asian ideology. The fact that most were also excellent candidates for war crimes trials must also have been an important consideration. Besides intelligence officers or members of the Kempeitai, any soldier associated with the construction of the notorious Burma–Siam Railroad knew he was likely to be tried for brutality or atrocities.[49]

A larger number of Japanese deserted because they had begun to suspect they might have to wait years before repatriation to Japan or saw no economic future for themselves once they did return. Others had married or were involved with Vietnamese women. Of thirty-five deserters captured by the French in 1945, sixteen had Vietnamese or Eurasian wives, and several had children.[50] Vietnamese women working in hospitals or as interpreters for the Japanese Army reportedly also acted as recruiters for the Vietminh. Some soldiers joined the Vietminh reluctantly through force or blackmail or the promise of relatively high pay—which Japanese deserters did receive.

Soldiers of the Vietminh Army in the south were short of weapons and largely untrained; many were armed only with axes or bamboo staves. The addition of experienced Japanese soldiers to their ranks provided an enormous boost in military effectiveness. Japanese officers and NCOs trained Vietnamese in the use and maintenance of weapons, small unit tactics, and communications. Specialists provided training in field medicine, staff work, and administration. Junior officers were trained in company and battalion exercises. Japanese instructors introduced Vietnamese soldiers to the guerrilla tactics they had intended to use against the superior Allied invaders in the last months of the war. Japanese officers also led Vietminh forces in battle. Nguyen Thi Tuyet Mai's platoon had a Japanese adviser referred to as "Brother Hai" and had been armed by the Japanese one day after the surrender.[51] A French intelligence report concluded that "arms, cadres, specialists and instructors furnished by the Japanese were of very great combat value" to the Vietminh. "As fighters they represent the most aggressive and formidable elements among the rebels."[52]

The French did their best to convince the British and Americans that Japanese help to the Vietminh was part of a larger Japanese scheme to reestablish their empire. "The Japanese are continuing the great War of Asia clandestinely," concluded one French report. "They have created an environment that is conducive to hatred between the French and the Indochinese. They have made efforts to break down the solidarity of the Occidental powers in Asia. They have given military help to the rebels, such as military training, weapons etc."[53] Interestingly enough, the Vietnamese shared the same paranoia about the Japanese. Vietminh cadres were reminded that "we already know both the Japanese and the French mind-set. Local units must be careful in their use of the Japanese. If they act well, they will be well treated, if not they will be punished. Japanese troops must be kept in their respective regions so they may not be in contact with one another."[54] A few weeks later, a Vietminh commander observed that "all Japanese have the same goal, to rebuild the Japanese nation. Some Japanese troops have joined the French and some have joined us, this is why we cannot trust them. We must use their knowledge but not follow their principles and instincts."[55]

The September 23 French takeover of Saigon and its aftermath completely soured relations between the OSS and the British. Dewey went to Gracey's office to protest French behavior, but the general refused to see him. The next day, Dewey reported, "Cochinchina is burning. The French and British are finished here and we ought to clear out of Southeast Asia."[56] Two days later Dewey was shot and killed at a Vietminh roadblock by men who probably took him for a Frenchman. Ironically it was the day he was scheduled to leave the country.

Dewey's murder caused a minor sensation. Members of his OSS team unanimously blamed Gracey for refusing to let Dewey fly an American flag from his jeep (although there was nothing that would have prevented him from painting it on). The British observed privately that Dewey had been reckless and a troublemaker. The inability to recover his body added to the general unease and embarrassment. Dr. Pham Ngoc Thach wrote to Dewey's father to express his sorrow at the loss of "our great friend" and announced that the Vietminh had decided to erect a memorial to Dewey on the street where he had had his house and to rename the street after him.[57]

A further irony came to light decades later. The fatal roadblock had been manned by a band of Advance Guard Youth led by a man named Muoi Cuong. After killing Dewey they burned his jeep and dumped the body into a nearby well. Later, after learning the identity of his victim, Muoi Cuong apparently panicked. He removed the body from the well and buried it in a small village nearby. Both Muoi Cuong and his second in command, Bay Tay, who wore Dewey's Colt 12 pistol on his hip, later died fighting the French. Dr. Pham Ngoc Thach, Dewey's closest Vietnamese confidant, was the founder of the Advance Guard Youth.[58]

Reports of Dewey's death reached Hanoi just as the Allies were preparing for the long-delayed Japanese surrender ceremony scheduled for September 28. Informed about the incident by Patti, Ho Chi Minh rushed to General Gallagher's headquarters to express his regrets and to assure him that such an event would occur in the north only "over my dead body." Although Gallagher and certainly Patti may have been concerned at news of Dewey's death, their immediate problem was the impending surrender ceremony. The French government had sent General Marcel Alessandri from Kunming to be their official representative. Chinese Combat Command had signaled Gallagher that the Chinese government had agreed to have a French representative participate in the surrender. Gallagher had already been advised that the Chinese government recognized French sovereignty in Indochina "and desired that its own commanders in Indochina facilitate the resumption of French administration." As for American policy, "it remains 'hands off.' "[59]

While he was still puzzling over the meaning of "hands off," General Gallagher learned that General Lu Han had no intention of taking any action on behalf of the French. Alessandri could be present at the ceremony, but not in an official capacity because of his "unclear position." The Chinese general also refused to have the French flag flown alongside those of the other Allied nations at the ceremony, on the grounds that to do so might incite violence. In reply to Gallagher's remonstrance, Lu pointed out that the French had collaborated with the Japanese in their war against China.[60] Alessandri himself had been prominent among the collaborators until the coup of March 1945, when he managed to escape to Yunnan at the head of a band of colonial troops. Thoroughly frustrated, Gallagher appealed to his superiors in Kunming and was confidentially informed that the Chinese government would instruct Lu that the French flag should be flown at the ceremony. Whether or not Lu ever received such an order, no French flag was visible at the surrender, and Alessandri was seated 155th among the guests.

At the beginning of October, as Alessandri was leaving Hanoi in a rage, Chinese chief of staff General He Ying-jin arrived, accompanied by the head of Chinese Combat Command, and Gallagher's boss, Major General Robert McClure. Officially, General He was in Hanoi to assess the state of discipline among the occupation troops. More important, he had two confidential assignments from Chungking. The first was to secure Lu Han's agreement to accept his cousin Lung Yun's sudden removal as governor of Yunnan, a post that General He now offered to Lu in return for acceptance of Chiang Kai-shek's authority in the south. The second was to impress upon the two generals, Lu Han and Hsiao Wen, the importance of ensuring that parties friendly to China played a major role in any future Vietnam government. Lu decided to accept Chiang's offer of the leadership of Yunnan and over the coming weeks became increasingly preoccupied with affairs in Yunnan. In late October he visited Chungking to confer with Chiang and solidify the new arrangement.[61]

Meanwhile, Lu and Hsiao brought increasing pressure on Ho to broaden his government by giving a greater role to the nationalist parties, which they favored. With the arrival of the Chinese, the Dong Minh Hoi and the Dai Viet had taken on new energy and confidence. Nguyen Hai Than, the aged but cantankerous head of the Dong Minh

Hoi, openly referred to "Ho and his gang of cutthroats."[62] The nationalist opposition controlled an influential and articulate press including the Vietnam Quoc Dan Dang's newspaper, *Vietnam*, and the Dong Minh Hoi's *Alliance*. These organs regularly attacked Ho's government for infringement of freedom of speech, misuse of power, and desire to compromise with the French.[63] The VNQDD also operated its own radio station.[64] The nationalists were not united, however, and their support from the Chinese had an on-again, off-again quality.

On November 19, General Hsiao Wen organized a meeting between the Vietminh and the nationalist parties that inaugurated a month of often acrimonious discussions on creating a broad coalition government with a unified program for independence. Finally, on December 19, Ho and the opposition agreed on the election of a new government in early January. Because the Vietminh was in firm control of most areas of the north, they were expected to sweep the elections. To placate the opposition, however, the VNQDD was guaranteed 50 seats in the new National Assembly and the Dai Viet 20, out of a total of about 350.

DESPITE HIS SUCCESS in fending off the Chinese and temporarily neutralizing the opposition, Ho understood that his situation was still precarious. It was now clear that the Americans would be of no real help, although Ho continued to address plaintive letters to Truman and Secretary of State James Byrnes through Patti and Gallagher. At a farewell dinner for Patti at the end of September, Ho said that he could not understand why the principle of self-determination set forth in the Atlantic Charter and other Allied declarations should not apply to Vietnam and why the United States remained passive while the French and British re-erected the old colonial system.[65] The Chinese had given the back of their hand to the French in Hanoi, but Ho knew that in Chungking and Paris, negotiations were ongoing about trading an early end to the occupation for French concessions to China. As for the French, reports of their actions in the south could leave little doubt about their ultimate intentions.

At the beginning of October, as the bloodshed continued in Saigon, Gracey and his newly arrived political adviser H. N. Brain of the Foreign Office decided that it might be a good idea to talk to the Vietnamese after all. The Vietnamese agreed to a cease-fire, and talks were held between Cédile and representatives of the southern revolutionaries. Neither side had much to offer the other. The Vietnamese leaders knew that only a promise of independence would satisfy their followers. The French declared that Paris had an enlightened program for Indochina but that French officials in Indochina, even Leclerc, were not empowered to discuss the question of independence or make any modifications to French policy.

Meanwhile, reinforcements poured in. Gracey got the remaining units of his division sent to Saigon together with their heavy weapons and an authorization to use Spitfires against Vietminh ambushes or roadblocks. Leclerc arrived on October 6, and French warships steamed up the Saigon River to land the rest of the 5th Colonial Infantry. To Leclerc, the French challenge in Indochina was clear: "Our adversaries obviously represented a minority; but an aggressive, decisive, dynamic minority, who had had time to install its men and committees, raise troops under its authority by tough methods using very Asiatic, very Nazi means and who had persuaded the population that France was incapable of reinstalling itself in Indochina."[66]

The French of Saigon turned out in large numbers to welcome "the liberator of Paris." French flags flew and portraits of de Gaulle appeared in the same shop windows that had earlier displayed pictures of Marshal Pétain.[67] Two weeks later, the cruisers *Gloire* and *Suffren* brought the first elements of the French 2nd Armored Division. Their tanks and other heavy equipment arrived at the end of the month aboard the aircraft carrier *Béarn*.[68] The Vietnamese could not help noticing that some of the cargo ships bringing French troops and supplies flew the American flag and that much of the equipment and weaponry used by the French, which they had received from the Americans under Lend-Lease during the war, still bore U.S. markings. American merchant seamen told U.S. intelligence agents that the use of American shipping was "bitterly resented by Asians whether in Saigon, Singapore or Batavia."[69]

On October 10, a British Indian reconnaissance party was ambushed outside Saigon, convincing Gracey that the truce was at an end. British, French, and sometimes Japanese forces now took the offensive against the Vietnamese in order to "clear" Saigon and its surrounding areas. By late October, French forces had swept into the Mekong Delta, establishing control of the towns of My Tho, Vinh Long, and Can Tho.[70] As if to signal a return to normalcy, the "Cercle Sportif," the center of French colonial social life, was reopened, and French sportsmen could sip their drinks "while the sound of cannon fire boomed regularly in the background and ashes from burning Vietnamese villages drifted down on the tennis courts."[71]

Throughout November, French troops continued to arrive. French Foreign Legionnaires, many of them former members of Rommel's Afrika Korps, spent their off-duty time in bars and cafés singing German drinking songs. If the presence in Indochina of these former adherents to the Nazi cause embarrassed the French, they hid that embarrassment well. Only 30 percent of the Legion in Indochina were German, they pointed out. Former SS men who could be identified were refused enlistment. "The others, by asking to enlist in the Legion must absolutely abandon their beliefs about 'race' and adopt the tradition of their corps which are solely the traditions of the soldier." There could be no comparison to the Vietminh recruitment of former Japanese soldiers; those who joined the ranks of the Vietminh were "working toward the establishment of a totalitarian regime."[72]

During the autumn evenings, "the streets of Saigon would fill with French soldiers and sailors and civilians, Indian soldiers, a few British tommies, a few scattered Chinese. French or metisse girls would pair off with the troops walking arm-in-arm or sitting across tables at the few open bars and cafes. Housewives, carrying their children with them, would comb the few open markets where fruits and vegetables could be had from Chinese vendors. . . . When the occasional straggling lines of trussed up or manacled Annamite prisoners would pass, French men and women would stop to stare. . . . 'It is really nothing,' said a Frenchman watching, 'some agitators brought by the Japanese. We'll kill them off.' "[73]

Captured Vietnamese who had now begun replacing the French and Legonnaires in the prisons usually received a ten-minute trial. American newsmen covering the trials reported that "often the proceedings in court and sometimes the indictment itself are not understood by the accused persons. . . . The average defense plea, as timed by the correspondents, takes under 4 minutes. In many cases the accused appear to have been subjected to very severe 3rd degree measures and some of them made the plea that they had signed their confessions under conditions of duress." Those found guilty of circulating subversive leaflets received on average five years' hard labor. Those convicted of possessing arms got ten to twenty years.[74] The French correspondent for *Paris-Presse,* an experienced journalist named Desaurrat, claimed to have witnessed the brutal beating and murder of a prisoner and the cold-blooded killing of sixteen wounded Vietnamese by French troops. "Returning to Saigon, Desaurrat went to Leclerc protesting as a veteran of World War I and of the Resistance of World War II. He told Leclerc he was ashamed to be a Frenchman and that Germans were being condemned to death for the same atrocities. Leclerc exploded in rage and ordered Desaurrat from his office. Desaurrat cabled [his paper] to either print his entire story or consider him no longer on the payroll."[75]

By the middle of November, the OSS was reporting that "both British and French are of the opinion that organized Resistance of the Vietminh Revolution has been almost completely dispersed." French troops had taken control of Tay Ninh to the north of Saigon and had moved into the central highlands by occupying Ban Me Thuot. Yet the war in the south, touched off by Gracey's anxiety to "restore law and order," was to continue until 1954. As French strength increased, Ho Chi Minh replaced Tran Van Giau with Nguyen Binh as leader of the Vietminh resistance in the Saigon area. Binh was an experienced military leader of considerable talent, but he had an unfortunate proclivity toward kidnapping or murdering other Vietnamese who appeared not to be so warm in the cause. During one month in the single area of My Tho, forty-one intellectuals, former government functionaries, rich proprietors, and landowners were killed or kidnapped, including a man who was executed along with his wife for having a French flag in his possession.[76] Among Binh's victims was Huyn Phu So, the founder and prophet of the Hoa Hao religion, whose followers subsequently became the most inveterate enemies of the Vietminh. Binh laid the groundwork for protracted war in the south, establishing large guerrilla bases in strategically located but inaccessible swamps and jungles around Saigon and in the Mekong Delta, bases that would serve Ho's forces well in both their eight-year war against the French and their ten-year struggle with the Americans.

With French troops arriving steadily, the Southeast Asia Command could at last see the end of the tunnel. Field Marshal Count Terauchi completed the formal Japanese surrender on November 30, by which time the British had completed plans to begin concentrating the Japanese at Cape St. Jacques for repatriation back to Japan. Mountbatten and Admiral Thierry d' Argenlieu, the newly arrived French high commissioner for Indochina, announced that on January 28, 1946, France would assume responsibility for all military operations in Indochina except for the repatriations from Cape St. Jacques. The bulk of the British forces would begin their withdrawal on that date.

On the day of his departure, Gracey took the salute on the steps of the Saigon city hall, flanked by Leclerc and Cédile. The British general was presented with a special scroll and named a Citoyen d'Honneur of the city, the first time in eighty years that such a distinction had been conferred on any individual. Gracey's mission may have been as delicate and complex as he always insisted it was, but to the cheering crowd of French colonials gathered in front of the city hall, there was no question whose side the general had been on. "The 20th Indian Division under General Gracey was friendly toward us," read Leclerc's final report, "and we much appreciated their aid."[77]

CHAPTER SEVEN

"JUST SAY YOU DON'T KNOW ANYTHING ABOUT IT"

In contrast to their frequent squabbling over Indochina, American and British leaders gave little attention to Korea during the war. Except among a handful of Christian missionaries, American knowledge and interest concerning Korea was low. (Secretary of State Stettinius reportedly had trouble finding the country on a map.) Yet though Americans knew little about Korea, they did know one thing: They wanted to keep the Soviets out. A Korea liberated from the Japanese but under the domination of the Soviets could pose a threat to the security of the entire north Pacific region, in the view of State Department planners and many of the president's advisers.[1]

In keeping with the general view of Roosevelt and his advisers that all colonial peoples deserved independence but few were "ready" for it, the preferred American solution for Korea was some sort of multinational trusteeship. This idea the president had raised on occasion with Stalin, who was noncommittal, and Churchill, who detested the whole trusteeship concept as a potential threat to Britain's empire. All three leaders had already announced at the Cairo Conference in December 1943 that, "mindful of the enslavement of the Korean people," they were "determined that in due course Korea should become free and independent." Korean patriots in exile rejoiced at the prospect of freedom but were uneasy about the "in due course" part. No one in Washington seemed able to say what that meant.

As the war neared its end, no final agreement about Korea had been reached, but it was apparent that the Russians would get there first. At the time that the Soviets were expected to enter the war, American troops would be concentrating for their invasion of the Japanese Home Islands, while Soviet forces would be moving into Manchuria, which bordered on northern Korea. General Order No. 1, hastily drafted in Washington after Japan's unexpected surrender offer, nevertheless provided for U.S. forces to occupy the southern part of Korea, even though they would arrive much later than the Soviets.

Two army planners, Colonel Charles H. Bonesteel and Colonel Dean Rusk, a future secretary of state, were given the task of recommending appropriate occupation zones for each country's forces. The colonels were War Department General Staff specialists on political-military issues but not experts on Korea. Unlike Stettinius, however, they were able to locate it on the map, and they noted that the 38th parallel divided the Korean Peninsula almost exactly in two. The area south of the parallel contained the capital, Seoul, and two-thirds of Korea's population as well as ports on the Yellow Sea and the Sea of Japan. Bonesteel and Rusk recommended the 38th parallel as a temporary dividing line, an idea that was quickly approved by the representatives of the State, War, and Navy Departments.

Surprisingly, the Soviets accepted the American proposal. Newly opened Soviet archives make clear that Stalin had no plans to annex Korea, but intended to keep it from falling into unfriendly hands and preventing any single power from gaining complete control.[2] The division at the 38th parallel may have appeared to the Soviet leader as a workmanlike balancing of interests on the peninsula. In any case, while recognizing that the United States and China would probably play a role, the Soviets remained most concerned to ensure that Japanese influence and power were eradicated and that Japan would have minimal influence in postwar Korea. A Soviet Foreign Ministry study concluded that "Japan must be forever excluded from Korea since a Korea under Japanese rule would be a constant threat to the Far East of the USSR."[3] While Japan might be permitted to trade with Korea after the war, she was to be wholly excluded from business investment, industry, or mining.

If the Japanese never again set foot in Korea, that would have been fine with most Koreans. When Japan annexed Korea in 1910, it established its rule over a country with a cohesive common culture, history, and language, one that had been an independent self-governing state for centuries. Indeed, the Koreans were accustomed to thinking of themselves as culturally superior to the Japanese, who had traditionally borrowed or adapted many aspects of Korean civilization.

In 1919, Korean students, religious leaders, intellectuals, and other prominent citizens, mistakenly believing that Woodrow Wilson's words about freedom and self-determination somehow applied to them, organized mass demonstrations throughout the country and read a "Proclamation of Independence" for Korea. The movement was ruthlessly suppressed by the Japanese, and more than two thousand people were killed. Nineteen thousand went to jail and thousands more fled the country. Many who fled established independence groups abroad in China, the United States, and the Soviet Union. The Korean exiles were united only in their determination to rid Korea of the Japanese. Some factions had strong ties to the Soviet Union, where there were substantial Korean communities in Siberia and the Maritime Province. Others were Christian converts with connections to American missionaries and church groups. In China there were Korean nationalist groups attached to both the Kuomintang and the Communists. Divided by ideological, regional, and family differences, the exiles also had little connection with nationalists and intellectuals inside Korea.

Japanese rule in Korea lasted only thirty-five years, but it left an indelible legacy. The economy was relentlessly modernized, an extensive railway network was constructed, telegraph lines crisscrossed the country, and banks and other financial institutions were established. The Japanese also opened schools for primary and secondary education, built hospitals, and established an extensive public-health system.

Yet the standard of living of most Koreans improved little. Even the per capita consumption of rice by Koreans decreased during the 1940s as more rice was exported to Japan. Most of the money to be made in the new Korea was made by the Japanese. All of the best jobs were held by Japanese. In Indochina, the French colonial bureaucracy had numbered less than 3,000 with only about 10,000 soldiers in a country of 17 million people. Korea, population 21 million, had at least 246,000 Japanese in some way connected to the colonial government.[4] Through it all, the Koreans remained determined to regain their freedom. "I made a special trip to Ireland to find out what had happened to the

Gaelic tongue," a Korean educator told an American journalist. "I found it had almost entirely disappeared. Yet the Irish kept on fighting for so many hundred years to be free." Koreans could do the same.[5]

After the shocks of 1919, the Japanese liberalized their rule to a limited extent, allowing moderate nationalists to organize, speak, and write, but not to act. This relative moderation ended in the late 1930s, and the Japanese began a program to erase all aspects of Korean national identity. The Korean language press was suppressed, only Japanese could be taught in schools, and all Koreans were required to take Japanese names.

As Japan's conflict in China broadened into a world war, the pressures and demands on Koreans increased. About two and a half million Koreans were recruited or conscripted for work in Japan, often working in Japanese mines and factories under conditions that amounted to virtual slave labor. Three hundred fifty thousand Koreans served in the Japanese military or in its auxiliaries and support services, and one hundred fifty thousand died. Korean women were tricked or kidnapped into the Japanese system of military prostitution; they were often referred to as "comfort women." Young women from all areas under Japanese control were coerced into this network of sexual slavery, but the largest proportion, an estimated fifty thousand to two hundred thousand, were Koreans.[6]

ON THE MORNING of August 15, posters appeared on the walls of Seoul notifying the public that there would be an important announcement at noon on the radio. By early afternoon, Koreans knew that the war was over. Everywhere people shed their Japanese-style clothes and appeared in Korean dress for the first time in years.[7] Professionals and businessmen tore up their Japanese-language calling cards. Korean flags hastily manufactured from makeshift materials appeared everywhere. "Every street, every alley is packed with people waving flags, singing, shouting, greeting each other," recalled a resident of a northern Korean town. "Noises and sounds of all kinds fill the air—drums, bugles, whistles, buckets, pots and pans."[8] "Crowds rushed up the steps [of Shinto shrines] past the torii gates carrying axes and ropes. They tore down the wooden shrines, hacked them to pieces, and right there on the wide courtyard they burned them to the ground."[9] "This was too unbearable for us," one Japanese is reported to have remarked. "The Koreans treat us as if we were foreigners."[10]

The Japanese Government General was expecting a lot worse than that. The military calculated that the Soviets might be in Seoul within twenty hours. Russian planes were already bombing the city of Chongjin in the extreme northeast of the country. The Soviets would likely release all political prisoners and establish a Communist government. Koreans might riot and kill thousands of Japanese civilians. For several days the governor-general had been talking with Korean leaders about forming a transition government that would at least maintain law and order, thus safeguarding Japanese lives and perhaps their property as well. Unhappily, prominent Koreans whom the Japanese considered the most likely to be sensible and cooperative were also those with a record of collaboration and so most likely to be lynched if they made an agreement with the Japanese.

Having quickly exhausted the list of "moderates," the Japanese turned to Yo Un-hyong, a dapper Western-educated nationalist whose tweed and flannel wardrobe and carefully groomed mustache were so impeccable that according to one story, he had escaped the secret police in Shanghai by passing as a Westerner.[11] Yo was a left-leaning populist with unblemished patriotic credentials who had resisted the Japanese actively or passively for more than two decades. In addition to his striking appearance, Yo was a charismatic speaker with a strong following among students and intellectuals.

Meeting with Endo Ryusaku, the governor-general's secretary for political affairs, Yo laid out the minimum conditions for cooperation. These went much further than the Japanese had envisioned. Yo demanded the immediate release of all political prisoners, an end to food shipments out of the country, a guarantee that the Japanese would not interfere with preparations for Korea's independence, and no interference with the activities of student groups, labor unions, and agrarian organizations. Still under the impression that the Soviet would occupy all of Korea, the Japanese decided to accept Yo's demands.

The following day Yo announced the formation of the Committee for the Preparation of Korean Independence. The committee was composed of Seoul notables and nationalist leaders whose ranks were soon augmented by newly released political prisoners, many of them Communists. The independence committee soon had branches throughout the country and its own militia, the Chiandae, or "Self-Protection Corps," which did a surprisingly effective job at assuming many day-to-day law enforcement duties. Worker, farmer, and student organizations proliferated.

By late August, word had reached Seoul that U.S. troops would occupy the southern half of the country. The news brought feelings of relief to the Japanese and motivated the independence committee, which moved quickly to establish a de facto government that could be in place when the Americans arrived. September 6 saw the formation of the Korean People's Republic with a long list of Cabinet members representing a wide spectrum of political leaders, including many prominent exiles who were unaware that they had been nominated. Although the People's Republic was designed to look like a government of national unity, it was in fact dominated by two factions, Yo Un-hyong's Korean Independence League and the Communists, whose dominant faction was headed by Pak Hon-yong.

In a nation where even the Communists had feuding factions, it was no surprise that the Korean People's Republic soon found itself confronted by a rival coalition, formed a week later. This was the Democratic Party, led by well-to-do professionals, businessmen, and landowners, many of them educated in American or Japanese universities. Some were patriots who had spent their share of time in Japanese prisons, but others were tainted with suspicion—or more than suspicion—of having collaborated with the colonial authorities. The leaders of the Democratic Party saw Yo Un-hyong as an opportunist who had sold out to both the Japanese and the Communists. Mostly members of the affluent classes, they naturally resisted the more radical reforms called for by the Korean People's Republic. Had the Koreans been left to determine their own future, they might have found a basis for unity and independence, or they might have become embroiled in civil war. But the forces of the world's two most powerful countries were arriving on the peninsula. The fate of Korea was now entangled in the exigencies of Great Power rivalries, as it had been so often in the past.

On August 20, a platoon of Russian soldiers with a lone Soviet tank entered the old fortress town of Kapsan on the Korea-Manchuria border. The Kapsan People's Committee had organized a welcoming ceremony with an honor guard of the local Chiandae and citizens lining the streets waving homemade red flags. One old man waved a tattered copy of *Das Kapital* and was hoisted up to the tank. The Soviet soldiers, appreciative of their reception, passed out loaves of black bread that one Korean found "tough enough to be used as pillows but tasty."[12]

The Russian platoon belonged to a division of the Twenty-fifth Army, which had attacked the Japanese forces in northern Korea on August 10. The outnumbered and outmaneuvered Japanese surrendered five days later. On the twenty-fourth, the Soviets reached Pyongyang, the largest city north of the 38th parallel, where they were welcomed by cheering crowds and bottles of liberated Japanese liquor.[13]

The Koreans soon discovered that the soldiers of the Twenty-fifth Army, like their counterparts in Manchuria, seemed to have left any sense of self-restraint far behind them in the Soviet Union. Indiscriminate looting, rape, and robbery began almost immediately. The town of Songdo, which was occupied by the Soviets for only days because it was below the parallel, had eight million yen taken from the bank and sixty thousand pounds of expensive, highly prized ginseng lifted from local warehouses. As a souvenir of their stay, the soldiers also relieved most of the citizens of their wristwatches.[14] In the larger towns north of the parallel, the conduct of the Soviets was such that Korean women began disguising themselves as men. An Australian who visited Pyongyang to help in the recovery of Allied POWs reported, "The Russians, armed with tommy-guns, fire a few shots in the air, then break into the house, drag out what women (mostly young girls) they can find, put them into the truck along with furniture and any other objects that caught their eyes and drive off to their barracks. After a day or two the girls are thrown on the street."[15] Even in 1947, long after Soviet generals had cracked down on their troops' worst abuses, a single province in the north experienced seven murders, one assault, two rapes, and five robberies during one month, according to Soviet Army statistics.[16] Those statistics may safely be assumed to represent only a fraction of those types of offenses, since in the Russian Army, as in many armies, most such crimes went unreported.

Soviet appropriations of factories, industrial equipment, and machinery in Korea were somewhat less sweeping than in Manchuria, but the effort was nevertheless impressive. Everything movable at the Nippon Steel Company of Chung-jin, from furnaces, ovens, and chemicals to telephones, tables, and chairs, was loaded aboard twenty freight cars, which, over a ten-week period, hauled the equipment to waiting ships for transport to the Soviet Union. The Nippon Textile Company was left with only an empty building. Over half of the coal stocks of the northern Korean railroads were shipped to Vladivostok.[17] The same American survey mission that had visited Manchuria in September spent a week in northern Korea in the spring of 1946 and estimated that the Soviets had lifted at least one billion dollars' worth of capital goods, raw material, and food from the country.[18]

The Soviets brought minimal food supplies with them and generally lived off the land, requisitioning whatever they needed in exchange for army blankets, rubles, or often nothing at all. "I have seen Russians go into a field of vegetables and remove the lot despite the farmer's entreaties that he and his family will starve unless they pay him," wrote the Australian observer, "but the Russians don't pay for the food they collect. At least I have never seen them pay and Koreans have told me they have received nothing for the animals and vegetables the Russians have taken."[19] By 1946, Koreans were also complaining that Soviet soldiers were bringing their families to Korea and "taking the homes of the Korean people as well as public buildings." In Hamhung alone they were said to have taken more than two thousand houses and buildings.[20]

Despite the behavior of their troops, which soon prompted an order from the high command that soldiers at night must travel in groups of three for safety, the advent of the Russians was far from completely unwelcome in the north. Land rents were drastically reduced, and over the next few months land formerly owned by Japanese or absentee landlords was confiscated and distributed to former tenants or other landless farmers. Many larger landowners fled to the south. Those who remained were permitted to retain only as much land as they could cultivate themselves. Japanese troops were quickly disarmed and sent north to prisoner of war camps. Japanese officials, police, and bureaucrats promptly found themselves out of a job. Most soon joined the streams of thousands of other Japanese refugees headed for the port of Wonsan or to southern Korea. Prominent Korean collaborators were swiftly rounded up.

Colonel General Ivan Chistiakov, a hero of the Battle of Stalingrad, commanded the Soviet Twenty-fifth Army in Korea. Chistiakov knew nothing about Korea, but he did know from the purges of 1937–38 what could happen to generals who became involved in political matters. He preferred to leave those to the Twenty-fifth Army's senior political commissars, particularly N. G. Lebedev, the senior political officer.[21] Despite their unfamiliarity with Korea, the Soviets were not dependent on Japanese technical experts and translators as the Americans would be in the south. Thousands of Soviet citizens of Korean descent were available to act as interpreters and technical advisers; some were already serving in the Red Army, and as many as thirty thousand were soon on their way south from Siberia to join the Twenty-fifth Army.

AFTER A FEW YEARS, as the Cold War hardened and the division of the peninsula evolved into a permanent condition, many Americans and their allies came to see Soviet actions in Korea as a product of a carefully developed plan to bring about the sovietization of the north, a region where the Korean Communist presence was weak to nonexistent. (Most of the real fire-breathing Communists were in the south, while the north was a stronghold of the nationalist right, the Christians, and indigenous socioreligious movements.)

Actually, Soviet actions in the north were driven by no guiding plan, nor was any needed. Soviet officers knew only one political and social system, and they had been assured since early childhood that Russian-style Communism represented a scientific blueprint for human progress. The Soviets kept the local People's Committees in place but brought them firmly under control. In Pyongyang they retained the Provisional People's Political Committee, headed by Cho Man-sik, a widely respected Christian nationalist. A graduate of Meiji University in Japan, Cho was sixty-three years old in 1945 and had been active in nationalist causes since the 1920s. He had become particularly famous during the war years for publicly refusing to comply with the Japanese order that all Koreans adopt Japanese names.

The Soviets were ready to work through Cho, but they found him stubborn and hard to fathom. General Chistiakov recorded in his diary that at a meeting with Cho and other nationalist leaders, the Korean patriarch sat almost silent, occasionally giving a slight nod of his head to statements or questions. Cho's demeanor was in keeping with what Koreans might expect from a man of his years, prestige, and attainments, but Chistiakov found such behavior mainly annoying, observing that Cho appeared to believe that "the less he says the more impressive he will seem."[22] More than his inscrutable behavior, Cho's Christianity and conservative connections gave the Soviets second thoughts about the possibilities for his long-term cooperation.

By late September, the Russian leaders in Pyongyang had chosen another candidate to balance Cho and if necessary replace him. This was Kim Il-sung, who had led an anti-Japanese guerrilla band in Manchuria during the late 1930s before being forced to retreat to the Soviet Far East in 1940. There he served in an international regiment of the Red Army composed mainly of Chinese and Koreans and rose to the rank of captain.[23] Much of what North Korean propagandists would assert about Kim's career as a guerrilla leader was largely fantasy, but there is solid evidence that he was successful and respected for his accomplishments in leading his "army" of fewer than three hundred men in raids against the Japanese in Manchuria. His most famous exploit was a 1937 raid on the small town of Poch-onbo, just inside the Korean border with Manchuria. Kim's band of about two hundred men destroyed the local Japanese police post and some Japanese offices before withdrawing back across the border a few hours later.[24] This insignificant skirmish had enormous psychological impact on both the Koreans and the Japanese. For a guerrilla unit even to succeed in penetrating the heavily guarded Korea-Manchuria border was itself an impressive achievement. The raid was reported in the press, and the news soon spread all over Korea. The Japanese authorities were sufficiently alarmed to form a special "Kim Il-sung Activities Unit."

Kim appears to have been happy in his new career as a Soviet Army officer, and according to some accounts he left the military with considerable regret. One Soviet political commissar recalled Kim as "very frustrated" at his new role, declaring, "I want to command a regiment, then a division. What is this for? I don't understand anything and I don't want to do this." Yet from the Soviet perspective, Kim must have appeared an ideal choice. The local Communist factions in the north were weak. The well-known leaders were in the south. Kim was a Korean Communist with a reputation as a fighter and patriot but with close ties to the Soviets. (Later stories, viewed with skepticism by many scholars, claimed that he had visited Moscow and received the nod from Stalin himself.)[25]

Whatever their expectations, the Soviets lost no time inserting Kim into the leadership ranks of Koreans in Pyongyang. On September 30, he met with Cho Man-sik. On October 14 he was present at a mass rally in honor of the Soviet Army "as a representative of the grateful Korean People" and delivered a speech prepared for him by the Twenty-fifth Army's political department. This was the first of a number of public appearances by the man the Soviets referred to as a "national hero" and "an outstanding guerrilla leader."

An American officer who witnessed one of Kim's public appearances more than a year later was unimpressed. "He is a fat, dissipated-looking, pasty creature of about 35 years of age who sat throughout the meeting slouched in his chair with a stupid-looking glassy stare noticing absolutely nothing that was taking place."[26] Like many Koreans of the time, the American observer believed the postwar Kim to be an impostor. "He is impersonating a true revolutionary hero of the same name. . . . The true Kim Il-sung has mysteriously disappeared. He is a man of about 50 years of age. . . . However the Soviets are ramming this farce down the throats of the Koreans." Whether the public Kim was truly an impostor, an assertion doubted by most contemporary scholars, it was a fact that the North Koreans were going to see a lot more of him.

WHILE THE SOVIETS went about their task of assuring a friendly political regime in northern Korea, Japanese and Koreans below the 38th parallel uneasily awaited the arrival of the Americans. The Japanese were having second thoughts about having granted such wide latitude to the nationalists, and they reinforced their well-armed police with detachments from the army. Either ignorant of or ignoring the fact that Japan had surrendered unconditionally, Japanese officials in Korea insisted that the future of Korea would be decided at a coming "peace conference" with the Allies. Endo, speaking for the governor-general, explained, "The Japanese sovereign power in Korea still majestically exists . . . in a sense only hostilities have ceased. The matters about Korea will be decided only after the treaty has been signed."[27]

In the meantime, the Japanese did their best to prepare for an uncertain future. Civil servants sold off government property and helped themselves to any government funds within reach. The Seventeenth Area Army authorized soldiers to sell weapons to "trustworthy" civilians. There was a run on the banks. The government countered by assuring depositors that their accounts would be honored by banks in Japan and by churning out quantities of banknotes. Depositors were reassured, but prices soared. Inflation, already a serious problem before the end of the war, now roared out of control. American economic experts later estimated that in 1945, rice cost about a hundred times what it had in 1941.

Many Japanese officials, technical experts, and businessmen took the first opportunity to return to their homeland. With General MacArthur's permission, two Japanese merchant ships regularly made the short run from Pusan to Japan. Many other Japanese departed aboard smaller, privately owned vessels. By early September, the number of those leaving was estimated by the Americans to have reached a high of four to six thousand a day. With them went much of the technical, financial, agricultural, and administrative expertise that Korea would sorely need in the months ahead.[28]

The U.S. Army's XXIV Corps, which had fought in the bloody campaign of Okinawa, was designated by MacArthur as the occupation force for Korea. Like the Marines on Okinawa, the soldiers of the XXIV Corps' three divisions had been expecting an early return to the United States now that the war had ended. Instead they got Korea. While even the newest Marine in Tsingtao, Tientsin, or Peking had consumed an ample stew of fact, sea stories, and half-remembered history about China before he embarked from Okinawa, there was nothing of the sort about Korea—no gossip, no rumors, no colorful or bloodcurdling stories. Nothing. Almost no one in the army spoke Korean except for a handful of Americans of Korean descent and the sons of missionary families. Thousands of soldiers had been trained in Japanese at the U.S. Army Military Government School in Charlottesville, Virginia, but "policy prohibited the study of Korean in Army schools."[29] The XXIV Corps had almost no intelligence on Korea. Aerial reconnaissance missions were flown over the peninsula and Koreans captured with the Japanese Army were interrogated, but with "little result."[30] Donald MacDonald, a graduate of the Military Government School, where he had been trained in intensive Japanese, arrived at Inchon aboard a troopship. "On the way a few of us dug out of the ship's library a book entitled 'Terry's 1905 Japanese Empire' which had a few pages on Korea. . . . We copied that on the ship's typewriter and then mimeographed it. That was the total of our knowledge about Korea when we arrived at Inchon."[31]

Lieutenant General John R. Hodge commanded the XXIV Corps. He came from a farm family in southern Illinois and entered the army during World War I. Hodge was a general who specialized in fighting. He had served in the last stages of the Guadalcanal campaign, on New Georgia, and on Bougainville before leading the XXIV Corps in the protracted and bloody battle for Okinawa. He lacked MacArthur's charisma and Mountbatten's wit and charm. While the latter two occupied opulent and stately living accommodations, Hodge shared his quarters with two of his senior officers. He was not a West Pointer. He was tough, plainspoken, and impatient. But he learned fast.

On August 30, XXIV Corps radio operators began calling Korea on all frequencies and call signs. Two days later, radio contact was established with Seoul, but it took some time before the Japanese could find a radio operator who could transmit English-language messages. Three days after contact was established, an advance party of thirty-seven men under Brigadier General Charles M. Harrison left Okinawa for Korea.[32] Major Charles M. Strother, a member of the advance party, found "the thought of entrusting the lives of a dozen American officers to the Japanese Army" unsettling.[33] But his misgivings quickly eased as the Americans began their meetings with the Japanese, who appeared polite and cooperative.

Many Koreans, however, found the behavior of the newly arrived Americans troubling. The advance team seemed to spend most of their working time meeting with the Japanese and the balance closeted in their hotel. They met few Koreans and were rumored to have treated those few rudely. In contrast, their relations with the Japanese appeared polite and friendly.[34] The brief visit of the advance party was to set the tone for much of the later conduct of the Americans and the Japanese during the autumn of 1945.

At the time that General Harrison's advance party began their talks with the Japanese, the ships carrying the first elements of Hodge's corps were already at sea. Twenty-one ships of the Seventh Amphibious Force carrying soldiers of the 7th Infantry Division left Okinawa in bad weather on the afternoon of September 5 and arrived off Inchon three days later. As the transports waited outside the harbor for the once-a-day tide that would permit them to enter during daylight, troops of the 7th Division lined the decks to have a first look at their unexpected destination. Many were new recruits recently assigned to the division to replace the losses of Okinawa and prepare for the invasion of Japan, but some of the enlisted men and more of the officers had fought with the division in the Aleutians and Kwajalein, Leyte, and Okinawa. Just before embarking, the men of the occupation force had received a "Pocket Guide to Korea," which advised soldiers, "If there is one subject to avoid it is politics. Just say you don't know anything about it, which is undoubtedly the truth."[35]

Before noon on September 8, troops of the 2nd Battalion, 17th Infantry regiment, climbed down the ships' cargo nets into waiting landing craft. Once loaded, the landing craft formed slowly moving circles off the bows and quarters of the transports, the preliminary formation for an amphibious assault. On a signal from the flagship, the landing craft stopped circling and headed for the Inchon docks in successive waves. First Lieutenant John Bliss's F Company was the first to come ashore. Bliss and his men were astounded to see Japanese sentries with fixed bayonets lining the docks and streets. "Further up and off the dock on the main road was a Japanese officer also fully uniformed and armed on horseback. . . . It was truly a shock as every man in the company had fought through the Okinawa campaign and had never seen a Japanese soldier in a full clean uniform. We were amazed and a lot of muttering and swearing started which had to be stopped with several loud commands."[36]

Earlier in the day, Japanese police had killed a number of Koreans while trying to break up demonstrations to welcome the coming of the Americans.[37] Lieutenant Bliss "noticed men lying in the streets whom we thought were drunks but after a few more were seen, I told one of my squad leaders to check it out while we continued our march. He came running back to me and said, 'They have cut their heads off.' The word passed along fast and the swearing became loud and meaningful and I didn't try to stop it. We saw seven bodies in all. We were not surprised, just enraged."[38]

The following morning the first American troops arrived at Seoul. The air was crisp and clear—"football weather" to the Americans—and Seoul appeared relatively unscathed by four years of war. The modern sections of the capital "looked almost like an American city." Yet the city had no electric power. All power plants were in the north where the Soviets had cut off the flow of electricity to the south. There was a strong smell of gas everywhere, a product of the acetylene lamps that were used at night for illumination. Among the people on the streets, "nobody wore anything that was not tattered and torn. That was true of coats and ties, if anyone had them. This was true even of the upper middle class. They too were dressed shabbily. . . . Creature comforts were not in existence. The few cars that did run were old. . . . Taxis had open hibachis in the back seat for heat. Streetcars and buses were always overcrowded."[39]

The American entry into Seoul was made in silence. Heavily armed Japanese police lined the principal streets, and those Koreans who dared turn out for the American arrival were prudently quiet. That afternoon, however, as General Hodge and Admiral Thomas C. Kincaid, commander of the Seventh Fleet, drove through Seoul on their way to accept the Japanese surrender, the previously silent Koreans broke into wild cheering. The surrender ceremony was held in the capitol building, in a chamber that had been used as a throne room for the emperor of Japan on imperial visits to Korea. That evening, Koreans danced and celebrated in the streets.

Korean exuberance was soon cut short by Hodge's announcement at a news conference that, for the present, the Japanese Government General would continue to function under American supervision and that all of its personnel from Governor-General Abe to the lowest ranking policeman would remain in their jobs. This declaration, which surprised even the Japanese, unleashed a blast of criticism in the media.[40] Editorial writers in U.S. papers reacted to Hodge's announcement in the same manner as Lieutenant Bliss's soldiers had to the sight of the bayonet-wielding Japanese sentries at Inchon, although they used less colorful language. Koreans took to the streets in protest. *The Seoul Times* commented that Koreans would rather be ruled by "some chief from Borneo" than by the Government General.[41]

The State Department quickly disavowed any responsibility for leaving the Japanese in control, explaining to the press that it was a local decision of the theater commander. (In fact, State Department planning documents for Korea had discussed the desirability of continuing to utilize Japanese technicians and functionaries in the postwar era to fill positions where no qualified Koreans were available.)[42] On the advice of Undersecretary of State Dean Acheson, President Truman released a public statement saluting Koreans as "a freedom-loving and heroic people" and promising that all Japanese officials would quickly be replaced.[43] Exactly why Hodge made his ill-fated decision remains unclear. One possibility is that he was simply following MacArthur's occupation policy for Japan, which was based on utilizing the existing governmental structures to implement American policies. Whatever the reasons, MacArthur, anticipating instructions from Washington, directed Hodge to remove immediately the Government General and its officials.

Hodge might have attempted to work through the Korean People's Republic, which was already exercising governmental responsibilities in many areas and was far and away the strongest and best organized political group in southern Korea. Yet Hodge and his political adviser, H. Merrill Benninghoff, had only a sketchy idea of who was who in Korean politics during those first few weeks. When Hodge invited Korean political parties to send two representatives to meet with him, more than two hundred individuals appeared. By early October there were fifty-four political parties registered with the military government.[44] All Korean politics appeared chaotic and disorderly, and Korean politicians obstreperous and demanding, given to encouraging raucous demonstrations that sometimes seemed indistinguishable from riots. The leaders of the People's Republic shared these characteristics and in addition appeared to include many Communists or Communist sympathizers, probably with ties to the Soviets. Hodge opted for direct American control. He abolished the Government General, replacing it with a U.S. Army military government headed by Major General Archibald V. Arnold. English became the official language of the occupation.

Hodge's public relations difficulties were not over, however. The general and the correspondent for *The Christian Science Monitor,* Gordon Walker, had already developed a cordial dislike for each other, and it was Walker who wrote the most damaging story about Hodge, one in which the general had reportedly referred to the Japanese and Koreans as being "the same breed of cat." This statement was quoted endlessly in the media of the time and is still mentioned in many historical accounts of the period. The general later lamented that it would "probably bob up again" in his obituary. According to Hodge, he had been deliberately misquoted. He had been speaking about the police problem and had observed that there was little difference "between the Japs and those collaborator Korean police who have been working against their people. In the eyes of the Korean people these Koreans are about the same breed of cat as the Japanese." Hodge believed that Walker had maliciously shortened the quote to embarrass him.[45]

CHAPTER EIGHT

"HOPELESS AS A SOCIETY"

"SOUTHERN KOREA CAN BEST BE DESCRIBED AS A POWDER KEG READY to explode at the application of a spark," wrote H. Merrill Benninghoff, General Hodge's political adviser, in his first report to Washington one month after the Japanese surrender. Inflation continued. Thousands of Koreans were unemployed, either because they refused to work any longer in Japanese-owned businesses or because of the collapse of many war-driven industries. Refugees from the north swelled the population of the crowded cities. There was a critical shortage of rice and coal. Korean agriculture was a mess and had been so for years. About 3 percent of the population owned two-thirds of the arable land. Farms were small and farming methods primitive. More than half of all farmers were tenants who worked their rented land under conditions that made sharecroppers in the American South appear almost affluent by comparison.[1] All Korean political groups, Benninghoff concluded, "seem to have the common ideas of seizing Japanese property, ejecting the Japanese from Korea and achieving immediate independence. Beyond this they have few ideas . . . Korea is completely ripe for agitators."[2]

Having rejected the idea of recognizing any Korean government authority and pledged to repatriate the Japanese, the Americans now found themselves absolute rulers of a country about which they still knew next to nothing. One immediate response was to retain the ousted Japanese officials as advisers and interpreters. Oda Yasuma, who had represented the governor-general in carrying out the surrender arrangements with General Harrison's advance party, was a great favorite with Americans because of his excellent command of English.[3] He continued to be utilized as a key adviser, helped select translators, and wrote memoranda on the situation in Korea. Altogether the military government received 350 separate memoranda on Korean affairs from former Japanese officials between August and mid-September, when the last Japanese left Korea.[4]

Hodge and Arnold had twenty-eight military government teams, totaling about 230 officers and men, some of whom had landed with the first occupation troops in early September. A considerable proportion of soldiers in these teams had received extensive training for military government duties—in Japan. Few knew any more about Korea than did Hodge himself. "At the Civil Affairs Training School at Harvard, I studied Japanese intensively for six months and had a fairly good knowledge of Japanese history, politics and culture," recalled one civil affairs officer. "Had I gone to Japan I would have been moderately well equipped for a beginner, but as far as Korea was concerned I knew absolutely nothing."[5] "I don't think the military government was terribly successful," recalled another Japanese-language officer. "It was thrown together on the spur of the moment. . . . I don't believe it had a coordinated, thought-out plan . . . there were no language or area specialists. The American personnel, in the main, were either people who couldn't be used in Japan or second raters. . . . Moreover the Koreans themselves had no desire to have a military government. They considered themselves liberated and they were very anxious to have us go home so they could begin the self-government process."[6]

The Americans were almost entirely dependent on Korean translators in their communications with the public. American posters and leaflets in the Korean language often contained inappropriate characters, misspellings, and incomprehensible American colloquialisms. All-important public addresses and press conferences had to be translated by Koreans or Japanese. American newsmen labeled it "government by interpreter."[7] Many of the Korean translators employed by the military government were suspected Japanese collaborators. They were disliked and mistrusted by many Koreans, who wondered exactly what it was they were "translating" to the Americans.[8] A "Korean Relations and Information Section," which at first consisted of three officers with backgrounds in public relations and journalism, initially handled relations with the Korean public. None spoke Korean.

In their unfamiliar surroundings in the midst of a strange, apparently unreadable society, the Americans felt most comfortable with those few Koreans who spoke English, most of whom had been educated in the United States or in American mission schools. These people also tended to be among the wealthiest and most conservative elements in the country. Some had long records of collaboration or service in the Japanese-run bureaucracy. As Hodge's acting political adviser, William R. Langdon, put it, "It is quite probable that at the beginning we may have picked out a disproportionate number of rich and conservative persons. . . . For practical purposes we had to hire persons who spoke English and it so happened that these persons came largely from the moneyed classes because English had been a luxury among Koreans."[9] The handful of American officers who came from missionary families were also a critical source of advice and were granted broad authority.

It is easy to exaggerate the extent of right-wing bias on the part of the American military government, however. Hodge was always displeased with the boisterousness and disorder of Korean politics and deeply suspicious of the Communists and those he believed to be under their influence. Koreans, he told Assistant Secretary of War John J. McCloy, "are most narrow, selfish and confused in their political thought."[10] Yet the military government tolerated an extremely diverse array of political associations, journals, and activities. By November there were 134 different political parties registered with the American headquarters.[11] Unlike General Gracey in Indochina, Hodge maintained personal lines of communication with all factions, including with the Communist leader Pak Hon-yong.[12]

In the north, the Russians had retained the People's Committees after purging them of any elements likely to oppose Soviet rule. In the south, Hodge opted to demand the dissolution of the committees and established an "advisory council" of eleven "prominent Koreans including educators, lawyers, and businessmen 'patriots' as well as representatives of the two leading political groups." These worthy gentlemen had been recommended to Hodge by a member of his staff, Lieutenant Commander George Z. Williams, the son of a missionary, whose contacts were with well-to-do Korean Christians.

Aside from Cho Man-sik, who was in the north and consequently could not serve, Yo Un-hyong was the only appointee not described by the Americans as a conservative. The man elected chairman of the advisory council, Kim Song-su, had also sat on the Central Advisory Council to the Japanese Government General during the war years. Four of the council members belonged to the Korean Democratic Party. At the sight of the other council members, Yo Un-hyong quit in disgust, asking Hodge whether he thought a council tilted nine to one in favor of one side was a way to achieve cooperation.

Undeterred by the formation of the council and Hodge's invitation to them to disappear, the People's Republic and its allies continued to demand the ouster of those they labeled former pro-Japanese from high places in the civil service and police and charged that the Americans were "harboring traitors in the government general building."[13] Rumors, probably spread by the People's Republic, that a national election would be held on March 1 began to appear in the Korean press.

General Arnold responded with a statement to the press that as duly appointed military governor, his was the only government in Korea south of the 38th parallel. "Self-appointed officials . . . and the self-styled government of the Republic of Korea are entirely without any authority, power or reality. . . . If the men who are arrogating to themselves such high-sounding titles are merely play-acting upon a puppet stage . . . they must immediately pull down the curtain on the puppet show. If behind the curtain of these puppet shows there are venal men pulling the strings who are so foolish as to believe that they can take to themselves and exercise any of the legitimate functions of the government of Korea, let them pinch themselves and awake to the realities of the situation." Because freedom of the press had only recently come to Korea, "it is to be expected that many foolish and ill-considered statements will appear in the newspapers under amateur editorship. . . . Such boyishness even by old men will be allowed to evaporate like smoke in the air."[14]

When Arnold's statement, which all news publications were instructed to carry, was read to the assembled Korean correspondents and editors by an American public affairs officer, there was a stunned silence. "The effect was devastating," reported one American who was present at the time. "They felt if they were required to print it, freedom of the press in Korea was but a myth." When the unhappy journalists reassembled the next day, the editor of *Maeil Sinbo,* the leading Seoul paper, pointed out that only a few Korean politicians and journalists could be accused of acting irresponsibly, whereas Arnold's rather intemperate statement appeared to indict them all. Further, such words as "amateur," "venal," "boyishness," and "puppets" carried particularly unfortunate connotations in Korean. An unsympathetic American colonel told the group that Arnold had been angry and intended to use strong language. His blast was directed only at the guilty, but "if the shoe fits, wear it."[15] *Maeil Sinbo* refused to carry Arnold's statement and was closed down for several days. The Korean People's Republic replied to Arnold with a pamphlet quoting from the pro-Japanese speeches made by members of Hodge's advisory council during the war.

Having received this unhappy introduction to Korean political affairs, Hodge and Benninghoff looked forward impatiently to the return of the leaders of the Korean provisional government from their long exile in China and the United States. This, they had been assured by their conservative English-speaking informants, would be a great step toward stability in southern Korean politics. The two best-known members of the Korean provisional government were Kim Ku, who led the organization from China, and Syngman Rhee, its representative in the United States. Kim Ku had gained fame for masterminding a 1932 terrorist attack that killed a Japanese general and another high-ranking Japanese and gravely wounded the Japanese ambassador to China. He was a favorite of Chiang Kai-shek, who allowed the provisional government to set up shop in Shanghai and later in Chungking. Syngman Rhee was distantly related to the former royal family of Korea and had been active in nationalist causes since around 1900. After his imprisonment for political activities in the early years of the century, he spent many years in the United States, where he earned a Ph.D. from Princeton and lobbied tirelessly for Korean independence. At seventy, he was one of the few living Korean politicians who had been involved in the original resistance to the Japanese seizure of Korea.

During the war, Rhee and the provisional government had been brushed aside by the State Department but had received a warmer reception from the OSS, which had plans to organize Korean partisans to fight behind Japanese lines in China. Nothing came of that project, but Rhee made important friends and contacts in OSS and the War Department. One of these, OSS officer Colonel Millard Preston Goodfellow, became deputy director of OSS. Goodfellow added his voice to those calling for Rhee's return and arranged to join him in Korea as an unofficial adviser. Rhee arrived in Korea on October 11 amid considerable publicity, and Hodge welcomed him at a press conference in which he described Rhee as "a great man who has given his entire life to the freedom of Korea."[16]

Much to Hodge's gratification, Rhee appeared to be devoting his first weeks in Korea to attempting to unify the country's contentious political factions. The Korean Democratic Party, the People's Republic, and the Communists organized a unified "Central Council for the Rapid Realization of Korean Independence." That organization lasted less than two weeks. Rhee did not like the Korean People's Republic and refused to join. He would not join the advisory council either. Similarly, he declined overtures from the Korean Democratic Party, although he accepted money from its well-heeled backers. Above all Rhee disliked the trusteeship plan for Korea, and spent much of his time denouncing the plan and the Soviets, who he claimed were using the southern leftists to subvert Korean independence.

Having fanned the smoldering coals of Korean politics with the return of Rhee, Hodge and the military government now poured oil on the flames by facilitating the return of Kim Ku, known to many of his countrymen, not inappropriately, as "the assassin." Hodge told his staff that Kim was "the salt needed for the stew" and provided the returning patriot with American vehicles, a military police escort, and spacious quarters on the grounds of the Toksu Palace, the residence of the last king of Korea.[17] Other leaders and factions of the Korean provisional government arrived over the next few weeks.

How much salt Kim Ku added was unclear, but the stew kept boiling. His followers soon proved themselves even more obstreperous and unpredictable than Rhee. "The members of [Kim's] Provisional Government strained their status as private citizens to the limit," noted an official military government study. By mid-December, William Langdon, who had strongly advocated the quick return of the exiles two months before, was obliged to admit, "There is little apparent enthusiasm for either Kim Ku or Syngman Rhee." Notwithstanding their almost total lack of any mass following in Korea, the returned exiles "considered themselves to be the logical candidates to be a transition government." The provisional government's VIP treatment by the Americans appeared to give substance to these pretensions.[18]

Hodge's difficulties were not just confined to squabbling political factions in Seoul. The military government, having proclaimed itself the sole authority, had somehow to extend its control over the eight sprawling provinces of southern Korea. As had the Government General in Seoul, Japanese officials in the provinces kept Hodge supplied with continuing reports on the disorder and danger to lives and property in the countryside. This disorder and lawlessness were generally attributed to Communist inspiration.

BY MID-OCTOBER, Hodge had received his two additional divisions, the 40th Infantry Division and the 6th Infantry Division, from the Philippines. A portion of the 6th Division, having gained experience in the evacuation of the Japanese from the Philippines, took on the task of completing the embarkation of thousands of Japanese from the port of Pusan on the east coast of Korea. The rest of the division, together with the 40th, made their way into the countryside. Military government companies that were supposed to assume responsibility for supervising or implementing all local government functions followed the divisions a few months later.

As their trucks rolled down the dusty roads and byways into towns and villages, the GIs received a warm welcome. Koreans ran from their homes "pointing and waving in the direction of the oncoming Americans. They lined the streets, sometimes three deep, shouting and waving homemade American and Korean flags. . . . At the entrance to the larger towns archways garnished with fresh flowers were constructed across the road. Across the top were signs of all sizes and descriptions—'Welcome Americans,' 'Thank you Allied Force,' or 'America-Korea.' "[19]

This cordiality did not last. In many areas, American troops and military government detachments clashed with local People's Committees of the Korean People's Republic that had assumed governmental functions in towns and districts. In some larger towns People's Republic leaders occupied the city hall and other municipal buildings. Local

Japanese felt themselves to be under constant threat of violence and had most of their property appropriated. Korean and Japanese small boat owners carried on a thriving business in illegal emigrations to Japan.[20]

As in Seoul, the Americans brushed aside the People's Republic's claim to be the de facto government. The 40th Division's standard operating procedure provided that in cases where "a political party had expelled the former officials and taken over the government, the officials put in by the party were to be arrested and suitable substitutes appointed." That was accomplished by "running in armored personnel carriers in a big show of force, informing the People's Committees that they had been abolished and arresting some members as necessary."[21]

Who the "suitable substitutes" might be was left unspecified, but the division's orders allowed for the retention of Korean officials who had held office under the Japanese. Japanese heads of local government were to be relieved but might be retained as advisers. "Former police officials were to be used where they were available and suitable and backed up if necessary by the military."[22]

Leftists charged that these actions had the effect of maintaining the most detested collaborators in place together with the Japanese-created police and of safeguarding the position of the reactionary class of large southern landlords who had been among the most loyal collaborators with the Japanese. An officer of the 6th Infantry Division agreed. "The Governor of South Cholla Province who was initially named was a moderate physician who had been associated with the People's Party. He was soon displaced by a Korean landowner who was famous for his conservative anti-Communist views who spoke English very well and was therefore attractive to the anti-communist Americans. . . . [He] continued all these ex–Japanese Government General employees. What was done in effect was to continue the Japanese government structure."[23] In many provinces there were riots and mass demonstrations. "There was a major strike in a large coal mine near Kwangju which was something of a national cause celebre. . . . There were parades and counter-parades, demonstrations and counter-demonstrations."[24] Many local officials who had been appointed or retained in office by the Americans found it prudent to absent themselves from their offices for extended periods.

If many Koreans soon found the American presence in Korea tiresome, many Americans found Korea to be the farthest shore of nowhere. "I thought at the time that Korea was hopeless as a society," recalled a former American engineer officer at Inchon. "It was this curious mixture of more or less 20th century and 15th century. You could smell it forty miles at sea. . . . The only fertilizer they had was human excrement. Honey wagons were all over the place. . . . This was obviously a society totally alien to us young Americans. We had no comprehension of it."[25] The Koreans themselves "were not overly friendly." They appeared to lack the obsequiousness and good manners of the Japanese or the jovial and accommodating approach of those Chinese long accustomed to dealing with foreigners. Instead the Koreans appeared proud, stubborn, puritanical, and contentious, "the most independent, cocky, sassiest people in the world."[26] "The GIs in Japan have got heaven and don't know it," declared one of Hodge's soldiers after a short stay at a rest camp near Tokyo. "The Japanese are friendly. The Koreans are hostile. You try to take a picture of a Korean child and he runs away. You treat the Korean nice and he cheats you." Another soldier declared he would "sign up for ten years" if he could spend them in Japan rather than Korea.[27] "Here we are not dealing with wealthy U.S.-educated Koreans," observed General Hodge, "but with poorly trained and poorly educated Orientals strongly affected by forty years of Jap control who stubbornly and fanatically hold to what they like and dislike, who are definitely influenced by direct propaganda and with whom it is almost impossible to reason."[28]

Americans invariably referred to the Koreans as "gooks," a derisive term that GIs applied indiscriminately to Filipinos, Chinese, Japanese, and other Asians. Americans who did speak a little Korean "always used the very familiar forms even to the most respectable old men. This of course was an insult." For those soldiers who lacked any knowledge of the language, "the feeling [was] that if the Koreans didn't understand what was being said, the corrective was to shout louder."[29]

For the complex and delicate operations involved in rebuilding and reforming a foreign nation, Hodge had too few officers and enlisted men, and these were seldom of the highest quality. "General Hodge had great difficulty getting top-flight officers because the word was out that

Korea was a have-not theater. It was the end of the line," recalled a former officer of MacArthur's staff. "Nine out of ten officers [assigned to Korea] tried to get their orders changed."[30] There was an acute shortage of experienced sergeants and company-grade officers. Battle-weary enlisted men were being rapidly replaced by new recruits, many of them men of "seventeen to nineteen years of age with only five weeks training."[31] The commanding general of the 6th Infantry Division observed, "Men acting as 1st Sergeants are hardly qualified to be corporals. . . . Out of 19 company commanders in a regiment about 6 can be rated fair or better and platoon leaders are about the same."[32]

One of MacArthur's officers investigating morale and living conditions in Korea reported that "all of the recruits were agreed on one point, that War Department recruiting inducements had painted a picture of Korea so far from reality that newly arrived soldiers suffered pronounced let-downs."[33] Since February 1946, American soldiers had been prohibited from accepting or conveying dinner invitations to Koreans, and in May all Korean restaurants and bars were declared off limits because of health concerns.[34] As for romance, soldiers were forbidden to "associate with Korean women in public except where such an association is of an official nature."[35]

GI living conditions ranged from austere to primitive. Virtually all latrines and showers were located outside the barracks. Donald MacDonald's military government company lived through its first cold Korean winter in tropical barracks "where the screens had been sprayed with plastic. That was the winterization. Down the center of each barracks was a coal stove and they kept it red hot all winter long, and still it was freezing." Even in the station hospital at Taejon, temperatures in the corridors could drop to below freezing. On such days, temperatures in the hospital rooms would seldom rise above 50 degrees.[36] Many barracks had small oil-fueled space heaters. These were a considerable fire hazard. "There were four hotels out there [in Inchon]. We managed to burn them all down."[37] There was a shortage of fire extinguishers, and in the winter, water lines tended to freeze. Water collected in barrels would also freeze on very cold days. Whether frozen or not, the Americans considered all water in Korea to be polluted. It could not be used for drinking or cooking without chlorination or boiling.

Fire extinguishers were far from the only item in short supply in Korea. While GIs in China and Japan shopped for jewelry, custom-tailored clothes, jade, and silk, an inspection team found that as late as 1947, GIs in Korea were still short of "shoe polish, flashlights, bath sandals, cookies, and mirrors." The shortage of lightbulbs was so acute that "in many units it is necessary to bring bulbs from the squad room to the mess hall during meal hours."[38] One bright spot appeared to be the venereal disease rate, which was unusually low for troops stationed in Korea. One officer speculated that this may have been "because newcomers to the area were told that Korean men would not tolerate having their females 'mess around' with Americans and were likely to mutilate any soldier caught in the act."[39]

It seems doubtful that many GIs were cheered by the assurance of one member of MacArthur's staff that they were "living under conditions far superior to those which existed in most combat zones during the war."[40] They were unhappy with Korea—and they tended to take it out on the Koreans. General Hodge observed that many Koreans had been alienated by GIs who "act the part of the great conquerer and run rough-shod over the rights and customs of a liberated nation. This spirit was not shown to a great degree by those splendid combat soldiers who actually won the shooting war but has grown up among replacements." These soldiers made passes and whistled at Korean women, made fun of Korean men, and played childish pranks. Americans "literally push Koreans out of the way and lay hands on them unnecessarily." American vehicles seldom hesitated to drive through crowds of Koreans at streetcar stops or in the market. "They take joy in and laugh at making Koreans dive for safety and in splashing them with water from vehicle wheels in rainy weather."[41] Under these circumstances it could not have been surprising when 53 percent of Koreans polled by U.S. Army intelligence in early 1946 said that they held an unfavorable impression of Americans. A poll several months later revealed that 49 percent of Koreans preferred even Japanese rule to that of the Americans.[42]

Washington's solution for Korea's problems was to pursue the goal of an international, or at least U.S.-Soviet, trusteeship. The State Department argued that only Soviet agreement to an international trusteeship could guarantee the elimination of the 38th parallel barrier and the reunification of Korea.[43] In December 1945, Secretary of State Byrnes journeyed to Moscow for talks with the Soviets on the situation in Eastern Europe and the future of Korea. He carried with him an American proposal for a five-year Great Power trusteeship over Korea.

Trusteeship was the one issue about which Hodge, his political advisers, and Korean leaders of all types had found firm agreement. They all hated the idea. All Koreans "want their country to themselves in their lifetime," Langdon pointed out in a message from Seoul.[44] "The Koreans want their independence more than any one thing and want it now," Hodge asserted. "The general uncertainty and thwarted hopes of the Korean masses after the initial occupation are growing toward certainty and hopelessness that the allied powers were not sincere in their promise. By occidental standards Koreans are not ready for independence, but it grows daily more apparent that their capacity for self-government will not greatly improve under current conditions."[45]

Despite these strong warnings and growing Russian-American friction over Eastern Europe, Secretary Byrnes and the Soviets succeeded in reaching an accord at the Moscow Conference. Their agreement established a U.S.-Soviet Joint Commission for Korea. Commission members, representing the two military commanders, would deal with broad questions concerning an interim government for the country, economic integration of north and south, and questions concerning the future withdrawal of U.S. and Soviet troops. Korean politicians reacted explosively to the Moscow agreement with its provisions for continued Great Power rule, but in Washington there was optimism that the troublesome problems of Korea were finally on the way toward solution. As Byrnes might have said, had he lived in the twenty-first century, an "exit strategy" had been found at last.

CHAPTER NINE

"ON NO ACCOUNT BE DRAWN INTO INTERNAL TROUBLES"

THE NETHERLANDS WAS THE LAST OCCUPIED COUNTRY IN WESTERN Europe to be liberated from the Nazis. Two hundred eighty thousand Dutch civilians had died at the hands of the Germans in concentration camps or from starvation. Dutch industry was in ruins and the great ports and harbors mostly unusable. Dikes had been wrecked and thousands of acres of farmland were underwater. Dutch politicians, businessmen, and ordinary citizens counted upon their rich colonial holdings in the East Indies to help them repair their economy and recoup their losses. In the Netherlands Indies, the Japanese had offered the colonial authorities the same satellite arrangement they had made with the French in Indochina, but the Dutch had opted to fight and lost their colony in bloody if ineffective battles against the Imperial Army and Navy. With the collapse of Japan, the Dutch in the Netherlands, as well as the colonials in the Indies, who had suffered under more than three years of Japanese rule, looked forward to a speedy liberation by the Allies and a return to normal times.

Mountbatten was not looking forward to it. The Netherlands Indies ranked last on Southeast Asia Command's list of priorities, behind Indochina and Thailand, far behind Burma and Malaya. The Dutch had no military forces in East Asia, and involvement in Indonesia would require still more Commonwealth troops, almost entirely Indian troops, and the possibility of more casualties. British forces were not expected to arrive in the Indies before early October 1945.[1]

SEAC planners initially believed the major problem would be ensuring the good behavior of the Japanese armies in Java and Sumatra, who, like their comrades in Indochina, had never lost a battle, and recovering thousands of Dutch, British, and other prisoners of war and internees being held in scattered camps on Java. The Allies had never disagreed about the reestablishment of Dutch rule in the Indies. Nor did they expect that this would require much effort. The Dutch were widely considered, even by the Americans, to be the world's most scientific, progressive, and efficient colonizers.[2]

It was concern over the condition of the prisoners and internees that resulted in the first hints that life in the Indies was unlikely to return to the accustomed rhythms of the colonial past. In mid-September, Mountbatten instructed Rear Admiral W. R. Patterson to make contact with the Japanese and carry out a survey of conditions in the Batavia area. Aboard Patterson's flagship, HMS *Cumberland,* were SEAC's POW experts, Dr. Charles Olke van der Plas, a former governor of East Java representing the Netherlands government, and Lieutenant Colonel Kenneth Kennedy, the American military observer at Singapore. After only a few days in Batavia, Kennedy laconically reported, "The confident prediction of Mr. van der Plas that the Javanese would welcome back the Dutch was proved incorrect."[3] General Yamamoto Moichiro, the chief of the Japanese military administration, reported that the Indonesians had declared their independence three weeks before. The Indonesians, led by Sukarno and Mohammed Hatta, were determined to fight to defend their Republic. Though Admiral Patterson sternly reminded Yamamoto that the Japanese would continue to be held responsible by the Allies for maintaining law and order, he privately concluded that "Japanese control is undoubtedly deteriorating and the new Indonesian national flag is appearing in increasing numbers."[4] Colonel Kennedy reported, "Most of the natives in the NEI and especially in Java appear as strongly anti-Dutch as they are anti-Japanese. . . . The educated Indonesian seems to wish for nothing short of independence and have not been satisfied by Dutch promises. . . . The nationalists have a radio station which is disseminating anti-Dutch propaganda. . . . All over downtown Batavia, slogans, painted in English in three-foot letters for the benefit of the Allies, advocate independence."[5] Kennedy, who was probably with the OSS, met with nationalist leaders and learned that they were willing to cooperate with

Allied forces in disarming the Japanese and recovering POWs and internees, but they would not tolerate the return of Dutch troops or officials.[6] A recently released British prisoner of war, Colonel Laurens van der Post, told Admiral Patterson much the same thing.

Patterson's report cannot have made Mountbatten any more eager to become involved in the Indies, but he was under increasing pressure from London to move more quickly. Not only was the Netherlands government insistent, but the fate of the Allied prisoners of war in Indonesia, estimated to number at least seventy thousand, was becoming a growing concern. Like Wedemeyer, Mountbatten had dispatched small POW rescue missions by air into Japanese-occupied territory soon after the surrender. The rescuers were called RAPWI (Recovery of Allied Prisoner of War and Internee) teams; their mission was to try to contact the responsible Japanese authorities, alleviate conditions in the prison camps, and arrange the evacuation of the prisoners and internees. These teams were now reporting on the dire conditions in many of the camps where disease and malnutrition were common and the attitudes of the local Indonesian authorities and the Japanese uncertain.[7] Mountbatten decided to advance the date for the arrival of British forces in Java to the beginning of October.

To command the Allied forces in the Netherlands Indies, Mountbatten selected Lieutenant General Sir Philip Christison, one of the best generals of the Burma campaign. Christison was probably less than delighted with his new job. "Things look pretty rum in Java and Sumatra," Mountbatten's chief of staff, Lieutenant General F.A.M. "Boy" Browning, told him. "Are you prepared to carry the can for Dickie [Mountbatten]? If things go wrong he'll back you from the wings but full responsibility would rest with you. You are not being ordered to take this on but if you are prepared to carry the can for Dickie you will go as Allied Commander, NEI and command your old 15 Corps. . . . Think it over. Dickie is most anxious that you should take it on."[8] Christison agreed to "carry the can."

That the situation in the Indies was "rum" was clear enough. What the British were to do about it was less so. The British and Dutch had concluded a civil affairs agreement at the end of 1944 that provided that a Netherlands Indies Civil Administration (NICA) would follow closely behind SEAC fighting forces and assume responsibility for

Dutch territory recaptured from the Japanese.[9] Yet it was now obvious that this model would be quite inadequate to handle the actual conditions in Indonesia in September 1945. Mountbatten told Van der Pless that his command "would on no account be drawn into internal troubles on Java."[10] Mountbatten's views were endorsed by the secretary of state for war, Jack Dawson, who was on a visit to Singapore because of London's concern over Gracey's problems in Indochina. Dawson told Christison privately that he did not want to see a similar mess in Indonesia. "H.M. government are determined that nothing should be done to suggest that your troops are going to re-impose Dutch colonial rule. You must not take sides. Carry out your role. . . . The Dutch and any rebel factions must sort things out for themselves. You may though use your good offices to arrange meetings if this seems necessary."[11]

On September 28, a battalion of the Seaforth Highlanders, together with several hundred sailors and Royal Marines, came ashore at Batavia. Christison's mission was limited to occupying Batavia and the port of Surabaya in eastern Java, disarming and controlling the Japanese, and aiding Allied prisoners and internees. With his relatively small force of less than three divisions, there was no thought of his establishing control of all of the Indies. At a press conference in Batavia on the following day, Christison emphasized that his troops would occupy only a few key areas. He announced his intention to meet with nationalist leaders and expressed regret that the Netherlands government had not done the same.

Reports of Christison's press conference infuriated the Dutch, who lodged a strong protest, and even Mountbatten had to caution Christison that it was "certainly not [British government] policy to accuse the Dutch publicly of an intransigent attitude."[12] Dutch officials insisted that the Southeast Asia Command adhere to the letter of the Civil Affairs Agreement and maintain order until their own soldiers and police could arrive.

To the Dutch, some British, and even a few Americans, the Indonesian Republic seemed merely the creature of the Japanese. Sukarno and Hatta had toured the country making speeches and radio broadcasts on behalf of Japan. They had urged Indonesians to work with the Japanese and join Japanese-sponsored organizations. They had been to Tokyo, where they had received decorations from the emperor. Yet they were not simply part of a small band of traitors and collaborators. They were national leaders of long standing who had spent time in Dutch prisons and were connected to and acknowledged by all anti-Dutch and pro-independence factions, even those who had refused to cooperate with the Japanese.

During the war, the Japanese had encouraged Indonesians to form and join mass organizations, which they intended to use to indoctrinate them in the creed of hatred of the Dutch and the Allies along with support for Greater East Asia. The Indonesians had little trouble with the anti-Dutch part but could not help noticing the wide gap between the lofty goals of Greater East Asia and the everyday facts of Japanese rule. As in Malaya, the Japanese wrecked the economy, created food shortages and local famines, fueled runaway inflation, and imposed their own brand of casual cruelty and brutality on their rule in Indonesia. The ubiquitous Kempeitai arrested and tortured anyone thought to be a subversive or a spy. Indonesian women were drafted as "comfort women" to service army brothels, and perhaps as many as two hundred thousand men from Java were sent as "volunteer laborers" to all parts of the Japanese Empire. Only a fraction were still alive at the end of the war. The combination of Japanese mass mobilization and Japanese oppression helped to politicize millions of Indonesian farmers, craftsmen, small-business men, and clerks who before the war had had no political affiliations or interests.

As their defeats mounted, the Japanese increasingly turned to organizing young Indonesians to support their military efforts and perhaps serve as a first line of defense in the event of an invasion. In late 1943 the Japanese created a sort of Indonesian national militia called PETA, intended to fight as guerrillas against invading forces. Twenty-five thousand men served in the *heiho,* a Javanese auxiliary of the Japanese Army. They received the same training as regular army recruits but were not always armed. A larger number of men twenty-five to thirty-five years old served in the Keibodan (Vigilance Corps), which was intended to provide air raid wardens, firefighters, and auxiliary police. In the cities, youths aged fourteen to twenty-four were encouraged to join a Youth Corps.[13] Members of all of these organizations received a degree of military training and were indoctrinated in the Japanese military ideals of unconditional loyalty, "warrior spirit," and indifference to hardship or death.[14]

The Japanese, who had been reluctant to allow the nationalists any real political role, began to talk seriously about independence for Indonesia following their loss of the Marianas in June 1944. In September the government of Prime Minister Koiso Kuniaki promised independence for Indonesia at some unspecified future date. In March 1945, as Japanese forces in the Philippines began their final retreat to northern Luzon and U.S. Marines battled the last defenders of Iwo Jima, the Japanese military government in Indonesia invited nationalist politicians and intellectuals to participate in a Committee for Investigating Independence that would formulate plans and proposals for a future state. While the committee, under Sukarno's leadership, debated constitutions and boundaries, American heavy bombers began systematically to burn Japanese cities to the ground. As the Japanese Army prepared for an assault on the Home Islands, a Committee to Prepare for Independence in Indonesia succeeded the Committee to Investigate Independence. If Japan could not hold on to her Southeast Asian empire, she wished to leave behind an independent and strongly anti-Western state to confront the returning Dutch. On August 9, the day following the Soviet entry into the war and the day the second atomic bomb was dropped on Nagasaki, Sukarno and Hatta were flown to Indochina to meet with Field Marshal Terauchi, who received them with considerable ceremony at his headquarters in the city of Dalat in the central highlands of Vietnam. The marshal confirmed Japan's decision to grant independence to Indonesia. The official announcement was scheduled for the following month, on September 7.

Sukarno and Hatta returned to Batavia on August 14 excited and exultant, eager to share the great news with their colleagues. But there was even bigger news brought by Sutan Syahrir. A left-wing nationalist from Sumatra who had been educated in Dutch schools and universities, Syahrir had spent as much time in Dutch confinement as Hatta. Yet he detested Japanese imperialism and refused to be associated with Japanese-inspired proponents of Greater East Asia. He did, however, remain in close touch with Hatta, and both men saw themselves as continuing to work for independence, whether it be through cooperation with or opposition to the Japanese.[15] Through his secret shortwave radio, Syahrir already knew that Japan was about to surrender unconditionally, and he immediately informed Hatta. Both men went to Japanese Army and Navy headquarters to seek confirmation but were told to wait.[16] To Syahrir, however, the large number of drunken sailors at naval headquarters seemed confirmation enough.[17]

Others in Batavia with shortwave radios knew the news as well. While the politicians of the Preparatory Committee fretted over what to do, younger activists called for an immediate declaration of independence to unify the country and signal to all that the Indonesians were determined to take freedom for themselves. To emphasize their point, they kidnapped Hatta and Sukarno and brought them to a small town east of Batavia where the local PETA unit had already disarmed the small Japanese garrison and raised the red and white nationalist flag.[18] The young nationalist toughs appeared violent and threatening, but Sukarno and Hatta were much more worried about the Japanese and their reaction to any mass demonstrations or challenges to their authority. At this point Rear Admiral Maeda Tadashi, the head of Japanese intelligence in Java, who was close to the nationalists, intervened and sent word that if Sukarno and Hatta were released, the Japanese would not interfere with a declaration of independence.

That evening, Sukarno and Hatta returned to Batavia in a battered prewar sedan driven by Achmed Subardjo, a nationalist lawyer and friend of Sukarno. Arriving at Maeda's quarters, they immediately closeted themselves in the first floor dining room along with a handful of nationalist leaders. Other members of the Preparatory Committee and some of the would-be kidnappers paced up and down on the spacious lawn waiting for word from those within.[19]

At ten o'clock the following morning Sukarno and Hatta emerged and addressed a small waiting crowd. Sukarno looked tense and exhausted, Hatta serene and imperturbable. After an uncharacteristically short address, Sukarno read the hastily typed declaration:

> We the People of Indonesia hereby declare the independence of Indonesia.
>
> Matters concerning the transfer of power etc. will be carried out in a conscientious manner and as speedily as possible.

The proclamation was published in the Malay-language newspapers the following day, and Indonesians at the Japanese-controlled radio station risked their lives by broadcasting the news to the country.[20] Word of the declaration spread quickly in Java. "From cars, carts, windows, flag poles, roof tops and bicycles sprang up a forest of red and white flags."[21]

The Japanese refrained from any overt assistance to the Indonesian Republic, but nationalists had little difficulty in getting their hands on Japanese weapons.[22] The PETA and the *heiho* were officially disbanded, but many of their former members managed to retain some of their arms. One Japanese source estimated that the nationalists obtained, through theft, purchase, or donation, more than fifty thousand rifles, three thousand light and heavy machine guns, and a hundred million rounds of ammunition.[23] "The younger and more bellicose officials blossomed forth in pseudo military uniforms, Japanese swords, revolvers and even decorations," reported a rather unsympathetic British observer. "A travesty of the fascist salute with greeting, 'Merdeka'—freedom came into being. The mob in the kampongs arrayed itself in its thousands with Japanese swords and rifles."[24]

Despite ringing pronouncements, Sukarno remained cautious. He did not want to provoke the Japanese and was apprehensive about the expected arrival of the Allies. His younger supporters saw it differently. They were convinced that the new Republic would have to fight to survive. The most radical favored an immediate seizure of power from the Japanese. Others favored preparing for a more protracted conflict. They began to form what was in effect a Republican army, the Badan Keamanan Rakyat (People's Security Organization), usually known by its initials, BKR. Many of the leaders were former PETA officers.

While the founders of BKR wanted to organize those with military experience or advanced education, the radicals wanted to organize everybody else as well. They formed the leadership of the dozens of politicized youth groups called collectively *pemuda* in the kampongs, towns, and cities. They were allied with rural gang leaders and urban underworld bosses who saw their future as linked with the fortunes of the Republic. They operated a clandestine radio station calling on people to prepare themselves for the freedom struggle and encouraged the seizure of buildings and utilities in Batavia.[25]

Things came to a head on September 19 when radical leaders organized a mass rally to be held in the Lapangan Ikada, the former exercise ground and playing field of the Jakarta Athletics Association. An estimated two hundred thousand people attended the rally, which was quickly ringed by Japanese tanks and armored cars. Fearing a massacre, Sukarno hurried to the Lapangan Ikada and persuaded the Japanese commander to allow him to address the crowd. The commander, not eager for a confrontation that might lead to reprisals against Japanese civilians, agreed. Sukarno gave a brief address, then ordered the people to disperse. To the astonishment of many, they did so. Both the Japanese and the British were impressed with this demonstration of Sukarno's charisma and powerful oratory. He was "a whiz-bang demagogue," in the words of one American correspondent.[26]

Indonesians were not the only people in the Indies who considered themselves liberated. Dutch colonials who had spent the war confined in primitive, overcrowded, and disease-ridden internment camps presided over by draconian Japanese and Korean guards greeted the news of the Japanese surrender with relief and joy, but also with growing concern about why the Allied liberators had not arrived. Most of the Dutch took for granted that both the Japanese and the Indonesians would recognize that the Netherlands was to be counted among the countries that had won the war and that their old comfortable colonial lifestyle could soon be resumed.

Many Dutch civilians simply walked out of their prison camps and made their way back to their homes. "Some of them succeeded in re-opening their houses and employing their former servants, and shopkeepers were polite and helpful. Sometimes all was not quite so friendly, a brusque refusal would indicate a more independent frame of mind, a Dutch man with a punctured bicycle tire would be told to mend it himself, a former faithful house boy would scorn domestic service."[27] In the first weeks following the surrender there was relatively little violence against the Dutch but a large amount of theft, looting, and outright confiscation of Dutch and Japanese property. An American intelligence officer told of "a Dutch civilian who had been interned for three and a half years. [He] went over to inspect his former residence and found a Jap officer living in it using all the original furnishings. . . . The Jap officer agreed to move. The first night the Hollander slept in his house. In the morning he locked the house up and left for his duties in the city. Upon returning that night he found the house swarming with Indonesians busily engaged in carting off everything movable. One enterprising group had even backed up a truck. . . . As the truck drove out the gate a civilian policeman standing there gave the Indonesian salute and shouted 'Merdeka.' "[28]

Outside Jakarta there was considerably less restraint. Indonesians in rural areas took their revenge against small or isolated groups of Japanese and against local officials and police who were seen to have collaborated with them or were unpopular for other reasons. Chinese merchants, small landowners, and laborers were also a favorite target. Many Chinese thought of themselves as neutral in the confrontation between the nationalists and the Dutch. But neither the Sukarno government nor the *pemuda* fighters recognized neutrals. Chinese were frequently rounded up and put in some type of confinement. Others were assaulted, robbed, or murdered. In one district not far from Batavia, a local resident "recalled in those days that it was difficult to find a drink of fresh water . . . as most of the wells were stopped with the bodies of dead Chinese."[29]

As more Commonwealth troops continued to arrive, along with Dutch military and civilian officials, unease among the Indonesians grew. Rumors spread that the British were preparing to bring in Dutch troops and that the revolution was in grave danger. The atmosphere was scarcely improved by the actions of recently freed soldiers of the Royal Netherlands Indies Army (KNIL), who formed their own vigilante group called Battalion X. The battalion was composed mainly of Ambonese soldiers with Dutch and Eurasian officers. The Ambonese were Christian Indonesians from the island of Ambon, east of Sulawesi, and were viewed as loyal servants of Dutch colonialism. The trigger-happy soldiers of Battalion X behaved in much the same fashion as the freed French prisoners in Saigon.[30] On his first night in Batavia, General Christison and his aide-de-camp were sitting on the steps of their villa when they heard shooting. One round "smacked into the steps. We heard afterwards it was escaped prisoners of the KNIL settling old scores. . . ."[31] Christison had none of the sympathy for the colonialists possessed by Gracey. He knew that Indonesia was a powder keg and wanted every last Dutch soldier withdrawn from Java and deployed to less volatile areas in eastern Indonesia.[32]

It required no particular acts by the Dutch, however, to convince most *pemuda* that the Republic was in deadly peril from enemies like the Ambonese, Menadonese, and other ethnic groups associated with the Dutch, from the Chinese and British, from the large number of Eurasians, called "Indos," who spoke Dutch and wore European clothing, and from some members of the traditional aristocracy. The *pemuda,* ranging in age from youths in their late twenties to some as young as twelve, lived in a world of exaggerated hopes, patriotic and religious fervor, paranoia, and exhilaration. "They are smoldering with the repressions, privations and humiliations of the last three years," wrote Colonel van der Post. "They have also had a liberal education in the application of politics by violence. Human life seems a great deal cheaper to them than it did before 1941."[33] The *pemuda,* observed the Indonesian writer Idrus, "worshiped a new God in the form of bombs, submachine guns and mortars."[34]

By late September, the atmosphere in Java had turned from defiant gestures and vague menace to violence. People began to disappear, most never to return; others were attacked by roving gangs of youth and often hacked to pieces. Bodies floating in the canals and the Tjiliwoeng River near Batavia became a common sight. Europeans who had managed to reoccupy their old homes suddenly found themselves without water and electricity. Telephones ceased to work. *Pemuda* bands armed with knives and long bamboo spears patrolled the shops and markets enforcing a self-proclaimed boycott against selling to Dutch and Eurasians. Servants were threatened with dire consequences unless they left the employ of the Dutch. Some colonial families were gratified at the way their staffs loyally carried on under these difficult conditions, while others wondered whether their servants were secretly plotting to poison them.

Faced with the growing violence, many Dutch and Eurasians returned to the relative safety of their internment camps. They were joined by many Chinese, Ambonese, and other ethnic groups that feared that they would become victims of the *pemuda.* These "IFTUs" (Inhabitants Friendly to Us, in SEAC jargon) swelled the numbers in the camps far beyond what they had been during the war. Mountbatten estimated that there were about 147,000 IFTUs on Java.[35] Despite the efforts of a small number of SEAC POW teams and a few Red Cross workers, conditions in many camps remained little better than during the time before the surrender. Overcrowding, shortage of sanitary facilities, poor diet, and lack of medicines and medical care kept death rates high. One camp in central Java built around an old abandoned plantation housed four thousand women and children. "Before one crossed the threshold of this camp which was surrounded by a twenty-foot defensive wall, one was almost driven back by the appalling stench of the drains which flowed into open stagnant ditches. . . . Many of the sick were so ill and weak that they were unable to feed themselves even when food was left beside them. There were four hundred women and children in one barrack block, the size of a dormitory in the services which would normally accommodate about forty men. . . . Outside the cells harassed mothers, all of whom had aged at least ten years during the occupation, had got little fires going on which they heated water and whatever sparse Red Cross luxuries could be distributed. . . . Across the courtyard was stretched an indescribable array of old and tattered garments and filthy louse-ridden bedding put out to catch the fitful sunshine between rainstorms."[36]

As unrest increased, Christison made it clear to the Japanese that they would still be responsible for law and order in areas under their control, including most of the camps in the interior of Java. RAPWI teams did find the Japanese very cooperative in providing for the security of the camps. The Japanese furnished food and medical supplies transported to the camps in their own trucks and on one occasion made aircraft and pilots available to the POW teams. However, many Japanese commanders were reluctant to take any action to curb the activities of the Indonesians, fearing reprisals against Japanese citizens. They also believed that the Indonesians and not the Japanese should be responsible for the maintenance of law and order.[37] The immediate issue was the repeated demands by the nationalists that the Japanese turn over arms and ammunition. The RAPWI teams strongly objected to such actions and demanded that the Japanese continue to protect the camps. Despite British protests, the Japanese Sixteenth Army advised its commander in central Java, Major General Nakamura Junji, that arms could be transferred or "loaned" to nationalist police, army, and militia forces.[38] Nakamura instructed his troops accordingly.

One Japanese officer who refused to follow Nakamura's guidelines was Major Kido Shinishiro, who commanded a battalion of some two hundred men usually referred to as the Kido Butai. Kido refused to surrender his arms, and when it appeared probable that the Indonesians might attempt to obtain them by force, he ordered his troops, along with like-minded soldiers from other units, to take control of the town of Semarang in central Java. The Japanese launched their attack early on the morning of October 15. Most writers have explained Kido's actions as a response to requests from RAPWI to help protect the camps and as a result of his sense of military honor and obligation toward the prisoners and internees menaced by the Indonesians. However, in a 1986 interview with Indonesian scholar Han Bing Siong, Kido declared that his refusal to surrender his arms was due to the fact that Kido Butai's rifles bore the imperial chrysanthemum emblem, indicating that they were in fact the property of the emperor. Captured Dutch arms might be transferred to the Indonesians, but under the Japanese military code, imperial arms could never be given up or lost.[39]

Whatever his motives, Kido's actions infuriated *pemuda* elements in Semarang, who imprisoned about eighty Japanese Army workers with their families in a tiny cell without food, water, or facilities to relieve themselves. After the Japanese had spent one day in the stifling heat of the cell, ten *pemuda* hotheads dragged them out and shot all those still alive.[40] One hundred thirty other Japanese confined at the Bulu prison were savagely butchered and mutilated. "Some corpses were hanging from the roof and from the windows, others had been pierced through and through with bamboo spears. . . . Some had tried to write last messages in blood on the walls."[41]

Japanese troops had been attempting in a rather desultory way to retake control of Semarang from the nationalists, but their mood abruptly changed after they captured the prison and viewed the scenes of horror inside. "Every Japanese soldier in Semarang went fighting mad," reported a British RAPWI officer at Semarang. "They swept through the town regardless of danger or their own losses like one of the Mongolian hordes of Genghis Khan or Tamerlane."[42] Truckloads of Indonesian prisoners with their hands tied behind their backs were driven into the countryside and never seen again. As the Japanese soldiers captured more weapons from the *pemuda* they armed Japanese civilians, who joined in the killing.

Altogether at least two thousand Indonesians were killed by the vengeful Japanese. They were still at it on October 19 when a battalion of Gurkhas from the 23rd Indian Division landed at Semarang. Neither the Gurkhas nor the Japanese troops were aware of the others' presence until some of their forces met near the center of the town. Both sides opened fire, but the Japanese quickly realized their mistake, apologized, and offered to cooperate with the Gurkhas as they were already cooperating with the RAPWI. The British would need all the help they could get, for the bloodiest phase of the revolution was just beginning.

CHAPTER TEN

"BUILT UPON UNKNOWN GRAVES"

Revolutionary fervor and paranoia ran most strongly in Surabaya. Residents of the city knew that SEAC forces had landed at Jakarta bringing with them small numbers of Dutch military and colonial officials. They also knew that Australian forces in Timor and Kalimantan had brought with them a sort of interim colonial government, the Netherlands Indies Civil Administration (NICA). It was widely believed throughout Java that the Dutch planned to reestablish their authority in the rest of Indonesia as well. In fact, "NICA" became a kind of shorthand among nationalists to signify all types of plots, plans, and organizations aimed to reestablish colonialism. Those suspected of sympathy with the Dutch or of general disloyalty were often labeled "NICA spies." The arrival of Allied RAPWI teams, which included Dutch officers, fed the growing unease.

On September 19, 1945, a group of young Dutch former internees and Eurasians gathered outside the Oranje Hotel, where the RAPWI had established its headquarters. Some of these youths raised a Dutch flag on the building's flagstaff. In recent days, Dutch and Eurasian gangs had torn down Indonesian patriotic posters and ridiculed the Indonesian flag. This gesture was seen by many as the final outrage. A large crowd of Indonesians quickly gathered outside the hotel. Stones were thrown and several shots were fired. A few Indonesian students climbed to the hotel roof and managed to rip the horizontal blue stripe from the Dutch flag, converting it into the red and white flag of the Republic.[1]

Having won a symbolic victory at the Oranje Hotel, the nationalists now turned to more practical actions to secure their control of the city. The local Japanese commander, Vice Admiral Shibata Yaichiro, had long sympathized with the nationalists and was also concerned to prevent bloodshed against Japanese civilians.[2] Through a combination of negotiation, intimidation, and mob action, the Indonesian nationalists collected large quantities of Japanese arms and took over most governing functions in the city.[3] By the first days of October, nationalist control appeared complete, although Surabaya's new "government" was actually an unstable coalition of educated notables, impatient *pemuda* youth-group factions, and politicized vigilante groups drawn from the city's Indonesian neighborhoods.

Tensions increased as news spread that an Allied landing was set for October 14. "People were shocked and felt afraid as if they were anticipating some great danger," recalled an Indonesian writer. "Everywhere one could sense uneasiness: in the people, in the cars roaring past along the street, in the printing press, and in the dogs. The dogs barked themselves hoarse until their voices were gone . . . no one remembered to feed them. Everywhere people were saying the same thing. . . . Like a badly trained choir they shouted, 'We won't be treated like the people in Djakarta! We'll fight! We've got revolvers and knives.' "[4]

Fear and suspicion of Dutch and Eurasians in the city as probable NICA spies or operatives reached new heights. Sukarno's government in Jakarta ordered the Republican authorities in Surabaya to allow the Allies to land and to maintain "iron discipline" to prevent violence. This was an almost fanciful directive to a shaky municipal government whose police and militia were outnumbered by, and no better armed than, the thousands of *pemuda* extremists determined to defend the city to the death.[5]

In mid-October, members of the numerous and particularly militant Youth of the Republic (PRI) began a wholesale roundup of Dutch and Eurasians in the city. Many were taken from their homes at gunpoint and loaded onto trucks that hauled them to local prisons. Some were killed by infuriated mobs who followed the trucks shouting "Kill the NICA dogs!" and "Filthy Dutch!"[6] The PRI had established its headquarters at the Simpang Club, in prewar days an exclusive "whites only" colonial gathering place. It was here that several hundred Dutch and Eurasians and a few Indonesians were brought for questioning. The detainees were ordered to strip to their underwear. Many were kicked or beaten and had "NICA" painted on their backs. Then they were subject to questioning by a tribunal of PRI leaders. These hearings apparently became progressively more violent with some prisoners being tortured or beheaded.

Neighborhood mobs attacked Ambonese and Madurese who were widely believed to be agents of the colonialists.[7] In the midst of the rising hysteria a newly established radio station, "Radio Rebellion," headed by the young journalist and *pemuda* activist Sutomo, urged its listeners in several languages to prepare for a struggle to the death against all Europeans. That was the atmosphere in Surabaya when the first Allied troops came ashore on October 25.

Two battalions of the 49th Brigade of the 23rd Indian Division began debarking at the former Dutch naval base early in the morning while RAF P-47 fighters roared overhead. To one British officer, Surabaya "looked dilapidated and tawdry. Its paint was blistered and faded. Its streets dirty and unswept." Groups of *pemuda* in their various uniforms stood guard at improvised roadblocks throughout the city. Most of the roadblocks "were covered by partly hidden machine guns."[8] Perhaps inspired by American Westerns, the youths "wore revolvers and knives at their hips. The revolvers were for shooting rustlers, and the knives were for . . . decoration."[9]

Having ignored a signal from the Indonesians to wait for clearance from the local military commander, Moestopo, before landing, the British then commandeered a building at the naval base for their brigade headquarters and instructed the Indonesian military to vacate the premises and haul down their national flag. After this start, the British found nationalist leaders in a rather unreceptive frame of mind when they attempted to open talks. The regional governor, R.M.T.A. Soerjo, repeatedly refused to accompany a delegation of brigade officers to their ship for a conference. When the officers finally stood and silently left the room, they impressed the Indonesians with their boorishness and lack of decorum.[10]

The following day the brigade commander, Brigadier A.W.S. Mallaby, sent his deputy Colonel L.H.O. Pugh to call on Moestopo. Arriving at Moestopo's headquarters, Pugh and another officer were "shown into a large room brilliantly lit with unshaded electric lights. From behind a desk littered with the unfinished remains of a bowl of rice, a Japanese brandy bottle and a disordered stack of papers rose a slight, nervously smiling figure. This was Dr. Moestopo, the one-time dentist and now the most powerful man in East Java."[11]

Moestopo may have been educated as a dentist, but he was also a former company commander in the Japanese-trained PETA militia. He had graduated at the top of his class at officer candidate school and been marked for early promotion.[12] He was a fierce nationalist, but he understood the military odds. Moestopo and Soerjo agreed to a modus vivendi. The British would be responsible for disarming the Japanese and evacuating them through Surabaya and would "assist in the maintenance of peace and order," but the nationalist army and police would be responsible for controlling the other armed elements in the city.[13]

This understanding quickly collapsed one day later when British planes dropped leaflets prepared in Jakarta some weeks before. They explained the aims of the SEAC operations in Java and called upon the population to cooperate with the occupation forces. One paragraph declared that only Allied troops could bear arms and any other individuals bearing arms were liable to be shot. Indonesians were given forty-eight hours to turn in their weapons.

Hundreds of these leaflets had been dropped all over Java in the previous few days without causing any great reaction by the local people, many of whom most likely ignored them. Their reception in Surabaya, however, was explosive. The British were seen as having violated their recent assurances and to be intent on undermining the authority of the Republic. Although he was surprised and unhappy with the unexpected appearance of the leaflets, Mallaby saw no option other than to enforce their demands, although he was able to get the deadline extended.

Throughout the twenty-seventh, columns of Indian troops moved slowly through the city posting copies of the leaflets for all to see. In all neighborhoods and among all political factions there was anger and consternation. Moestopo, meeting with Pugh, "was frantic with emotion. . . . He had neither assimilated the terms of the proclamation nor understood the relaxations which could be made in their application by Brigadier Mallaby. . . . Faced with the alternatives of capitulation or war, surrounded by a hot-headed military clique, his honor and reputation impugned, it was obvious that he would fight."[14]

The following day, Moestopo broadcast a warning that independence was in danger and that the Indonesians would have to fight. But the people of Surabaya needed no persuading. In the late afternoon of the twenty-eighth they attacked the troops of the 49th Brigade everywhere in the city. The British claimed that the Indonesian forces numbered some twenty thousand veterans of PETA and other Japanese-trained militia organizations with about one hundred forty thousand untrained but well armed and very determined youth groups, gangs, and ordinary citizens. The Indonesian military, now called the TKR, was not only well supplied with individual arms and ammunition but had inherited numerous mortars, artillery pieces, antiaircraft guns, tanks, and armored cars from the Japanese.[15] The 49th Brigade had about four thousand men, many scattered in platoon- and company-size units throughout the city. All of these units were soon surrounded. Isolated officers or small parties simply disappeared.

A convoy of twenty trucks that had been carrying women and children internees to a hospital in the city for treatment was halted at a TKR roadblock. The TKR intended to block the entry of any more Europeans into the city and to take them into custody; however, the convoy was quickly surrounded by a large, angry mob, which opened fire on the four hundred civilians in the trucks.

There were only about sixty troops with the convoy, including the drivers, but they were veterans of the Burma campaign and had been in bad places before. The Indians managed to get their civilian passengers into some nearby houses along the side of the road and a stubborn firefight ensued until, after about two and a half hours, the Indian troops began to run short of ammunition. It was now dark and most of the trucks were on fire, but three plus the convoy sergeant's jeep were still intact. The men ran to the jeep and barreled their way through the roadblock, followed by the three trucks loaded with most of the surviving civilians. About three-quarters of the women and children in the convoy survived.[16]

Elsewhere in Surabaya there were equally bloody struggles. The scattered units of the brigade found themselves surrounded by vastly larger and sometimes better armed Indonesians. In one part of the city a Rajput soldier charged two tanks with grenades, all of which missed or bounced off. Undaunted, he climbed onto each tank and dropped a grenade through the firing aperture. Colonel Pugh was visiting the

Darmo Hospital when the attacks came. He quickly organized the medical personnel, stretcher bearers, and ambulance drivers into an improvised infantry unit that repelled all enemy attacks.[17]

October 29 dawned in Surabaya, another brilliant sunny day. Amid the bright red, blue, and white flowers and stately white colonial homes lay groups of bodies. Shell casings were scattered over the ground, smoke rose from burned-out vehicles, and the air smelled of cordite and corpses.

In Jakarta, General Christison summoned Sukarno and arranged for him to be flown to Surabaya with Major General D. C. Hawthorne, the Allied commander for east Java. Sukarno and Hatta reached the embattled city late in the morning. An Indian battalion was precariously holding the airport. Sukarno and Mallaby quickly agreed on a cease-fire, but sporadic fighting continued through the night.[18]

The following morning, Hawthorne went with Sukarno and Hatta to meet with local Republican officials and commanders at a government building. The young activist journalist Sutomo was also present. General Christison gave an account of the meeting in his memoirs: "On one side were Hawthorne, Sukarno and some elderly and moderate Indonesians, on the other side a collection of young hotheads, the dedicated revolutionaries who had already tasted blood."[19] The Indonesians were incensed over the cease-fire order and believed reports that the British were bringing in Dutchmen with their faces blackened, disguised as Indian soldiers.[20]

> Sukarno agreed to dividing Surabaya into three zones. The British would occupy the airfield dock areas and RAWPI camps south of the city while the city itself would remain in Indonesian hands. This brought Sutomo angrily to his feet. He was a veritable firebrand with fanatical protruding eyes which General Hawthorne told me rolled incessantly. He claimed that by this agreement his forces would be enclosed by ours. Finally General Hawthorne told him to shut up and that Mountbatten was perfectly willing to send his fleet and air force to reduce Surabaya to ruins unless he fell into line and agreed to the conference decisions.[21]

Hawthorne's statement may have been largely bluff at the time, but it became reality over the next few days after Brigadier Mallaby was murdered by an Indonesian while attempting to calm a new outbreak of fighting on the thirty-first. Each side blamed the other, the British incensed by what they saw as Indonesian treachery, the Indonesians convinced that Mallaby had been killed by gunfire from his own troops.[22]

Wing Commander Alan Groom, a former British prisoner of war who spoke Malay and had many Indonesian friends and acquaintances from the days when they had all enjoyed the Japanese emperor's hospitality in various prison compounds, went to meet with Governor Soerjo. Groom announced that the British had no thought of surrender and emphasized the danger that nationalist actions might soon bring destruction on the city. He naturally omitted to mention that the British and Indians were almost out of ammunition. Reluctantly, Soerjo finally agreed that the British could carry out their plans to withdraw and concentrate their troops in the dock and airport areas, where they were already beginning to receive reinforcements, including a squadron of tanks. Even more powerful help was on the way. The 5th Indian Division, from Malaya, which had earlier been ordered by Mountbatten to Indonesia, arrived off Surabaya on November 1 accompanied by a squadron of Royal Navy warships.

Indonesians in Surabaya felt elated. The British had been paid back for their treachery and secret collaboration with the Dutch. Rumors circulated that the British had surrendered and were only being "allowed to stay in the port area."[23] "Their succession of victories left the people even more intoxicated. . . . They fell in love with carbines and revolvers as if they were beautiful girls: they caressed them, kissed them and sold them at very high prices. Their faces looked very happy and proud. Their confidence in their own strength radiated from their rifle butts and from their mouths. People were in wonderful spirits, just like the Romans the day before Vesuvius erupted. Their mouths stank of tobacco and hot air."[24]

By the seventh of November most of the 5th Division was ashore together with their armor. "These tanks rolled down from the ships like the Angel of Death himself descending from the sky."[25] Two cruisers and three destroyers were on station offshore. In leaflets dropped from planes, General Christison demanded the immediate internment of all government leaders and the surrender of all unauthorized weapons. "I think it just a possibility . . . that if Sukarno or some accredited leader would encourage them to pack it in that it is an outside chance that they might do so,"[26] Major General Robert Mansergh, commander of the 5th Division, told General Christison.

The Indonesian did not pack it in, and on November 10 the British attack began. The battle that ensued equaled in intensity many of the urban battles of World War II. It far surpassed the extent of the land fighting between the Japanese and Dutch that had decided the fate of the Indies. On both sides were peoples whose warrior traditions stretched back centuries. Both sides were well armed with small arms, mortars, and machine guns. Both had tanks and artillery. Indonesians defended every street. The British responded to the stubborn defense with air strikes and naval gunfire.

More than five hundred bombs were dropped on the city during the first three days of the battle.[27] As they slowly withdrew, the nationalist fighters often set fire to the neighborhoods they were leaving. "The city was like Rebecca's house [in Daphne du Maurier's novel] which had been burnt down and where a terrible tragedy had occurred," recalled one eyewitness. "Smoke came off the scorched beams like the smoke of Zipper cigarettes. . . . The air stank of cordite and human and animal carcasses; the hospital stank of ether and rose water. Now and then an explosion could be heard followed by black smoke billowing up into the sky. The air was full of dirty black dust."[28] Thousands of refugees clogged the roads leading away from the burning city and were sometimes attacked by Allied aircraft. A British officer who arrived in Surabaya midway through the battle found "conditions reminiscent of the Burma campaign, with heat, flies, dirt, mosquitoes and foully chlorinated water . . . everywhere there is the sickening sweet smell of human bodies."[29] Naval telegrapher Ted Bates, who came ashore with a party of Royal Marines at the height of the battle, was billeted in a ruined Dutch house. "During the day one could hear the sounds of fighting in the city's suburbs. . . . At night these sounds seemed to increase in volume and I recall that there was a night bird there that sounded for all the world like a machine gun. The first time I heard it I jumped out of bed quite certain that the gun was very close to the house. This gave some of the other lads quite a laugh as they'd all heard the bird before."[30]

It was almost three weeks before the 5th Division could report that "the lawless Indonesian element has been cleared from the city."[31] Even then, "shelling, mortaring and sniping" continued.[32] Thanks to their superior firepower and slow, systematic advance, Allied casualties had been light, fewer than eighty killed and wounded. Indonesian casualties were estimated by the British at more than seven thousand. Around 90 percent of the city's population were now refugees.[33]

Surabaya was a tactical defeat for the Indonesians and may have been a strategic setback as well, because many of the most capable weapons acquired from the Japanese, which might later have been better employed against the returning Dutch, were expended in the battle. Politically and psychologically, however, none of that mattered. Surabaya showed to the world that Indonesians were determined to fight for their freedom and that they were pretty good at it. "Native peoples, despite the inferiority of their weapons, are not overawed by those of modern warfare," concluded an American military observer, "for they have found that when in sufficient numbers they can maintain themselves against the British in local fighting. . . . In addition the lack of organization and of any self-defined strategy in the guerrilla fighting of the Javanese and Annamese [Vietnamese] serves only to preclude the possibility of effective strikes at any concentrated points and to deprive British planes, artillery, and tanks of any worthwhile targets."[34] Stories of the battle filled the international press. After Indonesian antiaircraft guns shot down a British plane, some British correspondents breathlessly declared that the flak over Surabaya was as bad as that over Germany. In Indonesia, November 10 is commemorated as Heroes' Day, and the battle is remembered as a symbol of sacrifice, dedication, and unity in the cause of independence.

News of the fighting in Surabaya soon enflamed the nationalists all over central and east Java. Most immediately in danger were the large prisoner of war camps in central Java. These still housed thousands of former POWs and internees whose numbers had been swollen by an influx of Eurasians and other ethnic minorities fleeing the violence of the revolution. These IFTUs were sometimes hard to distinguish from genuine internees, and in any case British commanders were reluctant to leave them to the mercies of the nationalists.[35] By that point the Allies and the Indonesian government were largely talking past each other. The Allies were preoccupied with the fate of the Europeans and others living in desperate conditions in the camps. The Indonesians were obsessed with the danger of a Dutch reconquest and saw the small numbers of Dutch civil affairs officers, commandos, and medical personnel who often accompanied the RAPWI elements as a significant threat.

The camps in central Java were in three main areas: around Semarang on the Java Sea, Ambarawa in the mountains in the center of Java, and farther south at Megaleng, not far from Jogjakarta. These camps were guarded by small detachments of Allied troops, and their road communications to the other camps and to the sea ran through areas controlled by the nationalists or by local thugs and crazies. At Megaleng, Japanese general Nakamura had withdrawn his troops from the town, leaving behind a mountain of weapons and supplies for the Indonesians.[36]

A crisis soon developed at the beginning of November when fighting broke out in the town, which was garrisoned by part of a battalion of Gurkhas. One company was soon cut off, and their situation was judged desperate enough that Christison approved the first use of an air strike in the postwar conflict in Java. At nightfall the Gurkhas were still surrounded, but the Indonesians were not eager for a showdown with these formidable fighters. During the night a small relief force with antitank guns reached the surrounded company. Next day the Gurkhas received an airdrop of supplies, and Sukarno again flew in to face down the fanatics and hammer out a shaky cease-fire.[37] This gave the Allies time to evacuate the inhabitants of the camps to the questionable safety of Ambarawa and Semarang.

General Nakamura was sent to Tokyo to stand trial as a war criminal, but other Japanese fought alongside the Allies in the battles that developed around Semarang in mid-November. In the town, Indonesians were carrying on a strict boycott of food and other sales to Europeans, and pamphlets were being surreptitiously distributed to the Japanese urging them to join the nationalists. On the evening of November 17, three Indian officers were fatally shot by a TKR officer as they were escorting some local Dutch.[38] The British commander in Semarang, Brigadier Bethel, anticipating a full-scale attack by the Indonesians, took the governor, Wongsonogoro, into custody and began a sweep "to clear unruly elements from the northern part of the town."[39]

The "unruly elements" proved formidable. The British had only one battalion and part of a tank regiment. After only a day of fighting, Bethel's battalion was cut in two by the force of the Indonesian counterattack and his own headquarters surrounded. Bethel called on Major Kido's battalion, which had already fought the nationalists in October following the Bulu Prison massacre. The Kido Butai entered the battle and fought "magnificently" according to Brigadier Bethel, and Kido was actually recommended for a Distinguished Service Order.[40]

Six Thunderbolt fighter planes flew in to bomb and strafe the Indonesians. According to an American military observer, the Thunderbolts had difficulty identifying their targets, and some British and Japanese were also strafed. Nevertheless the air strikes were "a great psychological weapon against the Indonesians of whom thousands took to the fields at its inception."[41] On November 21 an additional battalion of Indian troops was flown into Semarang, and more troops arrived from Surabaya over the next few days.

South of Semarang, the camps at Ambarawa, their population swollen to more than ten thousand, were under siege by the nationalists. The Gurkhas in the town, supported by air strikes, managed to protect the larger camps, but people in smaller or more isolated places often fell into the hands of the Indonesians. Some of these isolated groups of internees, mostly women, children, and the aged, were tortured, dismembered, or murdered by the Indonesian extremists. At a convent near Ambarawa, the Indonesians found thirty internees, whom they lined up against a wall and used as targets for hand grenades.[42]

By the end of November, a relief column of two battalions, trucks, artillery, and tanks had reached Ambarawa from Semarang and the evacuation of the camps began. Long columns of trucks on the road from Ambarawa became the target of snipers and sometimes came under artillery fire as they stopped to clear roadblocks or to search for mines. Indian and Gurkha troops patrolled the roads and guarded the flanks of the convoys. By December 14, the camps at Ambarawa had been evacuated, and the Allied troops returned to Semarang, where sporadic fighting continued. During December 1945, when Semarang was described "as fairly quiet," the British cruiser HMS *Norfolk* still fired 140 high explosive rounds in support of operations in the city during one six-day period.[43]

The successful evacuation of Ambarawa still left close to eighty thousand former prisoners and internees living in camps scattered through Java. Another hundred thousand were living outside the camps, and thousands of others had disappeared or never been accounted for.[44] The Indonesian government made some attempt to protect the prisoners in the early weeks after the Japanese surrender, but as fighting with the British escalated, control of local governments passed into the hands of extremists, who ignored admonitions from Sukarno's government. The struggle against the British had long since attracted not only youthful patriots but thugs, criminals, young men attracted by violence, older men with old grudges, and freelance sadists of all backgrounds like the "prominent citizen and worker for the Cause" who lived in a town not far from Batavia. He "was a small dapper little man in white jacket and black striped trousers. He was most devout in his prayers every morning. He had to his credit six wives and over seventy murders and his favorite pastime was torture."[45]

As 1945 drew to a close, Dutch internees, Eurasians, Chinese, and other ethnic minorities who found themselves outside the camps remained in the most precarious situations. "All the blood spilt in Java since the Japanese occupation will never be known," wrote one British officer. "In remote districts terrible crimes were committed that will never be disclosed—burnings, killings, torturings, enslavings. History in Java, like history in any other part of the world, is built upon unknown graves."[46]

"British interests [in Indonesia]," observed an Australian diplomat, "are first to get home and second to keep good friends with Holland."[47] At the end of 1945, the British appeared nowhere near to achieving either goal. "The general disorder, the shootings, the street battles, the burning bitterness between Dutch and Indonesians are played down in official reports," concluded one observer. "During the last three days firing in Batavia has been almost continuous and officers and other ranks have been advised or ordered not to venture out after dark."[48] American OSS observers advised Washington that "the Nationalist cause has gained in prestige and power during recent weeks and its strength today is greater than ever. . . . It is probable that only with full scale support of British military forces will the Dutch be able to reoccupy the whole of the Netherlands East Indies by force."[49]

There was no possibility of SEAC's receiving the reinforcements necessary to impose military rule on Java. One British general estimated that complete military occupation of Java would require at least twelve divisions.[50] The arrival of Dutch troops, in Mountbatten's view, could only make the situation worse. There was widespread dismay at the continuing casualties to British and Indian troops. Questions were raised in Parliament. The government of India and Indian politicians expressed increasing unhappiness. Indian National Congress leader Jawaharlal Nehru was reportedly so concerned with the situation that he considered personally visiting the embattled nationalists on Java.[51] The Soviets brought up the question of Indonesia in the United Nations and called upon the Security Council to intervene.

British generals speculated and worried about the state of morale among Commonwealth soldiers, who had recently fought through one four-year war and now were committed to a new conflict after peace had been declared. "The great majority of British and Indian troops in Java had no idea why they were there," recalled one British officer.[52] Some doubtless adopted the view of one soldier of the West Yorkshire Regiment: "There was a job to be done and we got on with it."[53] Many others were impatient to return home and resentful of any delays. "The general feeling of frustration and bitterness out here is almost beyond belief," wrote Captain Sissons. "Several men have written to their MPs. . . . The MPs reply politely. As for Churchill's brilliant idea of compensating men with cash for staying out east too long—if the money were offered it would probably be thrown on the floor."[54] Admiral Mountbatten observed that "both by the Press and by letters from home the British troops are being made to believe that the imposition of Dutch authority by force of British arms is a wrong cause. They do not like fighting for this though they are quite ready to fight to secure the safety of European and Eurasian women and children."[55]

Indian troops, some of whom were Muslims, also sympathized with the Indonesians and were aware that their fight for independence in Java and Sumatra was not unlike the freedom struggle in India. In many cases, however, this general feeling of support was more than counterbalanced by anger at atrocities and murders committed by Indonesian extremists. "The Supreme Allied Commander refused to countenance retaliation, reprisal or revenge," wrote a British officer. "Indian soldiers had been kidnapped and held prisoner, some of them killed and the remainder finally released. They would return to their comrades and tell of their own hardships and the torture and death of their friends. . . . Comradeship among many Indian soldiers amounts sometimes to devotion, and for a man to remain inactive after his comrades had been killed beside him was an offence to his pride, his love and his sense of duty."[56] In December 1945, when a transport aircraft crashed near the town of Bekasi, not far from Batavia, the survivors were tortured and killed by Indonesian terrorists, "the Black Buffaloes." A column of Indian troops entered the town, killed all the Black Buffaloes they could find, and then burned the town of ten thousand people to the ground.

Whatever their attitude toward the Indonesians, the British and Indian soldiers were united in their dislike of the Dutch. "The British state that the Dutch are completely worthless with regard to the formulation of a policy and have shown themselves to be extreme cowards," wrote an OSS officer. "This latter observation extends from division staff officers down to enlisted men."[57] A British report on troop morale concluded, "There is a feeling that we are doing a job that should be done by the Dutch; the morale and behavior of Dutch troops, who are said to be 'trigger happy,' does not help."[58] Christison considered that "the majority of these unfortunate Dutch people are temporarily mentally sick."[59]

Nor did the Dutch enjoy a very good press. There were at least sixty-five accredited correspondents in Batavia. Described by one British diplomat as "a bunch of unreliable drunks," they nevertheless managed to send out a steady stream of reports about the bloody fighting on Java, the continued presence of armed Japanese troops, and the stubborn refusal of the Dutch to accommodate Indonesian aspirations for independence.[60] Stories of Dutch and Japanese troops riding around in American Lend-Lease trucks and tanks that still bore their U.S. markings incensed American readers and prompted a formal protest from the State Department.[61]

In the midst of this apparent stalemate, Mountbatten and Christison received some welcome news. The Republican government had been reconstituted. Sukarno remained as president but Sutan Syahrir became prime minister and minister of foreign affairs, while his close ally Amir Sjarifuddin became minister of defense and information. Syahrir and Sjarifuddin were Western-educated nationalists who had refused all collaboration with the Japanese during the war. Syahrir had retired to his country bungalow, claiming that he was suffering from tuberculosis, while Sjarifuddin had actually been imprisoned by the Japanese.[62] Shortly before forming his new government in November 1945, Syahrir had published a pamphlet highly critical of those politicians who had "kowtowed" to the Japanese and called for a "wholly democratic constitution" free of fascist influence.[63] A British officer described the new prime minister as "a very small man, not more, I should think, than four and a half feet tall with an awkward schoolboyish manner and a self-conscious smile. However he is a man of courage, integrity and tenacity."[64]

The appointment of Syahrir as prime minister resulted almost immediately in a more positive approach to the problems associated with the evacuation of the remaining prisoners and internees. Christison and the leaders of the Republic began talks on a plan to evacuate the remaining Dutch and Allied civilians from the interior of Java to British-controlled areas. Units of the TKR escorted the evacuation convoys that got under way in January when General Oerip Soemohardjo, a former TKR chief of staff, personally accompanied a trainload of evacuees to Jakarta.[65]

Syahrir's assumption of leadership of the Republic undermined the persistent Dutch position that it could not negotiate with a government headed by former collaborators. Syahrir's European education and his familiarity with the Western language of political rights and social change appealed to American and European journalists. To the British, for the first time, there seemed to be a real possibility that some sort of negotiated agreement between the Republic and the Dutch would allow them to escape the Indonesia quagmire. This possibility was especially welcome because by late 1945, revolutionary violence was spreading from Java to Sumatra.

CHAPTER ELEVEN

THE CHILDREN OF ANDALAS

Sumatra is the official name. . . . The island is also known as Andalas. To many of us born on the island, Andalas has a significant political meaning. It is intimately associated with our struggle against colonial rule when we proudly showed our fiery nationalism by calling ourselves Children of Andalas.

—ADAM MALIK,
In the Service of the Republic
(Singapore: Gunung Agung, 1980), p. 25

SIXTEEN HUNDRED MILES LONG, THE LARGEST ISLAND IN INDONESIA, Sumatra in 1945 was a patchwork of peoples and ethnic groups including Bataks, Acenese, Javanese, Malays, and Chinese. Aceh, the northern third of Sumatra, had been under colonial rule less than thirty years when the Japanese took the Netherlands Indies. Prior to that, the Dutch had waged a protracted and bloody war for over a quarter century to add Aceh to their empire. The Acenese, the most fearsome fighters in a land that produced many fierce warriors, fought mainly with traditional weapons against the modern Dutch colonial soldiers. The Acenese, wrote one colonial governor, possessed "a fanatical love of freedom reinforced by a powerful sense of race . . . and hatred for the infidel ruler."[1] As late as 1926, the Dutch were faced with a serious guerrilla war in one section of Aceh, and the guerrilla leaders were still at large in 1941.

Despite this history of resistance, the situation in Sumatra at the end of the Second World War seemed initially to bear out all the confident Dutch assertions about the ease with which the Indies would return to the good old days. News of the Japanese surrender did not reach most of the people of Sumatra until about August 25. By that time, Dutch commandos had flown in with the first SEAC POW teams and established themselves in the principal city of Medan, where they organized a police force of former Ambonese and Manadonese soldiers of the Netherlands colonial army. The leaders of the Nationalists in Sumatra, Teuku Mohammed Hasan, appointed by Sukarno as governor, and his lieutenant governor, Dr. Mohammed Amir, were not exactly fire-breathers. One was a distinguished lawyer, the other a psychiatrist, both educated in Europe and with strong ties to the traditional aristocracy.

Conservative Indonesian members of the old colonial bureaucracy and the local rajahs and their entourages had little fear of revolutionary nationalism in Sumatra, but saw as their main problem the task of explaining to the victorious Allies why they had cooperated with the Japanese and also of assuring the British and Dutch of their readiness to work with their returning European overlords. Indeed, members of the royal aristocracy and prominent professionals in Medan actually discussed forming a reception committee to welcome back the Dutch.[2] Hasan, profoundly discouraged with his colleagues' outlook, refrained even from announcing the news of the independence declaration signed in Jakarta weeks before.[3]

Impressions that the old order was returning were powerfully reinforced in early October by the coronation of the youthful new sultan of Deli. Members of the court aristocracy were present in their splendid court robes and turbans. The Dutch constabulary formed the guard of honor. Senior NICA officers and former high-ranking officials of the Dutch colonial administration were escorted under yellow umbrellas—the traditional symbol of royalty—to the dais where representatives of the Japanese Army and military administration in their dress uniforms were also seated. Hasan was relegated to the spectators' section. It was a colorful and impressive spectacle watched by thousands.[4] Within five months, many of the Indonesian grandees around the sultan's throne would be dead.

As in Java, youth groups and societies on Sumatra took the initiative in support of the Republic. There were already large numbers of young

Japanese-trained former soldiers, militia, police, and civil servants in the larger towns, where they had been hastily demobilized following the surrender and left to their own devices with no means to return to their home villages. Mutual assistance and support groups formed among these "trained youth" soon took on a political character as rumors multiplied concerning the proclamation of independence and the imminent return of the Dutch. On September 23, 1945, the most active groups came together to form an Indonesian youth organization dedicated to independence. At a rally on September 30 attended by some seven hundred youth leaders, Hasan finally confirmed that Indonesian independence had been declared. Three days later he informed the Japanese that he was assuming authority as governor and ordered the Republican flag to be flown from all public buildings. Indonesians began wearing flashes of red and white to signal their support for independence.

On October 9, a crowd of more than a hundred thousand people carrying banners and chanting slogans marched to the main square of Medan to demonstrate their support for the Republic. Everywhere street gangs, labor organizations, ethnic associations, and political groups mobilized to fight for independence—and occasionally with one another. Although they sometimes coalesced briefly into larger associations, these gangs fundamentally agreed on only one thing: that the Republic was in danger and needed to be defended.

The day after the mass rally, a brigade of the 26th Indian Division landed at the town of Belawan, near Medan, bringing with them a unit of the NICA. There had been no fighting in Sumatra, but Medan still showed the effects of four long years of war. The arriving troops saw "a city bright with tropical splendor of lush gardens filled with the deep scent of melatti . . . of boulevards lined with fan palms," but it was also "a scarred and shabby town. . . . Its streets were torn and gutted, its parks unkempt, its sidewalks littered with the refuse of an uprooted citizenry. . . . It had become a town of beggars and tramps, of undernourished children and black-market profiteers. . . . Postwar Medan emanated a curiously blended atmosphere of anxiety, adventure and social abandon."[5] The arrival of NICA along with the British forces added significantly to this anxiety and tension. Many saw it as evidence that the British were in league with the Dutch to suppress the Republic.[6]

Two days after his arrival, Brigadier General T.E.D. Kelly, the British commander, met with Hasan and other Republican leaders. Kelly expressed a desire to cooperate with the Republic but refused to recognize it. He declined to take any action to inhibit NICA and the Dutch-organized colonial police, saying that he could not interfere in the internal affairs of the country, but at the same time he asserted that the British would be responsible for law and order. This type of self-contradictory position was bound to cause trouble, as it had in Java.

That trouble was not long in coming. On October 14, rumors spread that one of the Dutch colonial policemen had ripped the red and white Republican emblem from the shirt of a child and trampled it on the ground. Fighting soon broke out but was halted by the arrival of Japanese soldiers and a representative of the Republic. Later that same afternoon, however, a large youthful crowd returned to the scene and attacked the police headquarters in a Dutch hotel. More than one hundred of the Ambonese and Menadonese police were killed or wounded. A Swiss family and the hotel manager also died at the hands of the mob.[7] Two days later, a detachment of five Dutch soldiers was wiped out by another mob in the nearby town of Pematang Siantar, along with ten Ambonese and three Swiss civilians.[8]

As additional Allied troops arrived in Medan and in Padang on the west coast, bringing with them dozens of additional Dutch officers and administrators, tensions increased. Young Indonesians who had received officer training under the Japanese were placed in charge of TKR military training camps in towns and villages throughout southern Sumatra. "Immediately there was a great demand for people like myself, who had received some military training during the occupation, to train the *pemuda*," recalled J. K. Sarumpaet. "I can remember instructing them how to take apart a Japanese paratroop rifle knowing full well that they might never come across that type of weapon in their lives. But that was what we had . . . at that time. All sorts of funny things happened in these crash courses."[9] Recruits were instructed to bring with them a supply of their own clothing, a 1.5-meter bamboo pole, writing materials, and plates for eating.[10]

The TKR and the much more numerous youth gangs began to arm themselves with Japanese weapons. As in Java, this was accomplished through bluff, threats, bribery, and sometimes the willing cooperation of the Japanese. Not a few Japanese soldiers and even some Indians were amenable to selling or bartering a few rounds of ammunition or a rifle or two if offered the right deal. At a Japanese Air Force storage facility guarded by only twenty-one Japanese, local youth bands surrounded the place and, after staging a mock battle in which no one was hurt, persuaded the guards to hand over thirty-four machine guns, several rifles, and a large store of ammunition. Elsewhere, Japanese defectors to the nationalists or sympathetic Japanese commanders often helped Indonesians obtain quantities of weapons from Japanese military stores. In the town of Belawan, where the Japanese had been ordered to dispose of their excess weapons by disassembling them and sinking them in the deep water of the harbor, Indonesian divers quickly recovered the parts. "A lively market sprang up in salvaged and reconstructed weapons. The 'syndicate' in charge of the salvage operations would sell to anyone and most of these arms probably went to the Republic."[11]

More alarming to the Allies than the seizure of Japanese weapons was the possibility that the Japanese themselves might join with the nationalists against the British and Dutch. A British intelligence report stated that a Japanese colonel was organizing "stay behind" units equipped with weapons from hidden arms caches to live in the villages. According to the report, the Japanese were promising the Indonesians that they would return in twenty years.[12] How many Japanese actually defected to the nationalists is still a matter of conjecture. A U.S. intelligence report mentions sixteen hundred deserters in Sumatra.[13] A British estimate gave a figure of two thousand on the east coast.[14] A 1980 survey, by a Japanese veterans' group, of men who stayed on in Indonesia after 1945 includes 780 individuals.[15] Contrary to British beliefs, there is no record of any officer above the rank of captain defecting to the nationalist cause. About half of the deserters were enlisted men, a quarter were noncommissioned officers, and almost a third were civilians: former bureaucrats and employees of the Japanese Army.[16]

Japanese made the decision to join the nationalists for varied reasons. Some acted on principle, wishing to carry on the fight for Greater East Asia or believing that Japan owed Indonesia its promised independence. Some defected because they feared being apprehended as war criminals. Others had married Indonesian women or believed that economic opportunities would be better in Indonesia.[17] Although relatively few in number, the Japanese deserters were highly valued for their knowledge of weapons and tactics. Japanese soldiers were believed by the British to have played a key role in organizing and deploying the nationalist forces at Surabaya, and Japanese bodies had reportedly been found among the dead.

News of the fighting at Surabaya had an enormous impact on the young activists of the youth gangs and proto-TKR units. Newspapers in Sumatra printed detailed accounts of the battle and of the heroic struggle of Indonesian patriots agains the heavily armed troops of the Allies. To many this was the conclusive evidence that the SEAC forces had come to reestablish Dutch rule and that the armed struggle against colonialism long predicted by young nationalist orators had indeed begun.[18] Sniping at SEAC troops increased. Looting and lawlessness were reported to be increasing even in British-controlled areas. The various youth corps and gangs paraded through the streets of Medan carrying flags and banners and armed with homemade spears.[19]

In the highland town of Berastagi in the Karo area, trouble flared between the local youths and a company of British soldiers sent to establish an outpost and search for Japanese weapons. The Karos complained that the soldiers were annoying local women with unwanted attention and firing their guns unnecessarily within the town. A British officer replaced the Republican flag at the principal hotel with a Union Jack, sparking widespread protests. The troops were harassed by blowpipe darts fired from concealed locations, and two soldiers were injured. On November 25, when the British moved to occupy key points in the town, local youth gangs and the local TKR struck back using hand grenades and improvised bombs. The British, forced to withdraw from the town, fought their way back to Medan with the loss of two men. The Indonesians had five casualties. The relatively light losses on both sides after an all-day battle reflected the relatively primitive armament of the Indonesians and the reluctance of the British to become involved in a full-scale engagement.

Following the incident at Berastagi, British troops in Sumatra were pulled back to shallow perimeters surrounding the towns of Medan and its port of Belawan, and Padang and Palembang with their important oil refineries. About ten thousand Japanese troops reinforced the defenses of Medan, while thirteen thousand more were deployed to guard the refineries in and near Palembang.[20] At Palembang they were under the control of the Burma regiment, which had a strength of three infantry companies, about 5 percent of the number of Japanese troops in the area.[21] "The British exhibit no plan in their actions in Sumatra. They state ad nauseam that their mission consists of (1) disarming the Japanese, (2) succoring RAPWI, (3) maintaining peace and order. They have done little except for the second point and feel themselves in an impossible situation with the other two," reported an American observer. "Whether there is peace or war in Sumatra depends primarily on the situation in Java."[22]

In Java, the Dutch and the nationalists had begun a glacial movement toward negotiations. Dr. Hubertus Van Mook, head of the NICA and chief Netherlands representative, had finally agreed to meet with Sukarno in mid-October for a few inconclusive talks. That was enough to touch off a minor explosion in The Hague, where the Dutch government promptly disavowed the talks and considered firing Van Mook. British exasperation reached a new high. "We have persuaded these bone-headed Dutch to see reason out here," wrote Mountbatten's chief of staff. "I only wish someone would persuade the Dutchmen at home to see reason."[23] Even Mountbatten's political adviser Esler Dening, who believed the Indonesians were "easily instigated to theatrical political displays . . . by a small handful of Nationalist leaders," warned that if the Netherlands government was "going to intervene in a manner likely to wreck our negotiations . . . they may have serious cause to regret their action. They may be entitled to jeopardize their own position but they are not entitled to jeopardize ours."[24]

On November 17, Syahrir met with Van Mook and Dening. Although Van Mook refused to make any specific commitments, Dening insisted that the Dutch attitude was "generous" and urged Syahrir to offer concessions. "He made me feel like a schoolboy being questioned by a policeman," Syahrir told an Australian diplomat.[25] Any hope that the Netherlands government had indeed adopted a "generous attitude" was quickly dispelled by a BBC interview conducted by well-known British journalist Chester Wilmott with the Dutch minister for overseas territories. The minister spoke of the Indonesian Republic in a dismissive fashion and declared that the Netherlands was ready to use military force to reestablish their rule in the Indies.[26]

Mountbatten impatiently asked London to "state unequivocally what HM government's policy is in the NEI so that we who carry out that policy will no longer be left in any doubt as to what our instructions are."[27] HM Government was still unable to "get an accurate picture," as Prime Minister Clement Attlee admitted some weeks later,[28] but the Cabinet decided to take two measures to deal with the situation. The Dutch prime minister would be invited to meet with Attlee at his official country estate, Chequers, and a special commissioner would be appointed to represent the British government in the Netherlands Indies and to encourage negotiations. At the same time, Christison, who had long angered the Dutch through his ill-concealed contempt for their colonial troops and his willingness to cooperate with the Syahrir government, was promoted to an important command in Europe and replaced by Lieutenant General Sir Montague Stopford.

British High Commissioner Sir Archibald Clark Kerr arrived in Batavia on February 1, 1946, a few weeks after the high-level talks between the British and Dutch prime ministers had produced only mutual recriminations. By this point the government of the Republic had been effectively transferred to Jogjakarta in south-central Java, far from the British military presence. (The government's relocation may have been encouraged by the fact that trigger-happy Dutch colonial troops not infrequently chose to use the houses of members of the Cabinet and their aides for target practice.)[29]

When talks resumed between Syahrir and Van Mook on February 10 with Clark Kerr as "broker"—London disliked the term "mediator"—the Dutch dusted off their proposals derived from a 1942 address by Queen Wilhelmina. A commonwealth composed of the three Dutch colonies, Surinam, Curaçao, and the Netherlands Indies, would be established with its own Cabinet. The citizens of the colonies would receive the right to determine their "constitutional destiny" following "a given preparatory period," and could conduct their own international affairs, subject to a Dutch veto. There was no acknowledgment of Indonesian independence, let alone recognition of the Republic. Clark Kerr described Van Mook's proposals as "extremely reasonable"—and so they would have been, in 1919. In 1946 they had no chance of success even with the more moderate members of the Jogjakarta government.

Syahrir's government fell a few weeks later, and a new Cabinet was formed only on March 12. A week before, nine battalions of Dutch Marines had landed at Batavia and Semarang. Some still wore the American uniforms and insignia they had received during their training at the U.S. Marine base at Quantico prior to the Japanese surrender. How much training the Dutch had actually absorbed in the United States was a matter of conjecture, but British observers agreed that they had thoroughly assimilated the American habit of constant gum chewing.[30]

In London, the government continued to dither. Some saw the arrival of Dutch troops as a favorable opportunity to begin closing out British involvement in what appeared to be an increasingly intractable situation. Others argued that news of British plans for withdrawal would encourage the "extremists" in the Republican government to take a much tougher line in negotiations.

In the midst of these unpromising developments, Van Mook and Syahrir unexpectedly reached an agreement. Their model was Sainteny's recent agreement with Ho Chi Minh, which appeared to both recognize Ho's government and preserve French prerogatives. Van Mook agreed to recognize the Republic headed by Sukarno as the de facto government in the areas it controlled in Java and Sumatra. The Republic in turn would agree to join an Indonesian federation to be organized by the Dutch.

In April, a delegation from the Republic journeyed to the Netherlands for negotiations with representatives of the Dutch government at Hoge Veluwe, a national park about a hundred kilometers from Amsterdam. No sooner had negotiations commenced than the Dutch began to renege. There was an election scheduled for the following month, and the government in power in The Hague did not want to chance losing votes by seeming to appease the Indonesians.

After a week of fruitless discussion, the Indonesian delegates returned to Java. Rumors about concessions Syahrir had reportedly been prepared to make leaked out in June. Militants in the Republican movement, angered at the news that Syahrir appeared ready to settle for less than total independence, took matters into their own hands. On

June 27, Syahrir was "arrested" by dissident army units while on a visit to Surekarta. Sukarno assumed emergency powers and went on the air in a nationwide radio broadcast to demand that Syahrir be released. He warned that the radicals who had carried out the kidnapping were actually playing into the hands of the Dutch, who would use the incident as proof that Indonesians could not govern themselves and had succumbed to anarchy and chaos.[31] Syahrir was quickly released, and an attempted coup by the dissidents a few days later ended in complete failure. But the deep divisions among supporters of the Republic had been starkly revealed, and only Sukarno's intervention had kept the contending factions from outright warfare.

Shortly before the opening of the Hoge Veluwe talks, the British government, believing, or perhaps wanting to believe, that the problems of the Netherlands Indies were about to be settled, agreed to retain nineteen thousand troops in Java until the end of 1946.[32] Mountbatten and his political adviser Lord Killearn, who had succeeded Clark Kerr, were appalled, particularly after it became clear that no Indonesian-Dutch agreement was in sight. Mountbatten wanted to pull British troops off Sumatra by June and begin closing out the British role in Java well before December. London never approved Mountbatten's plan, but the supreme commander persuaded Van Mook that in return for a free hand to conduct any military operations they wished in the Indies, the Dutch would assume responsibility for all areas outside the narrowly defined military zones held by the British in Java and Sumatra by June. After that date, the Dutch could not expect to call on SEAC for military support. Beginning in April 1946, Japanese troops began to be concentrated in Batavia and Surabaya for repatriation, and by the end of June most of them were on their way to Japan.[33]

To the troops in Sumatra, their disengagement could not come too early. In Sumatra as in Java, the more conservative established spokesmen of the Republic were progressively losing control to the leaders of the youth groups, advocates of holy war, and other young radicals. The younger leaders stood for active confrontation and resistance to the Dutch, hostility toward the traditional elites, and suspicion and impatience toward the Republic's officially appointed leaders.[34] The Sumatra press was consistently radical and encouraged suspicion of the British and hatred of the Dutch.[35]

General Albert C. Wedemeyer with Chinese Nationalist generals.

SIGNAL CORPS

The Japanese had spent millions on developing Manchuria. This Japanese postcard shows the main street of the city of Kirin (now Jilin) with its modern buildings.

The prison barracks at Hoten as they appeared in 2005. The highest-ranking Allied prisoners, including General Jonathan Wainwright, were confined here. The camp buildings are under restoration by the Chinese government to serve as a museum. RONALD SPECTOR

The former prison hospital at Hoten. RONALD SPECTOR

Monument to the victory over Japan erected by Soviet soldiers near the Mukden railroad station.

RONALD SPECTOR

The former Yamato Hotel in the center of Mukden, still in business, was the headquarters of the OSS "Cardinal Mission." RONALD SPECTOR

The Supreme Allied Commander, Southeast Asia, Lord Louis Mountbatten, reads the surrender proclamation on the steps of the Singapore Municipal Building. To Mountbatten's right is General William Slim. SIGNAL CORPS

General George C. Marshall arrives at Communist Party headquarters at Yenan. To his right is Chou En-lai.

SIGNAL CORPS

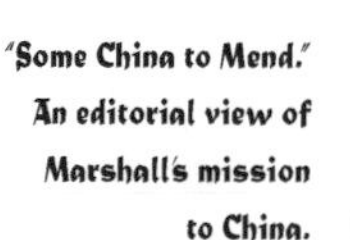

"Some China to Mend." An editorial view of Marshall's mission to China.

BY PERMISSION OF THE MARCUS FAMILY

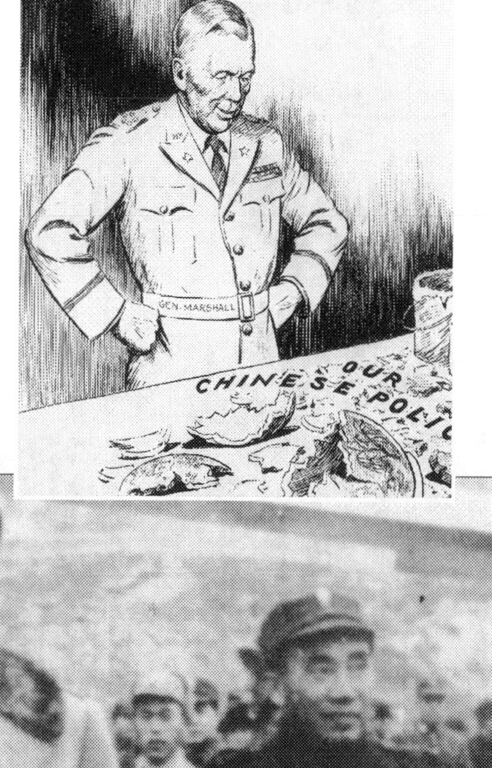

Two men not bothered by the heat: Sukarno of Indonesia and Ho Chi Minh of Vietnam.

SUKARNO: INDONESIAN PRESS SERVICE; HO: LIBRARY OF CONGRESS

Lieutenant General John R. Hodge with Korean leaders.

SIGNAL CORPS

American troops enter a Korean town. SIGNAL CORPS

Police attempt to break up a mass demonstration in Seoul protesting the U.S.-Soviet trusteeship plan.

SIGNAL CORPS

A GI receives a warm welcome from Koreans in the early days of the occupation. SIGNAL CORPS

DISPLACED PERSONS

Japanese soldiers leave Pusan for Japan. SIGNAL CORPS

A group of Japanese nurses in Korea awaiting evacuation. SIGNAL CORPS

Korean refugees from the north arrive in Seoul. SIGNAL CORPS

Dutch women internees in a camp in central Java.

SIGNAL CORPS

The British Royal Navy evacuates Dutch POWs and internees from Surabaya. SIGNAL CORPS

Commonwealth troops search an Indonesian town near Batavia (Jakarta). SIGNAL CORPS

A nationalist soldier mans an anti-aircraft machine gun during the battle for Surabaya. INDONESIAN PRESS SERVICE

Indonesian nationalist slogans cover a building in Batavia.

INDONESIAN PRESS SERVICE

Mountbatten visits troops in Java. Edwina Mountbatten is in the background.

SIGNAL CORPS

After the British had pulled back to the three towns that they garrisoned, fighting tapered off for a time and was confined mainly to sniping. In Medan, the radicals devoted their energies to organizing a boycott prohibiting sales of food or other goods to the British and Dutch or supplying them with services. Hasan was able to end the boycott and negotiated an agreement with the British to allow the Republic's police to patrol the city and carry a limited number of firearms.[36]

The police did little to protect the Chinese community in Medan, who now became a target of the radicals and criminal gangs. As they had in other parts of Indonesia, the Chinese in Medan formed their own self-defense force and were provided arms by the British. "The force . . . without doubt reduced the number of anti-Chinese incidents," a British report concluded, "but at the same time sowed the seed of a deep resentfulness on the part of the extremist Indonesians who saw in our actions the wish to recruit to our side the large and influential Chinese community. This resentment was the cause of intermittent fighting in the Chinese quarter involving our troops for many months to come."[37]

The nationalist revolution in Sumatra entered a new phase in January 1946, when a well-armed militant Muslim group called PUSA (Presatuan Ulama Seluruh Aceh, the All-Aceh Ulama Association) carried out a purge of the traditional ruling elite of Aceh called the *uleebalang*. Originally war leaders and petty rulers, the *uleebalang* under the Dutch had become village and district administrators with authority to administer justice and collect taxes. Even before the Second World War, their blatant corruption and use of their positions to enrich themselves through extortion, intimidation, and embezzlement had eroded much of the respect and deference paid to them by the community. After the Japanese surrender, many of them were suspected of having pro-Dutch leanings. PUSA, a movement that combined nationalism and religious fundamentalism with social and economic reform, had taken the *uleebalang* as its targets.

Captain Ushiyama Mitsuo, a young Japanese officer, witnessed the first violent clash between PUSA and the *uleebalang* in the town of Sigli in the Pidie District near the northern tip of Sumatra. "A large number of PUSA members were gathering in Sukon village. . . . Soon [we] could see a long column of people six or seven abreast crossing the

Sukon Bridge and marching toward us. They seemed not to have many rifles and were jogging along with parangs held aloft. This forest of parangs glittered in the sunshine." As they marched, the people chanted verses from the *Hikayat Perang Sabil,* the long Achenese battle song that spoke of the rewards in heaven awaiting a warrior who died in a holy war. "It was quite uncanny, sounding like the humming of an enormous swarm of bees. . . . It was weird and unnerving that these people should be chanting passages from the book and rousing their emotions to a state of rapture."[38] In Pidie District, twenty-three of twenty-five local rulers were killed along with large numbers of lesser officials and court functionaries. Sometimes entire families disappeared. Other *uleebalang* were arrested or fled.[39]

The British expected initially that the Japanese might help to stabilize Aceh, but the Japanese were eager only to leave, and it soon became obvious that their continued presence could only mean a bloody showdown with PUSA and other militants. Beginning in late December, Japanese forces were rapidly withdrawn from points in Aceh and concentrated around the town of Langsa, which they seized from the Indonesians after stubborn fighting. By the end of the month, all Japanese had been evacuated by sea or moved southeast out of the province. Neither the Japanese nor the Dutch ever returned to Aceh. During January and February, evacuation of Japanese forces from the Medan and Palembang also began, going into high gear in March, April, and May, when around two-thirds of the approximately seventy thousand Japanese in Sumatra left the island.[40]

Fighting flared again in March between the British and the nationalists. On March 8, the 26th Indian Division used artillery for the first time, and from April through June there were numerous clashes between British and Indian patrols and well-armed nationalists. A British analysis concluded that because the buildup of Indonesian armed groups in Sumatra had been relatively slow, with little of the suicidal fanaticism of the early battles in Java, "the result has been that they have been able to gain experience and develop their tactics and organization on a sound basis, strongly influenced by Japanese methods."[41] By August, nationalist attacks were reported to have become bolder and better coordinated, with frequent use of mortars and grenade launchers.

Meanwhile, nationalist radicals in eastern Sumatra had carried out their own "social revolution" against the rajas and sultans whom they accused of being in secret league with the Dutch and of standing in the way of government by the people. Many radical leaders must also have been aware that with the overthrow of the ruling houses, their considerable wealth would be up for grabs. Some sultans and high-ranking court officials were able to escape to the safety of the British-held areas, but many others were killed along with their families and retainers and their houses plundered.[42]

To Syahrir and Sjarifuddin even more than to the British, it appeared that parts of Sumatra were sinking into anarchy. Events there could serve to discredit the entire Republic. In April, Sjarifuddin flew to Java with a delegation of Republican leaders. The first members of the government to visit Java, they received a tumultuous welcome. Everywhere he went, Sjarifuddin addressed large, enthusiastic crowds with his message of unity and support for the duly constituted government and the army. Privately he counseled Hasan to get a grip and rein in the extremists. Many political leaders in Sumatra were now growing weary of the excesses of the "social revolution" and the spectacle of gang leaders profiting from the looting of the sultans' treasuries. Even Marxist leaders denounced the radical gangs as "infantile anarcho-syndicalists."[43]

By May 1946, a kind of tenuous order had returned to most of Republican-controlled Sumatra. In Palembang, the Republican governor, Dr. A. K. Gani, a well-known nationalist politician with strong ties to Sukarno and Hatta, had reached a tacit agreement with the British to develop the port and nearby refineries. As Gani saw it, in any prolonged struggle with the Dutch, the Republic would need money, and oil exports would provide it. In Padang and Medan, however, intermittent hostilities between the British forces and the nationalists continued. By September, British patrols had to be supported by artillery and armored cars. During the summer of 1946, almost all the remaining Japanese had been evacuated, and in October the first Dutch troops landed in force in Sumatra.

The last British troops left Indonesia at the end of November 1946. General Gracey had received full military honors and a key to the city from the French when he left Indochina. The Dutch felt little inclination to do the same for any British general, and the Indonesians likewise held no overwhelming feelings of gratitude toward the Southeast

Asia Command. Yet by 1949 Indonesia was independent and at peace, while Vietnam was in the first phase of a thirty-year conflict. These contrasting stories may have been due in some degree to the actions and decisions of Mountbatten's generals in the ruins of Southeast Asia's colonial empires.

As for the British and Indian troops, their thoughts on leaving Java and Sumatra probably echoed those expressed in a song sung by Scottish soldiers at the conclusion of the Sicilian campaign:

There's no jock will mourn the loss a'ye
Poor bloody soldiers are weary.

As their troubles multiplied on Java and Sumatra, Mountbatten's staff could feel grateful that responsibility for the rest of the Netherlands East Indies, the large islands of Borneo (now Kalimantan), the Celebes (now Sulawesi), and other eastern island groups that together constituted two-thirds of the Dutch colony's territory were, at least for a time, the responsibility of the Australians. About fifty thousand Australian troops of the 7th and 9th Divisions and the 26th Brigade, veterans of battles in North Africa and New Guinea, had been fighting in Borneo since May 1945, when the 26th Brigade took the oil-rich island of Tarakan, close to northeast Borneo, in one of the bloodiest operations of the war. That was followed by large-scale landings on Borneo's northern coast at Brunei Bay in former British Borneo and at the city of Balikpapan on the east coast.

With the surrender of Japan, Australian forces found themselves responsible for disarming the Japanese and maintaining order in Borneo and the neighboring Celebes, across the Makassar Strait, plus all of the smaller islands of eastern Indonesia. "Peace has come at last," wrote Corporal William J. Gambier on Tarakan. "Being stuck in Borneo . . . watching wounded men die it's hard to realize how gay everyone is at home. . . . We still have plenty of work to do cleaning up the smashed towns, rounding up and guarding thousands of Jap prisoners. . . ."[44]

There were eight separate Australian occupation forces deployed across an area stretching from Borneo to the easternmost part of New Guinea.[45] Throughout the region, the Australians accepted the Japanese surrender and assisted Allied prisoners and internees. Landing at

Makassar, the advance element of an Australian brigade was met at the pier by an honor guard composed mainly of Royal Navy sailors from HMS *Exeter,* a cruiser that had been sunk along with other Dutch and U.S. ships in the futile defense of Java in 1942.[46] Later, in the reception room of the Celebes governor's palace with its highly polished wood walls, ornate hanging chandeliers, and gleaming tile floors, the commander of Makassar Force, Brigadier I. N. Dougherty, received the swords of a Japanese vice admiral and his entourage.

Unlike the British, who were trying to placate the Indonesians, satisfy the Dutch, and keep a wary eye on American anticolonialists, Australian soldiers suffered from no confusion about their mission. Australian forces were in the Indies only to accept the surrender and to maintain law and order until "the lawful government of the Netherlands East Indies is once again functioning."[47] Units of the NICA were quickly installed as civil administrators wherever possible. The sole Australian aim was to hand over all responsibilities in the islands to the Dutch as soon as possible. "Officers commanding detached units will take all measures practicable to establish the orders of the NICA and ensure that its orders are carried out," read one instruction from Australian headquarters.[48]

The Australians would as soon have handed over to Martians or anyone else likely to relieve them of their occupation duties at an early date. Aside from a handful of bureaucrats and politicians in Canberra and Melbourne, Australians had no geopolitical interest in the Netherlands Indies. Their soldiers, like other Allied soldiers from Seoul to Singapore, wanted above all to go home. "A wave of disorderliness and stealing had broken out among the men," the 2/25 Battalion Diary noted in October. "It appears to be a phase through which the whole army is passing, due, it is thought, to the discontent felt at not being returned to Australia as soon as the fighting job was done."[49]

The Australian soldiers' understanding of Indonesia was on a par with that of American GIs' understanding of Korea. Knowledge of Malay was almost nonexistent, although older Indonesians later recalled that the Australians "were ingenious at miming their needs, flapping their arms and cackling when they wanted a chicken."[50] A Royal Australian Air Force guide divided the indigenous peoples into three categories: the Malays, who were "an easy-going and rather lazy race";

the Chinese, who were "shrewd" and very progressive but "not reliable"; and the Eurasians, "a very useful community often employed as teachers, nurses, clerks and typists."[51] Most soldiers never bothered with even these distinctions but referred to all Indonesians as "the natives" or, less politely, "the boongs." "These people are best left to the simplicity of their own lives that seem to change ever so slowly," declared radio newscaster Frederick Simpson. "They are somewhat indolent, are these Indonesians, and in days to come their plays and dances will tell of the Jap invasion with the childlike humor of a simple people."[52]

But things were becoming less simple, and the movement for Indonesian independence had a firm foothold in the eastern islands by the time the Australians arrived. Higher headquarters was not having any nonsense about that. Commanders were instructed that "any attempt on the part of the civil population to prevent [NICA's] orders being carried out will be treated as offenses against law and order. Processions and demonstrations will not be permitted."[53] The problem was, as the Australian official history noted, that "in the eyes of Indonesian leaders, Indonesia was already an independent state." Nationalists urged the Australians to deal directly with the Republican leaders in the islands and argued that their administration was perfectly capable of carrying on civil government functions without any help from the Dutch.

Despite the stern tone of the directives from army headquarters, local commanders had, in practice, great latitude in their decisions about maintaining order and in their relations with the nationalists. Some officers did attempt to crack down hard on nationalist activities. "As soon as the red-white [Republican] flag went up we pulled it down," one company commander recalled. When nationalist leader Dr. Sam Ratulangi, the Republican-appointed governor of Sulawesi, visited Bone to give a speech, this same officer confiscated Ratulangi's car and told him to walk back to Makassar.[54]

In the larger urban areas, Australians could not be so cavalier. Besides, they were learning that the Dutch could also be a source of trouble. After a brawl in Makassar between nationalists and Ambonese soldiers of the Dutch Colonial Army that resulted in at least eighteen deaths, Brigadier Dougherty ordered the Ambonese confined to their barracks and instructed NICA personnel not to harass Indonesians wearing nationalist badges.[55] At Makassar and at Samarinda and Sanga

Sanga in eastern Borneo, Australian commanders met informally with Indonesian leaders. No public meetings or demonstrations were permitted, and no flags. However, private meetings of nationalists were permitted, and Indonesians could wear Republican badges and emblems.[56] As reports of the fighting on Java reached the islands, fears of similar outbreaks in Borneo and Celebes increased. Dire rumors and reports circulated, such as one that the 7th Division had intercepted a message to all Indonesians in the islands "warning them to be ready to go into action at the sounding of a bell or gong."[57]

Violence against the Australians would not have been surprising, given their formal support for the restoration of the old colonial administration and their tendency to limit or suppress nationalist activities. Yet few incidents occurred, and the Australians remained on good terms with the Indonesians until the end of their occupation. In Makassar, 2/27th Battalion remained so popular that "various sections of the community sponsored farewell socials" for the departing Australian troops.[58] An Australian general later attributed the relative peace and orderliness of the occupation to "our patent impartiality in regard to their political problems . . . the magnificent bearing, patience and discipline of the members of the force . . . and to their innate qualities of kindness and sympathy with all sections of the community."[59]

Nationalists leaders would have had trouble recognizing the Australians' "patent impartiality," but Australians and Indonesians did develop a certain amused tolerance of each other. Though the Diggers' utter cluelessness about the country they were in was equal to that of any of Hodge's troops in Seoul, Australian soldiers were not isolated from the civilian population as were American GIs in Korea. Australians and Indonesians played frequent games of football and soccer. Because the Dutch style of soccer was not widely played in Australia at that time, the locals were often amused at the efforts of the Diggers to master the sport.

The main basis for personal relationships between soldiers and Indonesians was not so much kindness and sympathy as the ubiquitous barter system. Australian troops brought with them to Indonesia tens of thousands of canned rations that they were heartily sick of eating. To the Indonesians, however, these tins of meat, butter, and condensed milk, as well as Australian clothing, watches, pens, and lighters, represented luxuries that had not been available since the beginning of the war. The Indonesians, on the other hand, had fresh fruits, meat, and vegetables, which many of the Australians had not seen in months. A widespread and lively trade soon sprang up between the locals and the Diggers.

The constant trading sometimes led to personal relationships. "We made friends with an Indonesian family and we took them food," recalled W. J. Sodin, who served with the Royal Australian Air Force at Tarakan. "In return they would cook us bananas and other native fare which made a nice change from squadron meals."[60] When the NICA outlawed Japanese occupation currency, many Indonesians found themselves with no money, and barter became even more important. Nor were food and clothing the only items bartered. One Australian officer entered a local store and was greeted in English with the proposal, "You fuck my wife for some butter?"[61] Venereal disease rates climbed steeply.

Overshadowing all local developments in Borneo and the Celebes, the continued goodwill of the Indonesians was ensured not through any actions of the occupation forces but because of the activity of Australians at home. On September 24, the Communist-dominated Waterside Workers' Federation of Australia voted to refuse to load Dutch ships in Australian ports that they believed were carrying "supplies and troops for the suppression of the independent Indonesian government."[62] The boycott produced strong protests from the Dutch, but Australian prime minister Ben Chifly, himself a former union organizer, refused to intervene.

News of the Waterside Workers' strike quickly spread to Indonesia. One Australian soldier recalled, "The Indonesians used to make their own very rough paper and produce a news-sheet on the only typewriter available to them. Copies were carried by courier to different localities and in some towns that possessed typewriters more of the news-sheets would be typed out. The contents were read to meetings to overcome the illiteracy problem. In this way the Indonesians in the Celebes were informed that the Australian unions were supporting in action the Indonesian Republic."[63]

The federation also financed and produced a movie, *Indonesia Calling*, designed to explain the Indonesian situation to the Australian public. The film decried the exploitation of the Indonesians by the Dutch, pointed out that other unions had joined the boycott, appealed to the Atlantic Charter, and featured statements by Nehru of India, the president of the Philippines, and the Soviet foreign minister against Dutch suppression of the Republic.[64] The film's soundtrack, quickly translated into Indonesian, was played widely over nationalist radio. Many Indonesians in Borneo and the Celebes interpreted the developments in Australia as a sign that the Australians they met were on their side.

Most Australian soldiers would have been surprised to learn that they were champions of Indonesian independence. Yet some did express sympathy for the Indonesians, and many more voiced their dislike of the Dutch. The distinguished historian of Southeast Asia Anthony Reid, who interviewed a number of veterans about the occupation, observed, "It seems that every Australian soldier who served in Indonesia has anti-Dutch stories to tell."[65] The Australians resented the way the colonial bureaucrats who had fled from the Indies in 1942 had now been commissioned as instant military officers. They saw the Dutch as arrogant and pompous and believed that Dutch behavior toward the Indonesians was unduly harsh and overbearing. "We in the 7th Division were conscious of the anti-Dutch feelings of the Indonesians that these people didn't want to be bossed about," recalled one soldier.[66] "The vast majority of our chaps here have a tremendous amount of sympathy for these people here, whose life is one of continuous squalor under the harsh domination of the Dutch imperialists," wrote one Digger. "To quote the most frequently used phrase among our chaps, 'The Dutch are a mob of bastards.' "[67]

A small minority of Australian soldiers went beyond expression of antipathy for the Dutch and actively aided the nationalists. These soldiers were mostly members of the Australian Communist Party, which claimed to have fourteen hundred members in the Australian occupation forces in eastern Indonesia.[68] Probably the most important activity of Party members in the army was to distribute leaflets supplied by Indonesian nationalists in Australia. A news correspondent in east Indonesia reported that "Communists in the 7th Division are stirring the local people against the Dutch" and that pro-independence leaflets had been widely distributed in Bandjarmasin, Tarakan, Samarinda, Balikpapan, and other towns in Borneo.[69] A handful of Australian soldiers were reported to have incited or joined nationalist demonstrations, though none were ever apprehended.[70]

In February 1946, the last Australian units left the Indies. The Australians had suffered few losses and left behind few enemies. Without any conscious plan, partly through accident, they had been able to convince all factions that they were on their side. The army's firm support and cooperation with NICA satisfied the Dutch, while the longshoremen's strike in Australia and the evident anti-Dutch feelings of most Australian soldiers convinced the Indonesians that Australia was supporting their cause.

For the Indonesians there was a less happy ending. The Dutch returned. Ratulangi went to jail in the spring of 1946, to be joined by the local rulers who had supported the Republic. Resistance to Dutch rule continued, and at the end of 1946, Captain Raymond "Turk" Westerling, an early practitioner of the use of death squads as a counterinsurgency measure, arrived with his special unit in South Sulawesi. He is reported to have killed more than three thousand women and children within a few months. When the Netherlands finally conceded independence to Indonesia in 1949, Westerling tried unsuccessfully to sabotage the deal. Then he retired to the Netherlands and wrote a book about fighting terrorism.

CHAPTER TWELVE

WARS POSTPONED

DESPITE THE CONTINUED MAYHEM IN INDONESIA, THE WINTER and early spring of 1945–46 was a time that seemed to promise hope for a peaceful resolution to the incipient conflicts in China, Korea, and northern Vietnam. In Korea the Joint U.S.-Soviet Commission held its first meeting. In Hanoi the Vietminh and the French agreed upon a plan for the peaceful return of French troops and recognition of Ho's Democratic Republic of Vietnam. But it was in China that the most spectacular success appeared about to be achieved.

The weather was cold, windy, and dreary when General George C. Marshall's plane touched down at Chungking airport just before Christmas 1945. Rain the night before had turned the areas near the runway into slimy mud. "People huddled in small groups saying nothing. Marshall looked grim, unsmiling, tired. The Generalissimo was grim, unsmiling, but if he was tired it did not show."[1] Two days before Marshall had presented his credentials and held his first extended meetings with Chiang at Nanking, the prewar capital of China, to which the Generalissimo had recently returned. Wedemeyer found the meetings "remarkable for the deference Marshall showed Chiang Kai Shek."[2] The Generalissimo, however, recorded in his journal, "With respect to our internal problems and the conspiratorial nature of the Communists, he really has no understanding."[3]

The groups that welcomed Marshall at the Chungking airport representing the government, the American embassy, and the Communists all harbored varying views about Marshall's mission. Almost all of the Americans expected only failure. Chiang and his close advisers resented the arrival of still another American envoy who, they believed, had little understanding of China and might be unresponsive to the Generalissimo's attempts to enlighten him. Chen Li-fu, the leader of the right-wing faction of the Nationalists, the so-called CC clique, urged Chiang to refuse outright to accept Marshall as mediator. The government-controlled press blossomed forth with editorials complaining of American meddling in China's internal affairs. Madame Chiang told foreign diplomats that "in Chungking everyone is scared of the Americans." Their attitude, formerly altruistic, had changed into one that threatened "domination" of China.[4] Conservative elements within Chiang's regime believed that the mission might rob the Nationalists of the opportunity to crush the Communists militarily before they grew any stronger.

Chiang himself "was in an exuberant state of mind," recalled V. K. Wellington Koo, then China's ambassador to the United States. "[He] felt that the struggle which he led personally, of resistance to the Japanese enemy . . . had been crowned with success. That China had at last been put on the map, so to speak, and had earned her place in the councils of the world. He was not in the mood to accept advice from a foreign friend, even one from the most friendly country. He was not disposed to accept any control or even appearance of control of China's affairs by a foreign representative."[5]

Nevertheless the Nationalists had little choice but to accept President Truman's offer of Marshall's good offices. Marshall's towering prestige made his appointment unchallengeable, and behind him was the enormous economic and military power of the United States, which, if it did not "dominate" Chiang's regime, was vital to his survival. In addition, Chinese of all political persuasions as well as ordinary citizens strongly desired peace and the avoidance of civil war after years of struggle against the Japanese. Under these circumstances both Nationalists and Communists found it expedient to demonstrate their peaceful intentions by engaging in negotiations. Those negotiations, they hoped, could also be used to highlight the intransigence of their opponents.

Despite the fact that Mao believed he had been burned by Hurley's earlier blunders as a mediator, the Communist leadership welcomed Marshall's mission. Truman's recent statement suggested changes in U.S. China policy and appeared to signal a willingness to exert U.S. power to avert civil war. In contrast to the "reactionaries" like Hurley and Wedemeyer, Mao saw Marshall as a representative of the "progressive" faction within the American ruling elite. The Politburo took a highly positive view, informing cadres, "Our resolute three month struggle has already brought about Hurley's downfall and caused Truman to issue his China policy statement of December 15."[6]

At the time of Marshall's arrival, Mao was recovering from an illness. Day-to-day negotiations in Chungking were handled by Chou En-lai, a man of great charm, persuasiveness, and subtlety. Urbane and witty, with a talent for public relations, he was already a favorite with many members of the foreign press. The Nationalists were represented by General Chang Chun, wartime governor of Szechuan Province, who had been a classmate of Chiang's at the Military Preparatory School in Tokyo, which they had both attended in 1907.

In Chungking the general met with members of various parties, factions, and movements, and with politicians, journalists, intellectuals, and writers.[7] To all of them he listened patiently and courteously, giving no hint of his own views. "Marshall has this country in a stew by the simple expedient of not saying anything and not reacting when he is asked a question," noted diplomat John F. Melby. "Even to our own people who are explaining something and who artlessly and tentatively inject an 'Of course I don't yet know just what you have in mind or just what your objective is and so . . . uh . . .' he graciously and unsmilingly refuses the proffered opportunity to explain by simply telling them to proceed with what they were saying."[8] Marshall believed that neither the Nationalists nor the Communists had the military strength to defeat the other decisively but that they could force China into a ruinous civil war that might last years, invite foreign intervention, or lead to the division of the country. The two sides might be amenable to a negotiated solution, but their mutual distrust was so strong that they were unlikely to reach agreement without the mediation of a third party.[9]

At the close of the year the negotiators got down to business. Around the table with Marshall were the representatives of two factions who had known and hated each other with a murderous single-mindedness for almost twenty years. They were always agreeing in principle but disagreeing over details. There was continual squabbling over Communist and Nationalist military moves in Manchuria and its neighboring provinces. Many Nationalist leaders, especially the CC clique and some generals, believed that any agreement would be a dangerous diversion, that the Communists were controlled from Moscow, and that now was the best opportunity to crush them. The Communists were more interested in an agreement to lessen the military pressure on their forces and build up their strength, but they distrusted the Nationalists and suspected that Chiang's real objective was to destroy them. Consequently it was a surprise to all when, less than two weeks later, Marshall and the two negotiators submitted to Chiang and Mao an agreement for an immediate cease-fire, a halt to all troop movements except for Nationalist movement into Manchuria and south of the Yangtze River, and no further interference with the movement of railroads.

On January 10 the Political Consultative Conference—the constitutional advisory body composed of representatives of the government, the Communists, and various minor political movements agreed to in Chiang's meeting with Mao in October—finally met in Nanking. On the opening day of the conference, the Generalissimo informed the delegates that the two sides had approved the cease-fire agreement. To implement the truce, the agreement provided for an "Executive Headquarters" composed of one Nationalist, one Communist, and one American to be established in Peiping. Executive Headquarters would supervise a network of three-man field teams with the same tripartite composition to report on the effectiveness of the truce and investigate violations. All decisions and actions by the headquarters had to be unanimous, and the role of the Americans was theoretically limited to helping the Chinese of both parties implement the cease-fire. This principle of unanimity was the key consideration in Chou En-lai's acceptance of the cease-fire. The Communists believed that U.S. policy basically favored the Nationalists, but the requirement of unanimity would enable them to prevent any actions inimical to their interests.[10]

As the American member of Executive Headquarters, Marshall nominated Walter Robertson, the American chargé d'affaires in Chungking. Robertson was a former banker whose strongest wish was to return to private life. When he expressed this desire to Marshall, the general merely smiled and replied, "I want to go home too."[11] Colonel Henry Byroade, an engineer officer with wartime experience in China, was designated chief of staff. The Americans assigned about 120 soldiers and civilians to the headquarters, the Communists and Nationalists about 170 personnel each.

"I want Executive Headquarters to be opened and running in Peking by tomorrow," Marshall told Byroade on the afternoon the truce was signed.[12] Byroade commandeered every available American plane in China except General Wedemeyer's own transport and used them to airlift the Chinese and Americans from Chungking, Yenan, Nanking, and other parts of China to Peiping. There they were housed in hotels and set up offices in the empty Rockefeller Memorial Hospital Center. The first truce teams were in the field two days later, much to the amazement of the Chinese.[13]

Meanwhile, the Political Consultative Conference and its committees had approved a number of resolutions to reorganize and broaden the government. A National Assembly was to meet in the spring to consider a new constitution currently being drafted. In the interim, a Council of State that would include members from the Communists and the third parties would act as the highest organ of government. The legality and equality of all political parties was recognized, and all accepted Chiang Kai-shek as the national leader.

Among the other resolutions was a call for reorganization of the armed forces in order to create a single national army. Marshall had been careful to steer clear of any overt involvement in the political discussions between the Nationalists, the Communists, and the minor parties, but he did agree to the request of all parties to serve as the head of a military subcommittee of three composed of Chou, Marshall, and Nationalist general Zhang Zhi-zong to prepare a plan for the integration and reorganization of the armed forces.

Marshall's aim was to reduce the size of the Chinese military establishment in order to make it less of an economic burden on the country and to incorporate Communist military units into a single integrated army. His plan called for the organization of the armed forces into armies composed of three divisions, each including at least one Communist or Nationalist division. The number of divisions and armies would depend on the ultimate size of the reorganized forces.[14] Most important of all, the general believed, was to ensure that any new organization of the military would make it possible to free China from the grip of warlords and political generals. In lengthy sermons to Chou and Zhang he emphasized the importance of civil control of the military, using examples from British and American history.[15]

During January and February the subcommittee haggled over the ratio of Communist to Nationalist divisions, the timetable for reorganization and integration, and other important details. Nevertheless, by February 21 the three conferees had a draft agreement. Chou was flown to Yenan in an American plane to obtain Mao Tse-tung's commitment to the plan. At a special meeting of the Politburo, Chou outlined the terms of the agreement and pointed out its advantages. Mao grumbled that "the Americans and Chiang Kai-shek want to wipe us out by means of nationwide unification of troops. We want unification without being wiped out. . . . In principle we must support the nationwide unification of troops but we must look very concretely at what steps are being proposed to bring it about."[16] In the end the Politburo gave its consent, and Chou returned the next day with a statement of Mao's approval in principle.

On February 25, the military subcommittee announced an agreement labeled "Basis for Military Reorganization and for the Integration of the Communist Forces into the National Army." The reorganization, which was to be completed in just eighteen months, provided for a national army of fifty Nationalist divisions and ten Communist divisions. All other formations were to be demobilized. Within three weeks both parties were to submit lists of units to be retained or demobilized. General Chen Cheng, the Nationalist war minister, estimated that the reduction and reorganization of the army would result in a surplus of more than three hundred thousand officers.[17] The Communists were willing to accept the lopsided ratio for divisions because the agreement provided that all of their units could remain in the areas that they controlled in north China and Manchuria. At 4:00 P.M. on February 25 the Chinese and Nationalist representatives signed the integration agreement in the office of Chiang's aide.

It seemed that Marshall had done the impossible. In only two months he had brought about agreements to end the incipient civil war in China and unify the armed forces. General Zang Zhi-zong declared that "henceforth we are entering into a new period of peaceful reconstruction of the country and we will give up military force as an instrument for political supremacy."[18] "I believe with my head and with my heart that we here have seen the first long stride in a new march toward peace and greatness for China," concluded *Time* correspondent John Walker.[19] In Washington, Truman was jubilant. "I have just received another communication from General Marshall," he told a congressman, "and if things continue going as favorably as they are going now, I believe we can have all of our forces out of China before the year is out."[20]

Even the American embassy's China specialists were impressed. "When he [Marshall] pulled off the cease-fire, which nobody really thought he could do, we suddenly had this wild hope that maybe the great man can do it," recalled John F. Melby. "Then when he made the progress he did, which was done in an incredibly short period of time, toward a political settlement, again, it was, 'maybe he'll do it, maybe he really will.' "[21] Marshall himself was unaffected by the euphoria. At the conclusion of the signing, he observed, "The agreement, I think, represents the great hope of China. I can only trust that its pages will not be soiled by a small group of irreconcilables who for their own purpose would defeat the Chinese people in their overwhelming desire for peace and prosperity."[22]

The "small group of irreconcilables" was actually a sizable and very powerful faction of the Nationalists, the most visible of whom were the CC clique led by Chen Li-fu. They had the support of many in the army, who had no wish to diminish their wealth and prerogatives as war leaders and deal makers through any type of long-term settlement that might reduce the size and influence of the military. Chen Li-fu controlled the government's secret police and a network of spies, provocateurs, and thugs. He liked to describe himself to Americans as the Chinese equivalent of the head of the FBI and would tell all who would listen that the Communists could "be licked in three months."[23] Throughout the period of the negotiations there was an increasing number of public disorders, fights, riots, and demonstrations instigated or organized by the CC clique. Members of the Political Consultative Conference, independent politicians, and intellectuals were roughed up or had their houses wrecked. Plainclothes police broke up meetings and demonstrations in favor of the Consultative Conference. The offices of the Communist Party newspaper in Chungking were looted.[24]

Marshall and other Americans in China had little doubt about who was responsible. "The Tai Li Organization [controlled by Chen Li-fu] operates continuously to suppress free speech and writing," Wedemeyer observed. "Among the youth there is the Kuomintang Youth Corps which employs violence against young people in the schools when they critically discuss conditions in the country."[25]

Marshall was angered and annoyed at the efforts of the right-wing intransigents to sabotage his mission, but he was determined to press on. At the beginning of March, the Committee of Three left for a three-thousand-mile inspection trip to northern China to sell the agreements and check the effectiveness of the cease-fire. The most significant stop was Yenan, where Marshall met with Mao Tse-tung. "It was extremely cold," recalled General Alvan C. Gillem, Jr., who accompanied Marshall to the Communist headquarters. "It was zero or below. The winds were from the northwest desert and Gobi and the arctic. . . . At that time [Mao] occupied a very inferior type of dwelling—a typical Chinese house of the lower order. . . . We had our meeting first in this little anteroom with . . . a couch and one or two chairs—one of the chairs occupied by Mao, and the general and myself, and I think Chou En Lai sat on the couch. . . . Mao had on a blue type of peasant uniform, a semi uniform with earmuffs, and Chou had on the one coat I had seen him wear all winter."[26]

Mao promised to abide by the agreements reached in Chungking and praised Marshall's efforts. "Mao's eyes were totally without any type of interest," noted General Gillem, "more almost those of a reptile . . . no expression whatever."[27] Mao hailed "the durable cooperation between America and China, the Communist Party and the Nationalist Party," but the most substantial thing Marshall took away from his meetings at Yenan was a cold. He believed it was the result of watching a lengthy performance of traditional Chinese music and dance in an unheated auditorium.[28]

Even before departing on his swing through northern China, Marshall had told the president that he wished to return home in mid-March to lobby for increased aid to China, which he saw as both vitally needed and a useful prize to hold out to the quarrelling sides in pressing them to reach agreement. On March 11, Marshall boarded his plane for a four-week visit to the United States and turned over ongoing negotiations to General Gillem, who would serve as his personal representative during his absence.

Despite Marshall's excellent reasons for returning to Washington, his departure was a severe setback for the negotiations in China. "We all had a sense the minute he left, that the whole thing was going to blow up," observed John F. Melby. "I doubt seriously whether any other person in the world could have done so much in so short a time," observed Wedemeyer. "The permanence of his accomplishment, however, is in my mind contingent on his physical presence."[29] Mao and Chou were unhappy that Marshall would leave China while many of the most important questions concerning the implementation of the cease-fire and troop dispositions were still unresolved.[30] His departure increased the uneasiness and mistrust of both sides.

This was evident almost immediately. On the day of Marshall's departure, General Gillem recalled,

> I had spent all day on a number of principles with Chou En Lai and it seemed as if we had finally come to some sort of a conclusion. . . . At about six o'clock we went back to our quarters in Chungking and General Marshall said "Have you reached an agreement?" and Chou En Lai showed him that we had and so did I . . . and [Marshall] said, "Well I am going to depart for the States right away. I'm not going to remain for dinner." . . . No sooner had he left the house than there was a change of atmosphere. We had dinner and then went back to work on this thing to round out the figures and Chou En Lai was requested to sign the document with me and those of us responsible. He absolutely refused. Well we discussed this for a matter of hours. . . . He kept coming back with various and sundry comments that were most frustrating and most contradictory with the result that I eventually lost my temper and I must say that I did make comments to him that were most undiplomatic.[31]

Gillem was an extremely able officer with a distinguished record as a corps commander in the European Theater. "He was one of only two generals for whom I worked who got results without ever seeming to issue a direct order," one officer recalled, "a very warm, personable, down to earth person."[32] However, he had little experience of China and had to ask a member of the embassy staff to explain "this Kuomintang thing."[33] He also lacked Marshall's prestige and Marshall's recognized power to shape American policy. Yet it was not so much Marshall's ill-advised departure or Gillem's shortcomings that ultimately doomed all hopes of a compromise in China, but the course of events in distant Manchuria.

The cease-fire agreement had provided that the ban on troop movements called for in the agreement would not apply to "military movements of the forces of the National Army into or within Manchuria which are for the purpose of restoring Chinese sovereignty." Many Nationalist leaders read this to mean that the cease-fire did not apply at all to Manchuria.[34] They even disputed the need for Executive Headquarters field teams to be sent to Manchuria. The Communists were all for a cease-fire, but they intended to hold on to areas in Manchuria they already controlled and grab as much additional territory as they could before the cease-fire came into force.[35]

Then, in late March, the Soviets inadvertently raised the stakes by pulling their troops out of Manchuria. Since the end of the war, Stalin had had three aims in China: to loot Manchuria of its industrial riches, to establish a dominant economic influence for the Soviet Union in northern China, and to undermine the Americans without risking conflict. The looting part had gone pretty well, but Chiang had stubbornly resisted any new economic concessions to Stalin and continued to stay close to the Americans. The long-overdue Soviet troop withdrawal was intended to win Nationalist goodwill, provide an opportunity for the Communists, and bring pressure on the Americans to follow the Soviet example by removing their Marines from northern China.[36]

However sincere or insincere the Nationalists and Communists were in their desire for a cease-fire, Manchuria was a prize too great to resist. "The big jewel in the Chinese crown was Manchuria," observed a member of Wedemeyer's staff. "The Generalissimo felt compelled, even driven to recover [it]. To end World War II without recovering Manchuria was unthinkable."[37]

For the Communists, Manchuria had become the keystone of their power. They had been forced to yield many areas in central and northern China to the Nationalists, but in Manchuria, the Russian occupation, which delayed and obstructed the arrival of the Nationalist forces, had given the Communists the opportunity to expand.[38] Though the

Soviets were sometimes less than cooperative about making Japanese weapons available and continued to hold the large cities, the interregnum had enabled the Communists to move forces into Manchuria and recruit heavily from troops of the former Manchurian puppet army. "The CCP wants to cut off the northern four provinces from the central government," Chiang told one of his advisers. "If they openly continue to occupy this area, how can we say we are a united country . . . ? How can the goal of peace and unity be attained by a coalition government . . . ?"[39]

In early April, the Nationalists pushed into Manchuria and attacked the Communist-held city of Sipingjie (Siping), a key point on the rail line that connected Mukden in Liaoning Province with the provincial capital of Changchun in Jilin Province. Mao ordered his troops at Sipingjie to hold the city and directed his commanders to occupy Changchun and the major industrial city of Harbin, both recently vacated by the Soviets, who helpfully left behind large stocks of captured Japanese weapons and military supplies. On April 18, the day Marshall returned to China, the Nationalists began a monthlong siege of Sipingjie and Communist troops moved into Changchun.[40]

IN CHINA, CHIANG COULD rely on the belief that in the end, the United States would have no choice but to continue to help him. Mao Tse-tung and the CCP leadership believed that despite the abrupt zigs and zags in Soviet policy, they could ultimately count on help from Russia. In Hanoi, Ho Chi Minh and his government could count on help from nobody. The Americans in Hanoi were cordial and sympathetic, but Washington had shown no interest in Vietnam's problems. The Chinese were backing Ho's rivals. The Soviets were far away, and Stalin was preoccupied with the promising situation of the French Communists, who in the 1945 elections had obtained 25 percent of the vote and become the largest single party in France.

The shortage of food, even in Hanoi, remained critical. A U.S. intelligence report in November 1945 estimated that "if no relief arrives, 1,000,000 Annamites will starve to death this winter."[41] In areas of the countryside, armed clashes between the Vietminh and their nationalist rivals, the Vietnam Quoc Dan Dang (VNQDD) and the Dong Minh

Hoi, occurred with increasing frequency, while in Hanoi, the nationalist press continued to attack Ho and the nationalists organized boisterous antigovernment demonstrations.[42]

In the midst of all that, there was a financial crisis. The Chinese insistence that their money be accepted by the French and Vietnamese as legal tender had already led to economic dislocation, currency manipulation, and inflation. To make matters worse, the Chinese government demanded that the government of France assume responsibility for the expenses of the occupation of northern Indochina by providing loans and advances from the Bank of Indochina. The French agreed in principle, but the two governments had been dickering since the end of September over the amount of money to be paid.[43] Tired of waiting, the Chungking government on November 14 directed General Lu Han to order the two largest banks in Hanoi to pay forty million Vietnamese piasters a month toward the expenses of the Chinese occupation forces. Lu Han's financial expert, Xu Xie, informed Sainteny of the Chinese demands. He described the forty million, however, as "an advance," the money to be repaid later as determined by negotiations between the French and Chinese governments.[44]

Sainteny saw no alternative but to comply. Three days later, however, the French authorities in Saigon issued a decree intended to deal with the inflation caused by the Japanese printing of millions of piaster notes following their March takeover of Indochina. The target was the 500-piaster note, the most common currency unit of any significant value in Indochina. All 500-piaster notes printed between March and September 1945 were declared valueless, and the 500-piaster note would be withdrawn from circulation. Notes printed outside the March to September time period would be honored at 70 percent of face value, but only if deposited in banks.

The decree caused consternation in the north. Not only did the Chinese military and the ethnic Chinese merchant community hold large amounts of 500-piaster notes, but many Vietnamese small tradesmen and artisans commonly held much of their life savings in the form of these notes.[45] In Hanoi there was widespread panic among businessmen and small savers. There were large-scale demonstrations and riots. The Chinese told Sainteny that the French decree was invalid north of the 16th parallel and declared that they could not guarantee the safety of French banks in Hanoi.[46]

Sainteny flew to Saigon to confer with the French authorities. By the time he returned, a mass demonstration organized by the Vietminh was under way at the Bank of Indochina. In the midst of the demonstration, firing broke out, and two Chinese soldiers guarding the bank were wounded. Other Chinese guards opened fire on the demonstrators. When the Vietnamese appeared to return their fire, the Chinese tossed hand grenades into the crowd. Six Vietnamese were killed and ten wounded.[47]

The Vietminh then organized a boycott, in which Chinese merchants participated, on the sale of goods and food to the French in Hanoi. Sainteny could still offer nothing on the 500-piaster decree, which, he declared, was a financial policy of the French government. The Chinese responded by arresting the general manager and branch manager of the Bank of Indochina.

General Gallagher, who had spent most of the month at Haiphong supervising the loading of Chinese troops for transport to northern China, was called upon by the French to mediate. Gallagher knew that he was not authorized to intervene in local affairs, but he feared that a continuation of the crisis might lead to violence and the breakdown of order in the city.[48] Gallagher immediately obtained the release of the two bank officials by Lu Han's chief of staff, who claimed to be unaware of their arrest.

On December 1, Sainteny and the Chinese generals met at Gallagher's residence to try to reach agreement on financial matters. The most immediate problem was the boycott that was causing considerable hardship to the French civilians in Hanoi. The Chinese hinted that they could make the problem go away if the French would only be reasonable on the currency question.[49] Declaring that the two parties "could not solve the banking problem by having women and children go hungry," Gallagher asked the approval of both the French and Chinese to allow him to meet personally with Ho Chi Minh to seek an end to the boycott.

After the meeting temporarily adjourned, General Gallagher called on Ho, who agreed to try to end the boycott but asked that the French pay an indemnity to the families of the six Vietnamese killed in the demonstration at the bank. At the same time, Sainteny announced that French financial experts with full authority to reach an agreement would soon arrive from Saigon. After a few days of acrimonious debate, in the course of which General Gallagher warned darkly of a massacre being "narrowly avoided" and reminded the French that "blood has already been shed," the Chinese got most of what they wanted. The French decree on 500-piaster notes would not apply north of the 16th parallel.[50] To make some gesture toward controlling inflation, holders of amounts over five thousand in piasters were required to deposit them in bank accounts from which they could withdraw only 20 percent of their assets each month.[51]

With the financial crisis resolved, General Gallagher left Hanoi for China several days later. Most of the Chinese Combat Command staff had already departed, and the advisory headquarters was officially closed down on December 12. Unlike Gracey, Gallagher got no parades and no applause for his efforts. The French attitude was illustrated by an intelligence report that observed, "The evident sympathy and show of affection which the U.S. shows toward the Vietnamese will create ties between them. The role of moderator in this conflict has conveniently been assumed by the Americans who are especially interested in establishing future commercial relations. This is proven by the piaster incident."[52] Meanwhile, the Chinese generals returned contentedly to exploiting their opportunities and enjoying their newfound affluence. However, those happy days appeared likely to come to an end in the not too distant future. On January 8, 1946, the French and Chinese governments officially opened talks on the withdrawal of Chinese troops from northern Indochina.

In Hanoi and throughout the north, Ho and his advisers were busy preparing for the national elections called for in the December agreement. "Tomorrow our compatriots will freely choose and elect worthy people to represent them in the management of state affairs," the Vietnamese president declared on the eve of the January 6 voting.[53] To help the people with their choice, the Vietminh organization kept tight control of the election machinery. N. Khac Huyen recalled accompanying his mother to the polling place in Quang Binh Province:

> In the center of the hall where the voting took place there was a big table over which a huge portrait of Chairman Ho looked down and around which sat two solemn-faced officials who were also Vietminh agents. This was the polling "booth." Although a list of five candidates who were expected to run for the five seats allotted to the area had been circulated among the people, who were expected to memorize the names, the predominantly illiterate villagers were unable to remember them. To those who forgot the candidates' names the officials would ask: "Are you voting for A, B, X, Y and Z?" Invariably the answers were "yes" or "of course." . . . It was about noon. Some one hundred persons who had been busy chattering with each other had not voted. The presiding election official told them to leave their ballots on the table, promising to mark them as soon as he had time. The people obligingly thanked him for his helpfulness.[54]

With election practices such as these, few could have been surprised when the Vietminh candidates received 97 percent of the popular vote. No voting took place in provinces such as Vinh Yen, Viet Tri, Yen Bay, and Langson, where the nationalists, backed by their Chinese allies, predominated, but Vietminh candidates were nonetheless declared the winners in these provinces as well. Their sweep entitled the Vietminh to 300 seats in the 350-seat assembly, but as agreed, 70 seats were reserved for the two nationalist parties.[55] The national elections gave legitimacy and prestige to Ho's government and enabled them to present themselves to the Chinese and the French as the authentic representatives of the Vietnamese people.

Having prevailed in the election, the Vietminh now turned to neutralizing the opposition. Since August, the Vietminh had controlled the municipal police and the security services in the large cities and many parts of the provinces. The armed forces and militia were also firmly under their control. They used these organizations to control and disrupt nationalist activities and to infiltrate their leadership. Nationalists who appeared susceptible were pressured to defect to the Vietminh through persuasion and propaganda, family pressure, blackmail, kidnapping, or torture.[56]

In the countryside, the nationalists fought back with some success but were handicapped by disunity and lack of coordination. Their support from the Chinese was changeable and uncertain, while the French began to look with favor on the Vietminh as a faction with whom they might make a deal that would aid their return to power. "Thank goodness Ho Chi Minh is the boss," wrote one French general. "The Viet Minh have a solid grasp on power. He wants to get rid of the VNQDD, which can only help our cause."[57] Sainteny recalled that while Ho's nationalist rivals "demanded total and immediate independence as a condition of any negotiation, Ho Chi Minh declared that he understood quite well that he could not attain what he wanted immediately and that he would be content with relative independence and a gentlemen's agreement with France that would bring about, after a lapse of time, the total independence of his country."[58] Sainteny argued that it was better to make an agreement with "a worrisome government in Hanoi" than to have to deal with a government "entrenched in the mountain regions and waging a guerrilla war against the French."[59] A French intelligence report concluded that "in the military domain Tonkin is tending to return to the state of China in the 1920s, and the presence of Chinese occupation units and surviving bands of [nationalist] irregulars and auxiliaries does not simplify the chaotic situation. If this diversity, which engenders disorder and weakness, is favorable to our aims, it should not be lost sight of that the first effort at French military action in Tonkin will cause the fraternal enemies of the day before to coalesce against us."[60]

Since October, Sainteny and Ho had been meeting secretly for talks in a villa off Paul-Bert Square in central Hanoi. Sainteny was accompanied by his political adviser, Léon Pignon, a veteran colonial bureaucrat, Ho by Hoang Minh Giam, the minister of culture. Ho's tactic, reported Sainteny, "appears to be to discuss every subject point by point down to the last inch."[61] While he talked, Ho "smoked continually—Chinese cigarettes, American cigarettes, or the strong Gauloise cigarettes. Pignon smoked even more. . . . Our talks ended late at night in an atmosphere as thick with smoke as an opium den—but without the euphoria."[62]

The talks took on new urgency when the French negotiations in Chungking became known and as Leclerc assembled an expeditionary corps in southern Vietnam to reoccupy the north. The main points of contention were Ho Chi Minh's demands that France explicitly recognize the independence of Vietnam and use the word "independence" in any agreement, and also that France accept the unity of Vietnam as a nation. The French had divided Vietnam into three separate entities: Tonkin, the north; the protectorate of Annam (which included Hue) in the middle; and the colony of Cochinchina, ruled from Saigon, in the south. To the French, all three parts of Vietnam had separate administrative and legal status. While the talks continued, French troops landed on the coast of Annam at the seaside resort town of Nha Trang and other troops advanced overland from Cambodia to occupy Hue.

On February 20, a Reuters dispatch disclosed the terms of a Sino-French agreement soon to be signed in Chungking. Amid general unease and strident cries of alarm by their nationalist opponents, the Vietminh continued war preparations, enlarging the militia and beginning the evacuation of children and old people to the countryside. "There was tension under the surface," recalled one American observer, "with French troops on their way north from Saigon. And the mood of the city seemed gloomy and foreboding with gray faces in the gray streets under gray skies."[63]

Ho also moved to broaden his government. General Hsiao Wen, who had always distrusted the Vietminh but liked the French a good deal less, pressured the nationalists into forming a new coalition government.[64] Ho then convened the new National Assembly chosen in the January elections, which unanimously designated him president of the new government and chairman of a National Resistance Committee that would direct efforts to resist the French.[65]

In Chungking on February 29, the French and Chinese finalized their agreement on the "relief" of the Chinese occupation troops by the French. The French surrendered all extraterritorial rights and privileges in China and their concessions at Shanghai, Tianjin, and Xiamen. Ownership of the Chinese portion of the railroad from Hanoi to Kunming was to revert immediately to China, and Chinese exports passing through Haiphong were to be free of duty. In addition Chinese nationals in Vietnam were to enjoy most-favored-nation status. The date for the landing of the French expeditionary forces was set at March 5.

Three days later, French authorities met with the Chinese to sign the final agreement. At that point the Chinese military representative explained to the astonished French delegation that the Chungking authorities had determined that they could not sign the agreement without the approval of the supreme Allied commander, General MacArthur. There was some possible legal basis for this view, which was also held by General Wedemeyer, but the likelier Chinese motive was to stall.[66] The occupation command in Hanoi had always been uneasy about the Sino-French deal and had bombarded Chungking with warnings and objections. Some Chinese generals genuinely sympathized with Vietnam's struggle for independence, but all feared the consequences for the Chinese community in Tonkin if the French attempted to fight their way back into the north.[67] They may also have been concerned about the behavior of returning French troops and could not have been reassured by the statements of General Leclerc to the Chinese consul general in Saigon that the hooliganism, petty theft, and mistreatment of Chinese merchants engaged in by French troops in the south was "none of his affair. France was a great power and need answer to no one."[68]

By March 5, as the fleet carrying Leclerc's expeditionary corps steamed into the Gulf of Tonkin, Chungking had still sent no specific orders to Chinese commanders in Vietnam regarding a French landing, while Sainteny and Ho still had reached no agreement. General Raoul Salan, the French military representative at Hanoi, insisted that the French had to land on March 6. After that, the tides would be unfavorable for almost two weeks and the French ships carried insufficient supplies to enable them to wait.[69] Lu Han's chief of staff, General Ma Ying, insisted that the landing would have to be postponed and the French ships could be resupplied by boats from shore. He argued that without an agreement with the French, the Vietnamese, now united in a new coalition, would violently resist a French landing and that in the ensuing war and bloodshed the ethnic Chinese community would be at risk.

While the French and Chinese haggled, Sainteny and Ho came under increasing pressure to conclude an agreement, Ho from the Chinese and Sainteny from General Leclerc, who, according to Sainteny, urged him to do his utmost to reach an accord, "even at the cost of initiatives that could eventually be disavowed."[70] Just before dawn on the morning of March 6, Ho Chi Minh accepted Sainteny's final offer. In their agreement, France "recognized the Republic of Vietnam as a free state, having its own parliament, army and finances and forming part of the Indochinese Federation and the French Union." Matters concerning the unification of the three parts of Vietnam were to be settled by popular referendum. In return, the government of Vietnam agreed to "amicably welcome" the French army that would arrive to "relieve" the Chinese occupation troops.[71]

Three hours after Ho indicated his assent to the accord, landing craft from Leclerc's fleet headed for the port of Haiphong. The Chinese commander at Haiphong had not been informed of the latest round of agreements and had received no specific orders except to "remain on the alert."[72] As the French landing craft entered the river leading to the Haiphong docks, shots were fired from Chinese positions on shore. The French, under orders not to return fire, continued up the river. Then a large cache of captured Japanese ammunition on the docks blew up. The Chinese, convinced that the explosion was the result of fire from the French warships, intensified their fire. The French now returned the fire and withdrew to the mouth of the river. A cease-fire was soon arranged, but the two-hour battle had cost the French more than a hundred casualties, mostly wounded, and the Chinese about thirty.[73] It was an inauspicious start to the "amicable" French return.

The Vietminh staged a mass meeting in front of the municipal theater to explain the agreement with the French to a puzzled and surprised public. Nationalist activists in the crowd grumbled that Ho had been tricked into submitting to the French. Vo Nguyen Giap spoke first and compared the agreement to the Treaty of Brest-Litovsk, which the Bolsheviks had been obliged to sign with the Germans in 1918 to safeguard their revolution.[74] Ho spoke last, almost dwarfed by the huge red flag with a gold star that hung behind him. No country had so far recognized Vietnam's independence, he pointed out, but now the French had agreed that Vietnam was a free nation.[75]

To Sainteny, who witnessed the speech, Ho appeared "most thoroughly himself. He was an adroit speaker who knew how to argue a point and how to acknowledge his weaknesses. . . . His tone, his frankness, the fragility of his person and the humility of his attitude were very persuasive. He did not attempt to impress or intimidate. On the contrary he emphasized the difficulties that had to be overcome. . . . The indomitable will that flashed in his eyes illuminating his features made one understand that he would not hesitate to do anything to achieve his goal."[76] Ho concluded his talk by reminding his listeners that he had "fought alongside my compatriots all my life for the independence of our fatherland. I would rather die than betray my country." From the crowd there was a roar: *"Ho Chu Tich muon nam!"* (Long live President Ho Chi Minh!) Though few Vietnamese leaders were convinced that the bargain would lead to lasting peace (Party directives called it a means "to gain time"), they were still willing to trust Ho's judgment.[77]

On March 18, Leclerc led a long column of trucks carrying the troops of the French 2nd Armored Division in a parade through central Hanoi. French residents of the capital, "who thought the city had been liberated," lined the parade route cheering enthusiastically. "What they did not realize," wrote OSS cryptographer George Wickes, "is that it cost Leclerc considerable face before he was allowed to enter the city with a 'guard of honor' of 1,000 troops. Leclerc, whom I had last seen in all his glory in Saigon at the newly reopened Cercle Sportif or attending mass at the Cathedral, where the sermon appeared to be 'Leclerc, France and God,' cut a more modest figure in Hanoi."[78]

One week later, Ho met with Admiral Thierry d'Argenlieu, high commissioner for Indochina, aboard a French cruiser in Along Bay. A former Catholic monk as well as a naval officer, d'Argenlieu was a fervent disciple of de Gaulle. In politics he stood slightly to the right of Louis XIV; personally he was imperious, grandiose, and implacably stubborn and had inspired homicidal thoughts among the American officers who had encountered him as the Free French governor of New Caledonia during World War II. In a remark that was soon to become famous, he declared, "I am amazed, yes, that is the word, I am amazed that France has such a fine expeditionary corps and yet its leaders would rather negotiate than fight."[79]

D'Argenlieu's views faithfully mirrored those of the comparatively large French colonial community in the south. A colonial bureaucrat concisely summarized these beliefs in a memorandum addressed to General Leclerc:

> The Japanese are the cause of all Indochina's woes. . . . Access to the country ought to be denied to them for many years. . . .

> The French government ought to gather all pro-French Annamite patriots around itself. . . . We have committed ourselves to protecting certain ethnic minorities and we must uphold our role as vigilant guardians. . . . Cambodia, Laos and Cochinchina could become prey to Viet Minh imperialism. The same fate could be expected for the Meo, Tho and Nuong peoples. . . . It is true that the policies of the government since the Japanese capitulation have been based on procrastination and dilatory measures . . . but it is now time to shift strategies. Circumstances are now favorable to us, and if we do not seize this opportunity we will destroy what generations of French colonials and Annamite patriots have built together. There is one truth that no one can deny. France can only remain a first-rank power if it retains its sovereignty over its territories around the world.[80]

It took only a few hours' conversation with the admiral to convince Ho of the importance of holding further negotiations on the status of Vietnam and the implementation of the March accords in France, where d'Argenlieu would be out of the picture and the Vietminh could talk directly to the French government. Ho insisted on France, and Leclerc and Sainteny agreed with him. Ho did agree to d'Argenlieu's suggestion for a preparatory conference at the town of Dalat in the central highlands between colonial officials and Vietnamese representatives prior to the departure of the Vietnamese negotiators for France.[81]

The Dalat meeting, held in April and May, revealed how far apart the two sides were in their vision of Vietnam's future. The French interpretation of the powers to be exercised by a "free state within the French Union" was a narrow one that allowed for only local autonomy in Tonkin. Along with the other parts of Vietnam, Laos, and Cambodia, Tonkin would form part of an Indochinese federation. Within the federation, the governor-general would still control foreign affairs, the armed forces, transportation, immigration, hygiene, and other internal affairs. The Vietnamese representatives, led by Giap, replied that Vietnam was a single entity and should be considered as such. The division at the 16th parallel had no significance beyond demarcating the occupation zone of the Chinese. The Vietnamese argued that the March armistice included the south as well as the north and that settling the question of an armistice for the south was a precondition for any further progress toward an agreement.[82] Unable to reach agreement, the conferees adjourned to await the outcome of the talks in France.

Undeterred by the failure of the Dalat talks, Ho Chi Minh and the Vietnamese delegation boarded a French transport plane at Gia Lam airport on April 30 for the long journey to France. It was a journey made even longer by the French desire to delay the delegation's arrival until a political crisis resulting from the June 2 national elections in France could be resolved. Midway through the trip, Ho received word that d'Argenlieu had orchestrated the formation of an "Autonomous Republic of Cochinchina" with a prime minister and cabinet of very pliant assimilated Vietnamese. D'Argenlieu's reckless actions, which appeared to undermine the basic March understandings, had not been authorized by Paris, but the Colonial Ministry soon accepted the new entity. Ho pointedly expressed the hope that Cochinchina would not become "another Alsace-Lorraine."

Ho had time to cool off as Sainteny's guest at the coastal resort of Biarritz while he waited for the dithering political parties in Paris to put together a new government. After that, he went to Paris, where he gave newspaper interviews, attended receptions, and drew large crowds of onlookers. When the formal negotiations finally began at the Palace of Fontainebleau on July 6, they opened with a bang. In his opening statement, Pham Van Dong, the formal head of the Vietnamese delegation, blasted d'Argenlieu's recent seizure of the central highlands and protested "the mutilation of our fatherland" through the creation of a separate state in Cochinchina.[83]

After that, the two sides got down to hard negotiations. D'Argenlieu appeared briefly in Paris to urge the government to stand firm, warning that the Vietnamese would quickly capitalize on any sign of weakness. The French negotiators were the same men who had been at the Dalat meeting, and the issues were largely the same: the Vietnamese demand for an explicit French recognition of their independence and for a unified Vietnam that would include Cochinchina. Ho Chi Minh, not a formal member of the Vietnamese delegation, remained in Paris, making his case to the media and appealing to leaders of the Left and to anyone else who would listen.

On July 22, d'Argenlieu dropped another bombshell into the negotiations by announcing that he would convene a second conference at Dalat to discuss the future of the projected Indochina federation. The invitees were Laos, Cambodia, and the two "states" of Vietnam, Annam and Cochinchina, which the French had reoccupied. At one stroke, d'Argenlieu appeared to have unilaterally decided the fate of Cochinchina. The Vietnamese in Paris were furious and broke off the talks. If "the French authorities in Cochinchina are responsible for the fate of Cochinchina," declared Pham Van Dong, then "our conference at Fontainebleau has no further reason to meet." On the other hand, "if the 6 March convention must be put into effect . . . the Fontainebleau Conference is the sole appropriate forum for the discussion of these problems."[84]

The French government's response to d'Argenlieu's latest insubordination was to suggest timidly that he might perhaps shorten the conference a bit. Even this the admiral refused to do, declaring that it would be an affront to the monarchs of Laos and Cambodia, who were to attend, if he cut short the conference just because the Vietnamese in the north were unhappy.[85]

After d'Argenlieu concluded his conference in mid-July, the French government urged the Vietnamese to return to the negotiating table and offered agreement on a future referendum to decide the fate of Cochinchina. By now the Vietnamese position had hardened, and they demanded a firm date for the referendum as well as the explicit declaration on Vietnam's independence. The French said no, and the Vietnamese delegation sailed for Haiphong on September 13. Ho remained behind and succeeded in negotiating a modus vivendi with Marius Moutet, the colonial minister, two days later. The modus vivendi reaffirmed the March accords and called for a second round of negotiations at Fontainebleau in January. A cease-fire would go into effect in the south on October 30, and after order had been restored, citizens would be guaranteed their "democratic liberties."[86]

Whether Ho still hoped that further negotiations could avoid a war cannot be known, but most of his close associates were somber and pessimistic. Many had already begun to prepare for war. Nguyen Binh, who had more or less adhered to the cease-fire with great reluctance in the south, now saw his worst suspicious confirmed by d'Argenlieu's project to create a Cochinchina republic. In telegrams to Hanoi he advised Giap to prepare for a protracted guerrilla war against the French and to be prepared to destroy all of Hanoi if necessary.[87]

In France there was no sense of crisis and little concern. Other matters such as the developing Cold War abroad and the continued political upheavals at home claimed the most attention. France's vacillating policies toward Indochina risked war, but the Vietnamese could not, the French believed, stand up to a modern army and would not fight very long or effectively. As Maurice Thorez, a Communist member of the French Cabinet and a nominal supporter of Ho, declared, "If the Vietnamese do not respect these terms we will take the necessary measures and let the guns speak for us if need be."[88]

IN CHINA AND VIETNAM the contending parties had finally concluded broad agreements, which, it appeared, might slowly unravel. In Korea there was almost nothing to unravel. On January 15 a heavily guarded train from Pyongyang arrived in Seoul bearing General T. F. Shtikov and the Russian delegation to the Soviet-American talks provided for in the Moscow agreements. Attached to the train as a goodwill present were two carloads of coal. Almost all of Korea's coal was in the north, and the Americans had been importing coal from Japan to ease the severe shortage in southern Korea.

News of the Moscow agreements with their provision for a five-year trusteeship had unleashed a tidal wave of angry protest in the south. Businesses were closed in protest, and Korean employees of American military government offices walked out. All political factions organized mass rallies. There were terrorist bombs and political kidnappings.[89] The impetuous Kim Ku called a nationwide strike and proclaimed his Korean Provisional Government the only legitimate authority. Kim's bold power grab quickly fizzled and his star began to fade, but the opposition to trusteeship continued as strong as ever. Three days after the attempted coup, the Communists and some leftist parties suddenly switched from strident opposition to support for the Moscow accords. This drastic flip-flop was most likely dictated by instructions from Moscow, but whatever the cause, it served to completely discredit the Communists in the eyes of most Koreans and allowed the center and right-wing leaders, particularly Syngman Rhee, to assume the position of champions of immediate independence.[90] On the evening of the day of the Communists' sudden conversion, representatives of ninety-one different political groups meeting in conference passed resolutions calling for the execution for treason of Communist leader Pak Hon-yong. A news story claiming that Pak had expressed the hope that Korea might become one of the Soviet republics only increased the number of Koreans calling for his blood.[91]

The first round of talks with the Russians, referred to as the U.S.-Soviet Joint Conference, was intended to focus on economic and administrative problems with political questions to be left to the full U.S.-Soviet Joint Commission, which was scheduled to meet in March. The American delegation to the conference was led by General Arnold and included Benninghoff as well as nine additional military officers. It soon became apparent that the two sides held widely different assumptions about Korea, which colored even the most technical discussions. The Americans saw the 38th parallel as an inconvenient barrier to be removed as soon as possible and wished to treat Korea as a single economic unit. They wanted to unify the railroad system, establish a single power grid, and open direct trade across the 38th parallel. The Soviets came with the assumption that the principal issue was to establish appropriate economic and administrative relationships between two related but separate zones of responsibility.[92] They wanted to talk about barter. Specifically, the Soviets proposed to exchange coal and other raw materials from the north for rice from the south.

Southern Korea normally produced a surplus of rice, but at this time, the south had no surplus. The American military government's abrupt lifting of the long-standing Japanese controls on the prices and sale of rice introduced a free market system for the first time in Korea, but under the peculiar economic conditions of the time it also led to hoarding, speculation, smuggling, and inflation. Freed of the requirement to surrender most of their rice to the government, some chronically underfed farmers simply ate it themselves. The disorganization of the railways and shortages of coal and rolling stock created serious problems of distribution.[93] The Soviets greeted the American statements that they had no extra rice with anger and incredulity. General Shtikov declared that the Soviets would not discuss any exchange of commodities between the zones until the American command could promise to supply rice to the north. Arnold presented the conclusions of his technical experts that the north should be capable of producing as much rice as the south on a per capita basis.[94]

After fifteen meetings, the conference adjourned with agreement on only a few minor matters, such as the limited movement of mail, but no agreements were reached on matters of trade and exchange between the zones or the supply of electric power from the north to the south. "It was apparent from the tone and attitude of the Soviet delegation," reported Benninghoff, "that the USSR contemplates a lengthy occupation of at least the northern half of Korea. It was also apparent that the USSR will probably resist all efforts by the United States to open up the country and treat it as an economical and political unit."[95]

The shadow of the Moscow agreements led to new alignments among Koreans in the north and south. In the north, Kim Il-sung, with the support of the Soviets, moved to consolidate his authority. Cho Man-sik, who, like the nationalists in the south, had vehemently opposed the Moscow agreements, was arrested on charges of treason, and his party was placed under the leadership of one of Kim's loyal followers.

In February, Kim became head of a new North Korean Interim People's Committee, which assumed power in the north. Members of rival Communist factions held posts in the committee, but Kim and his longtime supporters were in control. Almost all non-Communist parties were folded into Kim's new North Korean Workers' Party or ceased to exist. The Party continued and strengthened earlier land reform programs and nationalized all large industries, banks, and businesses, touching off another exodus of landowners, businessmen, and Christian activists to the south. Among those who remained, however, the reforms were widely popular, and Kim declared that "the southern reactionaries are now very much afraid of the north wind."[96]

The "southern reactionaries" had also been busy. Washington was unhappy with the lack of progress in the Joint Conference, but that was insignificant compared to the problems that were likely to arise when the full-dress U.S.-Soviet Joint Commission convened. That commission was charged with the formation of a provisional government of Korea in consultation with Korean "democratic parties and social organizations."[97] The Soviets would undoubtedly insist that Kim Il-sung's North Korean People's Committee and North Korean Workers'

Party were just such organizations. What did Hodge have to offer? The State, War, and Navy Coordinating Committee instructed Hodge to "select a group of representative democratic Korean leaders for purposes of consultation with the Joint Commission in its preparation of proposals for the establishment of a Korean provisional government." All "democratic political parties and social organizations" were to be represented.[98]

Hodge's response was the Representative Democratic Council, which, as one of Hodge's junior officers later observed, "was neither democratic nor representative nor did it ever council [*sic*]."[99] Most of the parties and factions on the left, whose supporters probably still formed the majority in the south outside Seoul, were not represented, but the RDC did bring together the right and some of the center factions in an uneasy partnership in which Rhee played a prominent role. With this none-too-stable foundation in place, the Americans prepared to face the Soviets in the Joint Commission over the future of Korea.

CHAPTER THIRTEEN

WARS RENEWED

ON APRIL 12, 1946, GENERAL GEORGE C. MARSHALL LEFT WASHington for California and China accompanied by his wife, Catherine, who had been invited by Madame Chiang Kai-shek to return with him to Chungking. Marshall had spent most of his time during his brief visit to the United States testifying before the House and Senate Foreign Relations committees and lobbying the Export-Import Bank and other economic aid agencies. His message was invariably the importance of extending generous loans and credits to make possible the economic rehabilitation of China, still suffering from the devastation of war, plagued by regional famines, and facing ruinous inflation.[1] "All in all I think I have sold China," he told General Wedemeyer at the end of March.[2] The sale included congressional approval of a U.S. Military Advisory Group composed of several hundred army and navy officers and men to replace the China Theater Headquarters due to be deactivated in June.

The Marshalls' plane arrived at Long Beach Army Air Base on the evening of the twelfth, and the couple spent the next day in Hollywood with movie director Frank Capra, who had made the famous *Why We Fight* propaganda films for the U.S. Army. They continued on to Honolulu, Wake Island, and Tokyo, where they were guests of General and Mrs. MacArthur before flying on to Peiping.

While the Marshalls' plane crossed the Pacific, soldiers of the Nationalist New First Army and Seventy-first Army were advancing slowly toward the city of Changchun, which the Communists had recently seized following the withdrawal of the Soviets. With the capture of Shanhaikuan the previous November, Chiang Kai-shek had been able to assemble a formidable army in Manchuria supported by artillery and a small air force. Many of Chiang's troops were American-trained, and lavishly equipped by Chinese standards. The men of the Seventy-first Army had received "lined parkas, wind hoods, field jackets, mittens, mufflers, rubber snow boots, blankets and sleeping bags."[3] Chiang's objective was to expel the Communists from the cities they had taken over in the wake of the Soviet withdrawal and establish national government control over all of Manchuria. By April, Nationalist forces controlled the main rail line from the Great Wall to Mukden. Farther north were Changchun, the former capital of Japanese-controlled "Manchukuo," and Harbin, terminus of the former Chinese Eastern Railway.

General Lin Piao, a graduate of the Whampoa Military Academy and a veteran of the Long March, commanded the Communist Northeast Democratic United Army charged with defending the Party's gains in Manchuria. Lin was "held in first place by American officers of long experience in China as the best communist strategist," wrote an officer with one of the field teams; "he is cold, calculating, cruel and embittered by his years of struggle. He looks and acts like a soldier. . . . He can command a crowd or move a mob by his voice alone."[4] Lin Piao's mission was to hang on to Changchun and Harbin "at all costs" in the anticipation that Marshall would be able to bring about a renewed truce, at least for a time.[5] For Lin's troops this required the defense of the city of Sipingjie, a major rail junction on the line between Changchun and Mukden.

The first round went to the Communists. Lin's army caught one division of the Seventy-first Army about forty miles southwest of Sipingjie, isolated by a river from the rest of the Nationalist forces. On April 3 in the fading light, Lin's forty-thousand-man army surprised the Nationalists and threw them into panic. Some officers abandoned their men. The Communists reportedly captured half of the division's equipment and took a third of the Nationalists prisoner. When Lin tried to do the same to a division of the New First Army, however, he encountered hardened American-trained veterans who had fought the Japanese in Burma occupying more defensible positions. After several unsuccessful and costly attacks, Lin's force was obliged to pull back to Sipingjie.[6]

In a message to the Central Committee, Lin Piao pointed out that the Nationalists were continuing to pour more troops into the northeast. His forces could not simultaneously defend Sipingjie, hold Changchun, and fight the Kuomintang field army. He wanted to concentrate on destroying the Nationalist armies, not defending cities. Lin hoped to retain the initiative and avoid the practice of passively waiting for battles to develop. Mao turned down these recommendations. He told Lin Piao to "turn Siping into a second Madrid" (referring to the heroic three-year defense of the Spanish capital during the Spanish Civil War). Lin Piao replied resolutely that he would fight to the last man, something that his close associates believed he had no actual intention of doing.[7]

By the eighteenth of April, the Nationalists had Sipingjie completely encircled. The Communist defenders slightly outnumbered the attackers, but the Nationalists had artillery and air support and modern American weapons including new M-1 rifles. The Communists occupied the defensive installations built by the Japanese in and around the city. It was the first time that Mao's troops had ever fought a prolonged engagement from fixed positions, a tactical choice that one of Lin's commanders would later call "really stupid."[8] The terrain around the city appeared to one Nationalist general as a sea of endless mud often a foot or more deep.[9] The fight for Sipingjie was well under way as Marshall returned to Chungking.

Marshall stayed at Chungking only a few days, then moved with Chiang's government back to the former Chinese capital, Nanking, at the end of April. Here Marshall occupied the residence of the former German ambassador, which one of his aides described as the finest house in the city.[10] Built in the Chinese style but with a Western interior, it had a large room on the second floor that could be used for staff meetings and for watching evening movies, one of the general's only forms of relaxation.

Marshall was angry and frustrated by the escalating conflict in Manchuria. He blamed the Communists for their violation "of the plain terms of the cease fire agreement of January," but also blamed the Nationalists for their insistence that the agreement did not apply to Manchuria. Above all he blamed the delay in allowing field teams into Manchuria.[11] Marshall's first move was to try to defuse the situation in Manchuria by persuading the Communists to withdraw from Changchun and discouraging the Nationalists from attacking it. Instead, he proposed the city be turned over to representatives of Executive Headquarters. Neither side showed much interest, and by the end of April, Marshall was suggesting to the Nationalist and Communist negotiators that his usefulness as a mediator might be drawing to an end.

Meanwhile, the battle for Sipingjie continued to rage. Both sides brought in reinforcements, and Nationalist artillery pounded the city. By this time, Sipingjie had become crowded with troops. Artillery pieces, captured American trucks, and slow-moving, underpowered Japanese cars constantly clogged the single east-west street and the only one running north and south. Most shops had long since closed, but restaurants carried on a thriving trade with soldiers in grayish-yellow uniforms constantly coming and going at all hours. The restaurant owners were pleased with their profits but kept their essential possessions in the backroom packed and ready to go at a moment's notice.[12] Lin Piao directed the battle from his headquarters in a middle-school teacher's house in the southeast section of the city. Lin's desk faced a wall with a large map pierced by many small red and green flags that were frequently moved to show the progress of operations. On sunny days the general sometimes worked in the yard but returned frequently to gaze at the map on the wall.

During a period of thirty-one days the Communists repulsed ten major assaults. At one point Lin had reportedly "used all noncombatant political working staff . . . local cadre and even high school students" to stem the Nationalist advance. "They literally just threw them at the Kuomintang's crack troops. It was a massacre; more than five thousand noncombatants, who had never had any military training, were killed or wounded."[13] Early in May, General Tu Yu-ming (Du Yuming), who had been hospitalized for a kidney ailment, returned to the north to resume his post as commander in chief of the Nationalist armies in Manchuria. Tu arrived at the outskirts of Sipingjie aboard his special train and immediately held a conference with his commanders. The general, "in military uniform but wearing slippers and a scalp cap, presided over the conference while Mrs. Tu, who accompanied her husband in the train, constantly reminded him not to get excited." Tu was delighted that the Communists had decided to fight a set-piece battle. He promised to bring his American-trained New Sixth Army up from southern Manchuria to reinforce the attackers.[14]

Lin Piao learned of Tu's plan almost as soon as he made it, thanks to the Communists' efficient signal intelligence. Soon to be outnumbered five to one, he requested and received permission to withdraw. On the evening of May 18, as General Tu's troops completed their preparations for an elaborate encircling movement, Lin's forces silently withdrew and disappeared into the darkness. The following morning, Nationalist troops in their positions around Sipingjie "adjusted their eyes to the light of dawn and slowly peeked over their trenches. No rifle or machine gun fire spat out from the Red side. . . . With caution bred from keeping low in their trenches the Nationalist soldiers were not very fast in their movement forward. They reached the shattered town at about 7:30 A.M. A few Chinese and Japanese civilians crept out of their cellars to tell them that Lin Piao's entire army had closed out of the city about 1:30 that morning. This placed the rear Red echelons about six hours march away."[15]

None of the combatants who had fought at Sipingjie felt elated by the results. A Nationalist officer concluded that the government forces had "seemingly achieved nothing during the battle. The Communists had dispersed into small units and thus escaped capture." Troops who had fought Lin Piao's forces "were never again as spirited as when they entered Manchuria. They were simply horrified at the ghastly carnage involved in fighting the Communists."[16] Lin Piao had lost at least eight thousand and perhaps as many as forty thousand men killed or wounded. "During the battle our strategy was clumsy and at the end we felt exhausted," recalled one Communist commander.[17] Lin Piao himself appeared "dejected" when interviewed by newspapermen after the siege and "said he never again would fight a battle of fixed position until he had real troop strength."[18]

For the Communists, the loss of Sipingjie and Changchun, which fell easily a short time later, meant a long, hungry retreat across Manchuria pursued by the Nationalist armies. Many of the Manchurians and former puppet troops recently recruited to the Communist Army disappeared or defected to the Nationalists, along with not a few veterans. Soldiers exhausted by the fighting in Sipingjie walked for forty-two days. Wherever possible they took the most inaccessible routes. Sometimes the Nationalist forces were actually ahead of them and the Communist troops had to move in a long, circular march around or away from their enemy. Nationalist aircraft flew overhead dropping propaganda leaflets urging surrender. (That was probably the best use of the planes, since they could seldom hit any targets on the ground.) Lin Piao began to talk a lot about the Russian retreat before Napoleon's invasion that eventually led to the destruction of the French. Privately, he cabled the Central Committee that the Communists would probably have to give up Harbin and return to guerrilla warfare.[19]

In Nanking there was jubilation. Marshall reported that the capture of Sipingjie "convinced the Nationalist generals that they could settle the Manchuria problem by force."[20] This belief grew even stronger as Nationalist troops approached Changchun. "I am almost certain by now that the Generalissimo is convinced he can settle China by force alone and intends to do just that," wrote an American diplomat in Nanking.[21] Chiang now suddenly announced that he was out of communication with his generals in Manchuria and had to fly to Mukden to assess the situation. Chiang probably knew that his forces had already retaken Changchun with slight resistance from the Communists and were urging a further offensive toward Harbin. In any case, the Generalissimo's absence precluded any serious negotiations to get the situation under control.[22] In the meantime, Communist propaganda grew more stridently anti-American and began to accuse Marshall of in effect siding with the Nationalists.

Marshall warned Chiang that "the continued advances of government troops in Manchuria in the absence of any action by you to terminate the fighting are making my services as possible negotiator extremely difficult and will soon make them virtually impossible." Three days later he repeated his warning and cautioned that if the integrity of his position as a mediator were compromised, his mission would be at an end.[23] "Marshall is beginning to get the idea he is being pushed around, made a tool of, and he doesn't like it at all," wrote diplomat John Melby in his diary. "In short he is about as angry as anyone I have ever seen."[24]

Marshall doubted that Manchuria was the key to a decisive Kuomintang victory over the Communists. Like other American generals who knew the Nationalists, he believed that the only alternative to a compromise settlement was a long and disastrous civil war giving rise to "utter chaos" in large areas of China.[25] The belief among many of

Chiang's advisers and generals "that the Communists can be quickly crushed" was, Marshall told President Truman, "a gross underestimate of the possibilities as a long and terrible conflict would be unavoidable."[26] Marshall was also concerned that a Kuomintang drive into northern Manchuria might encourage Soviet intervention in an area where the Russians had long believed they had special strategic and economic interests. The second secretary of the Soviet embassy in Chungking, Andrei M. Ledovsky, observed many years later that Stalin would indeed have had "reasons to send his army back to Manchuria . . . should Chiang Kai-shek choose to direct his troops into northern Manchuria."[27]

Chiang may have sensed that he had pushed Marshall as far as he could get away with, or he may have wanted time to regroup his forces. In any case, upon his return at the beginning of June, the Generalissimo agreed to a ten-day truce—later extended to fifteen days—and also to the establishment of Executive Headquarters Field Teams in Manchuria. Whether Marshall actually believed that these arrangements might lead to a permanent settlement even at this late stage must be a matter of conjecture. "This is a hell of a problem," he wrote to his Washington liaison officer, "but we will lick it yet, pessimists to the contrary notwithstanding."[28]

Marshall's short truce came as a welcome respite for the hard-pressed Communist forces in the northeast, providing them time to reorganize and hold on to Harbin and their base areas in northern Manchuria. For this reason, some writers, most recently Jung Chang and Jon Halliday, have suggested that Marshall's intervention was responsible for the Nationalist defeat in Manchuria and ultimately in the entire civil war.[29] While it is impossible to assess events that never happened, the likelihood that Chiang would have won the civil war but for American meddling appears remote. Chiang's higher command was riddled with incompetents, and his headquarters at all levels was thoroughly penetrated by Communist agents. The Communists were skilled at gaining local support and at filling out their ranks with new recruits. More important, the Communist armies could move faster and remained far more agile than their Nationalist opponents. As a Nationalist official military history later observed, the Communists "had a marching capability which enabled them to attack, withdraw and make surprise attacks at will. They could deploy their strength flexibly, swiftly assembling and disassembling troops and moving back and forth freely. They could concentrate a troop strength ten or more times greater than our troops and attack one weak point."[30]

The U.S. military attaché at Peiping pointed out that the Communists "have almost unlimited room to maneuver, and while they cannot risk a decisive engagement with National Government Forces, the latter have never been able to fix the former into position and administer an annihilating blow." He predicted that the Nationalists "should be able to push the Communists around almost at will" for three to six months after the outbreak of a civil conflict. "Eventually, however, probably after about 6 months of full-scale civil war, it is believed the government offensive would bog down."[31]

BY THE SUMMER of 1946 there were already rumors and news stories in China that Marshall would soon depart, to be replaced by General Wedemeyer. In March, Marshall had in fact urged Wedemeyer to accept the post of ambassador. Secretary of State Byrnes and President Truman had approved the appointment, and Marshall had mentioned it in an off-the-record press conference.[32] While in the United States for medical treatment, Wedemeyer had already spent a large sum of money on suitable civilian clothes for his new position.[33] He expected to return to China as ambassador in May or June. At the beginning of July, however, Marshall requested that the State Department shelve the appointment of Wedemeyer in favor of Dr. John Leighton Stuart, a distinguished educator, former missionary, and president of Yenching University.

Marshall's abrupt change of mind arose from three considerations. The appointment of Wedemeyer, another general, might "raise doubts in Chinese minds that Marshall would stay, thus weakening his hand in the negotiations."[34] With the hope of successful negotiations still alive—at least in Marshall's mind—it seemed unlikely that Wedemeyer, with his record of close association with Chiang and other leaders of the Nationalist government, would ever be trusted as a mediator. As one American diplomat in Nanking observed, "It is inconceivable that the Communists will make or abide by an agreement in which he

[Wedemeyer] is involved."[35] Finally, Marshall believed he needed a man with Stuart's intimate knowledge of the Chinese political scene and wide acquaintance (many Nationalist and some Communist leaders were his former students) to advise him and to help him find his way through the thicket of Chinese political maneuvering.[36]

Wedemeyer, who had been anxiously following events in China and becoming increasingly puzzled over the delay in his appointment, received no prior word from Marshall, and it was left to Undersecretary of State Dean Acheson to inform the general of his change in status. He finally received a letter of apology from Marshall on July 24. Deeply embarrassed, harassed by newsmen, Wedemeyer kept silent; but twelve years later in his memoirs he bitterly characterized the episode as an "outrageous appeasement of the Chinese Communists" and Marshall as "physically and mentally too worn out to appraise the situation correctly."[37]

Ambassador Stuart plunged into the search for an agreement with an energy and persistence that belied his seventy years. But there was little left to be done. Efforts to extend the June truce failed, and fighting spread to central China. Nationalist armies were everywhere successful. Five Nationalist armies struck Communist forces under Li Xiannian in the area on the border of Honan and Hupeh provinces. The Communists split into two columns and began a withdrawal toward Yenan. They reached Shensi in September, having suffered heavy casualties, but the Communists told the American military attaché that they arrived at Yenan with approximately the same number of troops because they were able to recruit and conscript new recruits along their route. In Kiangsu Province, where eleven Nationalist armies faced about a hundred thousand men under General Chen Yi, the Communists lost their main base at Huai'an and suffered more than forty thousand casualties. A lucky minority broke through to Communist base areas in Shantung.[38] Virtually all of the provinces of Honan and Anhwei came under Nationalist government control. Smaller groups of Communists holding portions of central China were pushed out or destroyed. Nevertheless, large areas of the countryside remained under Communist control, and the Nationalists' far-reaching advances and captures of distant cities left them with long, vulnerable supply lines.

In the midst of the spreading conflict the Executive Headquarters Field Teams attempted to carry out their mission. The Nationalists and Communists had been slow to send representatives to staff the field teams, and when they finally began to function, the Americans discovered that the Chinese members of the teams "considered themselves representative of and subordinate to the local commanders rather than to Executive Headquarters. And on increasingly frequent occasions they refused to enter agreements or issue instructions until after they had conferred with local commanders." It was not surprising, then, that the teams frequently failed to reach a unanimous decision, and when they did, field commanders on both sides frequently ignored their warnings and instructions.[39] Communist and Nationalist members of the teams were frequently absent, and Communist members were accused of "spreading propaganda . . . by inciting people to mass meetings and local disturbances."[40] The teams' freedom of movement was often severely restricted, and on one occasion a field team quartered in the town of Pot'ou in Manchuria was invited to dinner at the nearby Communist headquarters and then held in custody there until the Communists had captured Pot'ou.[41]

As fighting grew more intense, members of the teams themselves came under threat. During June, the Nationalist liaison officers of two field teams were murdered by the Communists and the Communist member of another team disappeared, believed killed by Nationalist troops. At Chengte, capital of Jehol Province, a field team was isolated by the destruction of the airfield. The Communists denied the American member of the team the use of his radio, and his team was forced to leave with a Communist supply column, which was then strafed by Nationalist planes. The Nationalist member of the team was killed and the American member wounded.[42] Despite their increasing inability to affect the course of the fighting, the teams remained in northern China and Manchuria until February 1947.

Unable to dissuade Chiang from continuing his offensives, Marshall decided to bring pressure on the Generalissimo by indirectly arranging for a halt in certain types of aid to China. He deliberately refrained from putting pressure on congressional leaders to pass the China Aid Bill before their adjournment and recommended that requests from the China Supply Commission in Washington to purchase arms and ammunition from U.S. suppliers be deferred. Chiang's generals and diplomats protested vociferously, but the Generalissimo felt little real worry. Chiang firmly believed that ultimately the United States would have to back him in his struggle against the Communists, particularly in view of the steadily worsening state of American relations with the Soviets. He approved a new plan to capture Kalgan, a major transportation hub and the last major city still in Communist hands.

At the end of July, while fighting raged in northern China, a Marine convoy of nine trucks and several other vehicles traveling from Tientsin to Peiping was ambushed by about three hundred Communist troops forty-four miles from Tientsin, near the village of An Ping. It was a complete surprise. The road from Tientsin to the capital had been so quiet that regular patrols had been discontinued in March. No Communist units were known to be in the area.[43]

Most of the army and Marine personnel were traveling as passengers and were unarmed. The convoy was also outside radio range of the two cities. But there was a guard of thirty-one men from the 11th Marines and a 60-millimeter mortar section from the 1st Marines. A nasty firefight ensued. Four Marines were killed in the first minutes of the ambush, but the others kept the attackers cautious with well-directed mortar and machine-gun fire. Three Marines managed to turn a jeep around and race back to Tientsin. After about three hours, the Communists withdrew, leaving behind fifteen bodies. The convoy, abandoning three of its damaged trucks, continued on to Peiping and arrived an hour before the first relief forces from Tientsin left the city.[44]

The An Ping incident increased the level of distrust between the Americans and the Communists. Most American officers in northern China believed the ambush had been a deliberate effort by the Communists to put pressure on the Marines, encourage their withdrawal, and create opportunities for propaganda. The vociferous Communist denunciations of the American actions in "opening fire" on their forces in An Ping appeared to confirm these assumptions.[45] Chou En-lai initially proposed an investigation by an Executive Headquarters team. Marshall agreed, but arrangements soon bogged down through Communist obstruction. An investigation by the Marines and a second by an exclusively U.S. team from Executive Headquarters both concluded that the Communists had carried out a planned and unprovoked attack.[46]

Yenan initially believed the reports of its East Hibei Military District that U.S. forces had been supporting Nationalist troops in an attack on An Ping. They interpreted the incident as an indication that the United States was prepared to intervene militarily on the side of Chiang in the civil war. Chou En-lai speculated that perhaps the Marines had provoked an incident so as to justify their continued presence in China.[47] It was not until two weeks later that the East Hibei Military District admitted that its troops had first opened fire on the Americans. The Central Committee considered acknowledging the mistake but decided instead to stonewall, noting that many Chinese accepted the Communists' propaganda and blamed the incident on the Nationalists.[48]

Marshall angrily told Chou that he knew what had actually happened, but he chose not to make an issue of the incident. He was concerned that a public statement would only play "directly into the hands of the small group in the Kuomintang who are blocking me in my efforts to terminate the fighting." It would also mean the end of any role for Executive Headquarters in Hopeh and Jehol, where local Communist leaders were already bitterly anti-American.[49]

By this time, any chance of terminating the fighting appeared increasingly remote. Mao had concluded by June that "Chiang has made up his mind to conduct a total war."[50] The Generalissimo believed his hour had come and was disinclined to hold back. There were still numerous proposals and counterproposals by both sides. Chiang announced that he was prepared to call a halt to his advance on Kalgan for a limited time. Chou demanded an indefinite cease-fire. The Central Committee in Yenan now saw the negotiations as having only the goal of "thoroughly exposing the reactionary face of the U.S. and Chiang Kai-shek and educating the masses."[51] "This thing has blown up," Marshall concluded. "It's probably my fault but I'm just now too old and tired to go at it again."[52] In May, President Truman had offered Marshall the post of secretary of state. Marshall had accepted but had delayed his departure in the hopes of achieving a settlement. By early December, he finally indicated to the president his desire to be recalled.

Marshall left China on January 7. The following day, Truman announced his appointment as secretary of state, and on the ninth Marshall's report on his mission was released to the public. The general explained that the greatest obstacle to peace was the "complete and almost overwhelming suspicion" of the opposing parties, representing as they did drastically different political philosophies. He blamed the breakdown in negotiations on the influence of a "dominant group of reactionaries" within the Kuomintang and on the consistent "misrepresentation and abuse" of Communist propaganda, whose "purpose was to mislead the Chinese people and arouse a bitter hatred of America." He still saw hope for China, however, if "liberals in the government and in the minority parties" could assume the leadership of Chiang's Kuomintang.[53]

It is doubtful that anyone other than those "liberals" felt any regret at Marshall's departure. "America created this civil war," wrote Wang Zi-feng, a Manchurian party cadre, "by equipping Chiang, sending him military material worth four billion dollars and helping him establish his air force. America helped transfer troops from the south to the northeast and America sent troops to Peiping and other cities." The failure of the Marshall mission, he concluded, had "educated some of our cadres, removing their dream that the KMT and the Americans wanted peace. Now KMT and American actions have educated them."[54] Chiang Kai-shek recorded in his diary that "it was not difficult to sense that he [Marshall] felt more than a little bit guilty about his past attitude toward us. . . . He must be moved by our sincerity."[55]

WHILE MARSHALL'S PLANE was carrying him back to the United States, a young student and soldier, Xiong Xiang-hui, was desperately trying to find a ship to take him to the same destination. Xiong was a graduate of a provincial university in China who had joined the Youth Field Service Unit when Japan went to war with China in 1937. The Youth Field Service Unit was a kind of combination volunteer medical corps and YMCA staffed mainly by recent university graduates, doctors, and nurses. From there Xiong had been recruited as a staff officer by Hu Zhong-nan, one of Chiang's most capable and trusted generals.

Xiong remained with General Hu for almost eight years, serving as his confidential secretary and head of his personal security detail. Xiong was also a Communist agent, having been recruited by a fellow student in 1937. Chou En-lai, like General Hu, had been impressed by Xiong's ability and resourcefulness and had selected him to infiltrate the Nationalist Army high command.

In late 1945, General Hu encouraged Xiong to take a leave of absence in order to go to the United States for study. Xiong was delighted, but even with the general's backing, bureaucratic regulations and paperwork connected with his trip to the United States took up almost all of 1946. Xiong also had to sit for the American college entrance exams. In January 1947, Xiong was finally cleared to go, and during that same month he was married. The newlyweds moved to Shanghai so that Xiong could find a ship to the United States, but steamship tickets were extremely scarce.[56]

Xiong and his wife were still searching when he was suddenly summoned by no less than Mao Ren-feng, the head of the Shanghai underworld, to report to General Hu Zhong-nan for an urgent mission.[57] Chiang Kai-shek had approved a bold plan by Hu to strike into Yenan Province and capture the Party's central command. As Marshall had predicted, Chiang's armies had not been able to destroy the Communist forces in northern China and Manchuria. The capture of Yenan, however, promised to be an enormous propaganda victory and perhaps the long-desired decisive stroke of the civil war.

Hu's forces totaled 150,000 men and seventy-five aircraft, making this the largest operation of the war. The plans were made in great secrecy, and even the commanders who would actually be involved in the operation were kept in the dark until the last moment. Thanks to Xiong, however, Mao Tse-tung was kept fully informed of the Nationalist plans.

On March 14, Hu Zhong-nan, with the American-equipped First and Twenty-ninth Armies, brushed aside Communist opposition and within sight of Yenan in two days. Mao and the Party leaders, however, forewarned by Xiong, had left the city almost two weeks before. With them went the Party's most valuable weapons and equipment and key personnel.[58]

For several weeks, Chiang and the Kuomintang leadership basked in the glory of his spectacular victory, and journalists speculated that the war might be nearing its end. It was, but not in the manner they envisioned. Three months after the fall of Yenan, Communist forces in central China under General Liu Bo-cheng crossed the Yellow River and destroyed two Nationalist armies, inflicting casualties of eight to one. At the same time, Lin Piao launched the first of three summer offensives that succeeded in reoccupying much of southern Manchuria. During the fall and winter, the Communists gained control of the major rail lines and captured or encircled the large cities. By the end of 1947, Mao could proclaim, "The Chinese People's Liberation Army has now reached a turning point and the People's Liberation Army is on the offensive." Unfazed by these developments, the Generalissimo declared that the bandit suppression campaign against the Communists would be over in a year.[59]

WHILE THE LAST REMNANTS of the China peace agreements disappeared in the smoke of the battles in Manchuria and northern China, Ho Chi Minh was bringing his own peace agreement back to Vietnam, hoping to sell it to his increasingly skeptical countrymen. Ho's return to Vietnam aboard a French warship took more than a month. His reason for choosing this leisurely mode of travel over Sainteny's offer of an airplane has been the subject of endless speculation among his biographers. Sainteny guessed that the Vietnamese president might have feared sabotage if he went by air. Others have speculated that Ho may have wanted to give the Vietminh time to prepare the public to accept the modus vivendi, which was viewed with disappointment and suspicion by many Vietnamese. In France, members of the Vietnamese émigré community had denounced Ho as a turncoat. There was little danger of that happening in Vietnam, however. The Vietminh were now firmly in control, and public opinion manifested itself only in the manner they required.

During the time that the negotiations were proceeding, the Vietminh at home had taken advantage of the departure of the Chinese troops to complete the destruction of rival political parties and their armed militias. Some of the opposition forces, including those in Mong Cai Province, retreated with their Chinese sponsors into China. In other regions, Nationalist groups such as the Quoc Dan Dang, the Dai

Viet, and the Dong Minh Hoi still had considerable forces and controlled some key towns, but the factions, even when they were not fighting one another, seldom cooperated or coordinated their efforts. The Vietminh forces were also better armed and supplied. They had the acquiescence and sometimes the active support of the French, who were happy to see the defeat of the nationalist parties, whom they regarded as more dangerous than the Vietminh. A French report noted that the Vietminh were able to "eliminate the parties of the opposition who were hindering their efforts thanks to our indifference and, in some cases, with our aid."[60]

Between June and November, Giap's forces seized the nationalist strongholds at Langson, Viet Tri, Lao Cai, and Phu Yen. Some nationalist fighters managed to reach China. Others were "converted" to the cause or executed.[61] In the province of Quang Ngai, in central Vietnam south of Danang, French intelligence reports spoke of a "St. Bartholomew's [massacre] that cost the lives of a great number of Vietnamese, old civil servants, mandarins, Catholics, and members of the landowning classes."[62]

In a widely publicized incident, Vietminh agents who had infiltrated the nationalist parties in Hanoi reported a plot to carry out an attack on a French Bastille Day parade and have it appear to be the work of the Vietminh. Police raided the nationalist headquarters in Hanoi and claimed to have discovered "torture pits" and the bodies of several victims. Some later claimed that the torture pits had been dug for the occasion and that the bodies came from the morgue.[63] Whatever the facts, Giap seized on the incident to crack down on the nationalists and ban their activities.

At 4:00 P.M. on October 20, the sloop *Dumont Durville* steamed into Haiphong harbor flying the red flag with the gold star next to the tricolor on its mast. The ship sounded a long blast from its siren and was answered a few minutes later by a siren blast from the municipal theater. Ho Chi Minh stepped ashore to be met by French and Vietnamese dignitaries and an honor guard while a band played the Vietnamese and French national anthems. The Vietminh saw to it that the huge crowds that welcomed Ho back to Vietnam were suitably enthusiastic. At every station along his sixty-mile train journey from Haiphong to Hanoi, the old patriot was greeted by local farmers, women, and small children waving national flags and banners. At Hanoi he was greeted by an estimated eighty thousand people.

Three days after his arrival, Ho addressed the nation, explained the implications of the modus vivendi, and called for a second meeting of the National Assembly. As the president spoke, the Vietminh security organizations completed their roundup of opposition figures. When the Assembly convened on October 28, only thirty-seven of the seventy opposition seats were occupied. When a deputy inquired about the missing delegates, he was advised that they had been arrested "for crimes of common law."[64] The Assembly approved a new Cabinet that accurately reflected the new power alignment in the north: Vietminh ministers occupied all key positions. Ho was named prime minister as well as president. A draft constitution that declared the total independence of Vietnam without reference to the French Union was approved by the Assembly two weeks later.

In southern Vietnam, the cease-fire provided for in the modus vivendi went into effect as scheduled on October 30. It lasted about a week. The French interpreted the agreement to mean that they should not attack Vietminh forces but could still move into Vietminh-controlled territory. Since at this point almost three-quarters of the southern provinces appeared to be under some measure of Vietminh control, this was a sure recipe for trouble.[65] By late November, d'Argenlieu was reporting to Paris that hostilities in the south were once again at their old level.[66]

It was the north rather than the south, however, that was to be the flash point for all-out war in Indochina. It began ostensibly as a dispute over customs. Control of trade at Haiphong, the principal port for Hanoi and Tonkin, was of critical importance to the Vietminh. Arms and other military matériel smuggled in from China for Giap's growing army entered the country mainly through Haiphong. Customs duties at the port were one of the few sources of revenue left to the government after the economic devastation of the famine and the Chinese occupation. The French asserted that Haiphong was a port of the "Indochinese Federation" and claimed the right to control customs there.

Haiphong in 1946 was a smuggler's paradise. It had the largest Chinese community in northern Vietnam and attracted deserters from Lu

Han's occupation armies. There were Chinese pirates who were employed by both the French and the Vietnamese as spies, along with strong-arm men, a handful of Japanese deserters, and even some Koreans.[67]

As the last Chinese troops departed, the French became more assertive. In August, a French gunboat stopped and seized a Vietnamese customs boat, and at the end of the month, French troops accompanied by armored cars and tanks seized the customs house and the police station.[68] The Vietnamese government protested strongly, and anti-French demonstrations were held in Haiphong. Then, on November 20, a French patrol boat intercepted a Chinese junk reported to be carrying contraband petroleum products. Ignoring protests by the Chinese captain that his junk had been cleared by Vietnamese customs, the French took the junk in tow. Shortly after, firing broke out from the shore. Fighting quickly spread to various parts of the city and was halted only late on the following day when high-ranking French officers and Vietnamese officials arrived from Hanoi and negotiated a cease-fire. The French had lost twenty-three killed in the incident, and Vietnamese losses were reported by the Vietminh to have been about 240.[69]

Quiet had returned to Haiphong by the evening of the twenty-first, but the French government in Saigon had already determined to force a showdown. General Jean Valluy, the acting governor-general, believed that it was "absolutely necessary to take advantage of this incident to ameliorate our position in Haiphong."[70] The French commander in chief in Hanoi was General Louis Morlière, who had led French forces at Kasserine Pass in the North African campaign. He was an old soldier who alternately annoyed and amused Vietnamese officials with what they saw as his outmoded colonial mentality, but he believed independence for Vietnam was a desirable and attainable goal. Even Giap believed that he was "someone who meant well and desired peace."[71] Morlière warned Valluy that to force a showdown in Haiphong "would end up in a complete rupture of the March 6 agreement and the spread of fighting to all our garrisons in Tonkin."[72] Valluy, however, had already issued instructions to Colonel Debes, who commanded the French troops in Haiphong, to demand that all Vietnamese military forces withdraw from Haiphong and nearby villages.

Debes, who had been planning for a military takeover of Haiphong since September, quickly complied. On the evening of November 22, Debes delivered an ultimatum to the Vietnamese authorities in Haiphong calling for "all Vietnamese military and semi-military forces" to evacuate the city. Shortly after ten o'clock the following morning, French heavy artillery began their bombardment of the Vietnamese quarter of the city. The Vietminh government in Hanoi was not even informed of the ultimatum until after the French had opened fire.[73] "That the French could seriously have wished for a favorable reply to their ultimatum is incredible," observed American vice-consul James L. O'Sullivan.[74]

French 105-millimeter and 155-millimeter artillery, mostly acquired through American Lend-Lease, blasted the Vietnamese quarter, causing heavy casualties among those civilians who had not yet evacuated the area. Nung tribal mercenaries working for the French moved through the wrecked buildings methodically burning and looting the houses. One U.S. intelligence agent who witnessed the destruction concluded that "the French have made pillaging their military policy."[75] French Spitfires strafed refugees fleeing the fighting.

Vietnamese troops stubbornly held out for two days, even launching a counterattack that captured the municipal theater, which the French had occupied after the November 20 incident.[76] After two days the Vietnamese fighters were forced to withdraw. Many of the civilian refugees gathered in the village of Kien An, just outside the city. Kien An became the grave of many of these people when Debes's artillery and aircraft, supported by naval gunfire, attacked the village.[77] O'Sullivan labeled the destruction of the village "a terroristic measure."[78] At least three thousand Vietnamese died as the result of the French operations at Haiphong.

Morlière had predicted that an attack on Haiphong would lead to general war. It did, but not immediately. Neither side felt completely ready. The French were concerned about the danger to French civilians in isolated parts of Hanoi and the weakness of some of their outlying garrisons in Tonkin. They also hoped that the Vietnamese government could be bullied, persuaded, or bluffed into allowing the French to take control without a fight. Finally, the authorities in Paris insisted that if war broke out, the Vietnamese must appear as the clear aggressors.[79]

Another reason to go slowly may have been the pending visit of an American diplomat, Abbott Low Moffat, chief of the State Department's Division of Southeast Asian Affairs, to Saigon and Hanoi. The French government feared that the United States and perhaps Great Britain might feel the need to help mediate the Indochina disputes or perhaps bring the problem before the United Nations. They need not have worried. Moffat was instructed to tell Ho Chi Minh that the United States was "deeply concerned" about the recent outbreaks of fighting and had warned the French that intransigence by either side would only lead to further violence. However, Moffat was admonished to "keep in mind Ho's clear record as agent of international communism, the absence of evidence of any clear recantation of his Moscow affiliations. . . . The least desirable eventuality would be establishment of a Communist-dominated, Moscow-oriented state in Indochina." Moffat was also cautioned to "avoid the impression that the U.S. Govt was making a formal intervention at this juncture."[80]

The French government had already sensed that anti-Communism might be their high card in the Indochina poker game. Beginning in December, French officials suddenly began confiding their fears about the Communist character of the Vietminh government to American diplomats. They warned that Ho was "in direct contact with Moscow and is receiving advice and instructions from the Soviets," and that Chinese Communists were in Indochina helping the Vietminh.[81] O'Sullivan, who knew that the French had been aware of Ho's Communist connections since the 1930s, found it "peculiar" that French concerns should be brought to American attention "at the very moment . . . when the French may be preparing to force the Vietnamese government to collaborate on French terms or to establish a puppet government in its place."[82]

On the Vietnamese side, there was still hope on the part of Ho Chi Minh and some of his associates that war might be averted, or at least postponed, through further negotiations, but Giap was making all-out preparations for war. By this time his best-armed units had become the Army of the Democratic Republic of Vietnam. About 10 percent of the officers were reported to be former soldiers or noncommissioned officers of the French colonial army.[83] The Tu Ve, or militia, had grown to almost a million men, only some of whom had firearms. Three military schools had been opened in March in northern and central Vietnam, where officer candidates received basic infantry training, learned small-unit tactics and guerrilla warfare, and were drilled on Party theory and doctrine. Each regiment of the new army also established its own basic training school.[84] Beginning in the fall of 1946, the Vietnamese began moving their improvised armaments factories to the area northwest of Tonkin known as the Viet Bac, from which the Vietminh had originally waged guerrilla war against the Japanese.

Hanoi was quiet, but the atmosphere was "menacing." Vietnamese militia and army troops began to erect barricades and roadblocks at key points. The Vietnamese government began to evacuate all civilians able to leave. Most of the army redeployed to the city's outskirts, leaving behind the militia, youth assault squads, snipers, and saboteurs. Vietnamese suspected of being pro-French were taken into "protective custody." Government officials began to sleep outside the city, and one by one the ministries began to move their offices and records out of the capital.[85]

From the French authorities came a steady flow of demands that the Vietnamese referred to as "ultimatums." They began to refer to Morlière as "General Ultimatum." First the French demanded that the Vietnamese dismantle their barricades and roadblocks within the city. If they failed to comply, the French would clear them away. The same day, a French officer transmitted a statement that the Vietnamese police had shown itself incapable of maintaining law and order and that the French would take over that responsibility in the city. Two days later, on December 17, came a demand that the Vietnamese militia disarm and that the Vietnamese cease all preparations for war.

Ho Chi Minh addressed a final appeal to Léon Blum, the famous leader of the French Left, who had just taken office as prime minister. He appealed for a return to the conditions of the modus vivendi.[86] Blum had recently published an article calling for an "agreement on the basis of independence" with the Vietnamese and an end to decision making by "military authorities or civilian settlers in Indochina."[87]

Ho's message to Blum failed to reach Paris until December 20. By that time the Vietminh had decided that they had no choice but to fight. At 8:00 P.M. on the evening of December 19, the power supply in Hanoi was suddenly cut. Tu Ve units attacked French positions and troops throughout the city. A number of French civilians were taken as hostages, and some were brutally murdered. Throughout Tonkin, French military posts came under attack.[88] The American vice-consul reported that "it seems the French are faced with an almost completely hostile population."[89]

After three days of fighting, French troops were in control of the European part of the city and had captured the presidential palace. By that time, Ho Chi Minh and his ministers had withdrawn from Hanoi. On the twentieth, as the Vietminh radio station was being reassembled in its new clandestine location, Ho broadcast to the nation an exhortation to "fight with all the means at your disposal." It took the French more than two months to regain control of the Chinese and Vietnamese sections of Hanoi. The Vietnamese war with the French was to continue for more than seven years.

CHAPTER FOURTEEN

"THE LEAST DESIRABLE EVENTUALITY"

In the latter part of 1946, two events occurred that clearly signaled that the American military occupations in China and Korea had come to the end of their useful life, just as had the British and Commonwealth forces' occupations in Southeast Asia. One event began as a minor incident, the other as a massive wave of frustration and discontent.

As General Marshall was drafting his final report on his unsuccessful efforts to avert civil war in China, Corporal William Pierson and Private First Class Warren Pritchard of Headquarters and Services Company, 5th Marines, were preparing to celebrate Christmas Eve in Peiping. After a Christmas dinner at the YMCA and a visit to the ice rink near the Winter Palace, Pierson and Pritchard spent several hours drinking with fellow Marines at the Manhattan Club. At about 8:00 P.M. a group of Marines left the club for a party at the Peking Hotel, but the group split up after a minor fight among Pierson, Pritchard, and another Marine, all of whom had been drinking heavily, and the two continued alone toward the Peking Hotel. Passing the Pavilion Theater they encountered Shen Chung, a nineteen-year-old student in the preparatory course at Peking University. She had recently arrived in the city from Fukien Province and was living with her brother-in-law's family.[1]

The two Marines may have mistaken Shen for a prostitute, or they may have been too drunk to care. In any case, Pierson and Pritchard took her to the nearby polo grounds, where Pierson had sex with her while Pritchard looked on. After a while, Pritchard left for the Peking Hotel. Some time after that, Kuan Te-tsung, a Chinese police officer, responding to reports of a disturbance on the polo grounds, found Pierson with Shen. Summoning more police, Kuan attempted to restrain Pierson, who later claimed that the Chinese police hit him in the face with a rifle and in the stomach with a pistol. Pierson broke away and flagged down a jeep patrol of the Joint Sino-American Police. According to the military police report, Pierson complained that the Chinese police had assaulted him and taken away "his girl."[2]

The MPs took Pierson and Shen to the Joint Sino-American Police office for questioning. Early the next morning, Shen was examined by a Chinese doctor attached to the Peiping Police Department. Shen claimed that Pierson had raped her three times and that she had feared for her life while in his hands.[3] Later in the day she underwent two more medical examinations, including one by a U.S. Navy doctor. The findings were inconclusive. The doctors noted that while Shen had certainly had intercourse, she did not have the cuts and bruises normally associated with a struggle. However, her failure to resist more vigorously "could have been the result of shock, fear or intimidation."[4] Following an investigation, the 1st Marine Division provost marshal recommended disciplinary action against the two Marines, and four days after the incident, the Marines announced that Pierson and Pritchard would be tried for rape by a general court-martial.

Shen and her brother-in-law attempted at first to keep the incident secret, but a press informant in the police department passed the story to the newspapers.[5] The news electrified students all over China. To Chinese minds, rape was a crime more serious than murder. To make the offense even more heinous, Shen had been violated by a foreigner. There was a long tradition of student activism and protest in China, where students and teachers, though a small fraction of the population, were viewed as embodying the ideals and intellectual heritage of the nation. And Shen was not simply a student, but a student at one of China's elite universities in the intellectual center of the country. Her family background as the daughter of a midlevel official was similar to that of many students, who could easily identify with her.

The rape came at a moment when the country appeared to be sliding back into civil war, for which most people blamed the Kuomintang. In addition, there was the weary familiarity of foreign military forces in China. They had been there for more than half a century; first the gunboats and the detachments guarding the foreign settlements and concessions, then the Japanese, and even now—when China had finally won its war for freedom—there were the Russians and the Marines. "During eight years of war China sacrificed millions of lives because she did not want to see any more atrocities committed by foreigners on Chinese soil by virtue of their military power," declared a Shanghai newspaper. "One year and four months have now elapsed since V-J Day. . . . Yet a member of the Allied forces stationed in China has now violated a Chinese girl student."[6]

The Shen case "set off a protest movement that never saw its equal in Kuomintang China."[7] Students at Peiping universities declared a three-day strike, and ten thousand students turned out in protest. Students in Tientsin staged a ten-hour parade, carrying placards that read "Marines Go Home," "China Is Not a U.S. Colony," and "Stop Your Brutal Acts." In Nanking, thousands of students representing virtually every university in the city marched to the Foreign Office to present a petition calling for the withdrawal of all American troops from China.[8] Thirty professors in Shanghai published a statement with the same demand.[9] The American chargé d'affaires in Nanking, W. Walton Butterworth, observed that the rape of a student "was only the point of take-off. The underlying feeling was compounded of varying parts of economic misery, disillusionment at the war aftermath, recrudescence of the 'unequal treaty' psychology and simple envy. . . . The clearest thread of real emotion of these and other demonstrators, in fact, may be a simple hatred of the American soldier, perhaps as a symbol of their hatred of all soldiers."[10]

Only a small minority of student demonstrators were Communists, but by 1947 Communist student activists had assumed leadership of many campus organizations. Their organizational skills helped to increase the impact and effectiveness of the demonstrations.[11] Within a few days the protests had spread to universities throughout the country. Editorials and letters to the editor likened the violation of Shen to the longstanding violation of China by foreign nations and demanded that the Marines go home. Other writers expressed friendship for the United States but still called for the withdrawal of American troops.

Pierson's trial opened on January 17 in Peiping with the mayor, a representative of the Foreign Ministry, and the president of Peking University all in attendance as well as seventeen members of the Chinese and foreign press. Shen was accompanied by two law professors from the university, who acted as her advisers.[12] The prosecution was handled by Lieutenant Colonel Paul Fitzgerald, an able and aggressive lawyer.

Chinese newspapers closely followed the five-day trial, some even attempting to explain the rules and procedures for a court-martial.[13] A representative of the Foreign Ministry told an American diplomat in Peiping that if the trial appeared fair and "if Corporal Pierson receives a sentence of ten years or more, the public in general will be contented."[14] The trial's outcome amply met that prescription. Pierson was found guilty of rape and sentenced to fifteen years' imprisonment. Pritchard was found guilty of assault. Yet any positive effect the trial may have had on public opinion in China was nullified several months later when the secretary of the navy, on the recommendation of the Judge Advocate General, overturned the court-martial verdict and restored the two Marines to active duty.

By the time news of the dismissal of Pierson's conviction reached China in July 1947—where it infuriated political activists and intellectuals—the United States had already set in motion actions that would go far toward meeting the broader Chinese desire that the United States end its military presence in China. While the Marines did not "go home" as the editorials demanded, their numbers and area of operation had been much reduced by the summer of 1947.

Marshall had always been uneasy about the presence of the Marines in north China. The force was large enough to concern the Soviets but not powerful enough to put up "an effective fight against a determined Russian effort." Their continued stay in the area was thus "really an irritant and inasmuch as we do not have sufficient strength to cope with a serious Russian effort, it is better to remove the irritant."[15] By May 1946 all but a handful of the 540,000 Japanese in northern China had been returned to Japan and the Marines' missions had been reduced to protecting the lines of communication between Tientsin and Peiping, guarding the coal trains from Chinwangtao, and providing security for Executive Headquarters. This last assignment ended with the collapse of the Marshall peace effort and the closing of Executive Headquarters.

Planning began for the withdrawal of all Marine units from the area of Peiping.[16] In September 1946 the Marines turned over responsibility for the security of the rail lines to the Nationalist Army.[17] By that point, the strength of the Marine elements in China had been reduced from fifty-five thousand to twenty-two thousand men.[18] In May 1947 the last Marine units were withdrawn from the Peiping area. This left only the garrison at Tsingtao, now called Fleet Marine Force Western Pacific, with a strength of about four thousand men.[19] The Marines remained in China almost two more years but played no role in the titanic battles in which the Communists progressively destroyed the Nationalist forces. Their final mission was to help organize and protect the withdrawal of American citizens from China.

IN KOREA, THE EVENTS that signaled the crisis in American occupation policies were far more pervasive and dramatic than in China. The long-anticipated meetings of the U.S.-Soviet Joint Commission held from March to May 1946 failed to reach an agreement about the nature of a future government for a unified Korea. The commission adjourned for an indefinite period, and policy makers in Washington and Seoul began to consider the possibility of forming some sort of separate provisional government for the south.[20] While Hodge and his political advisers, at the direction of the State Department, maneuvered to form a right-left coalition among the feuding factions in Seoul, Korea exploded.

On September 23, railway workers in Seoul, Pusan, and Taegu went on strike. They were soon joined by electrical workers, telegraph workers, and postal employees. Students at some high schools boycotted classes.[21] The railway strike in Seoul was brought under control by September 30 after several violent confrontations between strikers and police, mass arrests, and the use of strikebreakers by the railway management, but by this point the uprisings and demonstrations had spread to the provinces. North and South Kyongsang, with the cities of Pusan and Taegu, experienced the most intense and widespread violence. More than one hundred cities, towns, and villages witnessed demonstrations, riots, and assaults on police stations.[22] The number of individuals involved was estimated at about seventy thousand.[23] In Taegu, Koreans infuriated by the killing of a demonstrator stormed the central police station. Most of the police fled, but about forty who fell into the hands of the mob were brutally murdered. An American report described how "the faces and bodies of the police were hacked by axes and knives. The hands of police were tied behind their backs and sharp-pointed slate rocks were thrown at them until they fell to the ground from the loss of blood. This was followed with dropping large boulders on their heads, crushing them beyond recognition." A police chief in one provincial town had his "eyes and mouth cut out with rice knives." Other captured policemen were "severely beaten, then buried alive."[24]

The causes of the violence, which in some places amounted to a full-scale insurrection, have been often debated. MacArthur and Hodge saw the uprisings as ordered and orchestrated by northern Korea or Moscow. Contemporary historians disagree about the extent of Communist involvement, northern or local, in organizing the uprisings. Bruce Cumings sees the uprisings as essentially spontaneous, "a classic instance of peasant rebellion" that local Communists sought to encourage but could not organize or control.[25] Allan Millett concludes that the question of northern Korean involvement remains uncertain but that "the timing and location of the incidents" as well as "the skilled use of prepared demolitions" and the targeted kidnapping of key individuals "suggest a degree of coordination that can be credited only to the [Communist-dominated] Democratic People's Front."[26] Concerning other and more important causes there is little disagreement. The primary concerns of the dissidents were the scarcity and rising cost of rice, a result of ill-advised agricultural policies followed by the American military government during the winter and spring of 1945–46, and hatred of the police, who were often involved in enforcing unpopular rice collection policies.[27]

Under Japanese rule, Korea's rice production, collection, and pricing were controlled by the colonial government. At least 80 percent of all Korean farmers rented all or part of their land. The yearly rent for agricultural land could run from 50 to 90 percent of the value of the expected annual crop. The American military government abolished the forced sale of rice to government agencies, limited rents to one-third of the crop value, and established a free market for rice.

These measures, admirable and progressive from an American viewpoint, had a disastrous effect. Korean farmers were not eager to exchange their rice for money, which could purchase little in an economy short of goods of all types. Some farmers made little effort to grow more; some simply retained their rice and ate it. Speculators and black marketeers bought up much of the rice that was available, some of it for sale to Japan. Unexpected bad weather also reduced the size of the harvest. By summer 1946 there were serious shortages of rice in urban areas. Prices skyrocketed. Within a few months the military government recognized the looming crisis and quickly shelved the "free market" for a system of rice quotas, price controls, and compulsory rice collection remarkably similar to the old colonial system.

Like the old system, the military government's rice collection program was administered by local notables and officials and enforced by the police. Police enforcement of the program was described by American observers, with considerable understatement, as "arbitrary, sometimes cruel, and dishonest." Farmers who failed to hand over their rice were jailed or beaten. Those who failed to meet their quota had their cattle and other possessions seized by the police, who sold them to purchase rice.[28] Farmers did not fail to see the similarities to the detested Japanese system and were angry and resentful toward the program. Left-wing organizers encouraged resistance, and in many areas trucks carrying rice or other food had to be escorted by armed guards.[29]

There were many other reasons for people in the southern provinces to join the rebellions. Union leaders, leftist politicians, and Communists saw the uprisings as their last chance to take a stand against an American administration that appeared increasingly determined to crush them. The corruption, incompetence, and venality of government functionaries at all levels was so widespread and so deeply detested that some hospitals reportedly refused to treat officials and police injured in the riots.

As the violence began to die down in the Kyongsangs in November 1946, new uprisings broke out in the provinces of North and South Cholla to the southwest. These attacks were less severe but better organized and planned. In one instance, police stations in six different towns within a radius of ten miles were attacked almost simultaneously.[30] In the end, about twenty-five hundred U.S. troops, mostly from the 20th Infantry Regiment, had to be committed to assist the Korean constabulary and police in suppressing the violence. Where they had the opportunity, the police vented their fear and anger on the population in their usual way. An American officer reported that a policeman struck "a Korean girl across the shoulders with a piece of steel tube one half inch in diameter." Another officer told Hodge's inspector general that he "saw a man whom I later identified as a detective in civilian clothes strike a kneeling Korean, who was a prisoner, with a stick approximately 2" in diameter and 2½ inches long. . . . I saw another instance [in which] a uniformed policeman was striking a young girl of approximately 14 years of age with his rifle using the barrel part to strike with."[31] At least 100 police and other security forces and 250 rioters were killed in the upheavals, which became known as "the Autumn Harvest Uprisings," and close to 6,000 residents of Kyongsang and Cholla were arrested.[32]

Although Hodge and the State Department continued to hatch new schemes to unite the dissident right and center factions in Seoul, the Autumn Harvest riots marked the dead end of American occupation policy in Korea. "To sum it up, I think if the Russians would come forward tomorrow with a proposition for us both to pull our troops out of Korea we would decide—and very properly, in my opinion—to haul our freight," observed the assistant secretary of state for occupied areas, General John E. Hildring, in November 1946.[33] Nevertheless, Washington was loath to simply let go of Korea in light of the hardening Cold War antagonism toward the Soviet Union. After considerable effort, the U.S.-Soviet Joint Commission was reconvened in June 1947, but its deliberations ended in deadlock five months later. The Soviets argued for a pullout of all foreign troops, with the question of Korea's political future left to the Koreans.

At that point, Joseph E. Jacobs, Hodge's new political adviser, suggested that the United States refer the problem of Korea to the United Nations as a means of gradually phasing out American involvement while still holding out the possibility of avoiding Soviet domination of the peninsula. The State Department endorsed the idea, and the Joint Chiefs of Staff confirmed that Korea lacked vital strategic importance to the United States, noting that American forces stationed there might actually be a liability in the event of a general war with the Soviet Union.

American influence in the United Nations was strong in 1947, and the United States had little difficulty pushing a resolution through the General Assembly over the vociferous opposition of the Russians. The resolution established an eight-nation U.N. Temporary Commission on Korea (UNTCOK) charged with organizing and monitoring nationwide elections in that country by early 1948. When the commission was denied entry into northern Korea, the U.N. made the decision to proceed with elections below the 38th parallel.

Syngman Rhee emerged victorious from the elections, which were marked by frantic political maneuvering, violence, and intimidation. The Communists and other left-wing dissidents boycotted the voting and held their own counterelection. Before the elections were concluded, a portion of the southern provinces centering on the island of Cheju-do was again experiencing riots and uprisings. American soldiers were told to stay out of the fighting.

On August 15, 1948, the formal independence of Korea was proclaimed in a solemn ceremony attended by General Douglas MacArthur. Providing security for MacArthur and his entourage "required more military policemen and infantry guards than did Seoul's liberation." The blazing August sunshine and humidity "wilted the general's unadorned khaki uniform and melted the starch in Rhee's yangban costume and Mrs. Rhee's hanbok."[34] On this day three years before, the Japanese had nominally transferred authority to Yo Unhyong and the Committee for the Preparation of Korean Independence. But Yo did not attend this independence ceremony. He had been gunned down by one of Kim Ku's thugs in 1947.

With the inauguration of the Republic of Korea, U.S. Army elements on the peninsula began to transfer their bases and some of their equipment to the Korean government and American troops began to embark for Japan. Left behind was a Provisional Military Advisory Group of about five hundred experienced officers and NCOs to assist in the organization and training of armed forces for South Korea. By June 1949 the last American military units had left Korea. No one anticipated that they would be back in a year.

ALMOST FIFTY YEARS after the last American occupation forces left East Asia, the United States found itself involved in another military occupation, far more costly and more controversial than any other in its previous history. The debate about Iraq has been frequently interlaced with discussions of past military occupations. Shortly before the war began, an army study prepared for the chief of staff reviewed past

American experiences with military occupations. The authors pointed out that even in well-planned occupations carried out by competent military forces, "strategic success is not guaranteed." They warned that "the possibility of the United States winning the war and losing the peace in Iraq is real and serious. Rehabilitating Iraq . . . threatens to consume huge amounts of resources without guaranteed results. . . . The longer the effort continues the greater the potent that it will disrupt [Iraqi] society rather than rehabilitate it."[35]

The study was famously ignored by the White House and the Defense Department. Proponents of a war to oust Saddam Hussein preferred instead to call attention to the experience of the postwar occupations of Germany and Japan as evidence that the aftermath of a U.S. victory would lead to the establishment of stable democratic government in Iraq. Little was heard about those successes in Germany and Japan after the first few months of the U.S. presence in Iraq. Instead, academic experts and policy analysts pointed out that historically the majority of military occupations have not achieved the aims set out for them. Political scientist David M. Edelstein, who provides a sort of scorecard for twenty-four military occupations over the last two hundred years, finds only seven that were unambiguous successes and more than half that were failures.[36]

The long stalemate in Iraq produced no shortage of "lessons" and recommendations by social scientists, talk show hosts, politicians, and policy analysts: Success requires lengthy occupations. Success requires short occupations, because long ones arouse the opposition of the locals. Totalitarian governments need to be reformed from the top down. Totalitarian governments should be reformed from the bottom up. Careful advance planning is essential. Too few troops in the occupation force can bring disaster. On all of these generalizations, the story of the liquidation of Japan's empire casts a bright light of ambiguity. The successes and failures in East and Southeast Asia in 1945 and 1946 were often the result of factors far beyond the power of generals and soldiers to halt or redirect.

"Success" and "failure" are, of course, relative terms. Were the Allied operations amid the ruins of the Japanese and the European colonial empires successful? Successful for whom? In what way? For how long? Viewed as an operation to liquidate the Japanese Empire, the Allied occupations succeeded brilliantly. Japanese forces throughout Asia surrendered in an orderly fashion, were disarmed, and were eventually sent home. There were no stay-behind guerrillas or underground networks. Yet many of the occupations fell somewhat short of the avowed objective of liberating Asia from the Japanese. In China and Southeast Asia, the Allies employed thousands of Japanese soldiers and civilians as technicians, advisers, guards, auxiliaries, police, and sometimes combat troops against the local inhabitants they had come to "liberate." A far smaller proportion of Japanese who threw in their lot with Southeast Asian nationalists played an important, perhaps critical, role in training, advising, and sometimes leading the anticolonial forces.

Viewed as an effort to establish peace and stability on the ruins of Japan's Greater East Asia, the occupations were a resounding failure. If Asia in 1945 was an enormous boiling pot, as General Wedemeyer insisted, then the Allies accomplished little to prevent the pot from boiling over. By 1948 all the states occupied by the Americans, British, and Russians were at war, either with their former colonial rulers or with political factions within their own country, sometimes both. Some wars were concluded by 1949, as was the case in China, where, between April and November, the Communists completed their chain of sweeping victories. Chiang and his remaining supporters retreated to Taiwan, while in Peiping on October 1, 1949, Mao announced the establishment of the People's Republic of China and proclaimed, "China has stood up."

In the Netherlands Indies, the Indonesian nationalists won few battles but won the war. A succession of agreements between the Republic and the Dutch from 1947 to 1949 each broke down a few months after signing and were followed by Dutch "police actions" that left the Dutch in control of most of Java's towns and cities by 1949. Sukarno and most of the government were captured by the Dutch, but part of the Republican army held out, waging war from central Java. By that point, time had run out for the Netherlands. The United States, impressed by the Republic's suppression of a Communist rising in 1948, was by now convinced that the Dutch were the aggressors, and, along with many other members of the United Nations, pressured The Hague into conceding full independence to the Indonesians in December 1949.

Other wars, like those between the Vietminh and the French in Indochina and in Malaya, where Chinese Communist veterans of the MPAJA had launched a new insurgency, were to drag on into the

1950s. The civil war in Korea escalated into a major international conflict in June 1950 after Kim Il-sung finally persuaded the Soviets and the new People's Republic of China to back an all-out military offensive against the South.

An army general with long experience in Iraq recently observed that "every army of liberation has a half-life after which it turns into an army of occupation."[37] That was certainly true of the Allied armies that liberated East Asia from the Japanese. Most arrived too late and stayed too long. All the occupation commanders saw their mission as one of restoring or maintaining law and order and of carrying out higher policies agreed to in the great wartime conferences at Yalta and Potsdam or as enunciated by their own governments in London, Moscow, and Washington. The problem was that the attempt to implement these policies often proved incompatible with the goal of maintaining order. In three countries the occupiers faced an armed insurgency by the time they departed.

Occupations proceeded most smoothly where soldiers of the occupation force found a basis for at least limited cooperation and friendship with the locals. Marines and Chinese shopkeepers, rickshaw pullers, prostitutes, bar owners, and household servants had their decades-old symbiotic relationship. Australians and Indonesians in Borneo quickly established one based on barter. In the last analysis, an occupation is not only a political and military event but a cultural process whose outcome may be shaped by the expectations, values, social interactions, and historical experience of both the occupier and the occupied.

In general, occupations of Japan's former empire appeared to work most successfully where the occupiers and the occupied shared common, or at least compatible, interests. Many scholars have explained MacArthur's success in Japan this way. Similarly, to a degree the Chinese in northern Vietnam, the Soviets in northern Korea, the British in Malaya, and the Americans in northern China all found common interests with the peoples they were charged with freeing from the Japanese. In all these countries, local leaders, or at least a sizable and powerful segment of the local leadership, believed that their interests and aspirations could be advanced through cooperation or partnership with the occupation authorities.

The actual, as opposed to the expected, consequences of the Allied occupations have often been explained in terms of the confrontation of

Asian nationalism with Western imperialism or as a by-product of the onset of the Cold War. In fact the situation was considerably more complicated, because the demise of Greater East Asia not only brought on a confrontation with the West but also stimulated old and new rivalries, ambitions, and regional and communal animosities that would be played out in 1945, 1946, and 1947 from Korea to Indonesia.

Leaders in the struggle for independence found themselves opposed to other leaders whose vision of independence and freedom differed radically from their own. In this situation it was natural that rival factions should seek to align themselves with one or more of the victorious Allies. As Allan Millett has observed of Korea, "The joint occupation . . . provided Korean politicians with an unusual opportunity to seek foreign endorsements and assistance."[38] This was true of rival political leaders in other occupied countries as well. Far from being unwillingly drawn into the Great Power rivalries of the late 1940s, political leaders and factions in all the "liberated" countries actively sought the moral and material support of the Soviets, the Europeans, or the Americans in their struggle for mastery.

The most deleterious effects of the Allied military presence developed not through blunders or misjudgments of those charged with carrying out the occupations, but when the highest levels of government acted indecisively, had mistaken notions or no notion at all about what was actually happening on the scene, and neglected or ignored reports from the field. Mountbatten had at least some idea of the formidable nationalist opposition the British were likely to face in southern Vietnam and Indonesia, but the government in London, preoccupied with retaining the goodwill of the Dutch and French, tended to downplay or ignore his warnings and those of his commanders in the field. The OSS and its successor, the SSU (Strategic Services Unit) provided detailed and highly accurate information on developments in Southeast Asia to the State Department and the White House, with no discernible result. Hodge and his political advisers tried repeatedly to alert Washington to the likely consequences of the establishment of a trusteeship for Korea but were ignored. It remains to be seen whether these patterns of behavior will be repeated in Iraq and Afghanistan. If they are, the experiences of half a century ago suggest what consequences we can expect.

ACKNOWLEDGMENTS

Research for this book in widely scattered archives was supported by generous travel grants from George Washington University's Sigur Center for Asian Studies and the Elliott School of International Affairs. A year as a guest professor at Keio University enabled me to undertake research in Japanese Foreign Ministry records in Tokyo with the indispensable assistance of archivist Atsuta Miruko and my two capable research assistants Yatsunami Noriko and Wakamatsu Yuriko. My friend Professor Sayuri Shimizu of Michigan State took time from her short visit to her family to spend an entire day with me at the Foreign Ministry Archives. I thank Professor Akagi Kanji and the other members of the Keio Faculty of Law for providing this opportunity. My research in the National Archives of Singapore was aided and encouraged by the capable staff of that organization and by my friends and colleagues at the National University of Singapore. Special thanks to Dean Tan Tai Yong of the Faculty of Arts and Social Sciences (FASS) and to the members of the history department who generously shared their time and expertise. Our friend Chng Huang Hoon, now assistant dean, FASS, as usual did her best to explain the mysteries of Singapore life to us, as did the students in my course, who endeavored with only indifferent success to ensure that I found the right buses and stopped eating in tourist restaurants.

An invitation from the Royal Australian Navy to deliver the 2005 Sir Anthony Synott Lectures in Naval History enabled me to undertake research in Canberra on the Australian occupations of eastern Indonesia. I thank Captain Richard McMillan and Dr. David Stevens of the RAN Sea Power Centre for this opportunity and for their warm hospitality.

For facilitating my research in Paris and London I am grateful to the helpful and knowledgeable staff members of the Imperial War Museum; the (British) National Archives, Kew; and the Liddell Hart Centre for Military Archives, Kings College, London; the Service Historique de l'Armée de Terre at Vincennes; and the Fonds du Maréchal Leclerc de Hauteclocque, Paris. In the Netherlands, Mariska Heijmans-Van Bruggen of the Netherlands Institute for War Documentation made it possible for me to attend the institute's conference on "Identity and Violence during the Early Revolution of Indonesia" held in Amsterdam in 2003.

Our good friends Laurel Steele and Doug Kelley of the U.S. Consulate General, Shenyang, hosted us on a visit to Dong Bai and helped locate key sites mentioned in the manuscript. I would also like to thank our friends Monique Novodorsque and Alain Deniau for their generous hospitality on our visits to Paris.

Like hundreds of researchers at the U.S. National Archives, College Park, from college students to veteran writers, I was fortunate to be able to call on the expertise of John Taylor and Tim Nenninger and other members of the staff of the Modern Military Records branch and the unfailing kindness of Sally Marks Kuisel of the Civil and Diplomatic branch.

This book could not have been completed as soon as it was without the invitation of the U.S. Army War College and the Army Heritage and Education Center to serve as Harold K. Johnson Visiting Professor of Military History in 2005–2006. This experience not only provided an opportunity to utilize the AHEC's unparalleled collection of manuscripts, oral histories, and rare books but enabled me to exchange ideas with the distinguished faculty and staff of the War College and U.S. Army Military History Research Center and to become acquainted with some of the Army's leading strategists and war fighters. I thank Major General David H. Huntoon, Commandant, Army War College; Colonel Robert Dalessandro, Director of the Heritage and Education Center; and Dr. Conrad Crane, director of the Military History Institute for their hospitality and encouragement. I am also grateful to the many knowledgable and helpful experts on the staff of the institute for their patience and assistance. Special thanks to the many members of the China Marine Association who generously shared their reminiscences with me and allowed me to attend their 2001 reunion.

Christopher Goscha, François Guillemot, and Allan Millett allowed me to see prepublication versions of their important articles and books. Professor Goscha and Professor Millett also read and commented on relevant parts of the manuscript, as did Gregg Brezinski, William H. Frederick, Paul Kratoska, Kirk Larsen, Edward McCord, Shawn McHale, Yasuyo Sakata, Odd-Arne Westad, and Daqing Yang.

At George Washington University I was fortunate to have the help of a number of hardworking and adaptable research assistants and translators. These included Casey Reivich, Briana Clifton, Kim Nguyen, Julie Butner, Jasmine Bai, and Momo Bi. Yuka Fujioka translated many of the Japanese memoirs and firsthand accounts cited in the book while Dianna Xuang did the same for Chinese-language materials. Special thanks to Leah Charpentier and Kate Hill, who worked on the project for two years and whose resourcefulness, intelligence, good nature, insight, and common sense proved invaluable in helping me complete this book. Amy Furches prepared the bibliography and calmly and efficiently guided the author through the mysteries of formatting.

I thank my agent, Gerard McCauley, and my editor, Robert Loomis, who were willing to support and encourage what began as a rather nebulous project about the aftermath of world war. I also thank Robert's able assistant, Cheryl Weinstein, and the other members of the Random House team who saw the book through to publication.

I thank my family for their usual patience and support. My sons, Daniel and Jonathan, maintained their active interest in the project, managed our affairs, and kept us out of trouble while we were outside the United States for extended periods. My wife, Dianne, acted as unofficial editor, proofreader, and research assistant. In the last capacity she discovered an important document in a file of records I assured her were of no possible interest.

NOTES

INTRODUCTION

1. Theodore H. White, *In Search of History: A Personal Adventure* (New York: Harper, 1978), p. 234.

CHAPTER 1 **"Shoot the Works!"**

1. Quoted in Marc S. Gallicchio, *The Cold War Begins in Asia: American East Asian Policy and the Fall of the Japanese Empire* (New York: Columbia University Press, 1988), p. 59.
2. Richard B. Frank, *Downfall: The End of the Imperial Japanese Empire* (New York: Random House, 1999), p. 300.
3. Letter, 11 August 1945, included in the unpublished memoir of David F. Earle. Courtesy of Mr. Earle.
4. Waldo H. Heinrichs, Jr., *American Ambassador: Joseph C. Grew and the Development of the American Diplomatic Tradition* (Boston: Little, Brown, 1966), p. 376.
5. Ibid. Barton J. Bernstein, "The Perils and Politics of Surrender: Ending the War with Japan and Avoiding the Third Atomic Bomb," *Pacific Historical Review* 46, November 1977, pp. 5–6.
6. Bernstein, "Perils and Politics of Surrender," p. 5.
7. Frank, *Downfall,* p. 301.
8. Bernstein, "Perils and Politics of Surrender," p. 5.
9. Heinrichs, *American Ambassador,* p. 378.
10. John M. Blum, *The Price of Vision: The Diary of Henry Wallace, 1942–46* (Boston: Houghton Mifflin, 1973).
11. Bernstein, "Perils and Politics of Surrender," pp. 7–8.
12. Harriman to Secretary of State, 29 August 1945, copy in Harry S. Truman Papers, Naval Aide to the President subject files, box 13, Harry S. Truman Presidential Library, Independence, Mo.
13. On the Japanese surrender deliberations, see Frank, *Downfall,* chap. 19; Robert J. C. Butow, *Japan's Decision to Surrender* (Stanford, Calif.: Stanford University Press, 1954); and Herbert Bix, "Japan's Delayed Surrender: A Reinterpretation," *Diplomatic History* 19, Spring 1995. Asada Sadao, "The

Shock of the Atomic Bomb and Japan's Decision to Surrender: A Reconsideration," *Pacific Historical Review* 64, November 1998.

14. Butow, *Japan's Decision to Surrender,* pp. 207–8.
15. David McCullough, *Truman* (New York: Simon & Schuster, 1992), p. 463.
16. Yuki Tanaka gives the figure of 132,134 Allied prisoners, of whom 35,756 died in captivity. Less than 5 percent of British and American POWs held by the Germans and Italians died in captivity. Uki Tanaka, *Hidden Horrors: Japanese War Crimes in World War II* (Boulder, Colo.: Westview Press, 1996), pp. 2–3.
17. Stanley L. Falk, *Bataan: The March of Death* (New York: W. W. Norton, 1962), pp. 205–11 and passim.
18. Memo for Chief of Staff, U.S. Forces China Theater, subject: Contact Teams for Allied Prisoner of War and Internee Camps upon Japanese Capitulation. Records of the Office of Strategic Services, National Archives Record Group 226, entry 148, box 6.
19. Ibid.
20. Memo by Col. Paul E. Helliwell, Chief Intel Div, OSS, China Theater, subject: Summary of Activities of Secret Intelligence Branch, 9 October 1945; Records of G-5, China Theater, National Archives Record Group 493, box 61.
21. Thomas Troy, *Donovan and the CIA: A History of the Establishment of the Central Intelligence Agency* (Frederick, Md.: University Publications of America, 1981), pp. 31–39 and passim.
22. Maochun Yu, *OSS in China: Prelude to Cold War* (New Haven, Conn.: Yale University Press, 1996), p. 21.
23. Helliwell, Summary of Activities.
24. Ibid.
25. Letter from Brig. Gen. Paul W. Carraway, Deputy Chief of Staff, China Theater, to CG Army Air Forces, China Theater, et al., subject: Emergency Liaison Teams for Allied Prisoners of War and Internee Camps, 14 August 1945, National Archives Record Group 493, box 61.
26. Message, Chungking (ComGenChina) to SOS, OSS, AGAS, 15 August 1945, National Archives Record Group 493, AGAS folder.
27. Donald Knox, *Death March: The Survivors of Bataan* (New York: Harcourt Brace, 1983), p. 443.
28. Major James T. Hennessy to SSO, Report on Cardinal Operation, 24 September 1945, National Archives Record Group 226, entry 154, box 187.
29. Ibid.
30. Ibid.
31. Peter Clemens, "Operation Cardinal: The OSS in Manchuria, August 1945," *Intelligence and National Security* 13, Winter 1998, p. 82.
32. Hennessy, Report on Cardinal Operation.
33. Ibid.
34. Memo, Helm to Heppner, 25 August 1945, National Archives Record Group 226, entry 154, box 187.
35. Knox, *Death March,* p. 444.

36. Hennessy, Report on Cardinal Operation.
37. Message, Helm to OSS Chungking, 211855, 21 August 1945, National Archives Record Group 226, entry 154, box 187.
38. Memo, Helm to Heppner, 25 August 1945.
39. W. E. Brougher, *South to Bataan, North to Manchuria: The Prison Diary of BG W. E. Brougher* (Athens, Ga.: University of Georgia Press, 1971), p. 186.
40. Message, Hennessy to SSO, Xian, 24 August 1945, National Archives Record Group 226, entry 154, box 187.
41. Clemens, "Operation Cardinal," pp. 92–93.
42. Message, Kunming to Peers, Davis, 18 August 1945, National Archives Record Group 126, entry 154, box 8.
43. Craig Nelson, *The First Heroes* (New York: Viking, 2002), p. 338.
44. Message, Nichols to Kunming, 23 August 1945, National Archives Record Group 226, entry 154, box 187.
45. Message, Nichols to Kunming, 30 August 1945, National Archives Record Group 226, entry 154, box 8.
46. OWI News Dispatch, attachment to Kraus to Heppner, 22 August 1945, National Archives Record Group 226, entry 154, box 187.
47. Message, Duck to Helm, Xian, 18 August 1945, National Archives Record Group 226, entry 154, box 187.
48. Message, Duck to Helm, Xian, 19 August 1945, National Archives Record Group 226, entry 154, box 187. Memo to Investigation Boards, U.S. Forces, China Theater, subject: Summary of Activities of Prisoner of War Humanitarian Teams, Records of G-5, China Theater, National Archives Record Group 493.
49. Message, Duck to Helm, Xian, 18 August 1945, National Archives Record Group 226, entry 154, box 187.
50. Message, Duck to Helm, Xian, 19 August 1945. Message, Duck to Krause, 25 August 1945. Both in National Archives Record Group 226, entry 154, box 187.
51. Message, Duck to Krause and Chungking, 29 August 1945, National Archives Record Group 226, entry 154, box 187. Memo to Investigation Boards, U.S. Forces, China Theater.
52. Letter, Lt. Col. A. R. Robinson to Lt. Col. Ainsworth, 13 August 1945, National Archives Record Group 226, entry 154, box 187.
53. Krause to Heppner, 27 August 1945, National Archives Record Group 226, entry 154, box 187.
54. Heppner to OSS Washington, 29 August 1945, National Archives Record Group 226, entry 154, box 187.
55. OSS Washington to Heppner, 1 September 1945, National Archives Record Group 226, entry 154, box 187.
56. Heppner to OSS Washington, 7 September 1945, National Archives Record Group 226, entry 154, box 187.
57. Krause to Heppner, 22 August 1945, National Archives Record Group 226, entry 154, box 187.

58. Memo to Col. Richard P. Heppner, Preliminary Report of Mission to Keijo, Korea, 23 August 1945, National Archives Record Group 226, entry 210, box 223.
59. Bird claimed in his report that Lieberman was "requested to accompany the mission by the Theater." Maochun Yu believes that Bird, "ever publicity conscious," brought Lieberman along "in violation of Heppner's specific orders." Yu, *OSS in China,* p. 233.
60. Henry R. Lieberman, "Japs Bring Up Tanks and Order American POW Relief Mission Out of the Country," OWI Dispatch, 22 August 1945. Copy in Eagle file, folder 6, National Archives Record Group 226, entry 210, box 223.
61. Ibid.
62. Preliminary Report of Mission to Keijo. "Summary of Activities of Prisoner of War Humanitarian Teams," Records of G-5, China Theater, National Archives Record Group 493, box 61.
63. Yu, *OSS in China,* p. 234.
64. Comments on Kahn, *The China Hands,* Albert C. Wedemeyer Papers, box 6, folder 6, Hoover Institution Archives, Stanford, Calif.
65. Yu, *OSS in China,* p. 234.

CHAPTER 2 "An Enormous Pot, Boiling and Seething"

1. Hayashi Shigeru et al., eds., *Nihon Shûsenshi [History of the Ending of the Pacific War],* vol. 1 (Tokyo: Yomiuri Shimbunsha, 1965), p. 98.
2. Louis Allen, *The End of the War in Asia* (London: Hart-Davis, MacGibbon, 1978), p. 235.
3. Magic Far East Summary, 16 August 1945, SRS513, National Archives Record Group 457.
4. "General Itagaki's First Refusal," *Singapore Straits Times,* September 4, 1945.
5. Hayashi et al., *Nihon Shûsenshi,* p. 117.
6. Message, CHAFX, Kunming to OSS, 16 September 1945, IN24307, National Archives Record Group 226, entry 53, box 4.
7. Arthur A. Thompson interview, Syonan Oral History Project, National Archives of Singapore, pp. 95–96.
8. G-2 Periodic Report, 26 October 1945, XXIV Corps G-2 Historical Section, National Archives Record Group 554, box 45.
9. Hayashi et al., *Nihon Shûsenshi,* p. 95.
10. XXIV Corps G-2 Periodic Report No. 46, 26 October 1945, cited in "History of U.S. Armed Forces in Korea," pt. 1, chap. 3. Copy in U.S. Army Center of Military History, Washington, D.C.
11. Message to all Consuls General, 25 August 1945, in "Japan's China Policy," 2 October 1941, SRH-093, National Archives Record Group 225.
12. OSS China, X-2 Branch Report, 2 September 1945, National Archives Record Group 226, entry 216, box 9.

13. Message, Forward Echelon, CCC, to CCC Chungking, 23 August 1945, Eyes Only file, Records of China Theater, National Archives Record Group 493.
14. Lt. Col. F. Spencer Chapman, D.S.O., Report on AJUF, 8 September to 12 October 1945, SOE, Far East, Malaya, HS1/120, Public Record Office, London.
15. Chin Sin Chong interview, Syonan Oral History Project, National Archives of Singapore, p. 44.
16. Tan Ben Chang interview, 000392/09, Syonan Oral History Project, National Archives of Singapore, p. 100.
17. Graham Peck, *Two Kinds of Time* (Boston: Houghton Mifflin, 1950), pp. 653–54.
18. Ng Seng Yong interview, A000283/11, Syonan Oral History Project, National Archives of Singapore, p. 110.
19. *Reports of General MacArthur: MacArthur in Japan, the Occupation: Military Phase,* vol. 1 supplement, pp. 170, 176, and passim.
20. Message, War Department to MacArthur and Wedemeyer, 17 August 1945, WARX 50537, ABC 387 (15 February 1945), National Archives Record Group 165, Records of General and Special Staffs.
21. For a detailed discussion of the drafting of General Order No. 1, see Gallicchio, *Cold War Begins in Asia,* pp. 75–92.
22. David M. Glantz, *August Storm: Soviet Tactical and Operational Combat in Manchuria, 1945,* Leavenworth Paper No. 8 (Leavenworth, Kan.: U.S. Army Combat Studies Institute, 1983), p. 33.
23. David M. Glantz, *August Storm: The Soviet 1945 Strategic Offensive in Manchuria,* Leavenworth Paper No. 7 (Leavenworth, Kan.: U.S. Army Combat Studies Institute, 1983), p. 229.
24. A thorough discussion of the importance of Manchukuo to Japanese political economic and cultural life can be found in Louise Younge, *Japan's Total Empire: Manchuria and the Culture of Wartime Imperialism* (Berkeley: University of California Press, 1998).
25. Hallett Abend, *Reconquest: Its Results and Responsibilities* (New York: Doubleday, 1946), p. 292.
26. "Principal Activities of Japanese in China, Manchuria and Formosa," Records of the Committee on the Far East, National Archives Record Group 59, reel 6.
27. Ibid.
28. Younge, *Japan's Total Empire,* pp. 356–58, 406.
29. Ibid., pp. 402–3.
30. Haruko Taya Cook and Theodore F. Cook, *Japan at War: An Oral History* (New York: New Press, 1992), p. 59.
31. Younge, *Japan's Total Empire,* pp. 406–7.
32. Umemoto Sutezo, *Kantogun Shimatsuki [Story of the End of the Kwantung Army]* (Tokyo: Hara Shobo, 1967), p. 44.
33. Cook and Cook, *Japan at War,* pp. 408–9.

34. Ono Eiko, *Ikiteita Yasui Manshu Touhikou, 300 Nichi [Memoir of a Three-Hundred-Day Escape from Northeast Manchuria]* (Osaka: Shoseki, 1985), pp. 48–66.
35. Younge, *Japan's Total Empire,* pp. 409–11.
36. Araragi Shinzo, *Manshu Imin no Rekishi Shakaigaku [Historical Sociology of Japanese Emigrants to Manchuria]* (Kyoto: Korasha, 1994), p. 53.
37. Umemoto, *Kantogun Shimatsuki,* p. 86.
38. Iijima Shiro, "Hoku-Man Kaitaku-Dan no Saiki" ["The Last Days of the Northern Manchukuo Settlers"], in Ito Masanori et al., eds., *Jitsuroku Taiheiyo Senso [Record of the Pacific War]* (Tokyo: Chuo Koronsha, 1960), p. 188.
39. Japanese Foreign Office Records, reel A-0116, frame 471, Foreign Ministry Archives, Tokyo.
40. Umemoto, *Kantogun Shimatsuki,* p. 55.
41. The Ambassador in Manchuria to the Minister of Foreign Affairs, 30 August 1945, in Jun Eto, ed., *The Ceasefire and the Suspension of Diplomatic Rights* (Tokyo: Ministry of Foreign Affairs, 1966), pp. 93–94.
42. Consular Report, 15 May 1946, Japanese Foreign Office Records, reel A-0116, frame 742, Foreign Ministry Archives, Tokyo.
43. Consular Report, 15 May 1946, Japanese Foreign Office Records, reel A-0116, frame 739, Foreign Ministry Archives, Tokyo.
44. Consular Report, 15 May 1946, Japanese Foreign Office Records, reel A-0116, frame 742, Foreign Ministry Archives, Tokyo.
45. Jung Chang, *Wild Swans: Three Daughters of China* (New York: Touchstone, 2003), p. 76.
46. Major R. Lamar, Team Cardinal, "Survey of the Mukden Area Situation . . .", 11 September 1945. National Archives Record Group 226, entry 148, box 6.
47. Hal Leith, *POWs of the Japanese Rescued!* (Victoria, B.C.: Trafford, 2003), pp. 60–61.
48. Japanese Embassy, Mukden, Report, [no date] August 1945, microfilm reel A-0116, frames 733–34, Japanese Foreign Ministry Archives, Tokyo.
49. Lamar, "Survey of the Mukden Area."
50. Ibid.
51. Ibid.
52. Umemoto, *Kantogun Shimatsuki,* p. 157.
53. Ibid.
54. U.S. Naval Attaché, Nanking, U.S.S.R.: Soviet Army of Occupation in Manchuria, 18 June 1946, National Archives Record Group 226, entry 108, box 378.
55. Leith, *POWs of the Japanese,* pp. 57–58.
56. Lamar, "Survey of the Mukden Area."
57. 1945–1946 microfilm records, microfilm reel A-0116, frame 774, Japanese Foreign Ministry Archives, Tokyo.
58. Brian Murray, "Stalin, the Cold War and the Division of China: A Multi-archival Mystery," Cold War International History Project, Working Paper

#12, (Washington, D.C.: Woodrow Wilson Center for Scholars, 1997), pp. 2–3.

59. Umemoto, *Kantogun Shimatsuki,* p. 166.
60. Ibid.
61. Abend, *Reconquest,* p. 67.
62. Personal Representative of the President on Reparations (E. W. Pauley), "General Summary of 'Report on Japanese Assets in Manchuria' " in *United States Relations with China with Special Reference to the Period 1944–49.* Department of State Publication 3578, Far Eastern Series 30. Reprinted as *The China White Paper,* ed. Lyman Van Slyke (Stanford, Calif.: Stanford University Press, 1967), p. 602.
63. Lamar, "Survey of the Mukden Area." Italics in original.
64. Pauley, "Report on Japanese Assets," p. 602.
65. Robert F. Seck, letter to author, July 21, 2001.
66. Tang Tsou, *America's Failure in China, 1941–50* (Chicago: University of Chicago Press, 1963), p. 335.
67. Abend, *Reconquest,* pp. 296–97.
68. Pauley, "Report on Japanese Assets," p. 599.
69. Military Information: Account of the Situation in Pingchuan After Soviet Invasion, Strategic Services Unit Report A-67256, 14 March 1946. National Archives Record Group 59.
70. Sergei N. Goncharov et al., *Uncertain Partners: Stalin, Mao and the Korean War* (Stanford, Calif.: Stanford University Press, 1993), p. 5.
71. John Paton Davies, Jr., *Dragon by the Tail* (London: Robson Books, 1974), p. 413.
72. Abend, *Reconquest,* pp. 55–56. Tang Tsou, *America's Failure in China,* p. 301.
73. George V. Underwood oral history interview, 1984, George V. Underwood Papers, box 1, pp. 14–15, U.S. Army Military History Institute, Carlisle, Pa.
74. Abend, *Reconquest,* p. 52.
75. Letter, Wedemeyer to Marshall, 1 August 1945, ABC 336 (26 January 1942) China, National Archives Record Group 218, section 1-B-4, box 243.
76. Franklin L. Ho oral history, vol. 1, no. 9, p. 164, Chinese Oral History Collection, Columbia University, New York.
77. Wu Kuo-chen oral history, p. 27, Chinese Oral History Collection, Columbia University, New York.
78. Ibid.
79. Herbert Feis, *The China Tangle: The American Efforts in China from Pearl Harbor to the Marshall Mission* (New York: Atheneum, 1965), pp. 337–38.
80. Feis, *China Tangle,* pp. 356–57.
81. Wedemeyer to War Department, CM-IN 12388, 12 August 1945, National Archives Record Group 218.
82. Marshall to Wedemeyer, WAR 49550, 14 August 1945, National Archives Record Group 165.
83. Wedemeyer to War Department, CM-IN 17460, 17 August 1945, National Archives Record Group 218.

84. CINCPAC to CNO CM-IN 15162, 15 August 1945, National Archives Record Group 218.
85. Message, Indiv to Davis, 25 August 1945, entry 148, box 7, National Archives Record Group 226.
86. Donald G. Gillin and Charles Etter, "Staying On: Japanese Soldiers and Civilians in China, 1945–1949," *Journal of Asian Studies* 42, May 1983, pp. 497–99.
87. Message CHAFX, Kunming to OSS, 4 September 1945, IN 23381, National Archives Record Group 226, entry 53, box 4.
88. Suzanne Pepper, *Civil War in China: The Political Struggle* (Berkeley: University of California Press, 1978), p. 12.
89. Odd Arne Westad, *Cold War and Revolution: Soviet-American Rivalry and the Origins of the Chinese Civil War* (New York: Columbia University Press, 1993), p. 104.
90. "China's Position Today," 19 August 1945, SRH-114, National Archives Record Group 457.
91. Pepper, *Civil War in China,* p. 12.
92. Message CCC FWD ECH to CCC Kunming, 23 August 1945, National Archives Record Group 493.
93. Louis Allen's summary of Imai's memoir, "Shina hakengun no kofuku" ["The Surrender of the Expeditionary Force in China"], in Allen, *End of the War in Asia,* pp. 238–40.
94. Herbert Bix, *Hirohito and the Making of Modern Japan* (New York: HarperCollins, 2000), pp. 362, 594–95.
95. Gillin and Etter, "Staying On," p. 499.
96. Message, CCC FWD ECH to CCC Kunming, 23 August 1945, National Archives Record Group 493.
97. John Hersey, "Letter from Peiping," *The New Yorker,* April 25, 1946, p. 90.
98. Gillin and Etter, "Staying On," p. 501.
99. Pepper, *Civil War in China,* p. 11.
100. Ibid.
101. Message, Redford to Indiv, 18 December 1945, National Archives Record Group 226, entry 210, box 156.
102. Report by Captain Hayes to Com. Seventh Amphibious Force, attachment to Memo by J. A. O'Neil, Flag Secretary, 11 December 1945, Daniel E. Barbey Papers, box 29, subject file "China," Naval Historical Center, Washington, D.C.
103. Gillin and Etter, "Staying On," p. 560.
104. Niu Jun, "The Origins of the Sino-Soviet Alliance," in Odd Arne Westad, ed., *Brothers in Arms: The Rise and Fall of the Sino-Soviet Alliance, 1945–1963* (Washington, D.C.: Woodrow Wilson Center Press, 1998), p. 51.
105. Lyman Van Slyke, "The Chinese Communist Movement During the Sino-Japanese War, 1937–1945," in John K. Fairbank and Albert Feuerwerker, eds., *The Cambridge History of China,* vol. 13, pt. 2 (Cambridge, U.K.: Cambridge University Press, 1986), p. 720.

106. "Sino-Soviet Relations in Manchuria Since the Defeat of Japan," JCS 1330/19 Sec. A, ABC 336China (24 January 1942), National Archives Record Group 218, section 1E, box 244.
107. Sergei N. Goncharov et al., *Uncertain Partners,* pp. 6–7.
108. Ibid., p. 7.
109. John F. Melby oral history interview by Charles Stuart Kennedy, June 1989, p. 2, Harry S. Truman Presidential Library, Independence, Mo.
110. Letter, Wedemeyer to Marshall, 1 August 1945, CM-IN 476, 1 August 1945, ABC 336China, 26 January 1942, National Archives Record Group 218, section 1-B-4, box 243.
111. Walter Millis, ed., *The Forrestal Diaries* (New York: Viking, 1966), p. 98.
112. Ross Terrill, *Mao: A Biography* (New York: Harper, 1980), pp. 181–82. Han Suyin, *Elder Brother: Zhou Enlai and the Making of Modern China, 1898–1976* (New York: Kodansha, 1994), pp. 188–89.
113. Yu, *OSS in China,* p. 236. Malcolm Rosholt to Paul Frillman, 4 January 1967, Paul W. Frillman Papers, box 3, Hoover Institution Archives, Stanford, Calif.
114. Memo for Major Gustave J. Krause, subject: Account of the Death of Captain John Birch, OSS Field Station Files, Chungking, National Archives Record Group 226, entry 14B, box 6.
115. Chu Teh to Wedemeyer, 18 September 1945, Albert C. Wedemeyer Papers, box 81, folder 81.5, Hoover Institution Archives, Stanford, Calif.
116. Yu, *OSS in China,* p. 237.
117. Minutes of Meeting Held at Ambassador Hurley's Home, 30 August 1945, National Archives Record Group 226, entry 144, box 6.
118. Untitled Comment on Kahn, *The China Hands,* Albert C. Wedemeyer Papers, box 6, folder 6.24, Hoover Institution Archives, Stanford, Calif.
119. Ross Terrill, *Mao,* p. 183.
120. Murray, "Stalin, the Cold War and the Division of China," p. 3.
121. Wang Zifeng, *Zhanzheng Niandi de Riji [Diary in Time of War]* (Beijing: Chinese Literature Publishing House, 1986), p. 171.
122. Westad, *Cold War and Revolution,* p. 83.
123. Ibid., p. 90.
124. Military Information: Account of the Situation in Pingchuan.
125. Goncharov et al., *Uncertain Partners,* p. 10. Murray, "Stalin, the Cold War and the Division of China," p. 3.

CHAPTER 3 "Graft and Corruption Prevail"

1. W. H. Brockintin, "An Airfield near Peiping, 1945," *Scuttlebutt,* June 2000, p. 10.
2. E. B. Sledge, *China Marine* (Tuscaloosa: University of Alabama Press, 2002), p. 3.
3. Ibid., p. 8.
4. Earle unpublished memoir.

5. Benis M. Frank and Henry I. Shaw, Jr., *Victory and Occupation: History of U.S. Marine Corps Operations in World War II,* vol. 5 (Washington, D.C.: Historical Branch, G-3 Division, Headquarters, U.S. Marine Corps, 1968), p. 534.
6. Calvin H. Decker oral history interview, p. 5, Marine Corps Historical Center, Washington, D.C.
7. Joseph T. Shipman, letter to author, June 29, 2001.
8. George H. Haertlein, letter to author, July 26, 2001.
9. Frank and Shaw, *Victory and Occupation,* p. 544.
10. Sledge, *China Marine,* p. 9.
11. John T. DeMoss, letter to author, July 20, 2001.
12. Earle unpublished memoir.
13. The Consul General at Tientsin (Mr. Ota) to the Foreign Minister (Yoshida), 25 August 1945, file A-0116, 532 (0198–0199), Foreign Ministry Archives, Tokyo.
14. Frank and Shaw, *Victory and Occupation,* p. 553.
15. Ibid., pp. 546–47.
16. Ibid., p. 546.
17. Ibid., p. 548.
18. George Moorad, *Lost Peace in China* (New York: E. P. Dutton, 1949), pp. 77–78.
19. Leo Bouchard, letter to author, August 3, 2001.
20. Earle unpublished memoir.
21. Otis Cary, ed., *Eyewitness to History: The First Americans in Postwar Asia* (Tokyo: Kodansha International, 1995), p. 90.
22. Ibid., p. 126.
23. Frank and Shaw, *Victory and Occupation,* p. 565. Captain Edwin Klein, "Situation in North China," *Marine Corps Gazette,* April 1946, p. 3.
24. Secret Intelligence Morning Meeting with Mayor Li Lien Liang, October 12, 1945. Secret Intelligence Morning Meeting with Mayor Li Lien Liang, October 13, 1945. Both in National Archives Record Group 226, entry 140, box 45.
25. Frank and Shaw, *Victory and Occupation,* p. 558.
26. John D. Druce, "China Reminiscences," unpublished memoir. Courtesy of Mr. Druce.
27. Westad, *Cold War and Revolution,* p. 105.
28. Letter, Acheson to Averell Harriman, 9 November 1945, W. Averell Harriman Papers, box 184, Manuscript Division, Library of Congress, Washington, D.C.
29. Gallicchio, *Cold War Begins in Asia,* pp. 76, 81, 84–87.
30. Westad, *Cold War and Revolution,* p. 102.
31. Ibid., p. 106.
32. Ibid.
33. Message, Com. 7th Flt. to Chungking, enclosing CTG 71 message, 5 Oc-

tober 1945, TS messages, China Theater, National Archives Record Group 493.

34. Barbey to Major General S. S. Wade, 8 November 1961, copy in Daniel E. Barbey Papers, box 32, subject file "1961–62," Naval Historical Center, Washington, D.C.
35. Message, Com. 7th Flt. to Chungking, 5 October 1945.
36. Frank and Shaw, *Victory and Occupation,* p. 559.
37. Ibid.
38. Jack D. McManus, letter to author, May 29, 2001. A notable exception was the observation of Pfc. William C. Wideman that after the island campaigns, China "reminded me of home," William C. Wideman, letter to author, July 11, 2001.
39. Edmund J. Bardy, letter to author, May 12, 2001.
40. Warren Beaster, letter to author, June 4, 2001.
41. Harold Henneman, letter to author, July 25, 2001.
42. Earle unpublished memoir.
43. William D. Huber, letter to author, July 21, 2001.
44. Louis R. Weibl, letter to author, June 22, 2001.
45. This conclusion is based on questionnaires completed by seventy-nine members of the China Marine Association during 2000–2001. Marines who received questionnaires were chosen at random (every twentieth name in the association's directory).
46. Of thirty-six members of the China Marine Association who gave an opinion about the Chinese in response to the author's questionnaire, twenty-six expressed positive views, three negative, and seven both positive and negative views.
47. Paul L. Nolan, letter to author, May 17, 2001.
48. William Hill, letter to author, June 26, 2001.
49. Donald C. Behrens, letter to author, July 18, 2001.
50. See Sledge, *China Marine,* p. 23.
51. Zhiguo Yang, "U.S. Marines in Qingdau: Society, Culture and China's Civil War, 1945–1949," in Larry I. Bland, ed., *George C. Marshall's Mediation Mission to China* (Lexington, Va.: George C. Marshall Foundation, 1987), pp. 186–87.
52. Robert Shaffer, "A Rape in Beijing, December 1946: GIs, Nationalist Protests and U.S. Foreign Policy," *Pacific Historical Review* 69, February 2000, pp. 35–36, 40, and passim.
53. Klein, "Situation in North China," pp. 2–3. The Consul General in Tientsin (Mr. Ota) to the Foreign Minister (Yoshida), 15 October 1945, file A-0116 532 (0207–0209), Foreign Ministry Archives, Tokyo.
54. The best discussion of Chieu-shou and its consequences may be found in Pepper, *Civil War in China,* pp. 16–28.
55. Paul Frillman and Graham Peck, *China: The Remembered Life* (Boston: Houghton Mifflin, 1968), p. 655.

56. Ibid.
57. Moorad, *Lost Peace in China,* pp. 55–56.
58. Franklin L. Ho oral history, vol. 3, no. 9, pp. 388–89.
59. Pepper, *Civil War in China,* p. 24.
60. Quoted in Tsou, *America's Failure in China,* p. 313.
61. Message, West Va. to Indiv, 19 March 1946, National Archives Record Group 226, entry 210, box 156.
62. Message, Redfern to Indiv, 20 December 1945, National Archives Record Group 226, entry 210, box 156.
63. Quoted in Li Huang oral history, p. 832, Chinese Oral History Collection, Columbia University, New York.
64. Wu Kuo-chen memoirs, box 20, Chinese Oral History Collection, Columbia University, New York.
65. Chang, *Wild Swans,* p. 80.
66. Wu Kuo-chen memoirs, box 20, p. 4.
67. Message, West Va. to Indiv, 14 March 1946, National Archives Record Group 226, entry 210, box 156.
68. Earle unpublished memoir.
69. Message, Kellis to Indiv, 1 November 1945, National Archives Record Group 226, entry 210, box 156.
70. Action report, ComTransDiv 59, 19 November 1945, copy in Daniel E. Barbey Papers, Naval Historical Center, Washington, D.C.
71. Ibid.
72. Ibid.
73. Wang Zifeng, *Zhanzheng Niandi de Riji,* pp. 171–72.
74. Zhang Zenglong, *Xie Bai Xue Hong [Blood and Snow]* (Hong Kong: Dadi Chu-banshe, 1991), pp. 33–34.
75. Ibid., p. 35.
76. Jung Chang and Jon Halliday, *Mao: The Unknown Story* (New York: Knopf, 2005), p. 288.
77. Zhang Zenglong, *Xie Bai Xue Hong,* p. 36.
78. Ibid., p. 35.
79. Wang Zifeng, *Zhanzheng Niandi de Riji,* p. 172.
80. Harold M. Tanner, "Guerrilla, Mobile, and Base Warfare in Communist Military Operations in Manchuria, 1945–1947," *Journal of Military History* 67, October 2003, pp. 1196–97.
81. USS *Catoctin,* Combat Intelligence Department, Chinese Political Supplement, copy in Daniel E. Barbey Papers, Naval Historical Center, Washington, D.C.
82. Message, CTG 7 to Com. 7th Flt., 6 November 1945, TS files, China Theater, National Archives Record Group 493.
83. Westad, *Cold War and Revolution,* pp. 125–26.
84. Ibid., pp. 125, 129–30.
85. Frank and Shaw, *Victory and Occupation,* p. 572.
86. Ibid., pp. 566–67, 585.

87. Joseph T. Shipman, unpublished memoir. Courtesy of Mr. Shipman.
88. Frank and Shaw, *Victory and Occupation,* pp. 585–86.
89. Westad, *Cold War and Revolution,* pp. 110–11.
90. Ibid., p. 111.
91. Frank and Shaw, *Victory and Occupation,* p. 586.
92. Ibid., p. 578.
93. Van Slyke, *China White Paper,* pp. 131–32.
94. Gary May, *China Scapegoat: The Diplomatic Ordeal of John Carter Vincent* (Washington, D.C.: New Republic Books, 1979), p. 82.
95. Meeting of the Secretaries of War, State, and Navy, 6 November 1945. *Foreign Relations of the United States (FRUS), 1945,* vol. 6, *The Far East: China,* pp. 606–7.
96. The best and most thorough discussion is in Gallicchio, *Cold War Begins in Asia,* pp. 118–27.
97. Memo by the Chief of the Division of Chinese Affairs to the Undersecretary of State, 16 October 1945, *FRUS, 1945,* vol. 6, p. 578.
98. Westad, *Cold War and Revolution,* p. 113.
99. Acheson to Representative Hugh DeLacy, October 9, 1945. *FRUS, 1945,* vol. 6, p. 577.
100. Gallicchio, *Cold War Begins in Asia,* p. 127.
101. The Ambassador to China to President Truman, 26 November 1945, Van Slyke, *China White Paper,* pp. 581–82.
102. Forrest C. Pogue, *George C. Marshall: Statesman, 1945–1959* (New York: Viking, 1987), p. 3.
103. Ibid., p. 29.
104. SMOF, Press Summaries, Rose Conway files, box 12, Harry S. Truman Presidential Library, Independence, Mo.
105. Statement by President Truman on United States Policy Toward China, December 15, 1945, Van Slyke, *China White Paper,* pp. 606–7.
106. Pogue, *George C. Marshall,* p. 75.

CHAPTER 4 "Freedom Is on the Offensive"

1. Samuel Eliot Morison, *Victory in the Pacific, 1945* (Boston: Atlantic, Little Brown, 1975), p. 368.
2. Philip Ziegler, *Mountbatten* (New York: Knopf, 1985), p. 21.
3. *Post-Surrender Tasks: Report to the Combined Chiefs of Staff by the Supreme Allied Commander, South East Asia, 1943–1945* (London: HMSO, 1969), p. 281.
4. Field Marshal Sir William Slim, *Defeat into Victory* (London: Cassell, 1956), p. 530.
5. Ibid.
6. SACSEA to Chiefs of Staff SEACOS 448, 21 August 1945, copy in CCS 901/8 ABC 387Japan (15 February 1945), National Archives Record Group 165, section 1C, box 505.

7. Slim, *Defeat into Victory,* p. 522.
8. Report on Morale of British, Indian and Colonial Troops, ALFSEA, August–October 1945. WO203/2268 Public Record Office, London.
9. Ziegler, *Mountbatten,* pp. 300–301.
10. Quoted in Paul H. Kratoska, *The Japanese Occupation of Malaya* (St. Leonards, Australia: Allen and Unwin, 1998), p. 306.
11. Thompson interview, p. 89.
12. Lee Tian Soo interview, Syonan Oral History Project, National Archives of Singapore, p. 78.
13. Cheng Kok Peng, "A Brief Study of the Situation in Batu Pahat During the Japanese Occupation," in Paul H. Kratoska and Abu Talib Ahmad, eds., *Pendukan Jepun Di Tanah Melayu* (Palau Pinang, Malaysia: Universiti Sains Malaysia, 1989), p. 31.
14. Ibid., p. 37.
15. Ahmed Khan interview, Syonan Oral History Project, National Archives of Singapore, p. 106.
16. Lee Kip Lin interview, Syonan Oral History Project, National Archives of Singapore, p. 171.
17. Gay Wan Guay interview, Syonan Oral History Project, National Archives of Singapore, p. 259.
18. F.S.V. Donnison, *British Military Administration in the Far East, 1943–46* (London: HMSO, 1956), p. 40.
19. Operational Report by Major J. L. Chapman, GLO to 7th Regt. MPAJA, Operation Siphon, 7 October 1945, HS1/120, PRO.
20. Lt. Col. F. Spencer Chapman, Report on AJUF, 12 October 1945, HS1/120, Public Record Office, London.
21. Ibid.
22. Kratoska, *Japanese Occupation of Malaya,* pp. 292–93.
23. Message, Mountbatten to Chiefs of Staff, 19 April 1945, WO203/4403, Public Record Office, London.
24. SACSEA War Diary, Clandestine Operations, 4 October 1945, WO172/1786, Public Record Office, London.
25. Operational Report by Lt. Col. D. K. Broadhurst, Galvanic GLO, [no date] 1945, SOE, Far East, Malaya, HS1/119, Public Record Office, London.
26. Ibid.
27. Lee Kip Lin interview, p. 162.
28. Cheah Boon Kheng, *Red Star Over Malaya: Resistance and Social Conflict During and After the Japanese Occupation of Malaya, 1941–1946* (Singapore: Singapore University Press, 1983), p. 167.
29. Operational Report by Major J. L. Chapman.
30. Chin Kee Onn, *Malaya Upside Down* (Singapore: Federal Publications, 1977), p. 183.
31. Mamoro Shinozaki, *Syonan—My Story: The Japanese Occupation of Singapore* (Singapore: Asia Pacific Press, 1969), p. 97.

32. Force 136 Report by Lt. Col. F. S. Chapman, 25 October 1945, cited in Kratoska, *Japanese Occupation of Malaya,* p. 302.
33. Quoted in Cheah, *Red Star Over Malaya,* p. 179.
34. Kratoska, *Japanese Occupation of Malaya,* p. 302.
35. "Views of a Malay on the Sino-Malay Differences," Appendix B to Malaya Command Weekly Intel. Report no. 30, WO172/9773, Public Record Office, London.
36. Ahmed Khan interview, p. 90.
37. Chin Kee Onn, *Malaya Upside Down,* p. 186.
38. Quoted in Cheah, *Red Star Over Malaya,* pp. 128–29.
39. Operational Report by Major J. L. Chapman. Operational Report by Major P. T. Thomson-Walker, subject: Galvanic Orange, SOE, Far East, Malaya, HS1/119, Public Record Office, London.
40. Kratoska, *Japanese Occupation of Malaya,* p. 302.
41. K.O.L. Burridge, "Racial Relations in Johore," *The Australian Journal of Politics and History* 2, May 1957, p. 163.
42. Lee Kip Lin interview, p. 164.
43. *Post-Surrender Tasks,* p. 302.
44. Richard Hough, *Mountbatten: A Biography* (New York: Random House, 1980), p. 203.
45. Ziegler, *Mountbatten,* p. 303.
46. C. M. Turnbull, *A History of Singapore, 1819–1975* (Kuala Lumpur: Oxford University Press, 1977), p. 218.
47. Thompson interview, p. 91.
48. Kratoska, *Japanese Occupation of Malaya,* pp. 307–8.
49. Andrew Gilmour, *My Role in the Rehabilitation of Singapore* (Singapore: Institute of Southeast Asian Studies, 1973), p. 6.
50. William L. Holland, ed., *Asian Nationalism and the West* (New York: Macmillan, 1953), pp. 299–300.
51. Tan Guan Chuan interview, 000414/10, Syonan Oral History Project, National Archives of Singapore, p. 127.
52. Shinozaki, *Syonan—My Story,* p. 103.
53. Evacuation of the Japanese to Rempang and Galang Islands, Appendix D to Weekly Intelligence Report no. 28 [no date], WO172/9773, Public Record Office.
54. Charlotte Carr-Greg, *Japanese POWs in Revolt* (St. Lucia, Australia: University of Queensland Press, 1978), p. 16.
55. Kratoska, *Japanese Occupation of Malaya,* pp. 320–21.
56. Turnbull, *History of Singapore,* p. 224.
57. Kratoska, *Japanese Occupation of Malaya,* p. 316.
58. Ibid., p. 320.
59. Ibid., p. 341. *Post-Surrender Tasks,* p. 284.
60. *Post-Surrender Tasks,* p. 284.
61. Tan Ben Chang interview, p. 106.

62. Tan Guan Chuan interview, p. 125.
63. Kratoska, *Japanese Occupation of Malaya,* p. 328.
64. Turnbull, *History of Singapore,* p. 228.
65. *Post-Surrender Tasks,* pp. 303–5.
66. Ibid., p. 306.
67. Message, SIGEX Kandy to Director, SSU, 28325, 13 November 1945, National Archives Record Group 226, entry 57, box 3.
68. SACSEA Weekly Intelligence Summary, 17 November 1945, WO203/2076, Public Record Office, London.
69. Cheah, *Red Star Over Malaya,* p. 237.
70. Malaya Command Intelligence Summaries, No. 53 and No. 55, 3 January 1946 and 5 January 1946, WO203/2585, Public Record Office, London.
71. Malaya Command Weekly Intelligence Report No. 31, 11 June 1946, WO172/9773, Public Record Office, London.
72. Ibid.
73. Cheah, *Red Star Over Malaya,* pp. 207–8.
74. Malaya Command Weekly Intelligence Report No. 31.
75. Ibid.; Malaya Command Weekly Intelligence Report No. 14, 2 February 1946, WO172/2773, Public Record Office, London.
76. Malaya Command Weekly Intelligence Summary No. 14.
77. ComGen India-Burma Theater, Weekly Intelligence Sitrep, 25 March 1946, Record Group 9, box 42, Douglas MacArthur Memorial Archives, Norfolk, Va.
78. SEAC War Diary, Intelligence Summary No. 16, 10 February 1946, WO172/9773, Public Record Office, London.
79. Malaya Command Intelligence Summary No. 87, 12 February 1946, WO203/2585, Public Record Office, London.
80. SEAC War Diary, Intelligence Summary No. 20, 16 March 1946, WO172/9773, Public Record Office, London. ComGen India-Burma Theater, Weekly Intelligence Sitrep, 25 March 1946.
81. Noel Barber, *The War of the Running Dogs* (New York: Weybright and Talley, 1972), p. 31.
82. Turnbull, *History of Singapore,* p. 225.
83. ComGen India-Burma Theater, Weekly Intelligence Sitrep, 4 December 1945, Radiograms India, Record Group 9, box 42, Douglas MacArthur Memorial Archives, Norfolk, Va.

CHAPTER 5 "Long Live Vietnam's Independence"

1. Fragment of letter, [no date] October 1945, V. M. Sissons Papers, Imperial War Museum, London.
2. Peter M. Dunn, *The First Vietnam War* (New York: St. Martin's, 1985), pp. 152–53.
3. Duong Van Mai Elliott, *The Sacred Willow: Four Generations in the Life of a Vietnamese Family* (New York: Oxford University Press, 1999), p. 131.

4. Archimedes L. Patti, *Why Vietnam? Prelude to America's Albatross* (Berkeley: University of California Press, 1980), p. 284.
5. Quoted in Christopher Thorne, *Allies of a Kind: The United States, Britain, and the War Against Japan* (London: Hamish Hamilton, 1978), p. 217.
6. Roosevelt to William Philips, 19 November 1942, cited in William Roger Lewis, *Imperialism at Bay* (New York: Oxford University Press, 1987), p. 180.
7. Elliott Roosevelt, *As He Saw It* (New York: Duell, Sloan and Pearce, 1946) p. 116.
8. "An Open Letter to the People of Britain," *Life,* October 9, 1942.
9. Davies, *Dragon by the Tail,* p. 276.
10. Wheeler to General George C. Marshall, 24 March 1945, OPD files, National Archives Record Group 165.
11. Halifax to Foreign Minister Anthony Eden, 4 February 1945, F2300/993/61, FO371/41746, Public Record Office, London.
12. Foreign Office to the Ambassador in Washington (Halifax), 29 January 1945, WO203/5621, Public Record Office, London.
13. Memo, Roosevelt to Secy. of State, 24 January 1944, *FRUS, 1943: The Conferences at Cairo and Tehran* (Washington, D.C.: GPO, 1961), pp. 872–73.
14. Thorne, *Allies of a Kind,* p. 348. The literature on this subject is extensive. In addition to Thorne, see Gary R. Hess, "Franklin Roosevelt and Indochina," *Journal of American History* 59, September 1972, pp. 353–68, and Walter Lafeber, "Roosevelt, Churchill and Indochina, 1942–45," *American Historical Review* 80, December 1975, pp. 1277–95. The most exhaustive discussion is in Stein Tonnesson, *The Vietnamese Revolution of 1945: Roosevelt, Ho Chi Minh and de Gaulle in a World at War* (London: Sage Publications, 1991).
15. Minute by Cavendish-Bentinck, 20 December 1943, F6656, FO371/35921, Public Record Office, London.
16. Foreign Office to the Ambassador in Washington, 29 December 1943, FO371/35921, Public Record Office, London.
17. Lafeber, "Roosevelt, Churchill and Indochina," p. 1291.
18. Memo, Roosevelt to Secretary of State, 16 October 1944, *FRUS, 1944,* vol. 3, *The British Commonwealth and Europe* (Washington, D.C.: GPO, 1963), p. 777.
19. See the works cited in note 14 above. Tonnesson believes that Roosevelt never abandoned his goal and may even have contemplated an American landing in Indochina.
20. George C. Herring, "The Truman Administration and the Restoration of French Sovereignty in Indochina," *Diplomatic History* 1, Spring 1977, p. 102.
21. Dening to Foreign Office, 6 March 1945, FO371/46304, Public Record Office, London.
22. Memo of Conversation, Enclosure to Foreign Office to the Ambassador in China, 24 April 1945, WO203/5621, Public Record Office, London.
23. Thorne, *Allies of a Kind,* p. 454.

24. Dening to Foreign Office, 9 December 1944, F5802, FO371/41746, Public Record Office, London.
25. Dening to Foreign Office, 8 February 1945, WO203/5561, Public Record Office, London.
26. Message, Wedemeyer to Marshall, 25 May 1945, FIC Book 1, National Archives Record Group 332.
27. Message, Wedemeyer to Marshall, 28 May 1945, FIC Book 1, National Archives Record Group 332.
28. Hurley to Truman, 28 May 1945, *FRUS, 1945,* vol. 1, *The Conference of Berlin,* p. 920.
29. Acting Secretary of State to Hurley, 7 June 1945, ABC 384 Indochina, 16 December 1944, National Archives Record Group 165.
30. Ronald Spector, *Advice and Support: The Early Years of the U.S. Army in Vietnam, 1941–1960,* (New York: Free Press, 1985), p. 49.
31. Ibid., pp. 49–50.
32. "Indochina," Briefing for the San Francisco Conference, F2431/G, 21 April 1945, FO371/46306, Public Record Office, London.
33. Memo by Mr. F. Jones, Foreign Office Research, Record of French in Indochina, 26 January 1944, F478/66/61, FO371/41723, Public Record Office, London.
34. John Gunther, *Inside Asia* (London: Hamish Hamilton, 1939), p. 380.
35. Memo, Foote to Secretary of State, Future of the Netherlands Indies, 6 July 1942, 8650.00/154, National Archives Record Group 59. "If his Dutch colonial friends and colleagues could have read [Foote's] cables and dispatches to the State Department," observes historian Francis Gouda, "they would not have objected simply because he recapitulated their own political views," in Francis Gouda and Thijs Brocades Zaalberg, *American Visions of the Netherlands East Indies/Indonesia* (Amsterdam University Press, 2002), p. 41.
36. Tonnesson, *Vietnamese Revolution,* p. 238.
37. Recent Political Developments in French Indochina, 6 April 1945, SRH-095, National Archives Record Group 457. Lt. Col. Sakai Tateki, "French Indochina Operations Record," Japanese Monograph No. 25, copy in U.S. Army Center of Military History, Washington, D.C.
38. David G. Marr, *Vietnam 1945: The Quest for Power,* pp. 133–34; Huyn Kim Khanh, "The Vietnamese August Revolution Reinterpreted," *Journal of Asian Studies* 30, 1971, pp. 761–82.
39. Nguyen Khang, "Uprising in Hanoi," in Nguyen Duy Trinh, ed., *In the Enemy's Net* (Hanoi: Foreign Languages Publishing House, 1962), p. 120.
40. Marr, *Vietnam 1945,* pp. 96–99.
41. Quoted in Nguyen Thi Anh, "Japanese Food Policies and the 1945 Great Famine in Indochina," in Paul H. Kratoska, ed., *Food Supplies and the Japanese Occupation of Southeast Asia* (Houndmills, U.K.: Macmillan, 1998), p. 211.
42. Elliott, *Sacred Willow,* p. 107.

43. Ibid.
44. Motoo Furuta, "A Survey of Village Conditions During the 1945 Famine in Vietnam," in Kratoska, *Food Supplies,* p. 237.
45. Nguyen Thi Tuyet Mai, *The Rubber Tree: Memoir of a Vietnamese Woman Who Was an Anti-French Guerrilla, a Publisher and Peace Activist* (Jefferson, N.C.: McFarland, 1994), p. 56.
46. Nguyen Thi Anh, "Japanese Food Policies," p. 221.
47. Ronald Spector, *Advice and Support,* pp. 39–42. Tonnesson, *Vietnamese Revolution,* pp. 308–10.
48. Spector, *Advice and Support,* p. 41.
49. Ibid.
50. Marr, *Vietnam 1945,* p. 366.
51. William J. Duiker, *Ho Chi Minh: A Life* (New York: Hyperion, 2000), p. 312.
52. French Indochina (Political Situation), 11 October 1945, SRH-094, National Archives Record Group 457. Marr, *Vietnam 1945,* pp. 516–17.
53. Patti to Indiv, 2 September 1945, National Archives Record Group 226, entry 154, box 199.
54. Patti to Indiv to Parrot, 4 September 1945. Patti to Parrot for Gallagher, 6 September 1945. Both in National Archives Record Group 226, entry 148, box 7.
55. François Guillemot, "Viêt Nam 1945–1946: l'élimination de l'opposition nationaliste et anticolonialiste dans le Nord: au cœur de la fracture vietnamienne," in Christopher E. Goscha and Benoît de Tréglodé, eds., *Le Viêt Nam depuis 1945: états, contestations et constructions du passé* (Paris: Les Indes Savantes, 2004), pp. 1, 5–9.
56. Ibid. Marr, *Vietnam 1945,* pp. 445–47, 518–19.
57. Elliott, *Sacred Willow,* pp. 120–21, 129. Duiker, *Ho Chi Minh,* p. 324.
58. Duiker, *Ho Chi Minh,* p. 324.
59. Spector, *Advice and Support,* p. 56.
60. Patti, *Why Vietnam?,* p. 122.
61. Ibid., pp. 238–39.
62. Françoise Martin, *Heures tragiques au Tonkin* (Paris: Editions Berger, 1948), p. 152.
63. Headquarters, Chinese Combat Command (Prov) to Commanding General I Army Group Command CCC (Prov), subject: Report on Hanoi, 15 September 1945, National Archives Record Group 226, entry 154, box 197. Patti, *Why Vietnam?,* pp. 174–75. Spector, *Advice and Support,* p. 58.
64. Surgeon General Bouvier to General Allessandri, 6 September 1942, subject: Situation à Hanoi, dossier 4, 10H161, Service Historique de l'Armée de Terre (SHAT), Vincennes, Paris.
65. Report on Hanoi, 15 September 1945, in Martin, *Heures tragiques,* p. 184.
66. Martin, *Heures tragiques,* p. 150.
67. Traduction de Telegramme, 19 September 1945, dossier, 10H161, SHAT, Vincennes, Paris.

68. Patti, *Why Vietnam?,* pp. 162, 192.
69. Patti to Indiv, 25 August 1945, 28 August 1945, 31 August 1945, National Archives Record Group 226, entry 154, box 197.
70. Patti, *Why Vietnam?,* p. 198.
71. Patti to Indiv, 25 August 1945, National Archives Record Group 226, entry 154, box 197.
72. Marr, *Vietnam 1945,* p. 485.
73. Ibid., p. 487.
74. Indiv to Kandy, No. 5902, 29 August 1942, National Archives Record Group 226, entry 154, box 189.
75. Patti, *Why Vietnam?,* p. 208.
76. Marr, *Vietnam 1945,* pp. 489–99.
77. Bulletin de renseignements no. 2660, 27 October 1945, dossier Section de Liaison Français en Extrème Orient, SHAT, Vincennes, Paris.
78. Davis to Heppner, 1 September 1945, National Archives Record Group 226, entry 154, box 199.
79. Heppner to Indiv for Patti, 3 September 1945, National Archives Record Group 226, entry 154, box 199.
80. Patti, *Why Vietnam?,* p. 254 and passim.
81. Patti to Strategic Services Officer OSS/CT, subject: Activity Report, OSS Hanoi Detachment, 5 September 1945, National Archives Record Group 226, entry 154, box 199.
82. Patti, *Why Vietnam?,* pp. 239, 301, 358.
83. Grelecki to Indiv, Activities Report, 5 September 1945, National Archives Record Group 226, entry 154, box 199.
84. Patti, *Why Vietnam?,* pp. 265–67.
85. Ibid., p. 281.

CHAPTER 6 **"Cochinchina Is Burning"**

1. Peter Worthing, *Occupation and Revolution: China and the Vietnamese August Revolution of 1945* (Berkeley: Institute of East Asian Studies, University of California, Berkeley, 2001), p. 67.
2. Headquarters, United States Forces, China Theater, Occupation of Indo-China North of 16° N. Latitude, 11 September 1945, copy in National Archives Record Group 226, entry 48, box 7.
3. Gallagher to Bernard Fall, 30 March 1956, Philip E. Gallagher Papers, U.S. Army Military History Institute, Carlisle, Pa.
4. 2ème bureau troups français en Extréme-Orient, Les Chinois en Indochine, 7 September 1946, 10H600, SHAT, Vincennes, Paris.
5. Elliott, *Sacred Willow,* p. 131.
6. SIGEX Kandy to Director of Operations, X-2 R&A, National Archives Record Group 226, entry 58, box 3.
7. John T. McAlister, *Vietnam: The Origins of Revolution* (New York: Center for International Studies, Princeton University, 1969), pp. 225–26.

8. Patti, *Why Vietnam?,* p. 291.
9. Spector, *Advice and Support,* p. 69.
10. Gallagher to Bernard Fall, 30 March 1956.
11. Gallagher to Maj. Gen. Robert B. McClure, 20 September 1945, FIC Files, Records of China Theater, National Archives Record Group 332.
12. Worthing, *Occupation and Revolution,* p. 70 and passim.
13. Memo for Record by General Gallagher, 21 September 1945, Philip E. Gallagher Papers, U.S. Army Military History Institute, Carlisle, Pa.
14. Report of Arthur Hale, November 1945, enclosure 2, Gallagher to Bernard Fall, 30 March 1945.
15. Patti, *Why Vietnam?,* p. 285.
16. Duiker, *Ho Chi Minh,* pp. 313–14.
17. Peter Dennis, *Troubled Days of Peace: Mountbatten and Southeast Asia Command, 1945–46* (New York: St. Martin's, 1987), p. 40.
18. War Office to SACSEA, 31 August 1945, WO203/4117, Public Record Office, London.
19. Memo by Colonel LeCompte, Projet d'emploi des premiers forces français en Indochine, 24 September 1945, dossier 3, 10H161, SHAT, Vincennes, Paris.
20. Dening to Foreign Office, 10 September 1945, WO203/5562, Public Record Office, London.
21. Dennis, *Troubled Days of Peace,* pp. 39–40.
22. Dunn, *First Vietnam War,* p. 154.
23. Cited in SACSEA Message SEACOS 488, 23 September 1945, CAB/162.
24. For a thorough and sympathetic discussion of the mind-set of these officers, based on extensive letters and interviews, see Dunn, *First Vietnam War,* pp. 169–72, 186–88, and passim.
25. Sissons letter, [no date] October 1945.
26. Spector, *Advice and Support,* p. 65.
27. Memo, Major George C. Sharp to Colonel G. Edward Buxton, Captain Albert Peter Dewey, 28 December 1943, National Archives Record Group 226, microfilm 1642, reel 73.
28. George Wickes, "Saigon 1945–Hanoi 1946." Courtesy of Professor Wickes.
29. Spector, *Advice and Support,* p. 66.
30. Wickes, "Saigon 1945–Hanoi 1946."
31. Dunn, *First Vietnam War,* p. 154.
32. Wickes, "Saigon 1945–Hanoi 1946."
33. Quoted in Dunn, *First Vietnam War,* p. 196.
34. Memo No. 1 of the Subcommittee of the High Commission for the Southern Zone, "Principles à observer à l'occasion de la reprise du travail," 23 September 1945, dossier 1, 10H161, SHAT, Vincennes, Paris.
35. Memo for Adm. Mountbatten, subject: FIC Political and Internal Situation, 3 October 1945, WO203/5562, Public Record Office, London.
36. Wickes, "Saigon 1945–Hanoi 1946."
37. Dunn, *First Vietnam War,* p. 200.
38. Ibid., p. 198.

39. Memo for the Secretary of State by William J. Donovan, 28 September 1945, National Archives Record Group 226, microfilm reel M1642.
40. Force 136 detachment, Saigon, to Headquarters, Force 136, subject: Saigon Control Commission, 19 October 1945, HS1/104, Public Record Office, London.
41. "The White Book of Vietminh Atrocities," #2868, Saigon, 6 June 1946, 10H602, SHAT, Vincennes, Paris.
42. Memo for the Secretary of State by William J. Donovan, 27 September 1945, National Archives Record Group 226, microfilm reel M1642.
43. Emery Plaice, *New York Daily Herald,* September 29, 1945.
44. Brigadier M. Hayaud Din, "With the 20th Indian Division in French Indochina," *Journal of the Royal United Service Institute of India* 78, July 1948, p. 253.
45. SIGEX Kandy, message, 9 November 1945, National Archives Record Group 226, entry 53, box 3.
46. SIGEX, Singapore to X-2 R&A, 27 December 1945, National Archives Record Group 226, entry 53, box 3.
47. Activités Japonaises, 22 March 1946, dossier "March 1946," 10H606, SHAT, Vincennes, Paris. Rapport sur la collusion nippo-vietnamienne, 9 August 1946, dossier 1E11224, 10H160, SHAT, Vincennes, Paris. "1,000 Deserters in Southern Indochina," Hayashi, et al., *Nihon Shüsenhi,* p. 118. Christopher E. Goscha, "Belated Allies: The Contributions of Japanese Deserters to the Viet Minh (1945–1950)," in Marilyn Young and Robert Buzzanco, eds., *A Companion to the Vietnam War* (Malden, Mass.: Blackwell, 2002), pp. 37–46. Draft version, courtesy Dr. Goscha.
48. Goscha, "Belated Allies," p. 19.
49. Hayashi et al., *Nihon Shüsenshi,* p. 120.
50. Le Problème Japonais en Indochine, 30 December 1946, 10H600, SHAT, Vincennes, Paris.
51. Nguyen Thi Tuyet Mai, *The Rubber Tree,* pp. 78, 80.
52. Rapport sur l'activité du Corps Expeditionnaire Français en Indochine, juin 1946, boite no. 18, dossier 1, travail Dronne, pp. 14–15, Fonds historique Leclerc, Memorial du Maréchal Leclerc de Hautclocque, Paris.
53. Rapport sur l'alliance nippo-vietnamienne, 8 September 1946, dossier "August 1946," 10H600, SHAT, Vincennes, Paris.
54. "Military Order of the Democratic Republic of Vietnam" by Hoang Van Thai, 24 November 1945, dossier 6, 10H602, SHAT, Vincennes, Paris.
55. Conference with a Vietnamese military personality, Hanoi, 16 December 1945, dossier 8, 10H602, SHAT, Vincennes, Paris.
56. Patti, *Why Vietnam?* p. 320.
57. Translation of a letter from Dr. Pham Ngoc Thach, 16 October 1945, National Archives Record Group 226, microfilm M1642, reel 73.
58. A Vietnamese refugee supplied this information to the U.S. embassy in Paris in 1980. See Spector, *Advice and Support,* p. 67.

59. Spector, *Advice and Support,* pp. 62–63.
60. Ibid. Worthing, *Occupation and Revolution,* p. 83.
61. Worthing, *Occupation and Revolution,* pp. 86–87.
62. Duiker, *Ho Chi Minh,* p. 338.
63. Guillemot, "Viêt Nam 1945–1946: l'élimination de l'opposition nationaliste et anticolonialiste dans le Nord."
64. Bulletin d'analyse des écutes effectuées du 20 juin au 20 juillet 1946. . . ., dossier "juillet 1946," 10H600, SHAT, Vincennes, Paris.
65. Patti, *Why Vietnam?,* pp. 368–69.
66. "Rapport sur l'activité du Corps Expeditionnaire."
67. Wickes, "Saigon 1945–Hanoi 1946."
68. Commandant Gilbert Bodinier, *Le retour de la France en Indochine, 1945–1946: textes et documents* (Vincennes: Service Historique de l'Armée de Terre, 1987), p. 13.
69. India-Burma Intelligence Sitrep, 18 December 1945, Record Group 9, box 42, Douglas MacArthur Memorial Archives, Norfolk, Va.
70. Ibid.
71. Wickes, "Saigon 1945–Hanoi 1946."
72. "Utilisation de la Légion étrangère" [no date], dossier 2, fiche no. 9, 10H602, SHAT, Vincennes, Paris.
73. Harold R. Isaacs, *No Peace for Asia* (New York: Macmillan, 1947), p. 136.
74. SIGEX, Kandy to War Department Special Services Unit, 10 November 1945, National Archives Record Group 226, entry 53, box 3.
75. Singapore to War Department Strategic Services Unit, 20 December 1945, National Archives Record Group 226, entry 53, box 3.
76. Dossier "Atrocities," 10H602, SHAT, Vincennes, Paris.
77. "Rapport sur l'activité du Corps Expeditionnaire," p. 14.

CHAPTER 7 "Just Say You Don't Know Anything About It"

1. Bruce Cumings, *The Origins of the Korean War: Liberation and the Emergence of Separate Regimes* (Princeton, N.J.: Princeton University Press, 1981), pp. 114–15. William Stueck, *The Korean War: An International History* (Princeton, N.J.: Princeton University Press, 1995), pp. 16–17.
2. Kathryn Weathersby, "Soviet Aims in Korea and the Origins of the Korean War, 1945–1950: New Evidence from Russian Archives," Working Paper No. 8, November 1993, Cold War International History Project, Woodrow Wilson International Center for Scholars, Washington, D.C., pp. 9–12.
3. Ibid., p. 11.
4. Cumings, *Origins of the Korean War,* pp. 11–12.
5. Isaacs, *No Peace for Asia,* p. 84.
6. Alexis Dudden, "U.S. Congressional Resolution Calls on Japan to Accept Responsibility for Wartime Comfort Women," April 25, 2006, www.zmag.org/content/showarticle.cfm?ItemID=10155.

7. Morita Yoshia, *Chosen Shusen no Kiroku [The End of the War in Korea]* (Tokyo: Genan-do Shoten, 1964), pp. 41–43.
8. Richard Kim, *Lost Names: Scenes from a Korean Boyhood* (New York: Praeger, 1970), pp. 164–65.
9. Hildi Kang, *Under the Black Umbrella: Voices from Colonial Korea* (Ithaca, N.Y.: Cornell University Press, 2001).
10. "History of U.S. Armed Forces in Korea," vol. 1, ch. 3, p. 2, ms. in U.S. Army Center of Military History, Washington, D.C.
11. Cumings, *Origins of the Korean War,* p. 474.
12. Young Sik Kim, *Eyewitness: A North Korean Remembers* (Korea Web Weekly E-books, www.Kimsoft.com).
13. "Akao Oboe Remembers," *Sankei Shimbum,* October 17, 1997.
14. Harold Isaacs, "Do We Run Korea Badly? Well, Look How Reds Do," *Newsweek,* September 24, 1945, pp. 59–60.
15. "Russian Occupation of Northern Korea," folder "Korean Reports, September 1945–February-March 1946," USAFPAC, Record Group 4, box 2, Douglas MacArthur Memorial Archives, Norfolk, Va.
16. Andrei Lankov, *From Stalin to Kim Il Sung: The Formation of North Korea 1945–1960* (New Brunswick, N.J.: Rutgers University Press, 2002), p. 6.
17. "Eye-witness reports from north of the 38th parallel in Korea by two former high level managers in the Railway Department, District of Hamhung until March 6, 1946," Millard Preston Goodfellow Papers, box 2, Hoover Institution Archives, Stanford, Calif.
18. Allan R. Millett, *The War for Korea, 1945–1950: A House Burning* (Lawrence, Kans.: University Press of Kansas, 2005), p. 49.
19. "Russian Occupation of Northern Korea."
20. "Eye-witness reports from north of the 38th parallel."
21. Lankov, *Stalin to Kim Il Sung,* pp. 2–3.
22. Ibid., p. 15.
23. Charles K. Armstrong, *The North Korean Revolution, 1945–1950* (Ithaca, N.Y.: Cornell University Press, 2003), pp. 27–32.
24. Lankov, *Stalin to Kim Il Sung,* pp. 53–54.
25. Ibid., p. 54. Armstrong, *North Korean Revolution,* p. 27.
26. Clyde Sargent to his parents, 6 July 1947, Clyde Sargent Papers, Hoover Institution Archives, Stanford, Calif.
27. "History of U.S. Armed Forces in Korea," pt. 1, ch. 8, p. 15.
28. Ibid., pp. 15–16, 22–24.
29. Carl J. Frederick, *American Experience in Military Government* (New York: W. Sloan, 1948), p. 356. C. Leonard Hoag, "American Military Government in Korea: War Policy and the First Year of Occupation," p. 15 (draft U.S. Army manuscript, 1970, U.S. Army Center of Military History Library, Washington, D.C.).
30. "History of U.S. Armed Forces in Korea," pt. 1, ch. 1, p. 56.
31. Donald MacDonald interview by Charles Stuart Kennedy, 25 January 1990,

"Frontline Diplomacy" oral history collection, Center for the Study of Diplomacy, Washington, D.C.

32. "History of U.S. Armed Forces in Korea," pt. 1, ch. 1, pp. 58–61.
33. Kenneth C. Strother, "Experiences of a XXIV Corps Staff Officer in the Occupation of Korea, September–November 1945," unpublished memoir, Kenneth C. Strother Papers, box 20, World War II Miscellaneous Papers, U.S. Army Military History Institute, Carlisle, Pa.
34. "History of U.S. Armed Forces in Korea," pt. 1, ch. 4, p. 5.
35. Hoag, "American Military Government in Korea," p. 110.
36. John Bliss, Jr., "My Most Memorable Day: Korea, September 8, 1945," *The Monadnock Ledger,* May 24, 2001, p. 10.
37. Cumings, *Origins of the Korean War,* p. 138.
38. Bliss, "My Most Memorable Day."
39. William C. Sherman interview by Thomas Stern, 27 October 1993, "Frontline Diplomacy" oral history collection, Center for the Study of Diplomacy, Washington, D.C.
40. Morita, *Chosen Shusen no Kiroku,* ch. 4.
41. Cumings, *Origins of the Korean War,* p. 136.
42. Ibid., p. 139. James A. Matray, "Hodge Podge: American Occupation Policy in Korea, 1945–1948," *Korean Studies* 19 (1995), p. 23.
43. "Draft Statement Prepared for President Truman," 12 September 1945, 740.00119-PW/9-1845, National Archives Record Group 59.
44. Richard J.H. Johnston, "Radicals in Korea Hit General A. V. Arnold," *New York Times,* October 30, 1945, p. 2.
45. Letter, Hodge to C. Leonard Hoag, 28 May 1947. Cited in Hoag, "American Military Government in Korea," p. 187. Hodge's version is supported by Langdon, who reported to Washington a few months after the incident that a check of the press conference transcripts appeared to show the newspaper reports to be incorrect. (Langdon to Secretary of State, 26 November 1945, *FRUS, 1945,* vol. 6, p. 1135.)

CHAPTER 8 **"Hopeless as a Society"**

1. Richard E. Lauterbach, "Hodge's Korea," *Virginia Quarterly Review* 23, June 1947, p. 359.
2. Benninghoff to the Secretary of State, 15 September 1945, *FRUS, 1945,* vol. 6, pp. 1049–50.
3. Allen, *End of the War in Asia,* p. 169; Cumings, *Origins of the Korean War,* p. 140.
4. Cumings, *Origins of the Korean War,* p. 140.
5. Donald MacDonald interview.
6. "History of U.S. Armed Forces in Korea," vol. 1, ch. 4, pp. 35–36.
7. John Gunther, *The Riddle of MacArthur: Japan, Korea and the Far East* (New York: Harper, 1950), p. 182.

8. "History of U.S. Armed Forces in Korea," vol. 1, pt. 1, pp. 187–88.
9. Langdon to Secretary of State, 26 November 1945, *FRUS, 1945,* vol. 6, p. 1135.
10. McCloy to the Undersecretary of State, 13 November 1945, *FRUS, 1945,* vol. 6, p. 1123.
11. NIS Survey of Political Parties, tab C JCS 1483, ABC 014 Japan, 13 April 1944, National Archives Record Group 165, entry 421, box 32.
12. Millett, *War for Korea,* p. 61.
13. Johnston, "Radicals in Korea Hit General A. V. Arnold."
14. "History of U.S. Army Military Government in Korea," vol. 1, pt. 1, p. 194, ms. in U.S. Army Center of Military History, Washington, D.C.
15. Ibid., p. 195.
16. Matray, "Hodge Podge," p. 23.
17. Cumings, *Origins of the Korean War,* pp. 192–93. Millett, *War for Korea,* p. 62.
18. "History of U.S. Army Military Government in Korea," vol. 1, p. 224.
19. "History of U.S. Armed Forces in Korea," pt. 1, ch. 6, p. 15.
20. For a detailed breakdown of American activities in the provinces based on American military records, see Cumings, *Origins of the Korean War,* ch. 9.
21. Donald MacDonald interview.
22. Cumings, *Origins of the Korean War,* pp. 49–51, 61.
23. Donald MacDonald interview.
24. Ibid.
25. Richard A. Ericson interview by Charles Stuart Kennedy, 27 March 1995, "Frontline Diplomacy" oral history collection, Center for the Study of Diplomacy, Washington, D.C.
26. Ibid. Lauterbach, "Hodge's Korea," p. 363.
27. Walter Simmons, "GI's Haven't a Kind Word to Say for Korea," *Chicago Tribune,* December 13, 1945.
28. MacArthur to JCS [enclosing letter from Hodge], 2 February 1946, *FRUS, 1946: The Far East,* vol. 8, p. 629.
29. David L. Olmstead, "Two Korean Villages: Cultural Contact at the 38th Parallel," in *Human Organization,* Fall 1951, p. 36.
30. Colonel Charles H. Donnelly, unpublished autobiography, p. 842, Charles H. Donnelly Papers, U.S. Army Military History Institute, Carlisle, Pa.
31. Ibid., p. 865.
32. Commanding General, 6th Infantry Division, to Hodge, 15 December 1945. Records of General Headquarters, Far East Command, entry A1, National Archives Record Group 554, box 1.
33. Donnelly unpublished autobiography, p. 866.
34. Headquarters, USAFIK, AG circular 14.13, 23 February 1946. AG circular 721, 4 May 1946. Both in National Archives Record Group 554, entry A1, box 50.

35. Headquarters, USAFIK circular 9, 25 January 1946, National Archives Record Group 554, entry A1, box 50.
36. Donnelly unpublished autobiography, p. 868.
37. Donald MacDonald interview. Memo to Deputy Chief of Staff, subject: Visit to Korea, 4 April 1947, tab R, copy in Charles H. Donnelly Papers, U.S. Army Military History Institute, Carlisle, Pa.
38. Ibid.
39. Donnelly unpublished autobiography, p. 867.
40. Ibid., p. 866.
41. Hodge to principal commanders, subject: Courtesy Drive, 6 November 1946. Headquarters XXIV Corps, subject: Message from CGUSAFIK, 17 January 1947. Both in National Archives Record Group 554, entry A1, box 1.
42. Lauterbach, "Hodge's Korea," p. 365.
43. Memo by the Director of the Office of Far Eastern Affairs to Colonel Russell L. Vittrup, 7 November 1945, *FRUS, 1945,* vol. 6, pp. 1113–14.
44. Langdon to Secretary of State, 20 November 1945, file 740.00119/11-1445. National Archives Record Group 59.
45. MacArthur to Joint Chiefs of Staff, enclosing report by General Hodge, 16 December 1945, *FRUS, 1945,* vol. 6, pp. 1144–47.

CHAPTER 9 "On No Account Be Drawn into Internal Troubles"

1. Dennis, *Troubled Days of Peace,* p. 81.
2. Gouda and Zaalberg, *American Visions,* p. 81 and passim.
3. Memo of Conversation by the Chief of the Division of Southeast Asian Affairs, 6 December 1945, *FRUS, 1945,* vol. 6, p. 1178.
4. Theodore Friend, *The Blue-Eyed Enemy: Japan Against the West in Java and Luzon, 1942–1945* (Princeton, N.J.: Princeton University Press, 1988), p. 215.
5. Director of Strategic Services, Memo for the President, 26 September 1945, Harry S. Truman Papers, Harry S. Truman Presidential Library, Independence, Mo.
6. Memo by the Chief of the Division of Southeast Asian Affairs, December 6, 1945.
7. See, for example, Wing Commander T. S. Tull, Report on Operation Salex-Mastiff, 10 September–15 December 1945, Tull Papers, Liddell-Hart Archives, King's College, London.
8. This conversation was reported in Christison's memoirs, written some years after the event. Mountbatten's biographer Philip Ziegler finds Christison's story unconvincing, but Peter Dennis finds that "Christison's account rings true." (See Dennis, *Troubled Days of Peace,* p. 87.)
9. Dennis, *Troubled Days of Peace,* pp. 78–80.
10. Ibid., p. 89.
11. "The Life and Times of General Sir Philip Christison, Bt," p. 176, unpub-

lished manuscript, General Sir Philip Christison Papers, Imperial War Museum, London.

12. Message, ACSEA to Christison, 30 September 1945, WO172/1785, Public Record Office, London.
13. M. C. Ricklefs, *A History of Modern Indonesia,* 2nd ed. (Stanford, Calif.: Stanford University Press, 1993), pp. 203–8.
14. Friend, *Blue-Eyed Enemy,* pp. 170–71.
15. Ricklefs, *History of Modern Indonesia,* p. 203.
16. Allen, *End of the War in Asia,* pp. 77–78.
17. Friend, *Blue-Eyed Enemy,* p. 117.
18. Robert Cribb, *Gangsters and Revolutionaries: The Jakarta People's Militia and the Indonesian Revolution* (Honolulu: University of Hawaii Press, 1991), pp. 49–50.
19. Allen, *End of the War in Asia,* p. 80.
20. U.S. Military Attaché, New Delhi, Summary of the Situation in Java, 11 October 1945, Appendix A, Army Intelligence Document File, National Archives Record Group 319.
21. David Wehl, *The Birth of Indonesia* (London: Allen and Unwin, 1948), p. 7.
22. "Allied Occupation of the Netherlands Indies," draft copy, General Sir Robert Mansergh Papers, folder 6, Imperial War Museum, London.
23. Friend, *Blue-Eyed Enemy,* p. 221.
24. Report by Major General L.H.O. Pugh, [no date] 1945, Pugh Papers, Imperial War Museum, London.
25. Cribb, *Gangsters and Revolutionaries,* pp. 51–52, 59–61.
26. Quoted in Gouda and Zaalberg, *American Visions,* p. 119. The source for this story is Sukarno's own account, which some scholars consider suspect. William H. Frederick, letter to the author, April 25, 2006.
27. Wehl, *Birth of Indonesia,* pp. 19–20.
28. Memo to Assistant Chief of Staff, G-2, War Department, subject: Observations in Java, 18 October to 27 October 1945, by Lt. Col. J. R. Galloway, National Archives Record Group 319.
29. Cribb, *Gangsters and Revolutionaries,* p. 53.
30. Isaacs, *No Peace for Asia,* p. 130.
31. Christison, "Life and Times," p. 177.
32. Ibid., p. 183.
33. U.S. Military Observer Singapore to Military Intelligence Division, WDGS, Summary of the Situation in Java, Appendix A, enclosing report by van der Post, 11 October 1945, Army Intelligence Document File, National Archives Record Group 319.
34. Gouda and Zaalberg, *American Visions,* p. 125.
35. Dennis, *Troubled Days of Peace,* p. 136.
36. Tull, Report on Operation Salex-Mastiff.
37. Han Bing Siong, "The Secret of Major Kido: The Battle of Semarang 15–19 October 1945," *Bijdragen tot deTaal-Land-en Volkenkunden* 152, 1996, pp. 399–401.

38. Ibid., p. 400.
39. Ibid., p. 404.
40. Allen, *End of the War in Asia,* pp. 94–95.
41. Tull, Report on Operation Salex-Mastiff, pp. 70–71.
42. Ibid.

CHAPTER 10: **"Built upon Unknown Graves"**

1. The most careful account of this incident, which became an icon of the struggle for independence, is in William H. Frederick, *Visions and Heat: The Making of the Indonesian Revolution* (Athens, Ohio: Ohio University Press, 1989), pp. 199–201.
2. Ibid., pp. 211–15, 267. Benedict R. Anderson, *Java in a Time of Revolution: Occupation and Resistance, 1944–1946* (Ithaca, N.Y.: Cornell University Press, 1972), pp. 154–55.
3. Allen, *End of the War in Asia,* pp. 89–92.
4. Idrus, "Surabaja," trans. S. U. Nababan and Benedict Anderson, in *Indonesia* 5, April 1968, p. 2.
5. William H. Frederick, *Visions and Heat,* p. 239.
6. Ibid.
7. Ibid., pp. 240–42.
8. Report by Major General L.H.O. Pugh, p. 10.
9. Idrus, "Surabaja," p. 1.
10. William H. Frederick, *Visions and Heat,* pp. 256–57.
11. Report by Major General L.H.O. Pugh, p. 8.
12. Anderson, *Java in a Time of Revolution,* p. 429.
13. William H. Frederick, *Visions and Heat,* p. 257. Dennis, *Troubled Days of Peace,* p. 123.
14. Report by Major General L.H.O. Pugh, p. 16.
15. Christison, "Life and Times," p. 182.
16. Ibid. William H. Frederick, *Visions and Heat,* pp. 259–60. Frederick says that the attack by the mob surprised the TKR, who ended up having to try to protect the civilians, some of whom they hid in nearby stores and homes. The accounts by Christison and the historian of the 23rd Indian Division do not differentiate between the TKR and the mob. The survival of the refugees is attributed entirely to the efforts of the Indians of the 49th Brigade.
17. Christison, "Life and Times," p. 184. A.J.F. Doulton, *The Fighting Cock: Being the History of the 23rd Indian Division* (Aldershot, U.K.: Gale and Polden, 1951), pp. 254–55.
18. William H. Frederick, *Visions and Heat,* p. 262.
19. Christison, "Life and Times," p. 184.
20. William H. Frederick, *Visions and Heat,* p. 275. British accounts do admit that Dutchmen were sometimes given British uniforms to try to safeguard them from the angry Indonesians. However, there is no mention of any Dutch disguising themselves as Indians or Gurkhas.

21. Christison, "Life and Times," pp. 184–85.
22. This version of the incident is still widely believed in Indonesia, although it is discounted by scholars elsewhere.
23. Wing Commander A. D. Groom, "Report on First Phase of British Occupation of Soerabaja, Appendix A to Report of Operations of 49th Indian Brigade," copy in General Sir Robert Mansergh Papers, box 79, Imperial War Museum, London. Idrus, "Surabaja," p. 3.
24. Idrus, "Surabaja," p. 3.
25. Ibid.
26. Mansergh, personal, to Christison, 9 November 1945, WO172/6965, Public Record Office, London.
27. William H. Frederick, *Visions and Heat,* p. 278.
28. Idrus, "Surabaja," p. 13.
29. Wehl, *The Moon Upside Down* (London: J. Barrie, 1948), p. 138.
30. Ted Bates, "Naval Party 2482, Java 1945–1946," www.britains-smallwars.com. I am grateful to Professor Marc Jason Gilbert for calling this source to my attention.
31. 5th Indian Division, Division Instruction No. 13, 30 November 1945, WO172/6965, Public Record Office, London.
32. Ibid.
33. Friend, *Blue-Eyed Enemy,* p. 228. William H. Frederick, *Visions and Heat,* pp. 278–79, says close to ten thousand.
34. SSU, Kandy to War Department, 10 November 1945, National Archives Record Group 226, entry 53, box 3.
35. Tull, Report on Operation Salex-Mastiff, p. 107.
36. Andrew Roadnight, "Sleeping with the Enemy: Britain, Japanese Troops and the Netherlands East Indies, 1945–1946," *History: The Journal of the Historical Association* 87, April 2002, p. 252.
37. Doulton, *Fighting Cock,* pp. 269–71. Dennis, *Troubled Days of Peace,* pp. 124–25.
38. Message, SSU, Kandy to War Department, 23 November 1945, National Archives Record Group 226, entry 53, box 3.
39. Doulton, *Fighting Cock,* p. 272.
40. Message, SSU, Kandy, 23 November 1945. Roadnight, "Sleeping with the Enemy," p. 255.
41. Message, SSU, Kandy, 23 November 1945.
42. Doulton, *Fighting Cock,* p. 274. Wehl, *Birth of Indonesia,* p. 76.
43. "Allied Occupation of the Netherlands East Indies, September 1945–November 1946 from the Point of View of the Royal Navy," General Sir Robert Mansergh Papers, folder 6, Imperial War Museum, London.
44. Memo of Conversation by the Secretary of State with Lord Halifax, 10 December 1945, *FRUS, 1945,* vol. 6, pp. 1181–82. Wehl, *Birth of Indonesia,* p. 92.
45. Wehl, *Birth of Indonesia,* p. 68.
46. Ibid., p. 69.

47. W. McMahon Ball to Australian Legation, Washington, D.C., No. 1762, 19 November 1945, file 401/1/2/3, Foreign Office Records, National Archives of Australia.
48. Ball to Burton, No. 405, 22 November 1945, *Documents on Australian Foreign Policy,* vol. 8, p. 211.
49. SSU, Kandy to War Department, 10 November 1945, National Archives Record Group 226, entry 53, box 3.
50. SSU, Singapore to War Department, 28 December 1945, National Archives Record Group 226, entry 53, box 3.
51. Marc Jason Gilbert, "Playing the Race Card: Vietnamese Appeals to Non-White Forces of Occupation, 1945–1975," p. 7, unpublished paper. Courtesy of Professor Gilbert.
52. Wehl, *Birth of Indonesia,* p. 95.
53. Private communication to the author by former officer of the West Yorkshire Regiment, July 14, 2005.
54. V. M. Sissons, unaddressed letter, 30 November 1945, V. M. Sissons Papers, Imperial War Museum, London.
55. Dennis, *Troubled Days of Peace,* p. 150.
56. Wehl, *Birth of Indonesia,* p. 94.
57. Department of State, Research and Analysis Branch, Field Memo No. 1199, 31 December 1945, Murphy Collection, National Archives Record Group 263, box 17.
58. Draft Report on Morale of British, Indian and Colonial Troops, ALFSEA, for November, December, January [1945–46], WO203/2268, Public Record Office, London.
59. Dennis, *Troubled Days of Peace,* p. 144.
60. Ibid., p. 156.
61. The Secretary of State to the Ambassador in the United Kingdom, October 13, 1945. *FRUS, 1945,* vol. 6.
62. Anderson, *Java in a Time of Revolution,* pp. 413–14.
63. Ibid., pp. 192–93.
64. Wehl, *Moon Upside Down,* p. 143.
65. Robert Cribb, "The Bersiap Violence in Historical Perspective," p. 5. Christison, "Life and Times," p. 189.

CHAPTER II The Children of Andalas

1. Anthony Reid, *The Blood of the People: Revolution and the End of Traditional Rule in Sumatra* (Kuala Lumpur: Oxford University Press, 1979), p. 9.
2. Ibid., p. 150.
3. Michael Van Langenberg, "National Revolution in North Sumatra: Sumatra, Timur and Tapanuli, 1942–1950," unpublished dissertation, University of Sydney, 1979, p. 114.
4. Ibid., pp. 301–2.

5. Hendrik L. Leffelaar, *Through a Harsh Dawn: A Boy Grows Up in a Japanese Prison Camp* (Barre, Mass.: Barre Publishing, 1963), pp. 182, 190.
6. F. Woodburn Kirby, et al., *The War Against Japan,* vol. 5: *The Surrender of Japan* (London: HMSO, 1969), p. 357.
7. Reid, *Blood of the People,* p. 159.
8. SSU to War Department, Sumatra: General Situation, 20 October 1945, National Archives Record Group 226, entry 409, box 400.
9. *The Indonesian National Revolution: Six Firsthand Accounts,* p. 22.
10. Van Langenberg, "National Revolution in North Sumatra," p. 320.
11. Reid, *Blood of the People,* pp. 166–67.
12. SIGEX, Kandy to X-2, Washington, 1 November 1945, National Archives Record Group 226, entry 53, box 3.
13. G-2 Sitrep, 27 January 1946, Radiograms, India File, Record Group 9, Douglas MacArthur Memorial Archives, Norfolk, Va.
14. SIGEX, Kandy to Washington, 6 November 1945, National Archives Record Group 226, entry 53, box 3.
15. Kenichi Goto, *Tensions of Empire: Japan and Southeast Asia in the Colonial and Postcolonial World* (Athens, Ohio: Ohio University Press, 2003), pp. 195–96.
16. Ibid., p. 195.
17. Report by Repatriation Office, 6 June 1946, microfilm reel K006, frame 1471, Japanese Foreign Ministry Archives, Tokyo.
18. Van Langenberg, "National Revolution in North Sumatra," pp. 325–27.
19. Department of State, Research and Analysis Branch, Field Memo No. 1199.
20. Singapore to SSU, 22 January 1946, IN 31625, National Archives Record Group 226, entry 53, box 7. War Office to SACSEA, 131150Z February 1946, Appendix A, WO203/4940, Public Office Record, London. Roadnight, "Sleeping with the Enemy," pp. 256–57.
21. Bisheshwar Prasad, ed., *Official History of the Indian Armed Forces in the Second World War, 1939–1945: Postwar Occupation Forces, Japan and Southeast Asia* (Delhi: Orient Longmans, 1958), p. 244.
22. Department of State, Research and Analysis Branch, Field Memo No. 1199.
23. Lt. Gen. F.A.M. Browning to Maj. Gen. W.R.C. Penney, 25 October 1945, Major General W.R.C. Penney Papers, Liddell-Hart Archives, King's College, London.
24. Dennis, *Troubled Days of Peace,* p. 139. Ball to Australian Legation, Washington, No. 1745, 16 November 1945, file 401/1/2/3, Foreign Office Records, National Archives of Australia.
25. Australian Legation, Washington, D.C., to Department of External Affairs, No. 1763, 19 November 1945, file 401/1/2/3, Foreign Office Records, National Archives of Australia.
26. Dennis, *Troubled Days of Peace,* pp. 146–47.
27. Ibid., p. 162.
28. Christison, "Life and Times," p. 194.
29. Anderson, *Java in a Time of Revolution,* p. 297.

30. Singapore to SSU Washington, 11 January 1946, National Archives Record Group 226, entry 53, box 7.
31. Anderson, *Java in a Time of Revolution,* p. 390.
32. Dennis, *Troubled Days of Peace,* p. 198.
33. Prasad, *Official History of the Indian Armed Forces,* pp. 254–55.
34. Reid, *Blood of the People,* p. 175.
35. History of the 26th Indian Division in Sumatra, 1945–1946, ALFSEA 328/2, WO203/6160, p. 23, Public Record Office, London.
36. Ibid., p. 21.
37. Ibid.
38. Ushiyama Mitsuo, "Record of Ending the War in the Northern Part of Sumatra," in Anthony Reid and Oki Akita, eds., *The Japanese Experience in Indonesia: Selected Memoirs of 1942–1945* (Athens, Ohio: Ohio University Monographs in International Studies, Southeast Asia Series No. 72, 1986), pp. 376–77.
39. Ibid., p. 20. Reid, *Blood of the People,* pp. 203–5.
40. Prasad, *Official History of the Indian Armed Forces,* pp. 256–57.
41. History of the 26th Indian Division, p. 18.
42. Reid, *Blood of the People,* pp. 230–38.
43. Ibid., pp. 240–44.
44. Papers of William John Gambier, Corporal, Wallet 2, PRO 4027, Australian War Memorial, Canberra.
45. Gavin Long, *The Final Campaigns* (Canberra, Australia: Australian War Memorial, 1963), pp. 568–69.
46. W. B. Russell, *The Second Fourteenth Battalion: A History of an Australian Infantry Battalion in the Second World War* (Sydney: Angus and Robertson, 1954), p. 312.
47. Long, *Final Campaigns,* p. 567.
48. Makassar Force Instruction No. 4, 6 November 1945, AWM-54 639/8/9, Australian War Memorial, Canberra.
49. 2/25 Battalion War Diary, October Summary, 8/3/25, Australian War Memorial, Canberra.
50. Anthony Reid, "The Australian Discovery of Indonesia, 1945," *Journal of the Australian War Memorial* 17, 1990, p. 34.
51. Ibid., p. 33.
52. Broadcasts by Frederick Simpson, 15 July and 20 August 1945, AWM-54 773/4/11, Australian War Memorial, Canberra.
53. Makassar Force Instruction No. 4.
54. Reid, "Australian Discovery of Indonesia," p. 37.
55. Long, *Final Campaigns,* p. 575.
56. 2/25 Battalion War Diary, November Battalion Commander's Summary, Australian War Memorial, Canberra.
57. Ibid.
58. 2/27 Battalion War Diary, January–March 1946, Monthly Summary, Australian War Memorial, Canberra.

59. Russell, *Second Fourteenth Battalion,* p. 313.
60. W. J. Sodin, "Tasmania to Tarakan," p. 93, unpublished memoir, MSS 1432, Australian War Memorial, Canberra.
61. Reid, "Australian Discovery of Indonesia," p. 34.
62. "What Is Behind Wharf Hold Up?" WWF handbill, Waterside Workers' Federation Records, Noel Butlin Archives Centre, Australian National University.
63. Rupert Lockwood, *The Black Armada* (Sydney, Australia: Australasian Book Society, 1975), p. 237.
64. Script of *Indonesia Calling,* pp. 3–6. Copy in Waterside Workers' Federation Records, Noel Butlin Archives Centre, Australian National University.
65. Reid, "Australian Discovery of Indonesia," p. 35.
66. Ibid., pp. 35, 38.
67. G. A. Kruger to James Healy, General Secretary, WWF, [no date], N114/190, Waterside Workers' Federation Records, Noel Butlin Archives Centre, Australian National University.
68. Lockwood, *Black Armada,* p. 242.
69. Department of External Affairs, Papers on Indonesia, file 401/1/2/3, Foreign Office Records, National Archives of Australia.
70. HQ 26 Inf Brigade to HQ, Queensland L of C Area, subject: Indonesian Unrest—Tarakan, 15 December 1945, AWM-54 617/7/26. AMF Morotai to HQ AMF, subject: Free Indonesia Movement, 1 November 1945, AWM-54 225/1/10. Both in Australian War Memorial, Canberra.

CHAPTER 12 Wars Postponed

1. John F. Melby, *The Mandate of Heaven: Record of a Civil War* (Toronto: University of Toronto Press, 1968), p. 53.
2. Pogue, *George C. Marshall,* p. 76, citing Wedemeyer's notes.
3. Ramon H. Myers, "Frustration, Fortitude and Friendship: Chiang Kai-shek's Reactions to the Marshall Mission," in Bland, *Marshall's Mediation Mission,* pp. 152–53.
4. Ibid., p. 58. Bulletin de renseignements, Conversations with Trevor Wilson, Carton de Wiarte, 27 December 1945, dossier 4, 10H161, SHAT, Vincennes, Paris.
5. "Dr. Koo's Comments on F. C. Jones 'The Far East' in *Survey of International Affairs,* 1947–48," pp. 4946–47, V. K. Wellington Koo loose material, V. K. Wellington Koo oral history, Chinese Oral History Collection, Columbia University, New York.
6. He Di, "Mao Zedong and the Marshall Mission," in Bland, *Marshall's Mediation Mission.*
7. Memo for the President by James Shepley, attaché to General Marshall, 28 February 1946, PSF subject files, box 110, Harry S. Truman Presidential Library, Independence, Mo.

8. Melby, *Mandate of Heaven,* p. 58.
9. Shepley memo.
10. Zhang Baijia, "Zhou Enlai and the Marshall Mission," in Bland, *Marshall's Mediation Mission,* p. 214.
11. Pogue, *George C. Marshall,* p. 76.
12. Henry Byroade oral history interview by Nial Johnson, 19 September 1988, p. 33, Harry S. Truman Presidential Library, Independence, Mo.
13. Ibid., p. 34.
14. Marc S. Gallicchio, "About Face: General Marshall's Plans for the Amalgamation of the Communist and Nationalist Armies in China," in Bland, *Marshall's Mediation Mission,* pp. 394–95.
15. Ibid. Pogue, *George C. Marshall,* p. 89.
16. He Di, "Mao Zedong and the Marshall Mission," p. 189.
17. *FRUS, 1946,* vol. 6, p. 339.
18. Pogue, *George C. Marshall,* p. 95.
19. Robert Edwin Herzstein, "Henry Luce, George Marshall and China: A Parting of the Ways," in Bland, *Marshall's Mediation Mission,* p. 128.
20. Truman to Representative Hugh de Lacy, 15 February 1946, PSF subject files, box 150, Harry S. Truman Presidential Library, Independence, Mo.
21. John F. Melby oral history interview, p. 128.
22. Pogue, *George C. Marshall,* p. 95.
23. John Robinson Beal, *Marshall in China* (New York: Doubleday, 1970), p. 88.
24. Melby, *Mandate of Heaven,* pp. 80, 83, 88–90, 94, 99.
25. Wedemeyer to Marshall, 7 January 1946, *FRUS, 1946,* vol. 9, p. 40.
26. Alvin C. Gillem, Jr., oral history interview by Dr. Eugene Miller, 1972, pp. 49–50, Alvan C. Gillem, Jr., Papers, U.S. Army Military History Institute, Carlisle, Pa.
27. Ibid.
28. Pogue, *George C. Marshall,* p. 102.
29. Wedemeyer to General Dwight D. Eisenhower, 11 March 1946, Albert C. Wedemeyer Papers, box 82, Hoover Institution Archives, Stanford, Calif.
30. He Di, "Mao Zedong and the Marshall Mission," p. 189.
31. Gillem oral history interview, pp. 40–41.
32. Underwood oral history interview, box 1, p. 19.
33. Melby, *Mandate of Heaven,* p. 101.
34. Ray Huang, "Some Observations on Manchuria in the Balance, Early 1946," *Pacific Historical Review* 27, Spring 1958, pp. 161–62.
35. Tanner, "Guerrilla, Mobile, and Base Warfare," p. 1206.
36. Odd Arne Westad, *Decisive Encounters: The Chinese Civil War, 1946–1950* (Stanford, Calif.: Stanford University Press, 2003), p. 35 and passim.
37. Underwood oral history interview, box 1, p. 16.
38. Westad, *Decisive Encounters,* p. 35.
39. Li Huang oral history, p. 771.

40. Tanner, "Guerrilla, Mobile, and Base Warfare," pp. 1208–11. Westad, *Decisive Encounters,* pp. 35–37.
41. SIGEX, Kandy to SI, 17 November 1945, National Archives Record Group 226, entry 53, box 3.
42. Guillemot, "Viêt Nam 1945–1946: l'élimination de l'opposition nationaliste et anticolonialiste dans le Nord," pp. 26–31. N. Khac Huyen, *Vision Accomplished? The Enigma of Ho Chi Minh* (New York: Macmillan, 1971), p. 104.
43. Singapore to War Department, SSU, 30 November 1945, National Archives Record Group 226, box 3, entry 53.
44. Worthing, *Occupation and Revolution,* pp. 185–87.
45. Ibid., p. 188; Spector, *Advice and Support,* p. 70.
46. King C. Chen, *Vietnam and China, 1938–1954* (Princeton, N.J.: Princeton University Press, 1969), p. 136.
47. Spector, *Advice and Support,* p. 70. Worthing, *Occupation and Revolution,* p. 190.
48. Gallagher to CGUSFCT, 25 November 1945, FIC Messages, China Theater, National Archives Record Group 493.
49. Memo for Record, Conference, Saturday, 1 December 1945, Philip E. Gallagher Papers, U.S. Army Military History Institute, Carlisle, Pa.
50. Memo for Record, Conference, Monday, 3 December 1945, Philip E. Gallagher Papers, U.S. Army Military History Institute, Carlisle, Pa.
51. Spector, *Advice and Support,* p. 71.
52. Bulletin de renseignements No. 2660, 7 décembre 1945, section de liaison français en Extrême-Orient, dossier 1, Fonds historique, Leclerc, Memorial du Maréchal Leclerc de Hauteclocque, Paris.
53. Quoted in Huyen, *Vision Accomplished?,* p. 106.
54. Ibid., pp. 108–9. For a similar story, see Elliott, *Sacred Willow,* p. 133.
55. Duiker, *Ho Chi Minh,* pp. 352–53.
56. Guillemot, "Viêt Nam 1945–1946: l'élimination de l'opposition nationaliste et anticolonialiste dans le Nord," pp. 16–19.
57. Ibid., p. 31.
58. Jean Sainteny, *Ho Chi Minh and His Vietnam: A Personal Memoir* (Chicago: Cowles, 1972), p. 57.
59. Ibid., p. 54.
60. Note de renseignements sur le forces annamites au Tonkin, 21 décembre 1945, état-major 2ème bureau, no. 800/2, boite no. 19, dossier 1, chemise 4, Fonds historique, Leclerc, Memorial du Maréchal Leclerc de Hautclocque, Paris.
61. Telegramme de Sainteny, Hanoi, 27 février 1946, in Bodinier, *Le retour de la France,* p. 216.
62. Sainteny, *Ho Chi Minh,* p. 58.
63. Wickes, "Saigon 1945–Hanoi 1946."
64. Duiker, *Ho Chi Minh,* p. 359.
65. Ibid., p. 361.

66. Worthing, *Occupation and Revolution,* pp. 253–55.
67. Ibid., pp. 268–69.
68. SSU Singapore to Director Ps-X2, 18 December 1945, National Archives Record Group 226. SSU Saigon to War Department, SSU, Estimate of Situation, 17 June 1946, National Archives Record Group 226.
69. A detailed account of these negotiations is in Worthing, *Occupation and Revolution,* pp. 276–92.
70. Sainteny, *Ho Chi Minh,* p. 62.
71. Texte de l'accord conclu à Hanoi, le 6 mars 1946, in Bodinier, *Le retour de la France,* pp. 221–22.
72. Worthing, *Occupation and Revolution,* p. 294.
73. Ibid., pp. 296–97.
74. Duiker, *Ho Chi Minh,* pp. 363–64.
75. Huyen, *Vision Accomplished?,* pp. 133–34.
76. Sainteny, *Ho Chi Minh,* pp. 65–66.
77. Duiker, *Ho Chi Minh,* p. 365.
78. Wickes, "Saigon 1945–Hanoi 1946,"
79. Philippe Devillers, *Histoire du Viêt-Nam de 1940 à 1952* (Paris: Editions du Seuil, 1952), p. 244.
80. W. Baze to General Leclerc, 11 November 1945, dossier 1, folder 3, box 19, Leclerc Papers.
81. Duiker, *Ho Chi Minh,* p. 367.
82. Conference de Dalat, 21 avril 1946, in Bodinier, *Le retour de la France,* pp. 248–49.
83. Martin Shipway, *The Road to War: France and Vietnam, 1944–1947* (Providence: Berghahn Books, 1996), p. 208.
84. Ibid., p. 212.
85. Ibid.
86. Déclaration conjointe des gouvernements de la République française et de la République democratique du Viêt-Nam, in Bodinier, *Le retour de la France,* pp. 287–91.
87. Christopher E. Goscha, "The Ambiguities of War in the South: Reflections on the Rise and Fall of Nguyen Binh," paper presented at the conference on "Le Viêt-Nam depuis 1945: États, marges et constructions du passé," 11–12 January 2001, pp. 20–21. Courtesy of Professor Goscha.
88. Sainteny, *Ho Chi Minh,* p. 71.
89. The Political Advisor in Korea to the Secretary of State, 23 January 1946, *FRUS, 1946,* vol. 8, *The Far East,* pp. 615–16.
90. For an elaborate—and, to this author, unconvincing—argument that the Communists were not following Moscow's orders, see Cumings, *Origins of the Korean War,* pp. 223–24.
91. Millett, *War for Korea,* p. 70.
92. The Political Advisor in Korea to the Secretary of State, 15 February 1946, *FRUS, 1946,* vol. 7, pp. 633–34.

93. The Acting Political Advisor in Korea to the Secretary of State, 27 December 1945. *FRUS, 1945,* vol. 6, pp. 1151–52.
94. Ibid., p. 636.
95. Ibid.
96. Cumings, *Origins of the Korean War,* p. 417.
97. The Ambassador in the Soviet Union to the Secretary of State, 27 December 1945, *FRUS, 1945,* vol. 6, p. 1150.
98. SWNCC, "Political Policy for Korea," 28 January 1946, *FRUS, 1946,* vol. 8, pp. 624–25.
99. Quoted in Cumings, *Origins of the Korean War,* p. 235.

CHAPTER 13 Wars Renewed

1. Marshall to General Alvin C. Gilles, Jr., 5 April 1946, in Bland, *The Finest Soldier,* p. 519.
2. Pogue, *George C. Marshall,* p. 110.
3. Huang, "Some Observations," p. 163.
4. Lt. Col. Robert B. Rigg, *Red China's Fighting Hordes* (Westport, Conn.: Greenwood Press, 1971), pp. 27–28.
5. Tanner, "Guerrilla, Mobile, and Base Warfare," p. 1208.
6. Huang, "Some Observations," pp. 163–64.
7. Zhang Zenglong, *Xie Bai Xue Hong,* pp. 154–56.
8. Tanner, "Guerrilla, Mobile, and Base Warfare," p. 1210.
9. "Civil War in China, 1945–50" (a translation prepared at field level under the auspices of the Office, Chief of Military History, U.S. Department of the Army), in Donald S. Detwiler and Charles B. Burdick, eds., *War in Asia and the Pacific, 1937–1949,* vol. 15 (New York: Garland Publishing, 1980), p. 24.
10. Beal, *Marshall in China,* p. 22.
11. Marshall to Harry S. Truman, 6 May 1946, in Bland, *Finest Soldier,* pp. 540–42.
12. Zhang Zenglong, *Xie Bai Xue Hong,* p. 157.
13. Liu Shaw Tong, *Out of Red China* (New York: Duell, Sloan and Pearce, 1953), pp. 122–23.
14. Huang, "Some Observations," p. 165.
15. Rigg, *Red China's Fighting Hordes,* p. 191.
16. Huang, "Some Observations," pp. 164–66.
17. Lu Zhengcao, *Hui Yi Lu,* p. 534.
18. Rigg, *Red China's Fighting Hordes,* p. 192.
19. Zhang Zenglong, *Xie Bai Xue Hong,* pp. 184–85.
20. Pogue, *George C. Marshall,* p. 113.
21. Melby, *Mandate of Heaven,* p. 115.
22. Marshall to Harry S. Truman, 22 May 1946, in Bland, *Finest Soldier,* pp. 563–64.
23. Ibid., pp. 576–77.
24. Melby, *Mandate of Heaven,* p. 128.

25. Marshall to Truman, 6 May 1946, in Bland, *Finest Soldier,* p. 544.
26. Marshall to Truman, 18 June 1946, in ibid., p. 599.
27. Andrei M. Ledovsky, "Marshall's Mission in the Context of U.S.S.R.-China-U.S. Relations," in Bland, *Marshall's Mediation Mission,* pp. 439–40.
28. Pogue, *George C. Marshall,* p. 115.
29. Chang and Halliday, *Mao,* pp. 295–97. See also Donald Gillin and Ramon Myers, eds., *Last Chance in Manchuria: The Diary of Chiang Kia-ngau* (Stanford, Calif.: Hoover Institution Press, 1989).
30. Detwiler and Burdick, *War in Asia and the Pacific,* p. 25.
31. J. Leighton Stuart to Department of State, enclosing Summary of Recent Military Developments by Acting Military Attaché, 29 September 1946, 893.00/9-2746, Records of the Office of Far East Affairs microfilm, National Archives Record Group 59. Westad, *Decisive Encounters,* pp. 46–47.
32. Wedemeyer to T. V. Soong, 10 August 1946, T. V. Soong Papers, box 36, folder 33, Hoover Institution Archives, Stanford, Calif. Beal, *Marshall in China,* p. 110.
33. Gillem oral history interview, pp. 38–39.
34. Beal, *Marshall in China,* p. 110.
35. Melby, *Mandate of Heaven,* p. 129.
36. Marshall to Dean G. Acheson, 5 July 1946, in Bland, *Finest Soldier,* pp. 620–21.
37. Albert C. Wedemeyer, *Wedemeyer Reports!* (New York: Holt, 1958), pp. 366–70.
38. Stuart, Summary of Recent Military Developments. Westad, *Decisive Encounters,* pp. 46–47.
39. Byroade to Marshall, 16 January 1946, *FRUS, 1946,* vol. 9, p. 359. "History of the Executive Headquarters, Peiping, China," Andrew C. Tychson Papers, U.S. Army Military History Institute, Carlisle, Pa. Memo for Director of Operations, Advance Section, Executive Headquarters, Changchun, Manchuria, enclosing Staff Study: What Authority Should Field Teams Possess?, Rothwell Brown Papers, U.S. Army Military History Institute, Carlisle, Pa.
40. Peiping Headquarters Group to Field Teams 3, 4, 6, 8, 9, 12, 13, 14, 15, 16, [no date], Rothwell Brown Papers, U.S. Army Military History Institute, Carlisle, Pa.
41. "History of Executive Headquarters, Peiping," p. 18.
42. Ibid., p. 21.
43. Frank and Shaw, *Victory and Occupation,* p. 612.
44. Ibid.
45. News Analysis of Chieh Fang Jih Pao Communist Party Organ, Period 6 August to 10 August 1946, Yenan Liaison Group, copy in Hoover Institution Archives, Stanford, Calif.
46. Frank and Shaw, *Victory and Occupation,* pp. 611–12.
47. Zhang Baijia, "Zhou Enlai and the Marshall Mission," pp. 226–27.
48. Ibid.

49. Marshall to Vice Admiral Charles M. Cooke, 12 August 1946; Marshall to Harry S. Truman, 16 August 1946, in Bland, *Finest Soldier*, pp. 653–55.
50. Westad, *Decisive Encounters*, p. 46.
51. Zhang Baijia, "Zhou Enlai and the Marshall Mission," p. 229.
52. Melby oral history interview, p. 131.
53. Marshall, "Personal Statement," 7 January 1947, in Bland, *Finest Soldier*, pp. 772–73.
54. Wang Zifeng, *Zhanzheng Niandi de Riji*, pp. 178, 182.
55. Quoted in Westad, *Decisive Encounters*, pp. 60–61.
56. The foregoing is based on Xiong Xianghui, *Wo de Qing Bao Yu Wai Jiao Shengya [My Life as a Spy in Foreign Affairs]* (Beijing: CCP History Publishing House, 1999), pp. 22–36 and passim.
57. Ibid.
58. This account of the Yenan campaign is based on Westad, *Decisive Encounters*, pp. 150–53.
59. Chester Roning, *A Memoir of China in Revolution* (New York: Pantheon, 1974), p. 122.
60. Conception personnelle au commandant Dronne sur la situation et sur le politique a Tonkin, [no date], boite no. 8, dossier 1, Fonds historique Leclerc, Memorial du Maréchal Leclerc de Hauteclocque, Paris.
61. Guillemot, "Viêt Nam 1945–1946: l'élimination de l'opposition nationaliste et anticolonialiste dans le Nord," pp. 26–31.
62. Note de renseignements sur le 6ème secteur du Viêt-Nam, 6 août 1946, dossier "août 1946," 10H600, SHAT, Vincennes, Paris.
63. Ibid., pp. 19–24. Duiker, *Ho Chi Minh*, pp. 383–84. The Vietminh version is given in Vo Nguyen Giap, *Unforgettable Days* (Hanoi: Foreign Languages Publishing House, 1975), pp. 281–84.
64. Duiker, *Ho Chi Minh*, p. 365.
65. The Vice Consul in Hanoi (O'Sullivan) to Department of State, 29 August 1946, 851g.00/8-2946, National Archives Record Group 59. Stein Tonnesson, "The Outbreak of War in Indochina, 1946," PRIO Report 3/84, Fall 1982, International Peace Research Institute, Oslo, p. 86.
66. Tonnesson, "Outbreak of War," p. 90.
67. O'Sullivan to Department of State, 1 December 1946, 851G.00/12-146, National Archives Record Group 59.
68. Giap, *Unforgettable Days*, pp. 219–21.
69. O'Sullivan to Department of State, 23 November 1946, 851G.00/11-2346, National Archives Record Group 59.
70. Tonnesson, "Outbreak of War," p. 140.
71. Reed to Department of State, 31 August 1946, 851G/8-3146, National Archives Record Group 59. Giap, *Unforgettable Days*, pp. 318–19.
72. Tonnesson, "Outbreak of War," p. 143.
73. O'Sullivan to Department of State, 24 November 1946, 851G.00/11-2446, National Archives Record Group 59.

74. O'Sullivan to Department of State, 1 December 1946, 851G.00/12-146, National Archives Record Group 59.
75. O'Sullivan to Department of State, 2 December 1946, 851G.00/12-246, National Archives Record Group 59.
76. Giap, *Unforgettable Days,* pp. 380–81.
77. O'Sullivan to Department of State, 24 November 1946, 851G.00/11-2446, National Archives Record Group 59.
78. O'Sullivan to Department of State, 1 December 1946, 851G.00/12-146, National Archives Record Group 59.
79. Tonnesson, "Outbreak of War," pp. 163–64.
80. The Acting Secretary of State to the Consul at Saigon for Moffet, 5 December 1946, *FRUS, 1946,* vol. 8, pp. 67–69.
81. The Ambassador in France (Caffery) to Secretary of State, 29 November 1946, ibid., p. 63.
82. O'Sullivan to Secretary of State, 3 December 1946, ibid., p. 64.
83. Notes de renseignement sur le 6ème secteur du Viêt-Nam, 6 août 1946, dossier "août 1946," 10H600, SHAT, Vincennes, Paris.
84. Giap, *Unforgettable Days,* pp. 239–40.
85. O'Sullivan to Secretary of State, 29 November 1946, 851G.00/11-2946, National Archives Record Group 59. Duiker, *Ho Chi Minh,* pp. 394–95.
86. Tonnesson, "Outbreak of War," pp. 197–98.
87. Shipway, *Road to War,* p. 259.
88. O'Sullivan to Department of State, No. 6903, 24 December 1946, 851G.00/12-2446, National Archives Record Group 59.
89. Ibid.

CHAPTER 14 "The Least Desirable Eventuality"

1. Provost Marshall, First Marine Division to Commanding Officer, Fifth Marines, Alleged Rape of Miss Shen Chung by Corporal William G. Pierson, Investigation of, 30 December 1946, enclosures A, B, and D. Copy in Marshall Mission Records, National Archives Record Group 59, entry 1102, box 27.
2. Ibid., enclosures F, H, and I.
3. Ibid., enclosure D.
4. Ibid., enclosure D, p. 3.
5. Gillem, 103, for General Marshall, 29 December 1946, Marshall Mission Records, National Archives Record Group 59, entry 1102, box 27.
6. "The American Marine Incident of Peiping," *Sin Wen Pao,* 4 January 1946. U.S. Consulate, Shanghai, Chinese Press Review, copy in Hoover Institution Archives, Stanford, Calif.
7. Westad, *Decisive Encounters,* p. 140.
8. American Consulate, Tientsin, to Department of State, No. 642, 3 January 1947, 893.00/1-247. American Embassy, Peiping, to Department of State,

No. 658, 3 January 1947, 893.00/1-347. Both in National Archives Record Group 59.

9. Robert Shaffer, "A Rape in Beijing," p. 37.
10. American Embassy, Nanking, to Secretary of State, 9 January 1947, 893.00/1-947, National Archives Record Group 59.
11. Westad, *Decisive Encounters,* pp. 99–100, 139–40.
12. J. Leighton Stuart to Department of State, No. 7, 30 January 1947, 811.22/3047, National Archives Record Group 59.
13. A good summary of the court-martial proceedings may be found in Shaffer, "A Rape in Beijing," pp. 48–51.
14. Stuart to Department of State, No. 7, 30 January 1947.
15. Wedemeyer to General Dwight D. Eisenhower, 11 March 1946, Alfred C. Wedemeyer Papers, box 82, folder 82.23, Hoover Institution Archives, Stanford, Calif.
16. Frank and Shaw, *Victory and Occupation,* p. 621.
17. Commander, Seventh Fleet, Memo for General Marshall, subject: Relief of Marines Along Railroad, 4 September 1946, Marshall Mission Records, National Archives Record Group 59.
18. Marshall to William L. Clayton, Gold 1556, 25 September 1946, 893.00/9-2546, National Archives Record Group 59.
19. Frank and Shaw, *Victory and Occupation,* pp. 628–29.
20. Alan R. Millett, *The War for Korea: A House Burning,* pp. 75 and 83.
21. Cumings, *Origins of the Korean War,* pp. 352–53.
22. The Political Advisor in Korea to the Secretary of State, 1 November 1946, *FRUS, 1946,* vol. 8, pp. 753–54.
23. Millett, *War for Korea,* p. 85.
24. History of USAFIK, vol. 3, pt. 1C, p. 23.
25. Cumings, *Origins of the Korean War,* pp. 351–35, 373–74.
26. Millett, *War for Korea,* p. 85.
27. History of USAFIK, vol. 3, pt. 1C, p. 19.
28. Ibid.
29. Ibid., p. 20.
30. The Political Advisor in Korea to the Secretary of State, *FRUS, 1946,* vol. 8, p. 770.
31. History of USAFIK, vol. 3, pt. 1C, p. 20.
32. Millett, *War for Korea,* p. 86.
33. Hildring, Memo to the Director of the Office of Far East Affairs, 8 November 1946, *FRUS, 1946,* vol. 8, pp. 764–65.
34. Millett, *War for Korea,* p. 160.
35. Conrad C. Crane and Andrew Terrill, *Reconstructing Iraq: Challenges and Missions for Military Forces in a Post-Conflict Scenario* (Carlisle, Pa: Strategic Studies Institute, 2003), pp. v, 42.
36. David M. Edelstein, "Occupational Hazards: Why Military Occupations Succeed and Fail," *International Security* 29, Summer 2004, pp. 57–58, 85–89.

37. Lt. Gen. David H. Petraeus, "Learning Counter-Insurgency: Observations from Soldiering in Iraq," *Military Review,* January–February 2006, p. 4.
38. Allan R. Millett, "The Korean People: Missing in Action in the Misunderstood War, 1945–1954," in William Stueck, ed., *The Korean War in World History* (Lexington, Ky.: University Press of Kentucky, 2003), p. 36.

BIBLIOGRAPHY

PRIMARY SOURCES

ARCHIVES AND REPOSITORIES

AUSTRALIA

AUSTRALIAN WAR MEMORIAL, CANBERRA

2/25 Battalion War Diary

AWM-54 773/4/11
AWM-54 639/8/9
AWM-54 617/7/26
AWM-54 225/1/10

Papers of William John Gambier
Papers of W. J. Sodin

NATIONAL ARCHIVES OF AUSTRALIA

Foreign Office Records

NOEL BUTLIN ARCHIVES CENTRE, AUSTRALIAN NATIONAL UNIVERSITY, CANBERRA

Waterside Workers' Federation Records

GREAT BRITAIN

IMPERIAL WAR MUSEUM, LONDON

General Sir Philip Christison Papers
General Sir Robert Mansergh Papers
Pugh Papers
V. M. Sissons Papers

Liddell-Hart Archives, King's College, London

Major General W.R.C. Penney Papers
Tull Papers

Public Record Office (now National Archives), London

FO371 (Foreign Office Records, 1945–46)
HS1 (Special Operations Records)
WO172
WO203

FRANCE

Memorial du Maréchal Leclerc de Hauteclocque, Paris

Fonds du Maréchal Leclerc de Hauteclocque

Service Historique de l'Armée de Terre (SHAT), Château de Vincennes, Paris

10H161
10H600
10H602
10H606

JAPAN

Japanese Foreign Ministry Archives, Tokyo

1945–1946 microfilm records

SINGAPORE

National Archives of Singapore

Syonan Oral History Project:

Ahmed Khan interview
Arthur A. Thompson interview
Chin Sin Chong interview
Gay Wan Guay interview
Lee Kip Lin interview
Lee Tian Soo interview
Minetomo Fumi interview
Ng Seng Yong interview

Tan Ben Chang interview
Tan Guan Chuan interview

UNITED STATES

Center for the Study of Diplomacy, Washington, D.C. (Copies in George Washington University Library)

Donald MacDonald interview by Charles Stuart Kennedy, January 25, 1990. "Frontline Diplomacy" oral history collection
Richard A. Ericson interview by Charles Stuart Kennedy, March 27, 1995. "Frontline Diplomacy" oral history collection
William C. Sherman interview by Thomas Stern, October 27, 1993. "Frontline Diplomacy" oral history collection

Columbia University, New York

Chinese Oral History Collection

Franklin L. Ho Oral History
Li Huang Oral History
V. K. Wellington Koo Oral History
Wu Kuo-chen Oral History

Douglas MacArthur Memorial Archives, Norfolk, Virginia

Record Group 4
Record Group 5
Record Group 9

Harry S. Truman Presidential Library, Independence, Missouri

Harry S. Truman Papers
Naval Aide to the President Subject Files
Henry Byroade Oral History
John F. Melby Oral History
Rose Conway Files
PSF Subject Files

Hoover Institution Archives, Stanford, California

U.S. Consulate, Shanghai, Chinese Press Reviews
Albert C. Wedemeyer Papers
Clyde Sargent Papers
Millard Preston Goodfellow Papers
Paul W. Frillman Papers

T. V. Soong Papers
Yenan Liaison Group

LIBRARY OF CONGRESS, WASHINGTON, D.C.

W. Averell Harriman Papers

MARINE CORPS HISTORICAL CENTER, WASHINGTON, D.C.

Calvin H. Decker Oral History

NATIONAL ARCHIVES, WASHINGTON, D.C., AND SUITLAND, MARYLAND

Record Group 59: Records of the Department of State, Records of the Committee on the Far East
Record Group 165: Records of General and Special Staffs
Record Group 218: Records of the Joint and Combined Chiefs of Staff
Record Group 226: Records of the Office of Strategic Services
Record Group 263: CIA Records
Record Group 319: Army Intelligence Document File
Record Group 332: Records of China Theater
Record Group 457: Special Research Histories
Record Group 493: Records of China Theater
Record Group 554: Records of General Headquarters, Far East Command

NAVAL HISTORICAL CENTER, WASHINGTON, D.C.

Daniel E. Barbey Papers

U.S. ARMY MILITARY HISTORY INSTITUTE, CARLISLE, PENNSYLVANIA

Alvan C. Gillem, Jr., Papers
Andrew C. Tychson Papers
Charles H. Donnelly Papers
Philip E. Gallagher Papers
Rothwell Brown Papers
Kenneth C. Strother Papers
George V. Underwood Papers

PUBLISHED PRIMARY SOURCES

Documents on Australian Foreign Policy, vol. 8.
Foreign Relations of the United States, 1943: The Conferences at Cairo and Tehran. Washington, D.C.: GPO, 1961.

Foreign Relations of the United States, 1944, vol. 3, *The British Commonwealth and Europe.* Washington, D.C.: GPO, 1963.

Foreign Relations of the United States, 1945, vol. 1, *The Conference of Berlin.* Washington, D.C.: GPO, 1960.

Foreign Relations of the United States, 1945, vol. 6, *The Far East: China.* Washington, D.C.: GPO, 1960.

Foreign Relations of the United States, 1946, vol. 8, *The Far East.* Washington, D.C.: GPO, 1971.

Post-Surrender Tasks: Report to the Combined Chiefs of Staff by the Supreme Allied Commander, South East Asia, 1943–1945. London: HMSO, 1969.

Reports of General MacArthur: MacArthur in Japan, the Occupation: Military Phase, vol. 1 supplement. Washington, D.C.: GPO, 1971.

United States Relations with China with Special Reference to the Period 1944–49. Department of State Publication 3578, Far Eastern Series 30. Reprinted as *The China White Paper,* ed. Lyman Van Slyke, Stanford, Calif.: Stanford University Press, 1967.

LETTERS TO AUTHOR

Bardy, Edmund J., May 12, 2001
Beaster, Warren, June 4, 2001
Behrens, Donald C., July 18, 2001
Bouchard, Leo, August 3, 2001
DeMoss, John T., July 20, 2001
Haertlein, George H., July 26, 2001
Henneman, Harold, July 25, 2001
Hill, William, June 26, 2001
Huber, William D., July 21, 2001
McManus, Jack D., May 29, 2001
Nolan, Paul L., May 17, 2001
Seck, Robert F., July 21, 2001
Shipman, Joseph T., June 29, 2001
Weibl, Louis R., June 22, 2001
Wideman, William C., July 11, 2001

MEMOIRS

Bates, Ted. "Naval Party 2482, Java 1945–1946," www.britains-smallwars.com.

Druce, John D. "China Reminiscences." Unpublished memoir, courtesy of Mr. Druce.

Earle, David F. Unpublished memoir, courtesy of Mr. Earle.

Kim, Young Sik. *Eyewitness: A North Korean Remembers.* Korea Web Weekly E-books, www.Kimsoft.com.

Shipman, Joseph T. Unpublished memoir, courtesy of Mr. Shipman.

Wickes, George. "Saigon 1945–Hanoi 1946," courtesy of Professor Wickes.

PUBLISHED WORKS

BOOKS

Abend, Hallett. *Reconquest: Its Results and Responsibilities.* New York: Doubleday, 1946.

Allen, Louis. *The End of the War in Asia.* London: Hart-Davis, MacGibbon, 1978.

Anderson, Benedict R. *Java in a Time of Revolution: Occupation and Resistance, 1944–1946.* Ithaca, N.Y.: Cornell University Press, 1972.

Araragi, Shinzo. *Manshu Imin no Rekishi Shakaigaku [Historical Sociology of Japanese Emigrants to Manchuria].* Kyoto: Korasha, 1994.

Armstrong, Charles K. *The North Korean Revolution, 1945–1950.* Ithaca, N.Y.: Cornell University Press, 2003.

Barber, Noel. *The War of the Running Dogs.* New York: Weybright and Talley, 1972.

Beal, John Robinson. *Marshall in China.* New York: Doubleday, 1970.

Bix, Herbert. *Hirohito and the Making of Modern Japan.* New York: HarperCollins, 2000.

Bland, Larry, ed. *George C. Marshall's Mediation Mission to China.* Lexington, Va.: George C. Marshall Foundation, 1987.

———, and Sharon R. Ritenour, eds. *The Papers of George Catlett Marshall,* vol. 5, *The Finest Soldier.* Baltimore: Johns Hopkins University Press, 2004.

Blum, John M. *The Price of Vision: The Diary of Henry Wallace, 1942–46.* Boston: Houghton Mifflin, 1973.

Bodinier, Commandant Gilbert. *Le retour de la France en Indochine, 1945–1946: textes et documents.* Vincennes: Service Historique de l'Armée de Terre, 1987.

Brougher, W. E. *South to Bataan, North to Manchuria: The Prison Diary of BG W. E. Brougher.* Athens, Ga.: University of Georgia Press, 1971.

Butow, Robert J.C. *Japan's Decision to Surrender.* Stanford, Calif.: Stanford University Press, 1954.

Carr-Greg, Charlotte. *Japanese POWs in Revolt.* St. Lucia, Australia: University of Queensland Press, 1978.

Cary, Otis, ed. *Eyewitness to History: The First Americans in Postwar Asia.* Tokyo: Kodansha International, 1995.

Chang, Jung. *Wild Swans: Three Daughters of China.* New York: Touchstone, 2003.

———, and Jon Halliday. *Mao: The Unknown Story.* New York: Knopf, 2005.

Cheah Boon Kheng. *Red Star Over Malaya: Resistance and Social Conflict During and After the Japanese Occupation of Malaya, 1941–1946.* Singapore University Press, 1983.

Chen, King C. *Vietnam and China, 1938–1954.* Princeton, N.J.: Princeton University Press, 1969.

Cheng Kok Peng. "A Brief Study of the Situation in Batu Pahat During the Japanese Occupation," in Paul H. Kratoska and Abu Talib Ahmad, eds., *Pendukan Jepun Di Tanah Melayu.* Palau Pinang, Malaysia: Universiti Sains Malaysia, 1989.

Chin Kee Onn. *Malaya Upside Down.* Singapore: Federal Publications, 1977.

Cook, Haruko Taya, and Theodore F. Cook. *Japan at War: An Oral History.* New York: New Press, 1992.

Crane, Conrad C., and Andrew Terrill. *Reconstructing Iraq: Challenges and Missions for Military Forces in a Post-Conflict Scenario.* Carlisle, Pa.: Strategic Studies Institute, 2003.

Cribb, Robert. *Gangsters and Revolutionaries: The Jakarta People's Militia and the Indonesian Revolution.* Honolulu: University of Hawaii Press, 1991.

Cumings, Bruce. *The Origins of the Korean War: Liberation and the Emergence of Separate Regimes.* Princeton, N.J.: Princeton University Press, 1981.

Davies, John Paton, Jr. *Dragon by the Tail.* London: Robson Books, 1974.

Dennis, Peter. *Troubled Days of Peace: Mountbatten and Southeast Asia Command, 1945–46.* New York: St. Martin's, 1987.

Detwiler, Donald S., and Charles B. Burdick, eds. *War in Asia and the Pacific, 1937–1949,* vol. 15. New York: Garland Publishing, 1980.

Devillers, Philippe. *Histoire du Viêt-Nam de 1940 à 1952.* Paris: Editions du Seuil, 1952.

Donnison, F.S.V. *British Military Administration in the Far East, 1943–46.* London: HMSO, 1956.

Doulton, A.J.F., *The Fighting Cock: Being the History of the 23rd Indian Division.* Aldershot, U.K.: Gale and Polden, 1951.

Duiker, William J. *Ho Chi Minh: A Life.* New York: Hyperion, 2000.

Dunn, Peter M. *The First Vietnam War.* New York: St. Martin's, 1985.

Elliott, Duong Van Mai. *The Sacred Willow: Four Generations in the Life of a Vietnamese Family.* New York: Oxford University Press, 1999.

Falk, Stanley L. *Bataan: The March of Death.* New York: W. W. Norton, 1962.

Feis, Herbert. *The China Tangle: The American Efforts in China from Pearl Harbor to the Marshall Mission.* New York: Atheneum, 1965.

Frank, Benis M., and Henry I. Shaw, Jr. *Victory and Occupation: History of U.S. Marine Corps Operations in World War II,* vol. 5. Washington, D.C.: Historical Branch, G-3 Division, Headquarters, U.S. Marine Corps, 1968.

Frank, Richard B. *Downfall: The End of the Imperial Japanese Empire.* New York: Random House, 1999.

Frederick, Carl J. *American Experience in Military Government.* New York: W. Sloan, 1948.

Frederick, William H. *Visions and Heat: The Making of the Indonesian Revolution.* Athens, Ohio: Ohio University Press, 1989.

Friend, Theodore. *The Blue-Eyed Enemy: Japan Against the West in Java and Luzon, 1942–1945.* Princeton, N.J.: Princeton University Press, 1988.

Frillman, Paul, and Graham Peck. *China: The Remembered Life.* Boston: Houghton Mifflin, 1968.

Furuta, Motoo. "A Survey of Village Conditions During the 1945 Famine in Vietnam," in Paul H. Kratoska, ed., *Food Supplies and the Japanese Occupation of Southeast Asia.* Houndmills, U.K.: Macmillan, 1998.

Gallicchio, Marc S. *The Cold War Begins in Asia: American East Asia Policy and the Fall of the Japanese Empire.* New York: Columbia University Press, 1988.

Giap, Vo Nguyen. *Unforgettable Days.* Hanoi: Foreign Languages Publishing House, 1975.

Gilbert, Marc Jason. "Playing the Race Card: Vietnamese Appeals to Non-White Forces of Occupation, 1945–1975." Unpublished paper courtesy of Professor Gilbert.

Gillin, Donald, and Ramon Myers, eds. *Last Chance in Manchuria: The Diary of Chiang Kia-ngau.* Stanford, Calif.: Hoover Institution Press, 1989.

Gilmour, Andrew. *My Role in the Rehabilitation of Singapore.* Singapore: Institute for Southeast Asian Studies, 1966.

Glantz, David M. *August Storm: The Soviet 1945 Strategic Offensive in Manchuria,* Leavenworth Paper No. 7. Leavenworth, Kans.: U.S. Army Combat Studies Institute, 1983.

———. *August Storm: Soviet Tactical and Operational Combat in Manchuria, 1945,* Leavenworth Paper No. 8. Leavenworth, Kans.: U.S. Army Combat Studies Institute, 1983.

Goncharov, Sergei N., et al. *Uncertain Partners: Stalin, Mao and the Korean War.* Stanford, Calif.: Stanford University Press, 1993.

Goscha, Christopher E. "The Ambiguities of War in the South: Reflections on the Rise and Fall of Nguyen Binh." Paper presented at the conference on "Le Viêt-Nam depuis 1945: États, marges et constructions du passé," January 11–12, 2001. Courtesy Professor Goscha.

———. "Belated Allies: The Technical Contributions of Japanese Deserters to the Viet Minh, 1945–1950," in Marilyn Young and Robert Buzzanco, eds., *A Companion to the Vietnam War.* Malden, Mass.: Blackwell, 2002.

Goto, Kenichi. *Tensions of Empire: Japan and Southeast Asia in the Colonial and Postcolonial World.* Athens, Ohio: Ohio University Press, 2003.

Gouda, Francis, and Thijs Brocades Zaalberg. *American Visions of the Netherlands East Indies/Indonesia.* Amsterdam University Press, 2002.

Guillemot, François. "Viêt Nam 1945–1946: l'élimination de l'opposition nationaliste et anticolonialiste dans le nord: au cœur de la fracture vietnamienne," in Christopher Goscha and Benoît de Tréglodé, eds. *Le Viêt Nam depuis 1945: états, contestations et constructions du passé* (Paris: Les Indes Savantes, 2004).

Gunther, John. *Inside Asia.* London: Hamish Hamilton, 1939.

———. *The Riddle of MacArthur: Japan, Korea and the Far East.* New York: Harper, 1950.

Hayashi Shigeru et al., eds. *Nihon Shūsenshi [History of the Ending of the Pacific War],* vol. 1. Tokyo: Yomiuri Shimbunsha, 1965.

He Di. "Mao Zedong and the Marshall Mission," in Larry I. Bland, ed., *George C. Marshall's Mediation Mission to China.* Lexington, Va.: George C. Marshall Foundation, 1987.

Heinrichs, Waldo H., Jr. *American Ambassador: Joseph C. Grew and the Development of the American Diplomatic Tradition.* Boston: Little, Brown, 1966.

Hoag, C. Leonard. "American Military Government in Korea: War Policy and the First Year of Occupation." Draft U.S. Army manuscript, 1970. Copy in U.S. Army Center of Military History Library.

Holland, William L., ed. *Asian Nationalism and the West.* New York: Macmillan, 1953.

Hough, Richard. *Mountbatten: A Biography.* New York: Random House, 1980.

Huyen, N. Khac. *Vision Accomplished? The Enigma of Ho Chi Minh.* New York: Macmillan, 1971.

Iijima Shiro. "Hoku-Man Kaitaku-Dan no Saiki" ["The Last Days of the Northern Manchukuo Settlers"], in Ito Masanori et al., eds., *Jitsuroku Taiheiyo Senso [Record of the Pacific War].* Tokyo: Chuo Koronsha, 1950.

Isaacs, Harold R. *No Peace for Asia.* New York: Macmillan, 1947.

Jun, Eto, ed. *The Ceasefire and the Suspension of Diplomatic Rights.* Tokyo: Ministry of Foreign Affairs, 1966.

Kang, Hildi. *Under the Black Umbrella: Voices from Colonial Korea.* Ithaca, N.Y.: Cornell University Press, 2001.

Kim, Richard. *Lost Names: Scenes from a Korean Boyhood.* New York: Praeger, 1970.

Kirby, S. Woodburn, et al. *The War Against Japan,* vol. 5, *The Surrender of Japan.* London: HMSO, 1969.

Knox, Donald. *Death March: The Survivors of Bataan.* New York: Harcourt Brace, 1983.

Kratoska, Paul H. *The Japanese Occupation of Malaya.* St. Leonards, Australia: Allen & Unwin, 1998.

Kratoska, Paul H., and Abu Talib Ahmad, eds. *Pendukan Jepun Di Tanah Melayu.* Palau Pinang, Malaysia: Universiti Sains Malaysia, 1989.

Lankov, Andrei. *From Stalin to Kim Il Sung: The Formation of North Korea, 1945–1960.* New Brunswick, N.J.: Rutgers University Press, 2002.

Leffelaar, Hendrik L. *Through a Harsh Dawn: A Boy Grows Up in a Japanese Prison Camp.* Barre, Mass.: Barre Publishing, 1963.

Leith, Hal. *POWs of the Japanese Rescued!* Victoria, B.C.: Trafford, 2003.

Lewis, William Roger. *Imperialism at Bay.* New York: Oxford University Press, 1987.

Lockwood, Rupert. *The Black Armada.* Sydney, Australia: Australasian Book Society, 1975.

Long, Gavin. *The Final Campaigns.* Canberra, Australia: Australian War Memorial, 1963.

Lu Zhengcao. *Hui Yi Lu [Memoirs of Lu Zhengcao].* Beijing, 1957.

Mamoro Shinozaki. *Syonan—My Story: The Japanese Occupation of Singapore.* Singapore: Asia Pacific Press, 1969.

Marr, David G. *Vietnam 1945: The Quest for Power.* Berkeley: University of California Press, 1995.

Martin, Françoise. *Heures tragiques au Tonkin.* Paris: Editions Berger, 1948.

May, Gary. *China Scapegoat: The Diplomatic Ordeal of John Carter Vincent.* Washington, D.C.: New Republic Books, 1979.

McAlister, John T. *Vietnam: The Origins of Revolution.* (New York: Center for International Studies, Princeton University, 1969.

McCullough, David. *Truman.* New York: Simon & Schuster, 1992.

Melby, John F. *The Mandate of Heaven: Record of a Civil War.* University of Toronto Press, 1968.

Millett, Allan R. "The Korean People: Missing in Action in the Misunderstood War, 1945–1954," in William Stueck, ed., *The Korean War in World History.* Lexington, Ky.: University Press of Kentucky, 2003.

———. *The War for Korea: A House Burning.* Lawrence, Kans.: University Press of Kansas, 2005.

Millis, Walter, ed. *The Forrestal Diaries.* New York: Viking, 1966.

Mitsuo, Ushiyama. "Record of Ending the War in the Northern Part of Sumatra," in Anthony Reid and Oki Akita, eds., *The Japanese Experience in Indonesia: Selected Memoirs of 1942–1945.* Athens, Ohio: Ohio University Monographs in International Studies, Southeast Asia Series No. 72, 1986.

Moorad, George. *Lost Peace in China.* New York: E. P. Dutton, 1949.

Morison, Samuel Eliot. *Victory in the Pacific, 1945.* Boston: Atlantic, Little Brown, 1975.

Morita, Yoshio. *Chosen Shusen no Kiroku [The End of the War in Korea].* Tokyo: Genan-do Shoten, 1964.

Murray, Brian. "Stalin, the Cold War and the Division of China: A Multiarchival Mystery." Cold War International History Project, Working Paper #12. Washington, D.C.: Woodrow Wilson Center for Scholars, 1997.

Myers, Ramon H. "Frustration, Fortitude and Friendship: Chiang Kai-shek's Reactions to the Marshall Mission," in Larry I. Bland, ed., *George C. Marshall's Mediation Mission to China.* Lexington, Va.: George C. Marshall Foundation, 1987.

Nelson, Craig. *The First Heroes.* New York: Viking, 2002.

Nguyen Khang. "Uprising in Hanoi," in Nguyen Duy Trinh, ed., *In the Enemy's Net.* Hanoi: Foreign Languages Publishing House, 1962.

Nguyen Thi Anh. "Japanese Food Policies and the 1945 Great Famine in Indochina," in Paul H. Kratoska, ed., *Food Supplies and the Japanese Occupation of Southeast Asia.* Houndmills, U.K.: Macmillan, 1998.

Nguyen Thi Tuyet Mai. *The Rubber Tree: Memoir of a Vietnamese Woman Who Was an Anti-French Guerrilla, a Publisher and Peace Activist.* Jefferson, N.C.: McFarland, 1994.

Ono Eiko. *Ikiteita Yasui Manshu Touhikou, 300 Nichi [Memoir of a Three-Hundred-Day Escape from Northeast Manchuria].* Osaka: Shoseki, 1985.

Patti, Archimedes L. *Why Vietnam? Prelude to America's Albatros.* Berkeley: University of California Press, 1980.

Peck, Graham. *Two Kinds of Time.* Boston: Houghton Mifflin, 1950.

Pepper, Suzanne. *Civil War in China: The Political Struggle.* Berkeley: University of California Press, 1978.

Pogue, Forrest C. *George C. Marshall: Statesman, 1945–1959.* New York: Viking, 1987.

Prasad, Bisheshwar, ed. *Official History of the Indian Armed Forces in the Second World War, 1939–1945: Postwar Occupation Forces: Japan and Southeast Asia.* Delhi: Orient Longmans, 1958.

Reid, Anthony. *The Blood of the People: Revolution and the End of Traditional Rule in Sumatra.* Kuala Lumpur: Oxford University Press, 1979.

Ricklefs, M. C. *A History of Modern Indonesia,* 2nd ed. Stanford, Calif.: Stanford University Press, 1993.

Rigg, Lt. Col. Robert B. *Red China's Fighting Hordes.* Westport, Conn.: Greenwood Press, 1971.

Roning, Chester. *A Memoir of China in Revolution.* New York: Pantheon, 1974.

Roosevelt, Elliott. *As He Saw It.* New York: Duell, Sloan and Pearce, 1946.

Russell, W. B. *The Second Fourteenth Battalion: A History of an Australian Infantry Battalion in the Second World War.* Sydney: Angus & Robertson, 1954.

Sainteny, Jean. *Ho Chi Minh and His Vietnam: A Personal Memoir.* Chicago: Cowles, 1972.

Shipway, Martin. *The Road to War: France and Vietnam 1944–1947.* Providence: Berghahn Books, 1996.

Sledge, E. B. *China Marine.* Tuscaloosa: University of Alabama Press, 2002.

Slim, Field Marshal Sir William. *Defeat into Victory.* London: Cassell, 1956.

Spector, Ronald. *Advice and Support: The Early Years of the U.S. Army in Vietnam, 1941–1960.* New York: Free Press, 1985.

Stueck, William. *The Korean War: An International History.* Princeton, N.J.: Princeton University Press, 1995.

Suyin, Han. *Elder Brother: Zhou Enlai and the Making of Modern China, 1898–1976.* New York: Kodansha, 1994.

Tanaka, Yuki. *Hidden Horrors: Japanese War Crimes in World War II.* Boulder, Colo.: Westview Press, 1996.

Terrill, Ross. *Mao: A Biography.* New York: Harper, 1980.

Thorne, Christopher. *Allies of a Kind: The United States, Britain and the War Against Japan.* London: Hamish Hamilton, 1978.

Tong Liu Shaw. *Out of Red China.* New York: Duell, Sloan and Pearce, 1953.

Tonnesson, Stein. "The Outbreak of War in Indochina, 1946." PRIO Report 3/84, Fall 1982, International Peace Research Institute, Oslo.

———. *The Vietnamese Revolution of 1945: Roosevelt, Ho Chi Minh and de Gaulle in a World at War.* London: Sage Publications, 1991.

Troy, Thomas. *Donovan and the CIA: A History of the Establishment of the Central Intelligence Agency.* Frederick, Md.: University Publications of America, 1981.

Tsou, Tang. *America's Failure in China, 1941–50.* Chicago: University of Chicago Press, 1963.

Turnbull, C. M. *A History of Singapore, 1819–1975.* Kuala Lumpur: Oxford University Press, 1977.

Umemoto Sutezo. *Kantogun Shimatsuki [Story of the End of the Kwantung Army].* Tokyo: Hara Shobo, 1967.

Van Langenberg, Michael. "National Revolution in North Sumatra: Sumatera Timur and Tapanuli 1942–1950." Unpublished dissertation. University of Sydney, 1979.

Van Slyke, Lyman. "The Chinese Communist Movement During the Sino-Japanese War, 1937–1945," in John K. Fairbank and Albert Feuerwerker, eds. *The Cambridge History of China,* vol. 13. Cambridge, U.K.: Cambridge University Press, 1986.

Wang Zifeng. *Zhanzheng Niandi de Riji [Diary in Time of War].* Beijing: Chinese Literature Publishing House, 1986.

Weathersby, Kathryn. "Soviet Aims in Korea and the Origins of the Korean War, 1945–1950: New Evidence from Russian Archives." Working Paper No. 8, November 1993, Cold War International History Project, Woodrow Wilson International Center for Scholars, Washington, D.C.

Wedemeyer, Albert C. *Wedemeyer Reports!* New York: Holt, 1958.

Wehl, David. *The Birth of Indonesia.* London: G. Allen & Unwin, 1948.

———. *The Moon Upside Down.* London: J. Barrie, 1948.

Westad, Odd Arne, ed. *Brothers in Arms: The Rise and Fall of the Sino-Soviet Alliances 1945–1963.* Washington, D.C.: Woodrow Wilson Center Press, 1998.

———. *Cold War and Revolution: Soviet-American Rivalry and the Origins of the Chinese Civil War.* New York: Columbia University Press, 1993.

———. *Decisive Encounters: The Chinese Civil War, 1946–1950.* Stanford, Calif.: Stanford University Press, 2003.

Worthing, Peter. *Occupation and Revolution: China and the Vietnamese August Revolution of 1945.* Berkeley: Institute of East Asian Studies, University of California at Berkeley, 2001.

Xiong Xianghui. *Wo de Qing Bao Yu Wai Jiao Shengya [My Life as a Spy in Foreign Affairs].* Beijing: CCP History Publishing House, 1986.

Younge, Louise. *Japan's Total Empire: Manchuria and the Culture of Wartime Imperialism.* Berkeley: University of California Press, 1998.
Yu, Maochun. *OSS in China: Prelude to Cold War.* New Haven, Conn.: Yale University Press, 1996.
Zhang Baijia. "Zhou Enlai and the Marshall Mission," in Larry I. Bland, ed., *George C. Marshall's Mediation Mission to China.* Lexington, Va.: George C. Marshall Foundation, 1987.
Zhang Zenglong, *Xie Bai Xue Hong [Blood and Snow].* Hong Kong: Dadi Chu-banshe, 1991.
Zhiguo, Yang. "U.S. Marines in Qingdao: Society, Culture and China's Civil War, 1945–1949," in Larry Bland, ed., *George C. Marshall's Mediation Mission to China.* Lexington, Va.: George C. Marshall Foundation, 1987.
Ziegler, Philip. *Mountbatten.* New York: Knopf, 1985.

PERIODICALS

"Akao Oboe Remembers." *Sankei Shimbum,* October 17, 1997.
Bernstein, Barton J. "The Perils and Politics of Surrender: Ending the War with Japan and Avoiding the Third Atomic Bomb." *Pacific Historical Review* 46, November 1977.
Bing Siong, Hang. "The Secret of Major Kido: The Battle of Semarang 15–19 October 1945." *Bijdragen tot de Taal-Land-en Volkenkunden* 152, 1996.
Bix, Herbert. "Japan's Delayed Surrender: A Reinterpretation." *Diplomatic History* 19, Spring 1995.
Bliss, John, Jr. "My Most Memorable Day: Korea, September 8, 1945." *The Monadnock Ledger,* May 24, 2001.
Brockintin, W. H. "An Airfield near Peiping, 1945." *Scuttlebutt,* June 2000.
Burridge, K.O.L. "Racial Relations in Johore," *The Australian Journal of Politics and History* 2, May 1957.
Clemens, Peter. "Operation Cardinal: The OSS in Manchuria, August 1945." *Intelligence and National Security* 13, Winter 1998.
Din, Brigadier M. Hayaud. "With the 20th Indian Division in French Indochina." *Journal of the Royal United Service Institute of India* 78, July 1948.
Edelstein, David M. "Occupational Hazards: Why Military Occupations Succeed and Fail." *International Security* 29, Summer 2004.
"General Itagaki's First Refusal." *Singapore Straits Times,* September 4, 1945.
Gillin, Donald G., and Charles Etter. "Staying On: Japanese Soldiers and Civilians in China, 1945–1949." *Journal of Asian Studies* 42, May 1983.
Han Bing Siong. "The Secret of Major Kido: The Battle of Semarang 15–19 October 1945." *Bijdragen tot deTaal-Land-en Volkenkunden* 152, 1996.
Herring, George C. "The Truman Administration and the Restoration of French Sovereignty in Indochina." *Diplomatic History* 1, Spring 1977.
Hersey, John. "Letter from Peiping." *The New Yorker,* April 25, 1946.

Hess, Gary R. "Franklin Roosevelt and Indochina." *Journal of American History* 59, September 1972.

Huang, Ray. "Some Observations on Manchuria in the Balance, Early 1946." *Pacific Historical Review* 27, Spring 1958.

Huyn Kim Khanh. "The Vietnamese August Revolution Reinterpreted." *Journal of Asian Studies* 30, 1971.

Idrus. "Surabaja." Trans. S. U. Nababan and Benedict Anderson. *Indonesia* 5, April 1968.

Isaacs, Harold. "Do We Run Korea Badly? Well, Look How Reds Do." *Newsweek,* September 24, 1945.

Johnston, Richard J. H. "Radicals in Korea Hit General A. V. Arnold." *The New York Times,* October 30, 1945.

Klein, Captain Edwin. "Situation in North China." *Marine Corps Gazette,* April 1946.

Lafeber, Walter. "Roosevelt, Churchill and Indochina, 1942–45." *American Historical Review* 80, December 1975.

Lauterbach, Richard E. "Hodge's Korea." *Virginia Quarterly Review* 23, June 1947.

Matray, James A. "Hodge Podge: American Occupation Policy in Korea, 1945–1948." *Korean Studies* 19, 1995.

Olmstead, David L. "Two Korean Villages: Cultural Contact at the 38th Parallel." *Human Organization,* Fall 1951.

"An Open Letter to the People of Britain," *Life,* October 9, 1942.

Petraeus, Lt. Gen. David H. "Learning Counter-Insurgency: Observations from Soldiering in Iraq." *Military Review,* January–February 2006.

Plaice, Emery. *New York Daily Herald,* September 29, 1945.

Reid, Anthony. "The Australian Discovery of Indonesia, 1945." *Journal of the Australian War Memorial* 17, 1990.

Roadnight, Andrew. "Sleeping with the Enemy: Britain, Japanese Troops and the Netherlands East Indies, 1945–1946." *History: The Journal of the Historical Association* 87, April 2002.

Sadao, Asada. "The Shock of the Atomic Bomb and Japan's Decision to Surrender: A Reconsideration." *Pacific Historical Review* 64, November 1998.

Shaffer, Robert. "A Rape in Beijing, December 1946: GIs, Nationalist Protests and U.S. Foreign Policy." *Pacific Historical Review* 69, February 2000.

Simmons, Walter. "GI's Haven't a Kind Word to Say for Korea." *Chicago Tribune,* December 13, 1945.

Tanner, Harold M. "Guerrilla, Mobile, and Base Warfare in Communist Military Operations in Manchuria, 1945–1947." *Journal of Military History* 67, October 2003.

INDEX

PHOTO: COURTESY OF GEORGE WASHINGTON UNIVERSITY

RONALD H. SPECTOR is a graduate of Johns Hopkins and Yale and served in the Marine Corps during the Vietnam War. He is currently professor of history and international relations at George Washington University. He has been a Fulbright lecturer in India and Israel, a distinguished visiting professor of strategy at the National War College, and the Harold K. Johnson visiting professor of military history at the U.S. Army War College, as well as a distinguished guest professor at Keio University in Tokyo. He is the author of six previous books, the last three of which have been History Book Club main selections, and one of which, *Eagle Against the Sun,* was a Book-of-the-Month Club main selection. He and his wife, Dianne, have two sons and live in Annandale, Virginia.